American Public Policy

Promise and Performance

SECOND EDITION

B. Guy Peters
Maurice Falk Professor
of American Government
UNIVERSITY OF PITTSBURGH

MACMILLAN
EDUCATION

This edition first published 1986.

Published by
MACMILLAN EDUCATION LTD
Houndmills, Basingstoke, Hampshire RG21 2XS
and London
Companies and representatives
throughout the world

Printed in the USA by
Hamilton Printing Company

IN MEMORY OF MY FATHER

BRITISH LIBRARY CATALOGUING IN PUBLICATION DATA
Peters, B. Guy
American public policy : promise and
performance.— 2nd ed.
1. United States—Politics and
government—1981-
I. Title
320.973   JK261

ISBN 0-333-41590-6
ISBN 0-333-41591-4 Pbk

Contents

Part Three: Substantive Policy Issues

Part Four: Policy Analysis

Tables

Figures

Preface to the Second Edition

Understanding public policy in the United States of the 1980s is a rather grand undertaking, although limited by both time and space. In a political system as large and as complex as that of the United States, understanding policymaking necessitates an explanation of the complex political system. Policymaking is not strictly a political undertaking, however; it also involves the skills and biases of economists, philosophers, engineers, and many other professionals outside the field of political science. To understand public policy in the United States the student must first have a firm grasp of what policy is and must understand the basic institutional and value structures in which it is made. Almost all the numerous definitions of public policy have some validity. In this book I attempt to focus on the effects that policy statements, declarations, and programs have on citizens, but I look too at more formal definitions of policy. Also, because policies are made within a set of institutions that limit their options and shape their outcomes, students must understand these institutions.

Public policy is also made by means of a complex, subtle, and not always formal process. That is, many agents who do not show up on any formal chart of government organizations may nevertheless influence the shape of policy, perhaps even more than many formal institutions do. The process of making policy begins in the mass society as problems and issues are defined, goes into the formal institutions for some policy decisions, and then is returned to the broader society for implementation and, eventually, evaluation.

All too often, the close connection between state and society, between the formal and informal actors in the policymaking process, is forgotten by both analysts and citizens, and the reality and subtlety of the relationships are reduced. It is also important to realize that policy problems are rarely if ever "solved"; solutions may be offered, but in all probability before long the problems will require new solutions. This is in part a result of changing circumstances and in part a result of the fallibility of policymaking institutions.

Understanding public policy also requires some knowledge of specific policy areas. The policy process is generic, but it varies substantially between policy areas. The technological, social, and institutional frameworks in which policies are made will influence their outcomes, and it is important to understand some of those differences. To that end, I have included chapters on specific policy areas. These have been selected because of my interests and expertise and because of the likelihood of significant modifications of the policies during the 1980s. Also, the policy areas that have been selected represent a variety of types, in terms of the technological and professional influences on policymaking. These policy areas are all domestic, and most lie in the broad area of social policy. But within that seemingly narrow set of policies is sufficient variation to demonstrate the importance of understanding the particular framework of each policy.

Finally, there must be some means of evaluating policies after they are made or proposed. This can be done on the basis of economic costs and benefits or on the basis of "softer," more humane values. I discuss both kinds of evaluation and, to some degree, the differences between them. As in many areas of policymaking, neither kind of evaluation is entirely right or entirely wrong; both are necessary to understanding policy in the fullest.

This second edition represents no major departures from the first, although it does contain a good deal of new material. Most important, it contains a chapter on defense policy, to balance the dominant concern of the book (and the author) with domestic and especially social policies. Also, the chapter on economic policy has been revised to take into account both the greater interest in an industrial policy in the United States and the centrality of tax policies in the mid-1980s. Finally, the impact of the Reagan administration on American public policy, at least during its first term, has been discussed and to some degree assessed.

As with the first edition, there are a number of people who should be thanked for their contributions to this volume. Again, my family had to put up with the inevitable pressures arising from the need to complete a manuscript. Again, students who have heard much of this provided a number of useful comments, although at times there were only dazed looks. Many colleagues in the profession provided useful feedback. Sandra Mathews typed the manuscript quickly and accurately — even the dreaded footnotes. If there are any differences in quality between the first and second editions, they may be attributed to having to listen to the Pirates rather than the Yankees.

PART ONE

The Nature of Public Policy

1. What Is Public Policy?

Government in the United States has grown from the small and simple "night watchman state" providing defense, police protection, and some education into an immense collection of institutions affecting the daily lives of all citizens. The size and complexity of modern government make it necessary for citizens to understand what policies in certain areas are, how those policies are made and changed, and how to evaluate the effectiveness and morality of the policies.

Government in the United States is large. Today it accounts for one dollar in three from the nation's revenue. This money is not wasted; most of it is returned to citizens through a variety of cash-benefit programs or in the form of public services. Likewise, one working person in every five is employed by government. But the range of activities of modern government in the United States is not confined to such simple measures as spending money or hiring workers. Governments also influence the economy and society in less obvious ways.

Government in the United States today is complex and is becoming more complex every day. The institutions of government are also becoming more complicated and numerous. More public business is now conducted through public corporations and quasi-autonomous public bodies, and nearly 83,000 separate governments now exist in the United States.[1] Also, the subject matter of government policy is more complex and technical now than it was years ago. Governments must make decisions about the risks of nuclear power plant accidents, the reliability of technologically sophisticated weapons systems, and the management of a huge economic system. Even when the subject matter of a policy is less complex, requirements for participation and accountability make managing a public program a difficult undertaking.

This book is intended to help the reader understand the fundamental processes and content of public policy that underlie the size and complexity of government. It is meant to increase knowledge about how policies are made, what the policies of the United States are in certain areas, and what standards of evaluation should be applied to policies. I begin with a discussion of the policy process in the United States — concentrating on the federal government — and

3

the impact that the structures and procedures of that government have on the content of policies. Second, I discuss the means that professionals and citizens alike can employ to evaluate the effects of public policies and the methods that will enable them to decide what they want and can expect to receive from government.

Defining Public Policy

Mark Twain once commented that patriotism was the last refuge of fools and scoundrels. To some degree "public policy" has become just such a refuge for some academic disciplines. As public policy studies are now popular, everything government does is labeled a part of the study of public policy. I adopt a more restrictive definition of public policy, but not too much more restrictive.

Stated most simply, public policy is the sum of the activities of governments, whether acting directly or through agents, as it has an influence on the lives of citizens. Within that definition, we can determine three levels of policy, defined by the degree to which they make real changes in the lives of citizens. At the first level we have policy choices—decisions made by politicians, civil servants, or others and directed toward using public power to affect the lives of citizens. Congressmen, presidents, governors, administrators, and pressure groups, among others, make such policy choices. What emerges from all those choices is a policy in action. At the second level, we can speak of policy outputs—policy choices being put into action. At this level the government is doing things: spending money, hiring people, or promulgating regulations that will affect the economy and society. Outputs may be virtually synonymous with the term "program" commonly used in government. Finally, at the third level we have policy impacts—the effects of policy choices and policy outcomes on citizens. Let us take as an example the policy choices made by the federal government on taxation. The administration of tax laws (policy outputs) produces a policy impact that takes more from the wealthy than from the poor. The overall policy on economic inequality in the United States is much less redistributive. When we take into account the effects of state and local taxation and the broad spread of expenditure programs, we see that the net effect is a very small improvement in the economic status of the poor.[2]

Several aspects of public policy require some explanation. First, although we are focusing attention on the federal government, we must remember that the United States has a federal system of government in which a large number of subsidiary governments also make decisions. In the best of all worlds, these governments often conflict. Even within the federal government itself the actions of one agency may conflict with those of another. The U.S. Department of Agriculture, for example, subsidizes the growing of tobacco, while the U.S. Office of the Surgeon General encourages citizens not to smoke.

Second, not all government policies are implemented by government employees. Many are actually implemented by private organizations or by individuals. We must understand this if we are to avoid an excessively narrow definition of public policy as concerning only those programs that are directly administered by a public agency. A number of agricultural, social, and health policies involve the use of private agencies operating with the sanction and in the name of government. Even the cabin attendant on an airplane making an announcement to buckle up seat belts is implementing a government policy.

Third, and most important, we are concentrating on the effects of government choices on the lives of individuals in the society. The word "policy" is commonly used in a number of ways. In one usage it denotes a stated intent of government, as expressed in a piece of legislation, for example. Unfortunately, any number of steps are required to turn a piece of legislation into an operating program, and all too frequently significant changes in the intended effects result from the difficulties of translating ideas and intentions into actions. In this analysis we evaluate policies on the basis of their effects rather than their intentions. We must also have some degree of concern for the legislative process, which produces good intentions that may or may not come to fruition.

Our definition recognizes the complexity and interorganizational characteristics of public policy. Few policy choices are decided and executed by a single organization or even a single level of government. Rather, policies—in terms of their effects—emerge from a large number of programs, legislative intentions, and organization interactions to affect the daily lives of citizens. The question posed many years ago by Harold Lasswell: "Who gets what?" is still useful in understanding public policy.

The Instruments of Public Policy

Governments have a number of instruments by which they can influence society and the economy and produce changes in the lives of citizens. The choice of which to employ in any particular instance may depend on the probable effectiveness of the instrument, its political palatability, and tradition. And some policy instruments may be effective in certain areas but not in others.

Law

Law is a unique resource of government. It is not available to private actors who have access to the other instruments of policy we will discuss. Governments have the right to make authoritative decrees and to back up those decrees with the legitimate power of the state. In most instances simply issuing the law is sufficient to produce compliance, but at times monitoring and enforcement are crucial to the effectiveness of this instrument. Citizens daily obey many laws without thinking about them, but both the police and the agencies that monitor environmental control, occupational safety, and product safety are also busy trying to ensure proper enforcement of legislation.

We should make several points about the use of laws as instruments of policy. First, laws are used as a means of creating the most important output of government for citizens: rights. Such laws are usually of a constitutional or fundamental nature and are central in defining the position of citizens in society. In the United States the fundamental rights of citizens are defined by the Constitution and its amendments, but rights have also been extended through a variety of other legislation. This has been especially true of the rights of nonwhites and women, as with the passage of the Voting Rights Act of 1965 and the Equal Employment Opportunity Act of 1972.

Second, the United States uses laws to regulate economic and social conditions to a much greater extent than most other countries do. The United States is frequently cited as having a small public sector in comparison with other industrialized countries, but if the effects of regulation are included in the comparison, government in the United States may be as pervasive as any European government.[3] The cost of government's intervention tends to be reflected in the price of products (an estimated $126 billion in 1980) rather than in the tax bills of citizens.[4]

Third, law can be used to create burdens as well as benefits. The most obvious example in the 1980s is the possibility of reinstituting the draft to fulfill military manpower needs. In effect, any action of government needs a legal hook on which to hang, but the ability of a simple piece of paper to create both rights and obligations is one of the essential features of public policy.

Services

Governments also provide a number of services ranging from defense to education to recreation. In terms of employment, education is by far the largest directly provided public service, employing over 6 million people. Defense employs another 3 million, both military and civilian.

The direct provision of services raises several questions, especially as there are pressures for governments to control their expenditures. An obvious question is whether direct provision of services is the most efficient means of ensuring that the service is delivered. Could it be contracted out instead? A number of public services have been contracted out to private corporations; these include traditional government services such as firefighting and tax collection.[5]

6

Contracting out removes the problem of personnel management from government, a problem made greater by the tenure and pension costs of public employees under merit systems. Also, there may be a tendency to build in a capacity for service to meet maximum demand, resulting in underutilization of expensive personnel. Such a situation could be corrected by the use of contracting.

Another interesting development in the direct provision of services is the use of quasi-governmental organizations to provide services.[6] Frequently there are services that the government does not want to assume entirely but that require public involvement for financial or other reasons. The best example here is the development of Amtrak and Conrail to allow government subsidy of declining railroads without a direct government takeover of these industries.

Money

Governments also provide citizens, organizations, and other governments with money. Approximately 45 percent of all money collected in taxes by the federal government is paid back out in transfer payments to citizens. Another 17 percent is given to other levels of government to support their activies. Transfers for citizens range from Social Security and unemployment benefits to payments to farmers to support the prices of certain commodities.

The use of money to attempt to promote certain behaviors is in many ways an inefficient means of reaching policy goals. The money paid out in Social Security benefits, for example, is intended to provide the basics of life for the recipients, but nothing prevents the recipients from buying food for their pets rather than food for themselves. And the claims made about how Aid to Families with Dependent Children (AFDC) payments are used are legion, if often inaccurate. Thus, while the direct provision of services is rather costly and requires hiring personnel and erecting buildings, many transfer plans are much less certain to reach the individuals and achieve the goals for which they were intended.

The use of money dispersed to other levels of government is both restricted and unrestricted. Of the $100 billion given in 1982 to state and local governments, 95 percent was given in categorical and block grants for specific purposes or for broad categories of purposes, while 5 percent was given as general revenue sharing with few strings attached. Both forms of transfers have been criticized by some and praised by others. Categorical grants do channel resources into the kinds of programs intended, but they also tend to centralize at the federal level most decision making about what is good policy.[7] Also, categorical grants tend to encourage local governments to increase their spending and to create clienteles that must be satisfied even after the federal grant money is exhausted. Revenue sharing, on the other hand, provides money to affluent suburban governments that may use the money for relatively frivolous purposes while the central cities of the nation are in dire need.

Taxes

The government giveth and the government taketh away. But the way in which it chooses to take away may be important in changing the distribution of burdens and benefits in society. In the United States we are familiar with tax loopholes or, more properly, tax expenditures. The latter term is derived from the theory that granting tax relief for certain expenditures is the same as subsidizing an activity directly through an expenditure program. For example, in 1984 the federal government did not collect $34 billion in income tax because mortgage interest payments and state and local property taxes were deductible. This is in some ways the same as the government subsidizing private housing by the same amount, a sum greater by far than the amount spent for public housing by the federal government.[8] The use of the tax system as a policy as well as a revenue collection system is perhaps even less certain in its impact than are expenditures, for the system is essentially providing incentives rather than mandating activities. Citizens have a strong incentive to buy homes of their own, but no program is established to construct housing.

Taxes may also be used more directly to implement policy decisions. For example, there are proposals to substitute taxes on pollution for direct prohibition and regulation of pollution. The logic is that such action could establish a "market" in pollution: Those willing to pay the tax price of polluting would be able to pollute, while those less willing (or more important, able), because of inefficient production methods, should either alter their modes of production or go out of business. The use of this market mechanism is assumed to direct resources in society toward their most productive use; regulations at many times inhibit production and economic growth. Critics argue that what is created is a market in death with the only real solution to the problem being the prohibition or severe restriction of pollution.

Tax incentives are a subset of all incentives available to governments to encourage or discourage certain activities. The argument for their use, as well expressed by Charles Schultze, is that private interests (e.g., avarice) can be used for public purposes.[9] If a system of incentives can be structured effectively, then demands on the public sector can be satisfied in a more efficient and inexpensive fashion than through direct regulation. Clearly, this form of policy instrument is applicable to a rather narrow range of policies, mostly those that are now handled through regulation, but even in that limited range the savings in costs in government and the costs imposed on society may be significant.

8

Also, this type of policy instrument would be much more in line with the Jeffersonian tradition in American thought, promoting the use of market mechanisms to solve public problems whenever possible, instead of relying on direct government intervention.

Other Economic Instruments

Government has a number of other economic weapons at its disposal.[10] Governments supply credit for activities such as farmers' purchases of land and supplies. When it does not directly lend money, government may guarantee loans, thus making credit available (e.g., for the Chrysler Corporation) when it would otherwise not be. Governments can also ensure certain activities and property. For example, flood insurance makes economically possible the development of some lands along the coasts of the United States. Almost all money in banks and thrift institutions in the United States is now insured by one of several insurance corporations within the federal government.

The above instruments share the attribute that although they may be important to their beneficiaries and may influence the spending of large sums of money, they do not show up in most government accounting systems as expenditures. Thus, as with regulation and its costs, the true size of government in the United States may be understated by looking simply at expenditure and employment figures. In addition, the ability of these programs to operate "off budget" makes them more difficult for political leaders and citizens to control.

Suasion

When all other instruments fail, governments can use moral suasion to attempt to influence society. Government as a whole or particular political officials are often in good positions to use such suasion. They have the ability to speak in the name of the public interest and to make those who oppose them appear unpatriotic and selfish. Suasion, however, is often the velvet glove disguising the mailed fist, for governments have formal and informal means of ensuring that their wishes are fulfilled. So, when Lyndon Johnson "jawboned" steel industry officials into rolling back a price increase, the patriotism of the steel officials was equaled by their fear of lost government contracts and Internal Revenue Service investigations of their corporate and personal accounts.

Suasion is an effective instrument as long as the people regard the government as a legitimate expression of their interests. There is evidence that the faith and trust of American citizens in their government is declining. This decline is a response to the excesses of Vietnam and Watergate and to the economic problems of the late 1970s and early 1980s. As governments lose some of their legitimacy, their ability to use this instrument naturally declines. In

9

this case, governments may have to use direct intervention after they have tried suasion without success. Intervention may mean an increase in the size of government taxation and employment and perhaps an increased downward spiral of the authority of government decrees.

Governments have a number of instruments with which they try to influence the economy and society. Using these instruments they distribute what they have at their disposal. The most fundamental things that governments distribute are rights. These are largely legal and participatory, but with the growth of large entitlement programs that distribute benefits to citizens, rights may now be said to include a number of cash-benefit programs as well.

Governments also distribute goods and services. They do this directly by giving money to people who fall into certain categories (e.g., unemployed) or by directly providing public services such as education. They also do this less directly by providing incentives to individuals to behave in certain ways and to make one economic decision rather than another. Governments also distribute goods and services through private organizations and through other governments in an attempt to reach their policy goals. A huge amount of money flows through the public sector where it is shuffled around and given to different people.[11] The net effect is not so great as might be expected, given the number of broad-scale expenditure programs, but the net effect of taxation and expenditure programs in the United States is to make the distribution of income and wealth more equal than the distribution produced by the market.

Finally, governments distribute burdens as well as benefits. They do this through taxation and through programs such as conscription, which take from individuals physically rather than taking from them financially. Like expenditures, taxes are distributed broadly, especially state and local taxes. Even the poorest citizens must pay a sales tax on what they buy, and they must pay Social Security taxes as soon as they begin to work. In other words, everyone in society benefits from the activities of government, but everyone also pays the price.

The Environment of Public Policy

Several characteristics of the political and socioeconomic environment influence the nature of the policies adopted and their effects on citizens. Policy is not constructed in a vacuum; it is the result of the interaction of all these background factors with the desires and decisions of those who make policies. Neither individual decision makers nor the nature of "the system" appears capable alone of explaining policy outcomes. Instead, policy emerges from the interaction of a large number of forces.

Conservatism

American politics is relatively conservative in policy terms. The social and economic services usually associated with the mixed-economy welfare state are generally less developed than those in Europe. This is especially true of government involvement in the management and ownership of economic enterprises such as public utilities and basic industries such as steel and coal. In general this is the result of the American belief in a limited government and in the effectiveness of the marketplace in encouraging economic production. As Anthony King has said: " . . . the State plays a more limited role in America than elsewhere because Americans, more than other people, want it to play a limited role."[12]

Several points should be brought out in opposition to the description of the American government as a welfare state laggard. In the first place, the government of the United States regulates and controls the economy in ways not common in Europe, and in some areas such as product safety it appears to be ahead of European governments. If the effects of regulation are tabulated along with more direct interventions into the economy, the government of the United States appears more similar to other industrialized countries. And we have a tendency to forget the activities of state and local governments, which frequently provide gas, electricity, and even banking services to their citizens.

Also, it is easy to underestimate the extent of the changes in public expenditures and the public role in the economy following World War II. Let us take 1948 as a starting point. Even in that relatively peaceful year, defense expenditures were 29 percent of total public expenditures and 36 percent of federal expenditures. At the height of the cold war in 1957, defense expenditures were 62 percent of federal expenditures and 37 percent of total expenditures. In contrast, in 1982 defense expenditures were 22 percent of total expenditures and 36 percent of federal expenditures, although they have continued to rise under the Reagan administration. Spending on social services—including education, health, social welfare, and housing—increased from 21 percent of total spending in 1948 to 47 percent in 1982. Even for the federal government, social spending now accounts for 27 percent of total expenditures. American government and its policies are conservative, but they are less so than commonly believed, and less so in the 1980s than in the 1950s.

It is also easy to overestimate the conservatism of the American public. Free and Cantril referred to Americans as "ideological conservatives" and "operational liberals."[13] Americans tend to respond negatively to the idea of a large and active government, but also tend to respond positively to individual programs (e.g., Social Security). For example, voters leaving the polls in California after voting *for* Proposition 13, which severely cut taxes in that state, had majorities in favor of reducing expenditures for only one program—social welfare. For most programs mentioned, larger percentages wanted to *increase expenditures* rather than reduce them.

Participation

Another attitudinal characteristic that influences public policy in the United States is the citizens' desire to participate in government. A natural part of democratic politics, participation has a long tradition in American politics. The cry of "No taxation without representation" was essentially a demand for the right to participate. In a large and complex political system that deals with complex issues, participation may be difficult to achieve. Some experts argue that the general public does not have sufficient information or the analytic capability to make decisions about things such as nuclear power. Citizens argue that they not only can make such decisions but that they should and must.

Government has increasingly fostered participation. The laws authorizing community action programs in 1964 were the first to mandate "maximum feasible participation" of the affected communities in the renewal decisions. Similar language was then written into a number of other urban and social programs. Also, the regulation process now has requirements for notification and participation that, in addition to their more salubrious effects, have slowed down the process significantly.

The desire to participate to some degree colors popular impressions of government. Citizens tend to demand local control of policy and to fear the "federal bulldozer" in Washington. Although objective evidence may be to the contrary, citizens tend to regard the federal government as less benevolent and less efficient than the local government. The desire to participate and to exercise local control then produces a tendency toward decentralized decision making and a consequent lack of national integration. In many policy areas such decentralization is benign and probably beneficial. In others, it may produce inequities and inefficiencies. But the ideological and cultural desires for local control may override any practical arguments.

Pragmatism

The reference to ideological desires belies another cultural characteristic of American policymaking that is usually, and quite rightly, applied. This characteristic is pragmatism, the belief that one shall do whatever works rather than follow a basic ideological or philosophical system. American political parties have tended to be centrist and nonideological, and perhaps the surest way to lose an election in the United States is to discuss philosophies of government. (Perhaps the major exception to that generalization has been Ronald Reagan, who has enunciated something of a philosophy of government and who has been successful politically.) This pragmatism tends to make American politics the scene of clashes of platitudes and narrow programs rather than clashes of ideas such as Marxism or fascism—perhaps mercifully.

One standard definition of what will work is "that which is already working," and policies tend to change slowly. The basic centrist pattern of political parties results in agreement on most basic policies, and each successive President and Congress tends to jiggle and poke policy but not to produce any significant changes. A crisis such as the Great Depression or a strong leader such as Lyndon Johnson during the war on poverty may produce significant innovations, but stability and gradual evolution are the most acceptable patterns for policymaking.

Wealth

Another feature of the environment of American public policy is the great wealth of the country. Although it is no longer the richest country in the world in terms of per capita income, the United States is the largest single economy in the world by a very large margin.

This great wealth is threatened by two factors. First, the U.S. economy is increasingly dependent on the rest of the world. This is true in terms of financial and monetary policy, but it is especially true in terms of raw materials. We are all familiar with this nation's dependence on foreign oil, but the economy is also heavily dependent on other countries for a range of commodities necessary to maintain its high standard of living.

Wealth in the United States is also threatened by the relatively slow rate of productivity growth and capital investment. The average American worker is still quite productive but is increasingly less productive than workers in other countries. Also, the factories of the United States are now outmoded when compared to others, and so competition in world markets is difficult. And since we must purchase raw materials on the same world market, the United States has experienced balance-of-payments difficulties, exacerbated by the continuing strength of the U.S. dollar in currency markets. While this may appear remote to the domestic concerns of most policymakers, it does seriously affect the ability of the nation to spend money for the programs that many politicians and citizens want.

Diversity

American society and economy are also diverse. This at once provides a great richness and strength to the country and presents policy problems. One of the most fundamental diversities is the uneven distribution of wealth within society.

Even with the significant shift toward social expenditures discussed above, 36 million people in the United States still live below the official poverty line. The persistence of poverty in the midst of plenty remains perhaps the most fundamental policy problem in the United States, if for no other reason than that it affects so many other policy areas, such as health, housing, education, and crime control.

Diversity of racial and linguistic backgrounds is also a significant policy problem in the United States. While racial unrest like that of the 1960s is now rather infrequent, the underlying problems of social inequality and racism persist. The concentration of minorities in urban areas, the influx of political refugees, and the economic recession of the early 1980s are all combining to exacerbate these underlying difficulties. Again, this diversity affects a number of policy areas, most notably education.

The social and economic characteristics of the country as a whole are also diverse. The United States is both urban and rural, both industrial and agricultural. It is a highly educated society, but it has 2 million illiterates. American policymakers cannot concentrate on a single class or group but must provide something for everyone if the interests of society are to be served. But, in so doing, the resources needed to rectify the inequalities of income and status get used for other services.

World Leadership

Finally, the United States is an economic, political, and military world leader. If America sneezes, the world catches cold, because the size of the American economy is so important in setting world economic conditions. Also, despite a major shift in the patterns of public spending in the United States, many NATO countries still exist under the American nuclear umbrella, and part of the reason for the relatively low military expenditures in other industrialized countries is the reliance on American strength.

The position of a world leader imposes burdens on American policymakers. This is true not only of the defense expenditures already mentioned but also of the need to provide political and moral leadership to the Western alliance. And the U.S. dollar is still the top currency in world financial circles, imposing special demands to keep that currency stable and strong.

The policies that emerge from all these influences are filtered through a large and extremely complex political system. The characteristics of that government and the effects of those characteristics on policies are the subject of the next chapter. Choices have to be made, and thousands are made each day in government, and the sum of these choices, rather than any one, will decide who gets what as a result of public policies.

Notes

1. U.S. Bureau of the Census, *Census of Governments, 1982,* vol. 1, *Government Organization* (Washington, D.C.: Government Printing Office, 1983).

2. Organization for Economic Cooperation and Development, *The Tax/Benefit Position of Selected Income Groups, 1972-79* (Paris: OECD, 1982).

3. Murray Weidenbaum, "The High Cost of Government Regulation," *Challenge,* November/December 1979, 32-39.

4. Murray Weidenbaum, *Business, Government and the Public,* 2d ed. (Englewood Cliffs, N.J.: Prentice-Hall, 1981), 344.

5. E.S. Savas, "Municipal Monopolies vs. Competition in Delivering Urban Services," in *Improving the Quality of Urban Management,* ed. W.D. Hawley and D. Rogers (Beverly Hills, Calif.: Sage, 1974).

6. See Ira Sharkansky, *Wither the State?* (Chatham, N.J.: Chatham House, 1979).

7. Michael D. Reagan and John G. Sanzone, *The New Federalism,* 2d ed. (New York: Oxford University Press, 1981).

8. Executive Office of the President, *Budget of the United States, 1983* (Washington, D.C.: Government Printing Office, 1982), table G1.

9. Charles L. Schultze, *The Public Use of Private Interests* (Washington, D.C.: Brookings Institution, 1977).

10. Christopher C. Hood, *The Tools of Government* (Chatham, N.J.: Chatham House, 1986).

11. Thomas Anton, *Moving Money* (Cambridge, Mass.: Oelgeschlager, Gunn and Hain, 1980).

12. Anthony King, "Ideas, Institutions and the Policies of Governments: A Comparative Analysis," *British Journal of Political Science,* April/July 1975, 418.

13. Lloyd A. Free and Hadley Cantril, *The Political Beliefs of Americans* (New York: Simon and Schuster, 1968).

2. The Structure of Policymaking in American Government

The structures through which public policy is formulated, legitimated, and implemented in the United States are extremely complex. It might be argued that American government has structures but no organization, for the fundamental characteristic of these structures is the absence of coordination and control. This absence of a central control structure was intentional. The framers of the Constitution were concerned about the potential for tyranny of a powerful executive within the federal government; they also feared the control of the central government over the constituent states. The system they designed divided powers among branches of the central government and further between the central government and state and local governments.

The absence of central coordination and control has some benefits for government. First, having a number of decision makers involved in each policy choice should help prevent errors, as all must agree to a proposal before it can be enacted into law or made into an operating program. Also, the existence of several decision makers should permit greater innovation, in both the federal government and state and local governments. And, as the framers intended, power is diffused, reducing the capacity of one central government to run roughshod over the rights of citizens.

Americans pay a price for this lack of coordination. It is sometimes difficult to accomplish *anything,* and elected politicians with policy ideas find themselves, and presumably popular opinion, thwarted by the large number of clearance points in the policymaking system. Likewise, programs may cancel each other out, as the progressive federal tax structures and regressive state and local taxes combine to produce a proportional tax system, or as the Surgeon General's antismoking policies and the U.S. Department of Agriculture's support for tobacco farmers please both pro- and antitobacco factions.[1] The apparent inability or unwillingness to choose among options means not only that policies will be incoherent but also that, since everything receives support from the public sector, taxes and expenditures will be higher than they might have been.

I have already mentioned the divisions that exist in American government. I now look at the dimensions of division and the ways in which they act and interact to affect policy decisions and real policy outcomes for citizens.

Federalism

The most fundamental division in American government has traditionally been federalism, or the constitutional allocation of the powers of government in the United States between the federal government and state governments. This division at once reserves all powers not specifically granted to the federal government for the states and establishes the supremacy of federal law when it conflicts with state or local law. Innumerable court cases and, at least in part, one civil war have resulted from this division of powers among the levels of government.

By the 1980s American federalism had changed significantly from the federalism described in the Constitution. The original constitutional division of power assumed that certain functions of government would be performed entirely by the central government and that others would be carried out by state or local governments. In this "layer cake" federalism, or the "separated powers model," the majority of activities were to be performed by the subnational governments, leaving the federal government with a limited number of functions, such as defending the country, minting money, and delivering the mail.[2]

As the activities of government at all levels expanded, the watertight separation of functions broke down, and federal, state, and local governments became involved in many of the same activities. The layer cake then began to be transformed into a "marble cake," with the several layers of government no longer so clearly isolated from one another. This form of federalism, however, still ruled in the majority of intergovernmental relations through central political officials. The principal actors were governors and mayors, and intergovernmental relations remained on the plane of high politics, with the representatives of subnational governments acting at once as ambassadors from sovereign governments and supplicants for federal aid. And in this form of federalism the state retained its role as intermediary between the federal government and local governments.

Federalism in the United States has been transformed from a horizontal division of activities into a set of vertical divisions. Whereas functions were once neatly compartmentalized by level of government, the major feature of "picket fence" federalism is the development of subsystems defined by policy area rather than by level of government.[3] So, major decisions about health policy, for example, are made by specialized networks involving actors from all levels of government, but those networks may be relatively isolated from other subsystems making decisions about highways, education, or whatever. The principal actors in these subsystems frequently are not political leaders but administrators and substantive policy experts. Local health departments work with state health departments and with the Department of Health and Human Services in Washington in making health policy and are less dependent on the actions of political officials as intermediaries in the process. This form of federalism, then, is as much administrative as political. In fact, in many ways it makes relatively little sense to talk about federalism in its original meaning; it has been argued that contemporary federalism is a facade rather than a picket fence.[4] A term such as "intergovernmental relations" more accurately describes the complex crazy quilt of overlapping authority and interdependence of relationships among levels of government. In addition to being more administrative and more complex, the contemporary system of intergovernmental relationships is more functionally specific and lacks the central coordination that occurs among levels of government.

Despite the complexity and overlapping that exist in intergovernmental relations, one can still argue that centralization of control has grown. State and local governments have become increasingly dependent on central government financing for their services, given the more buoyant characteristics of federal revenue—the progressive income tax, for example. With the distribution of money has come increased federal control over local government activities. In some cases this control is absolute, as when the federal government mandates that local governments provide equal access to schooling for the handicapped or sets water-quality standards for sewage-treatment facilities. Other controls on state and local governments are conditional, based on the acceptance of a grant; if the local government chooses to accept money, it must also accept the controls and requirements associated with that grant. And there are cases in which the failure of state and local governments to act in certain ways may result in the withholding of federal moneys for whole categories of grant funds. For example, if a state did not comply with the requirements of the Health Planning Act of 1974 to pass a certificate-of-need law for health facilities construction before 1980, the state was threatened with the cutoff of all federal health money. In general, the number of controls and conditions attached to federal grants has been increasing, even for grants such as general revenue sharing, which were originally conceived of as no-strings subventions of state and local governments. And even the very existence of a grant is something of a control, inasmuch as it directs the attention and the money of local governments in directions they might not have chosen had it not been for the presence of federal government.[5]

In addition to the controls exercised through the grant-giving process, the federal government has increased its controls through intergovernmental regulation and mandating.[6] These regulations required state and local governments to perform certain actions, such as wastewater treatment, whether or not there is a federal grant associated with the activity. Such regulations can be expensive and certainly are intrusive. One estimate had the state of New Jersey increasing its expenditures for water treatment by $62.54 per capita for capital expenditures and $31.42 for operating expenditures because of the mandates.[7] Further, the mandates change the nature of federalism significantly.

Thus, while the United States retains some features of a federal system of government, the balance of power in that system has been shifting in favor of the central government. With the grant system we have been purchasing a centralized system of government. The shift in control has resulted not from a power-hungry federal bureaucracy, but from the need to standardize many of our public services, such as pure drinking water, and from the need to enforce protection of equal rights for minority groups, to which end school desegregation was linked with continued federal funds for education. Finally, even though programs may have been intended as no-strings grants, the federal government has a natural tendency, especially in Congress, to demand the right to monitor the expenditure of public funds after it disperses them and to use the funds as levers to gain desired actions. And in an era in which the accountability of government is an important issue, such monitoring is very likely to increase.

One factor that further complicates intergovernmental relations in the United States is the proliferation of local governments. As fiscal restrictions on local governments have become more stringent, a number of new local governments have been created to circumvent those restrictions. States frequently restrict the level of taxation or the level of bonded indebtedness of a local government. When a local government reaches its limit, it may take the option of creating a new special authority to undertake some functions formerly performed by the general-purpose local government. For example, as Cleveland faced severe fiscal problems in 1979 and 1980, it engaged in a "city garage sale," in which it sold its sewer system and transportation system to special-purpose authorities. During the 1970s an average of 400 new local governments were created every year, primarily special districts to provide services such as transportation, water, sewerage, fire protection, and other traditional local government services.[8] These new governments present that many more problems of coordination, and they may pose a problem for citizens who want to control the level of taxation but who find that every time they limit the power of one government a new one is created.

The Separation of Powers

The second division of American government exists within the federal government itself and, incidentally, within most state and local governments as well. The Constitution distributes the powers of the federal government among three branches of government, each capable of applying checks and balances to the other two. In addition to providing employment for constitutional lawyers, this division of powers has a substantial impact on public policies. In particular, the number of clearance points in the federal government alone makes initiating any policy difficult and makes preventing change relatively easy. It also means, as we mentioned in our discussion of the incoherence of American public policy, that the major task involved in making public policy in the United States is forming a coalition across a number of different institutions and levels of government. Without such a coalition, either nothing at all will happen or the policy will be modified substantially. The United States is not an administered political system in which one actor makes a decision and all the other actors involved in the policy fall neatly into line; this country has an intensely political and highly complex policymaking system in which initiatives must be followed through the process step by step if anything positive is to result.

The President, Congress, and the courts are constitutionally designated institutions that must agree to a policy before it can be fully legitimated. The bureaucracy, however, although it is only alluded to in the Constitution, is now certainly a political force with which elected officials must contend. Despite its conservative and obstructionist image, the bureaucracy is frequently the institution of government that seeks to generate policy changes.[9] The bureaucracy, or more properly the individual agencies of which it is composed, has interests that can be served through legislation. The desired legislation may only expand the budget of the agency, but it usually has a broader public purpose as well. And administrative agencies, when they wish to, can also impede policy change or block it entirely. Almost every elected politician has had the experience of fighting the delaying tactics of nominal subordinates who disagree with a policy choice and want to wait for the next election or the next cabinet shake-up to see if someone whose policy ideas they prefer will come into office. Their very permanence and their command of both the technical issues and the procedural machinery give the agencies of the public bureaucracy a great deal more power over public policies than one would assume from reading the formal descriptions of government institutions.

One principal result of the necessity to form coalitions across a number of institutions is the tendency to produce a small, incremental change rather than a major revamping of policies.[10] This might be described as policymaking by the lowest common denominator. The need to placate all four institutions of the federal government—as well as many smaller organizations of individuals within each—and perhaps state and local governments as well, means there can be little change from established commitments to clients and producers if the policy change is to be successful.[11] The resulting pattern of incremental change has been both praised and damned. It has been praised as providing stability and limiting errors that might result from more significant changes in policy. If only small changes are made, and these changes do not stray far from established paths, it is unlikely that any major mistakes will be made.

The jiggling and poking of policy characteristic of incremental change is perfectly acceptable if the basic patterns of policy are also acceptable, but in some areas of policy, such as health and mass transportation, a majority of Americans have said (at least in polls) that they would like a significant change from existing policies.[12] The established system of policymaking appears to have great difficulty in producing the major changes desired. In addition, the reversibility of incremental decisions, assumed to be an advantage of that approach to policymaking, is often overstated. Once a program is implemented, a return to the conditions that existed before the adoption of a policy choice is difficult because clients and organizations are created by the choice and will exert powerful pressures for the continuation of the program.

The division of American government by the separation-of-powers doctrine represents a major institutional confrontation in the center of the federal government. Conflicts between the President and Congress over such matters as war powers, executive privilege, and budgetary powers represent conflicts over those ostensible issues as well as a testing and redefinition of the relative powers of the institutions. Is the modern Presidency inherently imperial, or is it subject to control by Congress and by the courts? Likewise, can the Supreme Court have a legitimate role as a rule-making body in the political system, as does Congress? Further, do the regulations made by the public bureaucracy really have the same force of law as the legislation passed by Congress or the decrees of the court system? These are the kinds of questions posed by the separation-of-powers doctrine, which influence not only relationships among institutions but substantive policy choices as well.

Subgovernments

A third division within American government cuts across the institutional divisions within the federal government and links the federal government directly with the picket fences of federalism. The results of this division have been described as "iron triangles," "cozy little triangles," "whirlpools," and "subgovernments."[13] The underlying phenomenon described by these terms is that the federal government rarely acts as one institution to make policy choices, but tends instead to endorse the decisions made by portions of the government. Each functional policy area tends to be governed as if it existed apart from the remainder of government, and frequently the powers and legitimacy of government are used for the advancement of individual interests in society rather than for a broader public interest.[14]

Three principal actors are involved in the iron triangles so important to policymaking in the United States. The first is the interest group. The interest group wants something, usually a favorable policy decision, from government and must attempt to influence the institutions that can act in its favor. Fortunately for the interest group, it need not influence all of Congress or the entire executive branch, but only the relatively small portion directly concerned with its particular policy area. For example, tobacco growers who want continued or increased crop support need not influence the entire U.S. Department of Agriculture but only those within the Agricultural Stabilization and Commodity Service who are directly concerned with their crops. Likewise, in Congress (although the politicization of the smoking issue may require a somewhat different strategy) they need to influence only the Tobacco Subcommittee of the House of Representatives Agriculture Committee; the Senate Subcommittee on Agricultural Production, Marketing and Stabilization of Prices; and the Agriculture and Related Agencies Subcommittees of both the Appropriations Committees of the Senate and House. In addition to the usual weapons of information and campaign funds, interest groups have an important tool at their disposal: votes. They represent an organization of interested individuals and can influence, if not deliver, votes for congressmen. They also have research staffs, technical information, and other support services that, although their output must be regarded with some skepticism, may be valuable resources for congressmen or for administrative agencies.

The second component of these triangles is the congressional committee or subcommittee. These bodies are designated to review suggestions for legislation in a policy area and to make a recommendation to the Senate or the House of Representatives as a whole. An appropriations subcommittee's task is to review expenditure requests from the President, then to make a recommendation on levels of expenditure to the whole committee and then to the whole House. Several factors combine to give these subcommittees substantial power over legislation. First, subcommittee members develop expertise over time, and are regarded as more competent to make decisions concerning a policy than is the whole committee or the whole House. And norms have been developed that support the subcommittee decisions for less rational reasons.[15] If the entire committee or the entire House were to scrutinize any one subcommittee's decisions, it would have to scrutinize all such decisions and then each subcommittee would lose its powers. These powers are important to individual congressmen, and each congressman wants to develop his or her own power base. Finally, the time limitations imposed by a huge volume of policy choices being made by Congress at the present time mean that accepting a committee decision may be a rational means of reducing the total work load of each individual.

Congressional subcommittees are not unbiased; they tend to favor the very interests they are intended to control. This is largely because the congressmen on a subcommittee tend to represent constituencies whose interests are affected by the policy in question. For example, in 1982 the Tobacco and Peanut Subcommittee of the House Agriculture Committee included three representatives from North Carolina and one each from Georgia, Kentucky, Oklahoma, South Carolina, Texas, and Virginia—all states that produce those commodities. There was also one representative from South Dakota. Similarly, the Cotton, Rice and Sugar Subcommittee had representatives from California, Georgia, Louisiana, Oklahoma, Tennessee, Texas, South Carolina, and Washington—all states that produce those commodities.[16] There was one representative each from Wisconsin and Minnesota. And the Housing and Community Development Subcommittee of the House Banking, Finance and Urban Affairs Committee has representatives from the major metropolitan areas of the United States. These patterns of committee and subcommittee membership are hardly random; they increase the ability of congressmen to deliver certain kinds of benefits to constituents through their committee assignments as well as the familiarity of congressmen with substantive issues. In addition, subcommittee members develop patterns of interaction with administrative agencies over which they exercise oversight. The individual congressmen and agency officials may discuss policy with one another and meet informally. And as both sides tend to stay in Washington for long periods of time, they may do so for twenty years or more. The trust, respect, or simple familiarity this situation produces further cements the relationships between committee members and agency personnel.

Obviously, the third component of the iron triangle is the administrative agency. The agency, like the pressure group, wants to promote its interests through the policymaking process. The principal interests of an agency are its survival and its budget. The agency need not be, as is so often assumed, determined to expand its budget. Agencies frequently do not wish to expand their budget share, but only to retain their "fair share" of the budget pie as it expands.[17] Agencies also have policy ideas that they wish to see translated into operating programs, and they need the action of the congressional committee

23

or subcommittee for that to happen. They also need the support of organized interests.

Each actor in the iron triangle needs the other two to succeed, and the style that develops is symbiotic. The pressure group needs the agency to deliver services to its members and to provide a friendly point of access to government, while the agency needs the pressure group to mobilize political support for its programs among the affected clientele. Letters from constituents to influential congressmen must be mobilized to argue that the agency is doing a good job and could do an even better job, given more money or a certain change. The pressure group needs the congressional committee again as a point of access and as an internal spokesman in Congress. And the committee needs the pressure group to mobilize votes for the congressmen and to explain to group members how and why they are doing a good job in Congress. The pressure group can also be a valuable source of policy ideas and research for busy politicians. Finally, the committee members need the agency as an instrument for producing services for their constituencies and for developing new policy initiatives. The agency has the research and policy analytic capabilities that congressmen often lack, so the committee members can profit from association with the agency. And the agency obviously needs the committee to legitimate its policy initiatives and provide it with necessary funds.

All those involved in the triangle have similar interests. In many ways they all represent the same individuals, variously playing the roles of voter, client, and organization member. Much of the domestic policy of the United States can be explained by the existence of these functionally specific policy subsystems and by the absence of effective central coordination. This system of policymaking has been likened to feudalism, with the policies being determined not by central authority but by aggressive subordinates — the bureaucratic agencies and their associated interest groups and committees. Both the norms concerning policymaking and the time constraints of political leaders tend to make central coordination and policy choice difficult. The President and his staff (especially the Office of Management and Budget) are in the best position to exercise this control, but the President must serve political interests, just as does Congress, and he faces an even more severe time constraint. Thus, decisions are rarely reversed once they have been made by the triangles.

One effect of this subdivision of government into a number of functionally specific subgovernments is the incoherence of policy I have already mentioned. All the interests are served by their own agencies, and there is little attempt to make an overall policy choice for the nation as a whole. And these functional subgovernments at the federal level are linked to functional systems in the intergovernmental relations I have already described. The result is that local governments and citizens alike may frequently receive contradictory directives from government and may become confused and cynical about the incoherence of their governments.

A second effect of the division of American government into a number of subgovernments is the involvement of large numbers of official actors in any policy area. This is in part a recognition of the numerous interactions within the public sector and between the public and private sectors in the construction of a public policy. For an issue area such as health care, the range of organizations involved cannot be confined to those labeled "health" but must inevitably expand to include consideration of the nutrition, housing, education, and environment that may have important implications for citizens' health. But the involvement of a number of agencies in each issue area also reflects the lack of central coordination so that agencies can gain approval from friendly congressional committees for expansion of their range of programs and activities. Periodically, a President will attempt to streamline and rationalize the delivery of services in the executive branch and in the process frequently encounter massive resistance from agencies with entrenched interests. For example, in creating the cabinet-level Department of Education, President Jimmy Carter sought to move the educational programs of the Veterans Administration into the new department.[18] In this attempt he locked horns with one of the best organized and most effective iron triangles in Washington—the Veterans Administration, veterans' organizations, and their associated congressional committees. The President lost.

As easy as it is to become enamored of the idea of iron triangles in American government—they do help to explain some of the apparent inconsistencies in policy—there is some evidence that the iron in the triangles is becoming rusty.[19] More groups are now involved in making decisions, and it is more difficult to exclude interested parties. The idea of "issue networks," involving large numbers of interested parties with substantial expertise in the policy area, is now said to be descriptive of policymaking. As important as these issue networks may be in the recruitment of personnel and in providing expertise, they remain an addendum to the underlying structure of subsystems.

American government, although originally conceptualized as divided vertically by level of government, is now better understood as divided horizontally into a number of expert and functional policy subsystems. These feudal subsystems divide the authority of government and attempt to appropriate the name of the public interest for their own private interests. Few if any of the actors involved in policymaking, however, have any interest in altering these stable and effective means of governing. The system of policymaking is effective politically because it results in the satisfaction of most interests in society. The basic patterns of decision making are logrolling and the pork barrel, through which — instead of conflicting over the allocation of resources — actors minimize conflict by giving one another what they want. For example, instead of conflicting over which river and harbor improvements will be authorized in any year, Congress tends to approve all the projects so that each representative can say that he or she produced something for the folks back home. Or congressmen from farming areas may trade positive votes on urban-development legislation for support of agricultural bills from inner-city congressmen. These patterns of policymaking are extremely effective means of governance as long as there is wealth and growth to pay for the subsidization of a large number of public activities without reducing the private consumption of individuals.[20] In an era of increasing scarcity during the 1980s, there is some cause for concern as to whether this pattern of policymaking can be sustained comfortably. But, given the divisions within the structures of American government, it is difficult for the policymaking system as a whole to make hard choices among competing goals and competing segments of society.

Public and Private

The final qualitative dimension of American government that is important in understanding the manner in which contemporary policy is made is the increasing confusion of public and private interests and organizations. These actors and actions have now become so intermingled that it is difficult to ascertain where the boundary line between the two sectors lies. The leakage across the boundary between the public and private sectors, as artificial as the boundary may be, has been occurring in both directions. Activities that were once almost entirely private have greater public-sector involvement, although frequently through quasi-public organizations that mask the real involvement of government.[21] Also, functions that are nominally public have significantly greater private-sector involvement. The growth of institutions for formal representation and for implementation by interest groups has given those groups an even more powerful position in policymaking than that described in the discussion of the iron triangle. Instead of vying for access, interest groups are being accorded access formally and have a claim to their position in government.

The blending of public and private is to some degree reflected in employment.[22] Table 2.1 shows public and private employment in some twelve policy areas, as well as the changes that have occurred from 1970 to 1980. In 1980, for example, only education had more than 80 percent public employees as a percentage of total employment. Even two presumed public monopolies — defense and police protection — had significant levels of private employment.

TABLE 2.1

PERCENTAGES IN PUBLIC EMPLOYMENT, SELECTED POLICY AREAS,

1970-80

Policy Area	1970	1980
Education	87	85
Post office	92[a]	73[a]
Highways	74[b]	68[b]
Tax administration	90[c, d]	60[c]
Police	85[e]	60[e]
Defense	63[f]	59[f]
Social services	26[g]	35[g]
Transportation	33	31
Health	26	30
Gas/electricity/water	25	27
Banking	1	1
Telecommunicatons	[h]	1

SOURCES: U.S. Bureau of the Census, *Census of Governments,* 1972;
U.S. Department of Defense, *Defense Manpower Statistics,* annual;
U.S. Employment and Training Administration, *Annual Report.*

a. Private employees are employees of private services, couriers, etc.
b. Contracting firms involved in highway construction.
c. Estimate of tax accountants and staffs, H&R Block employees,
    including seasonal employees.
d. Rough estimate.
e. Industry estimate of private guards, private policemen, etc.
f. U.S. Department of Labor estimate of employment generated
    by military purchases.
g. Private social work and philanthropy; large percentage employed
    only part-time.
h. Less than .5 percent.

These differ. Defense employment in the private sector is in the production of material for the armed forces, whereas in police protection a number of private policemen actually provide the service. The most interesting aspect of this table is the tendency of employment to go toward a "50-50" economy, with those functions that were more public becoming more private (e.g., police and the post office), and those that were more private becoming more public (e.g., health and social services).

The development of mechanisms for direct involvement of interest groups in public decision making is frequently referred to as "corporatism," or "neo-corporatism."[23] These terms refer to the representation of members of the political community not as residents of a geographical area but as members of functionally defined interests in the society—labor, management, farmers, students, the elderly, and so forth. Associated with this concept of representation is the extensive use of interest groups as instruments both of input into the policy process and as a means of implementing public policies. The United States has made less movement in the direction of corporatism than most industrialized societies have, but there is some movement in that direction nevertheless. For example, changes in the regulatory process and requirements that neighborhood organizations participate in urban programs have made interest groups legitimate actors in the policymaking process. Also, some crop-allotment programs of the U.S. Department of Agriculture have used local farmers' organizations to monitor and implement the programs for some time. Manifestations of movement in the corporate direction have included the use of labor and management organizations as the major participants in President Nixon's Wage and Price Stabilization Board. In health policy, county medical organizations have been used commonly as the Professional Service Review Organizations mandated in the Medicare and Medicaid programs as means of containing program costs and ensuring the quality of care. Also, local Health Systems Agencies organized under the Health Planning Act of 1974 were composed of affected interests as well as public-interest representatives. In addition, as of 1980, there were 3456 advisory bodies for the federal government, many containing interest-group representatives.[24]

Both the increasing use of quasi-public organizations and changes in the direction of a limited corporate approach to governance raise questions concerning responsibility and accountability. Both changes involve the use of public money and, more important, the name of the public by groups and for groups that may not be entirely public. In an era in which the public appears to be attempting to exercise greater control, the development of these patterns of policymaking at "the margin of the state"[25] may be understandable but can only exacerbate the underlying problems of public loss of trust and confidence in government.

The Size and Shape of the Public Sector

We have looked at some qualitative aspects of the contemporary public sector in the United States. What we have yet to do is to examine the size of that public sector and the distribution of funds and personnel among the numerous purposes of government. As already pointed out, drawing any clear distinction between public and private sectors in the modern mixed-economy welfare state is difficult, but let us concentrate on expenditures and personnel that are clearly governmental. As such, these figures inevitably understate the size and importance of government in the United States.

TABLE 2.2

GROWTH OF PUBLIC EMPLOYMENT AND EXPENDITURES, 1950-80

	Public Employment, Civilian (000 omitted)			Public Expenditures (000 omitted)		
Year	Federal	State and Local	Total	Federal	State and Local	Total
1950	2,117	4,285	6,402	$44,800	$25,534	$70,334
1955	2,378	5,054	7,432	77,842	35,645	113,487
1960	2,421	6,387	8,808	97,280	54,008	151,288
1965	2,588	8,001	10,589	110,129	92,553	202,682
1970	2,881	10,147	13,028	208,190	124,795	332,985
1975	2,890	12,083	14,973	341,517	218,612	560,129
1980	2,876	13,315	16,191	576,700	432,328	1,009,028
	As Percentage of Total Employment			As Percentage of GNP		
1950	3.6	7.3	10.9	15.7	8.9	24.6
1955	3.8	8.1	11.9	19.5	8.9	28.4
1960	3.7	9.7	13.4	19.2	10.7	29.9
1965	3.6	11.3	14.9	16.0	13.4	29.9
1970	3.7	12.9	16.6	21.2	12.7	33.9
1975	3.4	14.2	17.8	22.5	14.4	36.9
1980	2.9	13.1	16.0	20.0	16.4	36.4

Table 2.2 contains information about the increasing size of the public sector in the United States during the post-World War II era, and the changing distribution of the total levels of expenditures and employment. Most obvious in the table is that the public sector indeed has grown, with expenditures increasing from less than one-quarter to more than one-third of gross national product. Likewise, public employment has increased from 11 percent of total employment to 16 percent. The relative size of the public sector, however, has *decreased* from the mid-1970s, most notably in terms of percentage of employment. Although public employment increased by some 350,000, its share of employment dropped by 1.6 percent. It is interesting that this drop was occurring at about the same time as the greatest antigovernment sentiment in the United States (e.g., the vote for Proposition 13 and the election of Ronald Reagan). Government in the United States is big, but its growth certainly does not seem to be irreversible.

It is also evident that growth levels of public expenditure are more than twice as large, relative to the rest of the economy, as employment figures. This is largely the result of transfer programs, such as Social Security, which involve the expenditure of large amounts of money but require relatively few administrators. In addition, purchases of goods and services from the private sector (e.g., the Department of Defense's purchases of weapons from private firms) involve the expenditure of large amounts of money with little or no employment generated in the public sector. In 1980, however, those purchases did create 2.1 million jobs in the private sector, a figure that approximates the number of people in the armed forces.[26]

The distribution of expenditures and employment among levels of government has also been changing. In 1950 the federal government spent 60 percent of all public money and employed 57 percent of all employees. By 1980 the federal government was spending just over half of all public money and employed only slightly more than one-fourth of all public employees (including the military). This pattern reflects the continuing importance of the federal government as a funder of public activities, but it also shows that many of its programs are transfers (including those to state and local governments) or purchases from the private sector. In contrast, the programs run by state and especially by local governments are more labor intensive: The share of the total work force employed by local governments has increased by 100 percent, while the absolute number of local government employees has increased by 200 percent. Also involved in this declining share of total employment by the federal government is the shift away from defense and toward social programs: There were 1.6 million fewer uniformed personnel in the military in 1980 than there were in 1952. These data would appear to conflict directly with the many claims of the increasing size of the federal government in American society. Although the federal government is certainly a large institution, employing almost 5 million people in 1980, it has actually been declining relative to the total economy, with the major growth in the government in the United States occurring at the subnational level.

In addition to a shifting distribution of personnel and expenditures by level of government, a shift has occurred in the purposes of expenditures and em-

TABLE 2.3
SHIFTS IN PUBLIC EMPLOYMENT AND EXPENDITURES, 1952-80
(in percentages)

	1952		1980	
	Employment	Expenditure	Employment	Expenditure
Defense	49	46	17	16
Social welfare[a]	24	20	45	50
Other[b]	27	34	38	34

a. Including education.
b. E.g., commerce, agriculture, debt interest, general government.

ployment. Table 2.3 shows the distribution of employment and expenditures for a number of purposes in 1952 and in 1980. What is most noticeable in these data is the "welfare shift" or "antidefense shift" that occurred. In 1952 national defense accounted for 46 percent of all public expenditures and 49 percent of public employment. By 1980 defense expenditures had been reduced to 16 percent of all expenditures (up from 14 percent in 1978) and 17 percent of public employment. By contrast, the panoply of welfare state services (health, education, and social services) accounted for 20 percent of all expenditures in 1952 and 24 percent of public employment. By 1980 these services accounted for 50 percent of all expenditures and 45 percent of all public employment. Within the welfare state services, education was the biggest gainer, with 5 million more employees and $110 million more expenditures in 1980 than in 1952. The United States has frequently been described as a welfare state laggard, but the evidence here is that although it is still behind most European nations in range of social services, a marked increase has occurred in the social component of American public expenditures.

It can be argued that the landslide victories of the Republican party in the 1980 and 1984 elections were a repudiation of this pattern of change, and we should expect to see little increase, or perhaps an actual decrease, in the level of public expenditures for social welfare. This decrease may be difficult to obtain, however, given the nature of most social projects as entitlement programs. That is, once citizens have been made recipients of benefits, future governments may find it difficult to remove those benefits. This is especially true of programs for the retired elderly, as they cannot be expected to return to active employment in order to make up for losses in benefits. And the public expenditures of American government, especially the federal government, are increasingly directed toward the elderly. For example, in 1984, almost 40 percent of the federal budget went to programs for the elderly (Social Security, Medicare, housing programs, and so forth). As the American population continues to become older, on the average, expenditures for this social group can only be expected to continue. And although the elderly have greater claims to entitlement programs than do other groups, once a clientele has been created it is difficult to withdraw benefits. Therefore, cutting the size of government will be hard indeed.

Summary

American government in the 1980s is large, complex, and to some degree unorganized. Each individual section of that government, be it a local government or an agency of the federal government, tends to know what it wants, but the system as a whole is somewhat disorganized and lacking in overall co-ordination and control. An elected official coming into office and attempting to give direction to the system of government may well be disappointed by his or her ability to produce any desired results, by the barriers to success, and by the ways in which the probability of success can be increased.

Notes

1. Harvey M. Sapolsky, "The Political Obstacles to the Control of Cigarette Smoking in the United States," *Journal of Health, Politics, Policy and Law,* Summer 1980, 227-90.

2. Deil S. Wright, *Understanding Intergovernmental Relations,* 2d ed. (North Scituate, Mass.: Duxbury, 1982), 29-41.

3. Terry Sanford, *Storm over the States* (New York: McGraw-Hill, 1967), 80.

4. Wright, *Understanding Intergovernmental Relations,* 75.

5. Michael D. Reagan and John G. Sanzone, *The New Federalism,* 2d ed. (New York: Oxford University Press, 1981).

6. David R. Beam, "Washington's Regulation of States and Localities: Origins and Issues," *Intergovernmental Perspective* 7 (Summer 1981): 8-18.

7. U.S. Congress, "The Impact of Selected Federal Actions on Municipal Outlays," in *Government Regulations: Achieving Social and Economic Balance,* prepared for the Joint Economic Committee, 96th Cong., 2d sess., by Thomas Mueller and Michael Fix, 8 December 1980, 335.

8. U.S. Bureau of the Census, *Census of Governments* (Washington, D.C.: Government Printing Office, 1972, 1977, 1982).

9. Richard A. Goldwin, *Bureaucrats: Policy Analysts, Statesmen: Who Leads?* (Washington, D.C.: American Enterprise Institute, 1980); and B. Guy Peters, "The Problem of Bureaucratic Government," *Journal of Politics* 43, no. 1 (1981): 56-82.

10. For a discussion of "rationalization" in contemporary policymaking, see Lawrence D. Brown, *New Policies, New Politics: Government's Response to Government's Growth* (Washington, D.C.: Brookings Institution, 1983).

11. This corresponds to the idea that the United States has, not one government, but many. See Hugh Heclo, "Issue Networks and the Executive Establishment," in *The New American Political System,* ed. Anthony King (Washington, D.C.: American Enterprise Institute, 1978), 87-124.

12. "Alternative Health Care Systems Favored Over Present Private Plan," *Gallup Opinion Index,* February 1977, 26-27.

13. A. Grant Jordan, "Iron Triangles, Woolly Corporatism, or Elastic Nets: Images of the Policy Process," *Journal of Public Policy* 1, no. 1 (1981): 95-124.

14. See Theodore J. Lowi, *The End of Liberalism,* 2d ed. (New York: Norton, 1979).

15. David E. Price, "Congressional Committees in the Policy Process," in *Congress Reconsidered,* ed. Lawrence C. Dodd and Bruce J. Oppenheimer, 2d ed. (Washington, D.C.: Congressional Quarterly Press, 1981), 175-79.

16. Congressional Quarterly, *Washington Information Directory, 1981-82* (Washington, D.C.: Congressional Quarterly Press, 1982).

17. See Robert E. Goodin, "The Logic of Bureaucratic Backscratching," *Public Choice,* 1975, 53-68.

18. Rufus E. Miles, Jr., "A Cabinet Department of Education: An Unwise Campaign Promise or a Sound Idea?" *Public Administration Review,* March/April 1979, 103-10.

19. Hugh Heclo, "Issue Networks"; and A. Grant Jordan, "Iron Triangles."

20. Richard Rose and Guy Peters, *Can Government Go Bankrupt?* (New York: Basic Books, 1978).

21. Lloyd Musolf and Harold Seidman, "The Blurred Boundaries of Public Administration," *Public Administration Review* 40 (1980): 124-30.

22. B. Guy Peters, "Public and Private Provision of Services," in *The Private Exercise of Public Functions,* ed. Dennis Thompson (Beverly Hills, Calif.: Sage, 1986).

23. Phillippe C. Schmitter, "Still the Century of Corporatism," in *The New Corporatism,* ed. Frederick B. Pike and Thomas Stritch (Notre Dame, Ind.: University of Notre Dame Press, 1974).

24. Linda E. Sullivan, ed., *Encyclopedia of Governmental Advisory Organizations* (Detroit: Gale, 1980).

25. Ira Sharkansky, *Wither the State?* (Chatham, N.J.: Chatham House, 1979).

26. U.S. Bureau of the Census, *Current Industrial Reports,* Series MA 175 (Washington, D.C.: Government Printing Office, 1980).

PART TWO

Making Public Policy

Introduction

Part 2 deals with the processes through which policies are made in the United States. This is a much more complicated process than is sometimes assumed when political scientists discuss "how a bill becomes a law." It involves a great deal more than the legislative process, although certainly Congress and legislation are important elements in policymaking. But to begin and end at the congressional stage begs a number of questions. The first is how the bill came to be introduced into Congress originally and why it was drafted in a particular way. These two questions are discussed in chapter 3, Agenda Setting and Public Policy. Likewise, after Congress acts on a piece of legislation, several stages influence the extent to which the legislation is successful in producing the results intended. First, the proper form of organization must be developed in order to implement the legislation effectively. In addition, the bill and its attendant organization must be funded adequately through the budgetary process. These factors are discussed in chapter 5, Organizations and Implementation, and chapter 6, Budgeting. Finally, the effects of the legislation must be evaluated and, in all probability, the legislation will be modified to take into account the lessons learned during implementation. Few if any policies are ever successful as they come off the proverbial drawing boards. They require years of modification through trial and error to be translated into working programs. Even then, many programs are unsuccessful. As a result, it is important to understand how policies are evaluated and the ways in which policy change occurs. As the policy "space" of most industrialized countries, including the United States, is already crowded with programs and policies, it is especially important to understand the dynamics of policy change.

The description of the policy process is generic, and it is important to pay close attention to differences in the ways in which certain policies may be treated. Defense policy, social policy, new policy, and policy changes go through similar stages, but there are subtle and important differences. Not all of them are dealt with here; some are discussed in part 3, which deals with substantive policy issues.

3. Agenda Setting and Public Policy

This chapter discusses two aspects of the policymaking process that occur rather early in the sequence of decisions leading to the actual delivery of services to citizens but are nonetheless crucial to the success of the entire process. These two stages of policymaking—agenda setting and policy formulation—are important because they set the parameters for any additional consideration of the policy areas. Agenda setting is crucial, for if an issue cannot be placed on the agenda, it cannot be considered. Likewise, policy formulation begins to narrow the consideration of problems placed on the agenda and to prepare a plan of action intended to rectify the problem. Also, these two stages are linked, for in many ways it is necessary to have a solution ready before an issue is accepted on the agenda. In addition, the manner in which an issue is brought to the agenda determines the types of solutions that will be developed to solve the problem.

Agenda Setting

Before a policy choice can be made, a problem in society must have been accepted as a part of the agenda of the policymaking system—that is, as a portion of the range of problems deemed amenable to public action and worthy of the attention of policymakers. Many problems, if they are not perceived by authoritative actors, are not given further consideration. Although problems once accepted as a part of the agenda tend to remain for long periods of time, problems do come on and go off the policy agenda. One of the best examples of a problem being accepted as a part of the policy agenda after a long period of exclusion is poverty in the United States. Throughout most of this nation's history, poverty was perceived not as a public problem but as merely the result of the (proper) operation of the free market. The publication of Michael Harrington's *The Other America* and the growing mobilization of poor people brought the problem of poverty to the agenda and indirectly resulted in the launching of a war for its eradication.[1] And the relatively poor quality of American education, especially in science and technology, did not become an issue until the Soviet Union launched *Sputnik I.* The best example of an issue being removed from a policy agenda is perhaps the repeal of Prohibition, when the government said that preventing consumption of alcoholic beverages was no longer an issue for the federal government, although it retained some regulatory and taxing authority.

What causes an issue to be placed on the policy agenda? The cause is a perception that something is wrong and that something can be improved by public activity. But this forces a second question: What causes the changes in perceptions of problems and issues? Why, for example, did Harrington's book have such far-reaching influence when earlier books, such as James Agee's *Let Us Now Praise Famous Men,* had so little impact?[2] Did the timing of the "discovery" of the poverty problem in the United States result from the election of a young, liberal President who was followed by an activist President with considerable sway over Congress? When do problems cease to be invisible and become perceived as real policy issues for consideration?

Issues also seem to go through an "issue attention cycle," in which they are the objects of great popular concern for a short period and generate some response from government.[3] The initial enthusiasm is generally followed by a period of more sober realism about the costs of the policy options and the difficulty of making effective policy. This in turn is followed by a period of declining public interest as the public finds a new issue. The history of environmental policy and to some extent the women's movement illustrate this cycle very well.

This chapter discusses how to change and manipulate the public agenda. How can a problem be converted into an issue and brought to the agenda for consideration? In the role of policy analyst, one must understand not only theoretical points about agenda setting but also the points of leverage in such a system. Much of what happens in a policymaking system is difficult or impossible to control: the ages of the participants, personal friendships, constitutional structures of institutions and their interactions, external events, to name but a few variables. These factors may be important in explaining overall policy outcomes, but they are not pertinent when one confronts the task of bringing about the policy changes or initiatives one desires.

Kinds of Agendas

Until now we have been discussing "the agenda"—in the singular and with the definite article. There are, however, different agendas for the various institutions of government as well as a more general agenda for the system as a whole. The existence of all these agendas is to some degree abstract. The agendas do not exist in any concrete form; they exist only in a collective judgment of the nature of public problems, or as fragments of written evidence such as legislation introduced, the State-of-the-Union message, and notices of intent to issue regulations in the *Federal Register*.

Cobb and Elder, who have produced some of the principal writing on agendas in American government, distinguish between systemic and institutional agendas of government. The systemic agenda consists of "all issues that are commonly perceived by members of the political community as meriting public attention and as involving matters within the legitimate jurisdiction of existing government authority."[4] This is the broadest agenda of government, being all those issues that might be subject to action or that are already being acted on by government. The definition implies a consensus on the systemic agenda—a consensus that may not exist. Some individuals may consider a problem—for example, abortion—a part of the agenda of the political system (whether to outlaw abortion or to provide public funding for it), while others may regard this issue entirely as a matter of personal choice. The southern states' reluctance to include civil rights legislation on the agenda of the federal government indicated a conflict over what actions fell within the "jurisdiction of existing government authority." The setting of the systemic agenda is usually not consensual, as it is an important political and policy decision. If a problem can be excluded from consideration, then those who benefit from the status quo are assured of victory. It is only when a problem is placed on the agenda and made available for discussion that the forces of change have any opportunity.

The second kind of agenda that Cobb and Elder discuss is the institutional agenda—"that set of items explicitly up for active and serious consideration of authoritative decision-makers."[5] An institutional agenda is then composed of the issues that those in power actually are considering acting on. These issues may constitute a subset of all the problems they will discuss, as the latter set will include "pseudo issues," discussed just to placate clientele groups but without any serious intent to make policy choices.[6]

A number of institutional agendas exist—as many as there are institutions—and there is no reason to assume any agreement among institutions as to which problems are up for consideration. As with the discussion of conflicts over placing issues on the systemic agenda, interinstitutional conflicts will arise about moving problems from one institutional agenda to another. The agendas of bureaucratic agencies are the narrowest, and a great deal of the political activity of bureaucracies is directed at placing their issues on the agendas of other institutions. As an institution broadens in scope, the range of agenda concerns also broadens, and the supporters of any particular issue will have to fight to have it placed on a legislative or executive agenda. This is especially true of *new* problems seeking to be converted into active issues. Some older and more familiar issues will generally find a ready place on institutional agendas. Some older issues are *cyclical* issues: A new budget must be passed each year, for example, and a change in the debt ceiling must be adopted almost as frequently. Other older items may be *recurrent* issues, indicating primarily the failure of previous policy choices to produce the intended or desired impact on society. Even recurrent issues may not easily be placed on a specific institutional agenda, when existing programs are perceived as "good enough" or when no solutions are readily available. Walker classes problems coming on the agenda in four groups.[7] He discusses issues that are dealt with time and time again as either periodically recurring issues or sporadically recurring issues (similar to our cyclical and recurrent issues). He also discusses the role of crises in having issues placed on the agenda, as well as the difficulties in having new, or "chosen," problems selected for inclusion. With each institution, the supporters of issues must use their political power and skills to gain access to the agenda. The failure to be included on any one agenda may be the end of an issue, at least for the time being.

Who Sets Agendas?

Establishing an agenda for society, or even for one institution, is a manifestly political activity, and control of the agenda gives substantial control over ultimate policy choices. So, to understand how agendas are determined requires some understanding of the manner in which political power is exercised in the United States. As might be imagined, there are a number of different approaches to the ways in which political power is exercised. To enable us to understand the dynamics of agenda setting better, let us discuss three important theoretical approaches to the exercise of political power: pluralist, elitist, and state-centric.

Pluralistic Approaches

The dominant, though far from undisputed, approach to policymaking in the United States is pluralistic.[8] Stated briefly, this approach assumes that policymaking in government is divided into a number of separate arenas and that those who have power in one arena do not necessarily have power in others. The American Medical Association, for example, may have a great deal of influence over health legislation, but it does not have much influence over education or welfare policy. Furthermore, interests that are victorious at one time or in one arena will not necessarily win in another time or place. This approach to policymaking assumes that there is something of a marketplace in policies, with a number of interests competing for power and influence, even within a single arena. These competitors are perceived as interest groups that compete for access to the institutions of decision making and for the attention of the central actors in the hope of producing the desired outcomes. These groups are assumed, much as in the market model of the economy, to be relatively equal in power, so that on any one issue any one of the interests may win. Finally, the actors involved generally agree on the rules of the game, especially the rule that elections are the principal means of determining policy.

The pluralist approach to agenda setting would lead one to expect a relatively open marketplace of ideas for new policies. Any or all interested groups, as a whole or as a particular institution, should have a chance to influence the agenda. These groups may not win every time, but neither will they systematically be excluded from decisions, and the agendas will be open to new items as sufficient political mobilization is developed.

Elitist Approaches

The elitist approach to American policymaking contradicts the pluralist approach. It assumes the existence of a "power elite" who dominate public decision making and whose interests are served in the policymaking process. In the elitist analysis, the same interests in society consistently win, and these interests are primarily those of the upper and middle classes.[9] These analysts have pointed out that to produce the kind of equality assumed, the pluralist model would require relatively equal levels of organization by all interests in society. They then point out that relatively few of the interests of working- and lower-class individuals are effectively organized. While all certainly have the right to organize, the elitist theorists point to the lack of resources such as time, money, organizational ability, and communication skills among members of the working and lower classes. Thus, organization for many poor and working-class people, if it does exist, may be only token participation, as their voices will be drowned in the sea of middle-class voices Schattschneider describes.[10]

A variant of the elitist approach to American democracy is the neo-Marxist analysis. This approach is quite similar to that of the elitists, but it is phrased in terms of class domination.[11] The elite, who are assumed by neo-Marxists to be dominant, are the capitalists. In late capitalism, however, capitalists are said to be in collusion with big labor against the interests of "the people" and are thus able to control policymaking by government. According to this approach, government is merely an appendage to the capitalist class for whom it is essential to the process of accumulation.

Again, the implications of the elitist approach are rather obvious. If agenda formulation is crucial to the process of policymaking, then the ability of elites to keep certain issues off the agenda is crucial to their power. Adherents

43

of this approach believe that the agenda does not represent the competitive struggle of relatively equal groups, as in the pluralist model, but that it represents the systematic use of elite power to decide which issues the political system will or will not consider.

Bachrach and Baratz's concept of "nondecisions" are important here. They define a nondecision as follows:

> . . . a decision that results in suppression or thwarting of a latent or manifest challenge to the values or interests of the decision-maker. To be more nearly explicit, non-decision-making is a means by which demands for change in the existing allocation of benefits and privileges in the community can be suffocated before they are even voiced; or kept covert; or killed before they gain access to the relevant decision-making arena; or failing all these things, maimed or destroyed in the decision-implementing stage of the policy process.[12]

A decision not to alter the status quo is a decision, whether it is made overtly through the policymaking process or whether it is the result of the application of power to prevent the issue from ever being discussed.

State-Centric Approaches

Both the pluralist and the elitist approaches to policymaking and agenda setting assume that the major source of agenda items is the environment of the policymakers—primarily interest groups or other powerful interests in the society. It is, however, quite possible that the political system itself is responsible for its agenda.[13] The environment, in this analysis, is filled not with pressure groups but with "pressured groups."

Such a concept of agenda setting conforms quite well to the iron triangle in American government but would place the bureaucratic agency or the congressional committee rather than the interest group in the center of the process. Such an approach does emphasize the role of specialized elites within the government but, unlike the elitists, these government elites are not assumed to be pursuing policies for purposes of personal gain. Certainly their organization may obtain a larger budget and more prestige from the addition of a new program, but the individual administrator has little or no opportunity to appropriate any of that increased budget.

Also, the state-centric approach places the major locus of competition over agenda setting in government itself, rather than in the constellation of interests in society. Agencies must compete for legislative time and for budgets; committees must compete for attention for their particular concerns; and individual congressmen must compete for consideration of their favorite legislation.

One interesting question arises about the state-centric agenda-setting process: What are the relative powers of bureaucratic and legislative actors in defining the agenda? A 1980 study of the Advisory Commission on Intergovernmental Relations argued that the source of continued expansion of public programs was within Congress.[14] The authors of the study argue that congressmen, acting from a desire to be reelected or from a sincere interest in certain policy problems, have been the source of most new items on the federal agenda. Other analyses have placed the source of these new policy ideas in the bureaucracy as much as in Congress.[15] And it is difficult to distinguish congressional or bureaucratic ideas, given the degree of interaction between these institutions.

The agenda resulting from a state-centric process might be more conservative than one resulting from the pluralist model but less conservative than one from the elitist model. Government actors may be constrained in the amount of change from the status quo they can advocate on their own initiative; they may instead have to wait for a time when their ideas will be more acceptable to the public. Congressmen can adopt a crusading stance, but this choice is denied to most bureaucratic agencies. A government-sponsored agenda may be ahead of popular opinion—but just slightly ahead.

Which approach to policymaking and agenda formulation is best? The answer is probably all of them, for the proponents of each can muster a great deal of evidence for their position. More important, policymaking for certain kinds of problems and issues can be best described by one approach rather than another. For example, we would expect policies that are very much the concern of governments themselves and that have few domestic effects, such as foreign affairs and even defense, to be more heavily influenced by state-centric agenda setting than would other kinds of issues. Likewise, certain kinds of problems that directly affect powerful economic interests would be best understood by an elite analysis. Energy policy and its relationship to the major oil companies would fit that category. Finally, policy areas with a great deal of interest-group organization and relatively high levels of group involvement— of both clients and producers—might be best understood by means of the pluralist approach. Education might be a good example of the last kind of policy. Unfortunately, however, these are largely speculations, as the kind of detailed work necessary to track issues as they move on to and off of agendas has yet to be done.

From Problem to Issue: How to Get Problems on the Agenda

The nature of the problems themselves will have an influence on their being accepted as part of the agenda. A number of aspects of problems can affect their chances of becoming a part of the agenda.

The Effects of the Problem

The first aspect of a problem that may influence its placement on an agenda is whom it affects and how much. We can think about the extremity, concentration, range, and visibility of problems. First, the extremity of the effects of a problem should be related to its being placed on the agenda. An outbreak of a disease causing mild discomfort, for instance, is unlikely to produce public action, but the chance of an outbreak of a life-threatening disease, such as the swine flu scare in 1976 or AIDS in the 1980s, may provoke public action.

Even if a problem is not life-threatening, a concentration of unfortunate results in one area may produce public action. Unemployment of an additional 50,000 workers, while certainly deplorable, might not cause major public intervention if the workers are scattered across the country, but may well do so if the workers are concentrated in one geographical area. The concentration of unemployment in Michigan (approximately 25 percent of the work force in that state was unemployed in the summer of 1980 as a result of the slowdown in automobile production) merited a position on the agenda and a promise of action from a President.

The range of persons affected by a problem may also influence the placement of an issue on the agenda. In general, the more people affected or potentially affected by a problem, the greater the probability that the issue will be placed on the agenda. A problem may arise, however: An issue may be so general that no single individual believes that he or she has enough to gain from organizing action. Thus, an issue that has a broad but minor effect may have less chance of being on the agenda than a problem that affects fewer people but affects them more severely.

The intensity of effects, and consequently of policy preferences, is a major problem for those who take the pluralist approach to agenda setting.[16] Many real or potential interests in society are not effectively organized because few individuals believe that they have enough to gain from establishing or joining an organization. For example, although every citizen is a consumer, few effective consumer organizations have been established, whereas producer organizations are numerous and effective. The specificity and intensity of producer interests, as contrasted to the diffuseness of consumer interests, creates a serious imbalance in the pattern of interest-group organization in favor of the producer groups. An analogous situation would be the relative ineffectiveness of taxpayers' organizations as compared with clientele interests such as farmers or defense industries, at least until the 1970s.

Finally, the visibility of a problem may affect the placement of an issue on the agenda. This may be called the mountain-climber problem. Society seems willing to spend almost any amount of money to rescue a single stranded mountain climber but will not spend the same amount of money to save many more lives by, for example, controlling automobile accidents.[17] Statistical lives are not nearly so visible and comprehensible as an identifiable individual stuck on the side of a mountain. Similarly, the issue of the risks of nuclear power plants has been highly dramatized, while less visibly an average of 150 men die each year in coal-mining accidents, and many others die from black lung disease.

Analogous and Spillover Agenda Setting

Another important aspect of a problem that will affect its being placed on an agenda is the presence of an analogy to other public programs. The more a new issue can be made to look like an old issue, the more likely it is to be placed on an agenda. This is especially true in the United States because of the traditional reluctance of American government to expand the public sector, at least by conscious choice. For example, the federal government's intervention in medical-care financing for individuals in the Medicare and Medicaid programs was dangerously close to the much-feared "socialized medicine." It was made more palatable, however, at least for Medicare, by making the program similar to Social Security, which had already been legitimated. If a new agenda item can be made to appear to be an incremental departure from existing policies, rather than an entirely new venture, its chances of being accepted on the agenda are much improved.

Also, the existence of one government program may produce the need for additional programs. This spillover effect is important in bringing new programs onto the agenda and in explaining the expansion of the public sector. Even the best policy analysts in the world cannot anticipate the consequences of all the policy choices made by government. Thus, the adoption of one program may soon lead to other programs directed at "solving" the problems created by the first programs.[18] For example, the interstate highway program of the federal government was designed to improve transportation; it was also justified as a means of improving transportation for defense purposes. One effect of building superhighways, however, has been to make it easier for people to work in the city and live in the suburbs. Consequently, the roads assisted the flight to the suburbs by those who could afford to move. This, in turn, contributed to the decline of central cities. And in turn government has had to pour billions of dollars into Urban Renewal and Model Cities programs, Urban Development Action Grants, and so forth. The cities, of course, might have declined

47

without the federal highway program, but this program certainly aided that decline.

Policies in modern societies are now so tightly interconnected and have so many secondary and tertiary effects on other programs that any new policy intervention is likely to have results that seem to spread like ripples in a clear lake. To some degree analysts should anticipate these effects and design programs to avoid them, but they may never be totally successful in so doing. As a consequence, "policy is its own cause," and one policy choice may beget others.[19]

Relationships to Symbols

The more closely a particular problem can be linked to certain important national symbols, the greater its probability of being placed on the agenda. Seemingly mundane programs become involved in rhetoric about freedom and traditional American values. Phrased differently, a problem will not be placed on the agenda if it is clearly associated with negative values. There are, of course, some exceptions, and although the gay community is not a popular symbol for many Americans, the AIDS issue was successfully placed on the public agenda.

There are several interesting examples of the use of positive symbols to sell programs and issues that might not otherwise have been accepted. The federal government traditionally had eschewed any direct involvement with education, but the success of the Soviet Union in launching *Sputnik I* highlighted the weakness of American secondary and elementary education. This led to the National *Defense* Education Act, which associated the problem of education with the positive symbol of defense, a long-term federal government concern. In addition, although American government has generally been rather slow to adopt social programs, programs associated with children have been more favorably regarded. So, if one wants to initiate a social welfare program, it is well to associate it with children, or possibly with the elderly. It is perhaps no accident that the basic welfare program in the United States is formally labeled Aid to Families with Dependent *Children*.

Symbol manipulation is an extremely important skill for policy analysts. In addition to being rational calculators of the costs and benefits of their programs, analysts must also be capable of relating their programs and program goals to those of others and of justifying the importance of the problem and the program. Placing a problem on the agenda of government means convincing powerful individuals that they should take the time and make the effort to rectify the problem. The use of symbols may allow this when the problem itself is not likely to gain attention.

The Absence of Private Means

In general, governments avoid accepting new responsibilities, especially in the United States with its laissez-faire tradition and especially in a climate of scarcity. But there are problems in society that cannot be solved by private market activities. Two classic examples of problems of this type are social problems involving public goods or externalities.

Public goods are goods or services that, once produced, are consumed by a relatively large number of individuals and whose consumption is difficult or impossible to prevent. This means that it is difficult or impossible for any individual or firm to produce public goods, for they cannot be effectively priced.[20] If national defense were produced by paid mercenaries rather than by government, individual citizens would have little or no incentive to pay that group of fighters, for citizens would be protected whether they paid or not. Instead, citizens would have every incentive to be free riders and to enjoy the benefits of the service without paying the cost. In such a situation government has a remedy for the problem: It can force payment through its taxation powers.

Externalities are said to exist when the activities of one economic unit affect the well-being of another and no compensation is paid for benefits or costs created externally.[21] Pollution is the classic example of an externality. It is a by-product of the production process, but its social costs are excluded from the selling price of the products made by that process. Thus, social costs and production costs diverge, and government may have to impose regulations to prevent the private firm from imposing the costs of pollution—such as damage to health, property, and amenities—on the public. Alternatively, the government may develop some means of pricing the effects of the pollution and then imposing those costs on the polluter. All externalities need not be negative, however, and some activities create benefits that are not included in the revenues of those producing them. So, if a dam is built to generate electrical power, the recreational and flood-control benefits produced cannot be included as a part of the revenues of a private utility, but government can more easily include them in their calculations of undertaking such a project with public money.

Public goods and externalities are two useful categories for consideration, but they do not exhaust the kinds of social problems that have a peculiarly public nature.[22] Of course, the consideration of issues of rights and the application of the law may be regarded as peculiarly public. In addition, programs that involve a great deal of risk may require the socialization of that risk through the public sector. Thus, when banks were unwilling to lend the Chrysler Corporation money, the federal government decided to back those loans and thereby socialize the risk that the banks alone otherwise would have borne. This is only one example of the general principle that the inability of other insti-

49

tutions in the society to produce effective and equitable solutions may be sufficient to place an issue on the public agenda.

The Availability of Technology

Finally, problems will not be placed on the agenda until there is a technology
that is believed to be able to solve the problem. For most of the history of the
industrialized nations, it was assumed that economic fluctuations were much
like the weather: acts of God. Then the Keynesian revolution in economics produced what appeared to be the answer to these fluctuations, and governments
soon placed economic management on their agendas. In the United States this
was reflected in the Employment Act of 1946, pledging the U.S. government
to maintain full employment. The promise of "fine tuning" the economy, which
seemed possible during the late 1950s and early 1960s, has now become extremely elusive, but the basic point is still valid. There was a belief that Keynesian economics was capable of doing the job, and therefore it made sense to
attempt to solve the problem.

Another way of regarding this process of agenda setting is known as the
"garbage-can model" of decision making, in which solutions find problems,
rather than vice versa.[23] Problems may be excluded from the agenda simply
because of the lack of the instruments to do the job. And the example of economic management above illustrates the dangers involved in not excluding those
issues. If government announces that it is undertaking to solve a problem and
then fails miserably, the public confidence in the effectiveness of government
is shaken. Government must then take the blame for its failures as well as the
praise for its successes. The garbage-can model also illustrates the relationship
between agenda setting and policy formulation, because issues are not accepted
on the agenda until there is known to be a policy formulated, or one already
on the shelf, to solve the problem. Solutions may beg for problems, such as
a child with a hammer must find things that need hammering.

As with all portions of the policymaking process, agenda setting is an intensely political activity. It may well be the most political aspect of policymaking, as it involves bringing into the public consciousness an acceptance of a
vague social problem as something that government can, and should, attempt
to solve. It may be quite easy for powerful actors who wish to do so to exclude
unfamiliar issues from the agenda, and consequently there is a need for active
political mobilization. Rational policy analysis may play little role in establishing an agenda for discussion; such analysis will be useful primarily after it is
agreed that there is a problem and that the problem is public in nature. In
agenda setting the policy analyst is less a technician and more a politician,
understanding the policymaking process and seeking to influence that process

for a desired end. And agenda setting cannot be disregarded as a simple political process: It is the crucial first step in resolving any identified problem.

Policy Formulation

After the political system has accepted a problem as a part of the agenda for policymaking, the logical question is what to do about the problem. We can call this process *policy formulation,* meaning the development of a mechanism for solving a public problem. At this stage in the process a policy analyst can begin to apply some analytic techniques to attempt to justify one policy choice as superior to others. Economics and decision theory are both useful in assessing the risks of certain outcomes or in predicting likely social costs and benefits of various alternatives. But rational choice need not be dominant; the habits, traditions, and standard operating procedures of government may prevail over rational activity in making the policy choice. But even such a seemingly irrational choice may be, in its own way, quite rational, simply because the actors involved have had experience with the "formula," are comfortable with it, and consequently can begin to make it work much more readily than they could a newer and technically superior instrument in which they may have no confidence.

The federal government has followed several basic formulas in attempting to solve public problems. In economic affairs, for example, the United States, to gain its ends, has relied on regulation rather than on direct ownership of business; this has also been true of European democracies. But the reliance on this formula is declining, as the growth of public and quasi-public corporations indicates. In social policy, the standard formulas have been social insurance and the use of cash transfer programs rather than the direct delivery of services. The major exception to the latter formula has been the reliance on education as a means of rectifying social and economic inequality. And finally there has been a formula that involves the private sector as much as possible in public-sector activity through grants, contracts, and the use of federal money as "leverage" for private money and money from state and local governments. We should not, however, be too quick to criticize the federal government for its lack of innovation in dealing with public problems. Most governments do not use all the "tools" available in their tool kit.[24] In addition, there is very little theory to guide governments trying to decide what tools they should use.[25] Thus, a great deal of policy formulation is done by inertia or by intuition.

Who Formulates Policy?

Policy formulation is a difficult game to play, because any number of people can play and there are few rules. At one time or another almost every kind of policy actor will be involved in formulating policies. But several kinds of actors are especially important in formulating policies, and several are less important. Policy formulation is a political activity, but it is not always a partisan activity. Political parties and candidates, in fact, are not as good at formulating solutions to problems as they are at identifying the problems and presenting lofty goals for the society.

THE PUBLIC BUREAUCRACY

The public bureaucracy is the actor most involved in taking the lofty aspirations of political leaders and translating them into more concrete proposals. Whether one accepts the state-centric model of agenda setting or not, one must realize that bureaucracies are central to the process of policy formulation. Even if programs are formally presented by congressmen and the President, it is quite possible that the original formulation and justification came from a friendly bureau.

Bureaucracies are presumably the master of routine and procedure. This is at once their strength and their weakness. Bureaucracies do know how to use procedures and how to develop programs and procedures to reach desired goals. The problem is that agencies tend to know how to do these things too well, and they may develop an excessively narrow vision of how to formulate a particular solution for problems. As noted, certain formulas have been developed at the government level for responding to problems, and much the same is true of individual organizations that have standard operating procedures and rule books.

Certainly familiarity with an established mechanism can explain some of this conservatism in the choice of instruments to achieve ends. And faith in certain procedures may also explain part of the rigidity. One important component of the restrictiveness of policy choice, however, appears to be self-protection. That is, neither administrators nor their agencies can go wrong by selecting a solution that is only an incremental departure from an existing program. This is true for two reasons: First, such a choice will not have as high a probability of going wrong as a more innovative program; and, second, such an incremental choice will almost certainly keep the program in the hands of the existing agency. Hence, reliance on bureaucracy to formulate solutions may be a guarantee of stability, but it will not produce many successful policy innovations.

Also, agencies will usually choose to do *something*. Making policy choices is their business, and it is certainly in their interest to make some response to a problem. The agency personnel know that if they do not respond, some other agency soon will, and their agency will lose an opportunity to increase its budget, personnel, and clout. Agencies do not always act in the aggrandizing manner ascribed to them, but when directly confronted with a problem already declared to need solving, they will usually respond with a solution—one that involves their participation.

There is one final consideration about bureaucratic responses to policy problems: Agencies often represent a concentration of a certain kind of expertise. Increasingly this expertise is professional, and an increasing proportion of the employees of the federal government have professional qualifications.[26] In addition to assisting an agency to formulate better solutions to policy problems, expertise also narrows the vision of the agency and the range of solutions that may be considered. Professional training tends to be narrowing rather than broadening, and it tends to teach that the profession has *the* solution to a range of problems. Thus, with a concentration of professionals of a certain kind in an agency, it will tend to produce only incremental departures from existing policies. In addition, the profession of public manager itself is becoming more professional, so the major reference group for public managers will be other public managers, a factor that may also narrow the range of response to policy problems.

THINK TANKS AND SHADOW CABINETS

Other sources of policy formulation are the think tanks that ring Washington and the state capitals around the country. These are organizations of professional analysts and policy formulators. We would expect much greater creativity and innovation from these organizations than from the public bureaucracy, but other problems arise as to what kind of policy option they may propose. First, an agency may well be able to guarantee the kind of answer it will get by choosing a certain think tank. Certain organizations are labeled as more conservative and will usually formulate solutions relying more on incentives and the private sector, while other consultants might recommend more direct government intervention. These reports are likely to have a substantial influence, as they not only have been labeled as expert but they also have been paid for and therefore should be used.

Another problem that arises is more of a problem for the consultants than for the agency, but it certainly affects the quality of the recommended policy. If the think tank is to get additional business from an agency, the consultants believe—perhaps rightly—that they have to tell the agency what it wants to hear. In other words, a consulting firm that says the approach of an agency is entirely wrong and needs to be completely revamped may be technically correct and bankrupt all at once. Hence a problem of ethical judgment arises for

the consulting firm, as it might for individual analysts working for an organization: What are the boundaries of loyalty to the truth and loyalty to the organization?

Two particular think tanks have been of special importance in U.S. policy
formulation. They are the Brookings Institution and the American Enterprise
Institute. During the Nixon, Ford, and Reagan administrations, the Brookings
Institution has been described as "the Democratic party in exile." The Carter
administration did indeed tap a number of Brookings staff members for appoint-
ments; many of them had served previously in the Kennedy and Johnson administrations. On the other side of the political fence, the American Enterprise
Institute housed a number of Nixon and Ford administration personnel, although relatively few have been tapped by the even more conservative Reagan
administration. These two institutions are extremely important, for their publications are indicative of the ideas that people inside and outside government
have about solving policy problems, and they provide places for those who
have been and who may again be in government to think about ways of solving society's problems more effectively.

Universities may also serve as "think tanks" for government. This is true
especially for the growing number of policy studies programs across the country. As well as training the future practitioners of the art of government, these
programs provide a place where scholars and former practitioners can formulate
new solutions to problems. In addition to the policy programs, specializied
institutes such as the Institute for Research on Poverty at the University of Wisconsin and the Joint Center on Urban Studies at Harvard and MIT develop
policy ideas concerning their own specific concerns.

INTEREST GROUPS

Interest groups are also important sources of policy formulation. In addition
to identifying problems and applying pressure to have them placed on the agenda, successful interest groups have to supply ready cures for those problems.
Those cures will almost certainly be directed at serving the interests of the members of the groups, but that is only to be expected. It is then the task of the
authoritative decision makers to take those ideas about policy choices with as
many grains of salt as necessary and develop a workable plan for solving the
problem. And, given the iron-triangle relationships, a close connection is likely to exist between the policy formulation of the agency and that of the pressure group. The policy choices advocated by established pressure groups will
again be rather conservative and incremental and will not produce sweeping
changes from the status quo in which both agency and group have a decided
interest.

Some interest groups contradict the traditional model of policy formulation by interest groups. These are the public interest groups, such as Common Cause, the Center for Public Interest, and a variety of consumers' groups. Perhaps the major task of these groups is to break the stranglehold that the iron triangles have on policy and to attempt to broaden the range of interests represented in the policymaking process. These groups are geared toward reform of policy and policymaking. Some of the issues they have taken up are substantive, such as the reform of safety requirements for a variety of products sold in the marketplace. Other issues are procedural, such as the opening of the regulatory process and campaign reform. But, in general, no matter what issue these groups decide to interest themselves in, they will advocate sweeping reforms as opposed to incremental changes, and these groups are important in providing balance to the policy process and in providing a strong voice for reform and change.

CONGRESSMEN

Finally, individual congressmen are a source of policy formulation. We have previously tended to denigrate the role of politicians in formulating policy, but a number of congressmen do involve themselves in serious policy formulation instead of accepting the advice of their friendly bureaucratic contacts. Like the public interest groups, these congressmen are generally interested in reform, for if they were primarily interested only in incremental change, there might be little need for their activities. Some congressmen are also interested in using policy formation and advocacy as means of advancing their careers, adopting roles as national policymakers as opposed to the more common emphasis on constituency service.

Congress in the 1980s is much better equipped to formulate policy than it has ever been. There has been a significant growth in congressional staff personnel—both personal staffs of congressmen and committee staffs.[27] For example, in 1965 Congress employed just over 9000 people, whereas by 1985 the number of employees had increased to over 20,000. These employees are on the payroll at least in part to assist Congress in doing the research and drafting necessary to be more active in policy formulation, and they are quite important in rectifying what some see as a serious imbalance of the power of Congress compared with that of the executive branch.

How to Formulate Policy

The task of formulating policy involves substantial policy sensitivity and a potential for creative application of the tools of policy analysis. In fact, many problems faced by government require substantial creativity, because little is known about the problem areas. Governments may, however, have to act whether or not they know the best course of action. In many cases the routine response of the agency will be sufficient to meet most problems that arise, but if the response is unsuccessful, the agency will need a more innovative response and more active involvement of a range of actors in policy formulation. Phrased somewhat more abstractly, a routine or incremental response may be sufficient for most problems, but if it is not, the agency or the entire policymaking system must embark on a search for more efficacious alternative policies. Making policy choices that depart radically from the incremental response will require methods of identifying and choosing among alternatives.

Two major barriers block government's ability to understand the problems with which it is confronted. One is a basic lack of factual information. A number of situations can arise in which government lacks information about the basic question. Most obvious is defense policy, where secrecy prevents one side from knowing some facts about the other's capabilities and about the intentions underlying its actions. Similarly, in making risk assessments about dangers from various toxic chemicals or nuclear power plants, there is not enough empirical evidence to enable experts to determine the probabilities of the occurrence of undesirable events.[28]

Perhaps more important, government decision makers often lack adequate information about the underlying processes that created the problems they are attempting to solve. For example, to decide how to solve the poverty problem one should understand how poverty is created and perpetuated. But in spite of masses of data and information, there is certainly no accepted model of causation for poverty. This may be contrasted to decisions about epidemic diseases made by a public health agency that has a well-developed theory about how diseases are caused and spread. Clearly decision making to attempt to solve these two types of problems should be different.

TABLE 3.1
KINDS OF POLICY FORMULATION

| Information | Knowledge of Causation | |
	High	Low
High	Routine	Conditional
Low	Craftsman	Creative

Table 3.1 demonstrates possible combinations of the knowledge of causation and basic factual information. The simplest type of policy to make is the *routine* policy, such as Social Security. Making policies in such areas, with

adequate information and an acceptable theory of causation, requires primarily routine adjustment of existing policies, and for the most part the policy changes formulated will be incremental. This could change, however, if the basic theories about creating a desirable retirement situation or the mechanism for financing such a system were altered.

Creative policy formulation lies at the other extreme of information and knowledge for decision makers. Here we have neither an adequate information base nor an adequate theory of causation. Research and development operations in government, as in the National Institutes of Health or in the numerous agencies of the Department of Defense, provide an important example of policy formulation of this kind. Another may be the delivery of personal social services such as counseling. In these instances, a great deal of creativity and care must be exercised in matching the particular needs of the individual with the needs of the agency for scheduling and efficient management. Such policies require building in reversibility of policy choices so that no choice is irreversible.

In some situations there may be sufficient information but inadequate understanding of the underlying processes of causation. These situations require the formulation of *conditional* policies, in which changes in certain indicators trigger a response of some sort, even if that response is simply the reconsideration of existing policy. It may well be that a government can know that certain policies will produce desired results, even if the underlying processes are not fully understood. With the declining faith in Keynesian economic management, it could be argued that macroeconomic policy is made in this manner. There are several agreed-upon indicators of the state of the economy—unemployment rates, growth rates, and inflation, for example—and changes in those indicators may trigger relatively standard reactions, even though the policymakers may not fully understand the reasons behind those changes. Also, it would be advantageous to build a certain amount of automaticity into the policy response, or at least to provide some insulation against political delay and interference. As in economic management, on the average, countries with relatively independent central banks have been more successful than those with more political central banks.

Finally, in some policy areas governments may have a model of causation for the problem but lack sufficient information to have confidence in any policy response they might formulate. Defense policy might fit into this category of *craftsman* policies. Governments seem to understand quite well how to respond to threats and how to go to war, but they frequently have only limited and possibly distorted information about the capabilities and intentions of their opponents. Building policies of this kind depends on developing a number of contingencies and possible forms of response as well as finding means of assessing the risks of certain occurrences. In other words, formulating such policies may involve building a statistical basis for response instead of relying on the certainty that might be taken for granted in some other policy areas.

Tools for Policy Formulation

Given the difficulties of formulating effective policy responses to many problems, it is fortunate that some techniques have been developed to assist in that formulation. In general, these techniques attempt to make the consequences of certain courses of action more apparent to decision makers and to provide a summation of the probable effects of the policy along a single scale of measurement, usually money, so that different policy alternatives can be more effectively compared with one another. I discuss two of these techniques only briefly here, reserving a more detailed exposition and discussion of the methods for chapter 14. It is important, however, to understand at this time the considerations that one might take into account when choosing among policy alternatives.

COST-BENEFIT ANALYSIS

The most frequently applied tool for policy analysis is cost-benefit analysis (see chapter 14). The concept underlying this technique is to reduce all the costs and benefits of a proposed government project to a quantitative and economic dimension and then to compare available alternative policies, with those economic considerations paramount.

The analysis is in some ways deceptively simple. The total benefits created by the project are enumerated, including those that would be regarded as externalities in the private market (amenity values, recreation, etc.). The costs are also enumerated, again including social costs (e.g., pollution). The long-term costs and benefits are also taken into account, although they are discounted or adjusted because they are in the future. Projects whose total benefits exceed their total costs are deemed acceptable, and then choices can be made among the acceptable projects, generally leading to the adoption of the project with the greatest total net benefit (benefits minus costs).

Some of the more technical problems of cost-benefit analysis are discussed later, but it is important to talk about some ethical underpinnings of the technique here, as they will have a pronounced effect on the formulation of policy alternatives. The fundamental ethical difficulties are the assumptions that all values are reducible to monetary values and that the economic dimension is the most important for government to consider when making policy (see chapter 14). There may well be other values, such as civil liberties or human life, that many citizens would not want reduced to dollars and cents. Even if such a reduction were possible, it is questionable whether government is primarily in the business of maximizing economic welfare in the society.

DECISION ANALYSIS

Cost-benefit analysis assumes that certain events will occur. A dam will be built; it will produce X kilowatts of electricity; Y people from a nearby city will spend Z hours boating and waterskiing on the newly created lake; farmers will save Q dollars in flood protection and irrigation. Decision analysis is geared more toward making policy choices under conditions of less certainty. It assumes that in many or even most cases, government, with inadequate information, is making choices about what to do. In fact, in many instances, government may be almost playing a game, with nature or a human being as its opponent. As already pointed out, governments do not have a very good conception of the impacts of the policy instruments which they might choose, and that lack of knowledge, combined with a lack of knowledge of patterns of causation within the policy areas, is a sure recipe for disaster.

Take, for example, a situation in which a hurricane is forecast to be heading in the general direction of a major coastal city. On the one hand, the mayor can order an evacuation and cause a great deal of lost production as well as a predictable number of deaths in the rush to leave the city. On the other hand, if he does not order the evacuation and if the hurricane does strike the city, a larger loss of life will occur. Of course, the hurricane is only forecast to be heading in the general direction of the city, and it may veer off. What should the mayor do?

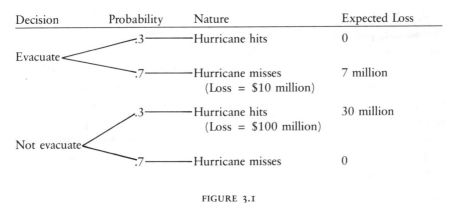

Decision	Probability	Nature	Expected Loss
Evacuate	.3	Hurricane hits	0
	.7	Hurricane misses (Loss = $10 million)	7 million
Not evacuate	.3	Hurricane hits (Loss = $100 million)	30 million
	.7	Hurricane misses	0

FIGURE 3.1
A DECISION TREE ON EVACUATION

This decision-making problem can be organized as a "decision tree" in which the mayor is essentially playing a game against nature (see figure 3.1).

He has two possible policy choices: evacuate or not evacuate. We can assign a probability to each of the two events based on the best information available from the weather bureau, and we have estimates of the losses that would occur as a result of each outcome. In this analysis we assume that, if the hurricane does strike, the loss of property will be approximately the same whether or not the city is evacuated. The mayor would make the smallest possible error by choosing to evacuate the city. By doing so, he might cause an expected unnecessary loss of $7 million ($10 million multiplied by a probability of the event of 0.70) if the hurricane does not hit, but he would cause an expected unnecessary loss of $30 million if he does not order an evacuation and the hurricane hits.

In a simple decision such as this, the decision is rather easy to make if enough information is available. In more complex situations, where many facts need to be considered simultaneously, the decision-making process becomes more difficult. It becomes still more difficult when one faces a human opponent rather than nature. But in these instances, as in cost-benefit analysis, the technique is only an aid to decision making and to policy formulation. Decisions still have to be made, and they can be made only by individuals who consider ethical, economic, and political factors before making a judgment as to what should be done. And, as the results of policy formulation will be felt in the future, the exercise of judgment is particularly important. When an issue is new on the agenda, the first formulation of a solution will to some degree structure future attempts at solution and therefore must be considered especially carefully.

Policy Design

All the aids that governments can use in formulating policy still do not create an underlying approach to policy design. That is, no means of addressing public problems relates the characteristics of the problem to criteria for evaluation, to the instruments that might be used to solve the problem. Without such an approach to design, much policy formulation in government is done by intuition or by analogy with existing policies and programs. This produces frequent mistakes and much wasted money and effort. Thus, one of the tasks of policy analysis is to develop a comprehensive approach to the problems of formulating policy.

Summary

This chapter has taken the policymaking process through its first stages: considering problems and then developing some mechanisms for solving them.

Both these exercises—and indeed also the exercise of policymaking—are political activities, but they also involve the application of techniques and tools for analysis. The tools for agenda setting are largely political and require the "selling" of agenda items to authorized decision makers who may believe that they already have quite enough to do. Agenda setting also requires a detailed knowledge of the issue in question, so that it can be related, first, to the known preferences of the decision makers and, second, to existing policies. Agenda setting is in many ways the art of doing something new so that it looks old.

The techniques that can be applied to policy formulation are more sophisticated in a technical sense, but they, too, require sensitive political hands that will use them effectively. And to a great extent the use of old solutions to new problems is a major means of searching for solutions. For both the agenda and the choice of policy instruments, incremental solutions appear to be in vogue. This produces a great deal of stability in the policy process, but it does make rapid response to changing considerations difficult. The solutions that emerge from these first stages of the policy process, then, are more readily accepted by legislators and administrators who must authorize and legitimate the alternative policies selected.

Notes

1. Michael Harrington, *The Other America: Poverty in the United States* (New York: Macmillan, 1963).

2. James Agee, *Let Us Now Praise Famous Men* (Boston: Houghton Mifflin, 1941).

3. Anthony Downs, "Up and Down with Ecology: The Issue-Attention Cycle," *Public Interest* 32 (1973): 38-50.

4. Roger W. Cobb and Charles D. Elder, *Participation in American Politics,* 2d ed. (Baltimore: Johns Hopkins University Press, 1983), 85.

5. Ibid., 86.

6. Ibid., 96.

7. Jack L. Walker, "Setting the Agenda in the U.S. Senate: A Theory of Problem Selection," *British Journal of Political Science* 7 (1977): 423-45.

8. See Robert Dahl, *Who Governs?* (New Haven: Yale University Press, 1961).

9. See C. Wright Mills, *The Power Elite* (New York: Oxford University Press, 1961).

10. E.E. Schattschneider, *The Semi-Sovereign People* (New York: Holt, Rinehart and Winston, 1960), 35.

11. See Ralph Miliband, *The State in Capitalist Society* (London: Weidenfeld and Nicolson, 1969).

12. Peter Bachrach and Morton Baratz, *Power and Poverty* (New York: Oxford University Press, 1970).

13. See, for example, Douglas Yates, *Bureaucratic Democracy* (Cambridge, Mass.: Harvard University Press, 1982).

14. Advisory Commission on Intergovernmental Relations, *The Federal Role in the Federal System: The Dynamics of Growth* (Washington, D.C.: ACIR, 1980).

15. B. Guy Peters, "The Problem of Bureaucratic Government," *Journal of Politics,* February 1981, 56-82.

16. James Q. Wilson, *The Politics of Regulation* (New York: Basic Books, 1980).

17. Guido Calabresi and Philip Bobbitt, *Tragic Choices* (New York: Norton, 1978), 21.

18. Aaron Wildavsky, "Policy as Its Own Cause," in Aaron Wildavsky, *Speaking Truth to Power* (Boston: Little, Brown, 1979), 62-85; and Brian Hogwood and B. Guy Peters, *Policy Dynamics* (New York: St. Martin's, 1983).

19. Wildavsky, "Policy as Its Own Cause," 63.

20. James M. Buchanan, *The Demand and Supply of Public Goods* (Chicago: Rand McNally, 1968), 3-7.

21. R.H. Coase, "The Problem of Social Cost," *Journal of Law and Economics,* October 1960, 1-44.

22. Charles Wolf, Jr., "A Theory of Nonmarket Failure: Framework for Implementation Analysis," *Journal of Law and Economics,* April 1979, 107-40.

23. Michael D. Cohen, James G. March, and Johan P. Olsen, "The Garbage Can Model of Organizational Choices," *Administrative Science Quarterly,* March 1972, 1-25.

24. Christopher Hood, *The Tools of Government* (London: Macmillan, 1984).

25. John Dryzek, "Don't Toss Coins into Garbage Cans," *Journal of Public Policy* 3 (1983): 354-68.

26. B. Guy Peters, "Public Employment in the United States," *Studies in Public Policy,* No. 63 (Glasgow: Centre for the Study of Public Policy, University of Strathclyde, 1980), 44-47.

27. See Harrison W. Fox, Jr., and Susan Webb Hammond, *Congressional Staff* (New York: Free Press, 1977).

28. W.D. Rowe, *An Anatomy of Risk* (New York: Wiley, 1977); and Susan G. Hadden and Jared Hazelton, "Public Policies toward Risk," *Policy Studies Journal,* Autumn 1980, 109-17.

4. Legitimating Policy Choices

Once it has been decided that a certain policy instrument is required, or is feasible, as a response to a policy problem, that choice must be made a legitimate choice. It is almost certain that no matter what course of action is decided on, some citizens will believe themselves disadvantaged by the choice. At a minimum, any public program or project will cost money, and those who pay taxes and receive (or perceive) no direct benefits from the expenditures will frequently believe themselves harmed by the policy choice. Because policy choices inevitably benefit some citizens to the detriment of others, considerable attention must be given to the process by which decisions are made. It is by means of these processes of government that the substantive policy decisions are legitimated, that is, have the legitimate authority of the state attached to them.

Legitimacy is a fundamental concept in the discipline of political science and is important in understanding policymaking. Legitimacy is conventionally defined as a belief on the part of citizens that the current government represents a proper form of government and a willingness on the part of those citizens to accept the decrees of that government as legal and authoritative.[1] A vast majority of American citizens regard the government of the United States as the proper set of institutions to govern the country. And most Americans consequently accept the actions of that government as authoritative (i.e., as having the force of law) as long as the actions are in accordance with the procedures set forth in the Constitution or are derived from the process described in the Constitution. It is understood that all policies adopted must be within the powers granted to government in the Constitution.

Several things should be understood about legitimacy as it affects contemporary policymaking. First, legitimacy is largely psychological. It depends on the majority's acceptance of the rightness of government. A government may come to power by all the prescribed processes, but if the population does not willingly accept that government, or the rules of the game as enumerated, then the government in practice does not have legitimacy. For example, many constitutions give governments the right to suspend civil liberties and to declare martial law, but citizens accustomed to greater freedom may find it difficult to accept the decrees of governments that operate in such a manner. And changes in government may cause some citizens to question the legitimacy of the new government's actions.

Legitimacy has substantive as well as procedural elements. It matters not only how things are decided but also what is decided. The government of the United States might decide to nationalize all the oil companies operating in the country. (It will not do so, of course, but just imagine for a moment.) The decision could be reached with all appropriate deliberation as prescribed by the Constitution, but it would still not be acceptable to the majority of citizens. In a more realistic example, the war in Vietnam was promulgated according to the procedures in the Constitution, but it nevertheless was not accepted by a significant share of the population. In addition, that conflict evoked a response from Congress, in the form of the War Powers Act, to conflicts of that sort.[2] If subsequent Presidents were to follow that act, their decisions would be less subject to legitimacy questions.

Legitimacy is a variable and not a constant. It works among individuals and across time. Some citizens of the United States may not accept the legitimacy of the current government. For example, some black leaders have specifically rejected the legitimacy of the government of the United States and have called for the formation of a black country within the country; some leaders of the antiwar movement during the 1960s and 1970s also rejected the legitimacy of government. A general decline in confidence in American institutions has been occurring, and that decline has been especially pronounced for government (see table 4.1). Even with an upturn in trust in 1982, the confidence

TABLE 4.1

CONFIDENCE IN GOVERNMENT *(in percentages)*

ANSWERS TO: *"How much of the time can you trust
the government in Washington to do what is right?"*

	1964	1966	1968	1970	1972	1974	1976	1978	1980	1982
None	0	3	0	0	1	1	1	4	4	2
Some of the time	22	28	36	44	44	61	62	64	69	62
Most of the time	62	48	54	47	48	34	30	27	23	31
Always	14	17	7	7	5	3	3	3	2	2
Don't know	2	4	2	2	2	2	3	3	2	3
TOTAL	100	100	99[a]	100	100	101[a]	99[a]	101[a]	100	100

SOURCE: "Opinion Roundup," *Public Opinion,* July/August 1978 and April/May 1983.
a. Rounding error.

that Americans feel toward their government is now much less than in the past. In some societies that are deeply divided ethnically or politically, the rejection of the sitting government by one or another element may be a constant fact of life. Even a government that is widely accepted may lose legitimacy, or strain its legitimate status, by some of its activities or some of its personnel. The Vietnam war and Watergate illustrate the low points to which the legitimacy of even a widely accepted political regime may be reduced.

Because of the variability of legitimacy, a fully legitimated government may gradually erode its legitimate status through time. A series of blatantly unpopular or illegal acts, committed by a widely accepted government, may reduce the authority of that government. That government may then become open to a challenge, whether of a revolutionary or a more peaceable nature. Or a government may lose legitimacy through incompetence, rather than unpopular activities. Citizens in most countries have a reservoir of respect, which they can gradually lose, for their governments. As a result, governments engage in a continuing process of legitimation for themselves and for their successors.

Finally, government must somehow legitimate each individual policy choice. No matter how technically correct a policy choice may be, it is of little practical value if it cannot be legitimated. Policy analysts, in their pursuit of elegant solutions and innovative policies, frequently forget this mundane point, but their forgetfulness is a real barrier to their success.[3] To legitimate a decision a policy analyst must understand the political process, for that political process may define the set of feasible alternatives in a more restrictive fashion than does the social and economic world. Thus it is the task of the policy analyst to be able to "sell" his or her decisions to those individuals who are crucial to their being legitimated.

In general, legitimation is performed through the legislative process, through the administrative process designed for the issuing of regulations, through the courts, and through mechanisms for direct democracy. As shown in table 4.2,

TABLE 4.2
KINDS OF LEGITIMATION

Majority Involvement	Majoritarian	Nonmajoritarian
Mass	Referenda	—
Elite	Congress	Courts; administrative regulations

these can be seen as combining characteristics of the decisions—majoritarian or nonmajoritarian—and the range of actors involved. The nonmajoritarian mass cell is empty in this table, but it may be filled by revolutionary or intense group activities. Let us now discuss each kind of legitimation and its implications for the kind of policy choices that may be feasible in each process.

Legislative Legitimation

In the United States we have traditionally equated lawmaking with Congress, the principal legislative body. As this section points out, this notion is now excessively naive, for the work load and the technical content of many subjects on which decisions must be made have overwhelmed Congress. This is true despite the massive growth of legislative staffs and the availability of increased advice for congressmen.[4] Governments are simply too large and involved in too many issues to permit a large and complex institution such as Congress to make all the decisions that are required to keep the society functioning.

Of course, Congress remains a crucial source of primary legislation. That is, although administrative bodies are responsible for writing regulations in large numbers, Congress must supply the basic legislative framework within which other bodies may operate. Congress tends to pass legislation written in relatively broad language, allowing administrators latitude for interpretation. Thus, in the 1980s, despite the resurgence of congressional power in opposition to the "imperial presidency," it is best to think about legitimation in Congress as the legitimation of relatively diffuse statements of goals and structures that allow the executive branch to fill in the details by writing regulations and by using the implementation process itself. Congress also retains its supervisory powers so that if the executive branch strays too far in writing the regulation, Congress can reassert its powers to explain what its intentions were when it constructed the legislation. Until 1983 Congress had at its disposal the "legislative veto," which required agencies issuing certain regulations to submit those regulations to Congress for approval. The Supreme Court, however, declared the veto to be excessive meddling by one branch of government in the affairs of another.

The Congress places a great deal of emphasis on procedural legitimation and has established elaborate sets of procedures for processing legislation.[5] In fact, its procedures have been so well developed that it is difficult for legislation to be passed. Typically, a bill must be passed by subcommittee, committee, and floor action in each house. And, as one house is unlikely to pass exactly the same version of the bill that the other house passed, conference committees will be necessary. Given the possibility of more arcane procedural mechanisms such as filibusters, amendments, and recommittals, legislation can be slowed down or killed at a number of points by failure to attract the necessary majority at the right time. Or, to put it the other way around, all that the opponents of a bill must do is to form a majority at one crucial point to prevent the passage of the legislation. These procedures are important as a mechanism to prevent unnecessary or poorly considered legislation from becoming law, but they also offer the possibility that good legislation can be frustrated. The ability of the opposition to postpone and block civil rights legislation during the 1950s and early 1960s demonstrates the use of legislative procedures to thwart the apparent majority will of the Congress.

Legitimation through the legislative process is majoritarian. It depends on the building of simple or special majorities at each crucial point in the process. The job of the policy analyst, or of the legislative leaders of a bill, is to construct such majorities. In addition to appealing on the basis of the actual qualities of the proposed legislation, such majorities can be formed in several ways. One method has been referred to as "partisan analysis."[6] This involves convincing members of Congress that the piece of legislation the analyst wants passed is also something the other members want. The trick here is to design the legislation in such a way that it will appeal to a sufficient number of interests to gain a winning coalition. For example, the National Defense Education Act of 1958 was passed by a coalition of congressmen interested in education and in defense. The title of the bill indicates that it was intended to serve two purposes, and it brought together liberals who favored federal aid to education and conservatives who were interested in improving the defense capabilities of the United States. Also, many social and housing programs have been "sold" to more conservative interests in Congress as benefiting business — as urban renewal certainly did — or as providing employment.[7]

Another strategy that is not dissimilar to partisan analysis is logrolling.[8] In logrolling, coalitions are formed not around a single piece of legislation but across a set of legislative initiatives. In the simplest example, Congressman A favors Bill A and is indifferent toward Bill B. Congressman B, on the other hand, favors Bill B but is indifferent toward Bill A. The logical thing for these two congressmen to do is to trade their votes on the two pieces of legislation, with A voting for Bill B and B voting for Bill A. The real world may not be so simple, though, and several bills may become involved in the trading of votes. In some ways logrolling is a rational activity, for it allows the passage of legislation that some congressmen, and presumably their constituencies, favor intensely and that might not otherwise be able to gain a majority. Logrolling, however, also has the effect of passing a great deal more legislation than would otherwise be passed, thus affecting the amount of public expenditure and taxation. It enables relatively narrow interests in the nation to develop coalitions for their legislation that may not be justifiable in terms of a broader concept of "the public interest."

As well as being a majoritarian body, Congress has universalistic norms that promote the spreading of government expenditures very broadly. This is commonly referred to as "pork-barrel" legislation. Legislation of this kind often concerns capital expenditures, the classic examples being river and harbor improvements. Obtaining capital projects such as these has become a measure of success for congressmen, and some argue that it, rather than policymaking on broad national issues, has become the dominant activity of congressmen.[9] Congressional representatives have to demonstrate to their constituents that they can "bring home the bacon" and produce tangible benefits for the voters. Thus, the tendency in designing legislation of this kind is to spread expenditures as broadly as possible geographically and to create a majority by benefiting virtually anyone who wants a piece of the "pork." As with logrolling, this kind of decision making tends to increase the costs of government. Arnold is quite correct, however, in pointing out that such legislation costs very little in comparison with national defense or major entitlement programs such as Social Security.[10] It may, however, stand as an example of the way government wastes money by funding projects with relatively low social benefit in order to ensure the reelection of incumbent congressmen.

The description of legitimation through the legislative process does not give the most favorable impression of Congress. Actually, a good deal of congressional decision making is done on the basis of the merits of the legislation. To the extent that partisan analysis, logrolling, and pork-barrel legislation do characterize the actions of Congress, however, the legislative process has certain effects on the rules that can be legitimated. It can be argued that the legislative process will inevitably produce broad and rather diffuse legislation. The necessity of building a coalition requires that one take care not to offend potential members, and it does result in benefits to individual congressmen. As a consequence, legislation must be designed that is amenable to partisan analysis and is not so clearly worded as to reduce the number of possible coalition members. This, of course, allows administrators to make more difficult and politically charged decisions on cases, thus deflecting criticism from Congress.

Also, it can be argued that legislative decision making is associated with an expanding government. Both logrolling and pork-barrel legislation are perhaps related to the expansion of government beyond the bounds that could be set if there were no possibility of vote trading. And with pork-barrel legislation there is the tendency to adopt public projects that are marginal in terms of their social productivity. We know quite well that the world of policymaking is by no means perfectly rational, but these patterns of institutional decision making appear to exacerbate the irrational character of politics.

These difficulties in congressional decision making also suggest some more general points concerning the problems of social decision making. In its simplest terms, the problem is this: How can a set of social preferences best be expressed in a single decision? Congress faces this problem when it attempts to combine the preferences of its members and their constituents in a single decision as to whether or not to adopt a piece of legislation; the same general problem arises in club, committee, and college faculty meetings.

One underlying problem facing decision makers is the issue of intensity. We faced this in discussing the logic of logrolling. In a majoritarian system, it may be possible to construct a majority composed of individuals who are not much interested in a proposal and who do not feel intensely about it. This is in part a function of having a single vote for each person, whereas in the market setting, individuals have more than one dollar and can apply their resources differentially depending on their preferences and the intensity of those preferences. Logrolling is one means of attempting to overcome the intensity problem, but it can work only in a limited set of circumstances with a certain distribution of preferences. In majoritarian institutions with one vote for each member, it is difficult to reflect accurately the preferences of the participants in a decision that creates the greatest net satisfaction for the participants. This is made additionally difficult if in a number of successive decisions (e.g., voting on amendments) the order in which options are eliminated affects the final preferences.[11] In examining the problems of making choices of this kind, Arrow argued that it is impossible to devise a social-choice mechanism that satisfies certain logical conditions for rationality.[12] The only way in which such decisions can be arrived at in his framework is to impose them, which he rejects on moral grounds. But the imposition of administrative regulations as another means of legitimating decisions has some characteristics of imposed solutions, although the regulatory procedures have been sanctioned legally.

Regulations and the Administrative Process

Most rule making in the United States, and in other industrialized societies, is now done through the regulatory process.[13] Here we are referring to the regulatory process in a rather broad context to include the actions of executive branch agencies as well as those of independent regulatory commissions. We will be discussing the process by which administrative or regulatory bodies issue binding regulations that are subsidiary to congressional legislation. These regulations are sometimes referred to as secondary legislation, and the issuance of such legislation is definitely a legislative or legitimating activity, as it

69

makes rules for the society, but it is pursuant to primary legislation adopted by Congress.

The volume of this activity is immense. It can be judged by the size of the *Federal Register,* a weekly publication containing all regulations and proposed regulations, and by the size of the *Code of Federal Regulations* containing all the regulations currently in force. One example of the volume of regulatory activity is provided by the Occupational Safety and Health Administration (OSHA), an agency of the Department of Labor. OSHA, which has been a frequent target of critics of government regulation, issued 4600 regulations during the first two years of its existence.[14]

Although conducted through a legal process, the decision making associated with adopting regulations is not majoritarian. If it were, most of the regulations adopted by OSHA or by many of the other regulatory bodies might never have been adopted. The decision making in the regulatory process can afford to be more technical and less tied to political considerations than can decision making in Congress, but political considerations cannot be neglected entirely. This is especially true for agencies that are a part of executive branch departments. Such agencies are responsible directly to the President and consequently must issue regulations that address the political priorities of the President. And even the regulations issued by independent regulatory commissions cannot afford to be too far from the basic political and ideological norms of the population; if they are, the agency will threaten its own survival.

If the making of regulations is not directly politicized, it is nevertheless open to public influence. The procedures mandated by the Administrative Procedures Act and several other laws affecting the issuing of regulations specifically require that the agencies accept advice and ideas from citizens as the process goes forward, and they require delays at each stage to allow time for affected interests in the society to respond. For some segments of the economy, in fact, the regulatory process may be more democratic than decision making in Congress. The regulatory process requires the direct access of affected interests to the decision makers, whereas in Congress those affected interests may be excluded from any involvement, especially if they are not considered representative of interests widely accepted as "legitimate" by congressmen. This does, not, of course, mean that the responses of the affected interests will be crucial to the decisions that are finally made. And this does not protect the interests of segments of the society that are not sufficiently well organized or alert to make their presentations to the agency. But it does indicate the openness of the regulatory process to ideas and options.

The writing of regulations goes through three basic steps. First, the agency is required to publish, in the *Federal Register,* a notice of its intent to issue a certain regulation. Then a period of three months is allowed during which those who believe themselves potentially affected can offer opinions and make suggestions about the content of the regulation. After the three months have passed, the agency may issue a draft regulation. This, as the name implies, is a draft of the regulation that the agency ultimately would like to see put into effect. It may be based on the suggestions received from affected interests, or it may be what the agency had planned all along. Then a three-month waiting period follows, during which the affected groups can respond to the draft regulation. They may respond to the agency in person, or they may respond indirectly—for example, by getting congressmen to put pressure on the agency to alter the draft regulation. Then, based on the response of the affected groups and its own beliefs about the appropriateness of the regulation, the agency will issue a final regulation that will have the force of law, a force derived from a statute passed by Congress and from following correct procedures in issuing the regulation. In general, the issuing of a regulation requires about eighteen months from beginning to end and allows for substantial representation of affected groups and individuals.

The role assigned to affected interests in responding to issues in the regulatory process brings up another point that pertains to social decision making. This is the point made by John C. Calhoun, in part as a means of justifying the continuation of slavery. Calhoun argued that a proper democracy would take into account not only a majority of individuals but also a majority of interests in the society. His idea of the "concurrent majority" would have assigned a greater importance to the role of pressure groups than is true in most American political thought and would have made the opinions of the groups in the regulatory process more crucial in the decisions.[15]

The role of pressure groups in regulatory decision making also has some relationship to the development of "neocorporatism" in Western Europe.[16] The principal difference is that interest groups in the United States usually are not accorded the quasi-official status they have in Europe. Further, the affected interest groups are rarely brought together to negotiate a compromise decision as they would in most European systems. Decision making in this country is still done largely within the agency, but there is now an attempt to use pressure groups as a means of improving the quality of the decisions made by government. In addition to protecting the interests of their members, these groups frequently make important substantive points about proposed regulations, and they can prevent agencies from making serious errors.

Finally, regulatory decision making is also threatened by the classic problem of the capture of regulatory agencies by the very interests they were designed to regulate.[17] Agencies that regulate a single industry have tended to become advocates of their industries rather than impartial protectors of the public interest. This results from the agencies' need to maintain political support when — especially in the case of independent regulatory agencies — the only logical source of support is the regulated industry itself. The public is too amorphous a body to offer the specific support the agency may need in defending its budget, or its very existence, before Congress. Thus the reforms intended to remove political pressures from regulatory decision making by making the agencies independent only substitute one form of political influence for another. In Lowi's phrase, the public interest is appropriated for private gain.[18] The capture argument is less relevant to the newer regulatory agencies, which act across a number of industries, than it is to single-industry regulatory bodies.[19] For example, either the Consumer Products Safety Commission or the Occupational Safety and Health Administration regulates virtually every industry in the country, and their advocacy of one industry would harm other industries. It is generally too difficult for an industry to capture these cross-cutting regulators, and they are more likely to act in the broader public interest. But, of course, the agency itself must still define "public interest."

Regulation is a central process of legitimation, although it is one that many citizens would challenge. Many popular writers comment on laws being made by bureaucrats without what the writers regard as the proper processes of legitimation. The procedures used are "due," however, and have been ordained by an act of Congress. In addition, each regulation issued must have a legislative peg to hang on. But, unlike legislation produced in Congress, these regulations tend to make specific judgments and decisions and by so doing to affect individual interests more clearly. Many regulations issued through this process may have been criticized as impractical and unnecessary: Everyone has his or her favorite silly regulation. But there is still the possibility of greater objectivity and the application of greater objective rationality in this process than in the more politicized arena of Congress. It may be, in fact, that this very attempt to apply strict criteria is the source of many objections.

The Courts

Another nonmajoritarian means of legitimating policies is through the courts. Along with the increasing role of the administrative process in legitimation, there has been an increase in the involvement of the courts in issuing legitimating decrees. And, along with the complaints against the administrative process, there have been a number of complaints against "judge-made law." Of course, the courts have been involved in legitimating actions and issuing law-like statements in the United States for some time, but perhaps because of the increasing litigation involving social issues and the willingness of the courts to make declarations on how to eliminate situations that violate the Constitution or federal laws, there is a greater popular awareness of the role of the courts in making rules for society.

The courts have as their constitutional basis for making legitimating decisions the supremacy clause, which says that all laws and treaties made in pursuance to the Constitution are the supreme law of the land. And in *Marbury* v. *Madison,* Chief Justice John Marshall decided that it was incumbent on the courts to decide whether a law conformed to the Constitution and to declare, if it did not, that the law was void. Following from that basic declaration of judicial power, the courts have been able to make rules based on their interpretation of the Constitution. Particularly crucial to their role in legitimating actions is their ability to accept or reject the remedies proposed by parties to particular disputes. If an action is declared unconstitutional, the courts frequently become involved in determining the actions necessary to eliminate that unconstitutionality. The involvement of the courts in disputes over school desegregation comes to mind immediately. In several cases, such as *Swann* v. *Charlotte-Mecklenburg Board of Education,* the courts have declared that the existence of boundaries between certain school districts constitutes an intent on the part of local government to maintain or create racial segregation of the schools; the courts have been willing to accept cross-district busing as the only remedy for the problem. Such decisions represent rather greater involvement of the courts in mandating state and local government action than has been true historically.

The role the courts have adopted in legitimating actions is twofold. In its simplest sense, the courts may further legitimate the actions of other decision makers by declaring that their actions are indeed acceptable under the Constitution. As mentioned, American society appears to be becoming increasingly litigious, so more and more issues are not fully decided until they have been ruled on by the courts. Litigation presents an important means of protecting individual rights in the policymaking process, but it can also slow down greatly the implementation of policy. Putting an issue into the courts is sometimes a means of winning a conflict simply by delay, as the attempts to block the construction of nuclear power plants indicate.

In a second sense, the courts take part in policy legitimation by deciding that certain conditions existing in the society are in contradiction to the Constitution and by then offering a solution to those problems. The role of the courts in school desegregation is an example of this kind of involvement. This has been true not only in the busing cases but also in the entire process of desegregation beginning with *Brown* v. *Board of Education* (1954). The courts have acted relatively independently of other political institutions and have been

73

active in making decisions and in offering remedies they believe are derived from sound constitutional principles.

Because the role of the courts is to judge the constitutionality of actions and to protect individual liberties against possible incursions by government or by other individuals, decision making in the courts can be expected to be different from decision making by a legislative body. In many ways the decisions made by the courts are more authoritative than other legitimating decisions, both because of the courts' connection to constitutional authority and because of the absence of any ready avenue of appeal, once appeals through the court system are exhausted. The courts leave less room for compromise and vote trading than does a legislative body, and they have a less clearly defined constituency, if they have any constituency at all. And the courts' decisions will be narrower, generally speaking to the particular case in question but not establishing a general statement of the principle to be implemented in other decisions. These decisions legitimate certain actions but leave any future decisions ambiguous, whereas decisions taken by both legislatures and administrative agencies are attempts to develop more general principles to guide further actions and decisions.

Popular Legitimation

The three methods of legitimation discussed so far have one point in common: They are performed by elites in the political process. A number of American states have mechanisms for direct democracy that allow voters to legitimate policy decisions. These constitute in part a way for state legislatures to "pass the buck" to the people on issues the legislators believe might be too hot to handle for the good of their future political careers. And in some instances the people can use these mechanisms to bypass the legislatures entirely or to prod them into action. Despite some agitation, these mechanisms for direct democracy have not been adopted at the level of the federal government.

The majority of states in the United States employ *referenda* for some policy decisions. Typically, approval of the voters is required to pass bond issues and to change the state constitution. A referendum is a vote of the people on an issue put to them by the legislature or by some other authoritative body. Approval of the popular vote is required before the measure in question can become law. In some states, in addition to passing on bonding issues and constitutional changes, referenda are used to pass other legislation. An issue thought by the legislature to be of sufficient importance, or highly charged politically, may be put to the voters for a decision. This certainly satisfies the tenets of democracy, but it may lead to relatively uninformed voters deciding on issues of great importance that would be better decided in more expert deliberative bodies.

The *initiative* is an even more extreme means of involving the mass of voters in policymaking. The initiative allows voters not only to pass on an issue put to them by government but also to place issues on the ballot. If the requisite number of signatures is obtained, the item will be voted on at the next election and, if approved, will become law. A number of significant policy issues—most notably Proposition 13, which limited property taxes in California—have been passed by initiative. The initiative has many of the same problems as the referendum. One difficulty is that complex policy issues such as nuclear power become embroiled in political campaigns so that the complex issues at question become trivialized and converted into advertising slogans. The initiative does offer an avenue for the expression of popular opinion, however, and it gives some real power to the voters, who may be absent from representative policymaking institutions.

Summary

Legitimation is at once the most difficult and the simplest component of the policymaking cycle. It involves the least complex forms of policy analysis, and the number of actors is relatively constrained unless initiative and referenda are used. The actors involved are relatively powerful, however, and have definite agendas of their own. Consequently, the task of the policy analyst seeking to alter perceptions and create converts is difficult. The barriers that the analyst faces are sometimes individual and political, as when congressmen must be convinced, through partisan analysis or through vote trading, to accept one concept of the policy world. Conversely, the task may be one of altering substantial organizational constraints on a vision of the appropriate policy response to a particular problem or a whole set of problems. Or the problem may be a legal one of persuading the courts to respond appropriately to a set of facts and to develop an appropriate remedy to the perceived problem. Or, finally, the problem may be political in the broadest sense of persuading the voters to accept or reject an issue. This is a great range of problems that demand a great range of skills.

No individual is likely to have all these skills, but someone must make strategic choices as to which arenas are most appropriate for a particular problem. If the problem is to get a dam built, then Congress is clearly the most appropriate arena, but if the problem is a civil rights violation, the best place to begin is probably the court system. Policies do not simply happen, they must be made to happen. This is especially true given the degree of inertia in American politics and the number of points at which any action can be blocked. As in so many problems, the major task of the policy analyst may be to define the problem that must be solved. Once that is done, the solution may not be simple, but at least it is potentially analyzable.

Notes

1. Eugene J. Kolb, *A Framework for Political Analysis* (Englewood Cliffs, N.J.: Prentice-Hall, 1978), 7-11.

2. I.M. Destler, "Executive-Congressional Conflict in Foreign Policy: Explaining It, Coping With It," in *Congress Reconsidered,* ed. Lawrence C. Dodd and Bruce J. Oppenheimer, 2d ed. (Washington, D.C.: Congressional Quarterly Press, 1981), 296-316.

3. Arnold J. Meltsner, "Political Feasibility and Policy Analysis," *Public Administration Review,* November/December 1972, 859-67.

4. James L. Sundquist, *The Decline and Resurgence of Congress* (Washington, D.C.: Brookings Institution, 1981), 402-14.

5. For a review, see Dodd and Oppenheimer, *Congress Reconsidered,* 332-48.

6. Charles E. Lindblom, *The Policy-Making Process* (Englewood Cliffs, N.J.: Prentice-Hall, 1968), 101-8.

7. Bruce Headey, *Housing Policy in the Developed Economy* (London: Croom Helm, 1978), 201-7.

8. James Buchanan and Gordon Tullock, *The Calculus of Consent* (Ann Arbor: University of Michigan Press, 1962), 120-44.

9. Morris P. Fiorina, *Congress: Keystone of the Washington Establishment* (New Haven: Yale University Press, 1977).

10. Douglas R. Arnold, *Congress and the Bureaucracy* (New Haven: Yale University Press, 1979).

11. William R. Riker and Peter Ordeshook, *Positive Political Theory* (Englewood Cliffs, N.J.: Prentice-Hall, 1973), 97-114.

12. Kenneth Arrow, *Social Choice and Individual Values,* 2d ed. (New York: Wiley, 1963).

13. Phillip J. Cooper, *Public Law and Public Administration* (Palo Alto, Calif.: Mayfield, 1983), 236-94.

14. Albert Nichols and Richard Zeckhouser, "OSHA after a Decade: A Time for Reason," in *Case Studies in Regulation,* ed. Leonard W. Weiss and Michael W. Klass (Boston: Little, Brown, 1981), 202-34.

15. John C. Calhoun, *A Disquisition on Government* (Charleston, S.C.: Walker and Jones, 1851).

16. Phillipe C. Schmitter, "Still a Century of Corporatism," in *The New Corporatism,* ed. Frederick B. Pike and Thomas Stritch (Notre Dame, Ind.: University of Notre Dame Press, 1974), 84-131.

17. See Colin S. Diver, "A Theory of Regulatory Enforcement," *Public Policy,* Summer 1980, 285-86.

18. Theodore J. Lowi, *The End of Liberalism,* 2d ed. (New York: Norton, 1979), 50-52.

19. William Lilley III and James C. Miller III, "The New 'Social Regulation,' " *Public Interest,* Spring 1977, 49-61.

5. Organizations and Implementation

Once a piece of legislation or a regulation has been accepted as a legitimate public law, in some ways the easiest portion of the policymaking process has transpired, for then government must put the legislation into effect. This requires the development of organizations that will apply the principles of the legislation to specific cases, monitor the performance of the policies, and, it is hoped, propose improvements in the content and method of administration of the policy. Even policies that are primarily self-administered or that rely on incentives rather than regulation require some organizational basis for administration, although the organizations can certainly be smaller than those needed for programs that depend on direct administration and supervision. For example, the collection of the income tax, which is largely self-administered, requires many fewer persons for each dollar collected than does collecting revenues from customs duties, even leaving aside the role of the customs agents in controlling smuggling.

Traditional American political thinkers have denigrated the roles of public administrators and bureaucrats in policymaking. The traditional attitude has been that policy was made by the legislative body and then the administrators were merely to follow the guidelines set forth in the legislation. Such an attitude fails to take into account the important role of administrative decision making and especially the importance of decision makers at the bottom of the organization in determining the effective policies of government.[1] The "real" criminal justice policy of the nation or city is to a great extent determined by the way in which the police enforce the laws, just as the "real" social welfare policy is determined by decisions made by caseworkers or even by receptionists in social service agencies. We have already noted that the bureaucrats play an important role in interpreting legislation and making regulations; they also play an important role in making decisions while applying laws and regulations to individual cases.[2]

It is also customary to regard government as an undivided entity and to regard government organizations as rather monolithic. In fact, this is not the case at all. We have already mentioned that American government is divided vertically into a number of subgovernments and horizontally into levels of government in a federal system. But within the federal bureaucracy, and even within single cabinet-level departments, there exist a number of bureaus, offices, and sections, all competing for money, legislative time, and public attention. Each organization has its own goals, ideas, and concepts about how to attack certain problems. As in the making of legislation, these ideas will also influence the implementation of legislation. Implementation will involve conflicts and competition rather than neat coordination and control, and struggles over policy will go on long after Congress and the President have enacted the legislation. Policies, as operating instruments, commonly emerge from these conflicts, as much as they do from the design of legislation.

Dramatis Personae

The organization of the federal government is complicated, not only because of the number of organizations but also because of the number of different kinds of organizations. There is no single organizational format for accomplishing the work of government, and the various organizations exist in different relationships to elective officials and even to government authority as a whole.

In addition to the three constitutionally designated actors—the President, the Congress, and the courts—there are at least eight different organizational formats in the federal government (see table 5.1).[3] One of these is a catchall category containing a number of organizations that are difficult to classify in accordance with the other major types. Again, the absence of a basic organizational format tends to lessen central coordination and to contribute to the incoherence of the policy choices made by the federal government. Further, the eight forms of organizations have a great deal of internal variation. As shown in table 5.1, they differ greatly in size; they can also differ greatly in their internal organization. For example, the Department of Agriculture is structured with almost fifty offices and bureaus, while the Department of Justice has only twenty-two.

The most familiar forms of organization are the *executive departments,* such as the Department of Defense and the Department of Health and Human Services. Each of these thirteen departments is headed by a secretary who is a member of the President's cabinet and who is directly reponsible to the President. These departments should not, however, be regarded as uniform wholes. Rather, they are collections or "holding companies" of relatively autonomous agencies and officies.[4] Departments vary in the extent to which their constituent agencies respond to central direction. Some, such as the Department of

TABLE 5.I

EXAMPLES OF EMPLOYMENT IN FEDERAL ORGANIZATIONS

Kind of Organization	Employment[a]
Executive departments	
Department of Defense (civilian)	1,018,098
Department of Education	5,783
Executive Office of the President	
Office of Management and Budget	658
Council on Environmental Quality	12
Legislative organizations	
Library of Congress	1,674
Architect of the Capitol	22
Independent executive agencies	
Veterans Administration	233,218
Arms Control and Disarmament Agency	183
Independent regulatory agencies	
Federal Communications Commission	2,008
Consumer Products Safety Commission	638
Corporations	
U.S. Postal Service	666,876
Neighborhood Reinvestment Corporation	197
Foundations	
National Science Foundation	1,404
National Endowment for the Arts	292
Other	
Smithsonian Institution	4,187
Advisory Commission on Federal Pay	3

a. Full- and part-time; permanent and temporary positions.

Defense, have relatively high degrees of coordination; some, such as the Department of Commerce, are extremely decentralized. In some instances, the individual agency may have more political clout than does the department as a whole. One such agency is the FBI, which is part of the Department of Justice. And in some instances it is not entirely clear why some agencies are located in one department rather than another; for example, why the U.S. Forest Service is best located in the Department of Agriculture rather than Interior, or why the U.S. Coast Guard is located in the Department of Transportation rather than the Treasury or Department of Defense.

Although the executive departments are linked to constituencies and provide services directly to those constituencies, the organizations within the *Executive Office of the President* exist to assist the President in carrying out his tasks of control and coordination.[5] The most important units within the Executive

Office of the President are the Office of Management and Budget, the Council of Economic Advisers, the National Security Council, the Domestic Policy Staff, and the White House Office. The first two assist the President in his role as economic manager and central figure in the budgetary process. The National Security Council provides advice and opinion on foreign and defense issues independent of the Departments of State and Defense, while the Domestic Policy Staff performs a similar role for domestic policy. The White House Office manages the complexities of just being President of the United States and employs a number of personal advisers for the President. The units within the Executive Office of the President now employ more than 1700 people—a rather insignificant number compared with a total federal work force of more than 2.2 million, but quite large when compared with the personal offices of the chief executives of other nations.[6]

The Congress has also created organizations to assist it in its role in policymaking. The two most important *legislative organizations* are the General Accounting Office and the Congressional Budget Office. Legislatures generally audit the accounts of the executive to ensure that the money is being spent legally. The General Accounting Office, for most of its existence, has been strictly a financial accounting body. In the 1970s, however, the organization began to expand its concerns to the cost effectiveness of expenditures.[7] For example, in one report the GAO agreed that the Internal Revenue Service had been acting perfectly legally in the ways it sought to detect income tax evaders, but recommended changing the IRS program to one the GAO considered more efficient. The Congressional Budget Office has its major impact on the preparation of the budget; its role is discussed thoroughly in chapter 6.

In addition to the executive departments responsible to the President there are a number of *independent executive agencies.* These organizations perform executive functions, such as implementing a public program, but are independent of the executive departments and generally report directly to the President. There are several reasons for this independence. Some independent executive agencies, such as the National Aeronautics and Space Administration, are mission agencies organized outside existing frameworks so as to have enhanced flexibility in completing their mission. Others, like the Veterans Administration, are organized independently to highlight their importance and in recognition of their political power. Others, such as the General Services Administration and the Office of Personnel Management, provide services to a number of other government departments, and their location in any one department might create management difficulties.

The fifth form of organization is the *independent regulatory commission.* Three such organizations are the Interstate Commerce Commission, the Federal

Trade Commission, and the Consumer Products Safety Commission. These commissions are different from the independent executive agencies in that they do not perform executive functions but act independently to regulate certain segments of the economy. Once the President has appointed the members of a commission, the application and formulation of regulations are largely beyond his control. The absence of political support tends to result, however, in the "capture" of the regulatory commissions by the interests they were intended to regulate.[8] Over time, lacking ties to the President or Congress, the agencies must seek the support of the regulated interests in order to get their budgets, personnel, or legislation from the other institutions in government. The tendency toward capture is not so evident in agencies that cross-cut industries — the Consumer Products Safety Commission, for example. Also, it must be remembered that not all regulation of the economy is conducted through the independent commissions, and some of the more important regulatory agencies such as the Occupational Safety and Health Administration and the Food and Drug Administration are in executive departments (OSHA is in the Department of Labor, and the FDA is part of Health and Human Services).

The government of the United States has generally avoided becoming directly involved in the economy, other than through regulations, but there are a number of *public corporations* in the federal government.[9] For example, since 1972 the U.S. Postal Service has been a public corporation rather than a part of the executive department, which it was before. This public corporation employs over 660,000 people, or approximately 25 percent of all federal civilian employees. Another public corporation, the Tennessee Valley Authority, has about 6 percent of the total electrical generating capacity in the United States. Some public corporations are very small, however. The Overseas Private Investment Corporation, for instance, employs only 100 people. Public corporations are organized much like private corporations, with a board of directors and stock issued for capitalization. The principal difference is that the board members are all public appointees and the stock is generally held entirely by the Department of the Treasury or by another executive department. There are several reasons for choosing the corporate form of organization. One is that these organizations provide marketed goods and services to the population and hence can be better managed as commercial concerns.[10] Also, this is a means of keeping some government functions at arm's length.

There are also several *foundations* within the federal government, the two principal examples being the National Science Foundation and the National Endowment for the Humanities. The foundation is intended primarily to separate the organization from the remainder of government. This is done because of a justifiable fear of creating a national orthodoxy in the arts or in science and thereby stifling creativity. The use of the more independent foundation enables government to support the activities while being removed from the decisions. This isolation is far from complete, however, as Congress has become involved in the decisions of the National Science Foundation, especially the support of textbooks for use in elementary and secondary schools.

In addition to the wholly owned government corporations described above, there is also a group of organizations that has been described as "quasi governmental," or as being in the "twilight zone." Examples of these organizations are the National Railroad Passenger Corporation (Amtrak), the Consolidated Rail Corporation (Conrail), the Corporation for Public Broadcasting, and the Federal Reserve Board. These organizations have some attributes of public organizations (most important, access to public funding), but they also have some attributes of private organizations. They are similar to public corporations except that a portion of their board of directors is appointed by private-sector organizations, just as the boards of Amtrak and Conrail are appointed in part by the member railroad corporations. Also, not all their stock may be owned by the public sector as is true for wholly owned corporations; instead, some may be owned by the cooperating private-sector organizations. For example, up to half of the stock of Comsat (Communications Satellite Corporation) may be held by communication common carriers.[11] Finally, employees of these quasi-governmental organizations are frequently not classified as public employees.

The justification for the formation of quasi-governmental organizations such as these is, again, to allow government to become involved in a policy area without giving it any real or apparent direct control. The federal government clearly subsidizes certain activities—passenger railroad service would almost certainly have vanished in the United States without the formation of Amtrak—but this intervention is not as obvious as other forms of intervention. Also, intervention by an organization of this sort gives the public a greater role in decision making and provides greater representation of private interests such as the affected corporations. And, as in the case of the Corporation for Public Broadcasting, this form of organization permits the federal government to become involved in an area from which it has traditionally been excluded. It is important to understand just how vital these organizations are to the federal government. For example, the Federal Reserve Board fits quite comfortably into this twilight zone, given its isolation from executive authority and its relationship to its member banks. But the Federal Reserve Board is responsible for making the monetary policy for the United States and thereby has a significant —if not the most significant—influence on this nation's economic conditions. Likewise, Amtrak and Conrail receive massive subsidies, but the public sector has no firm control over their policies.

Finally, there is a catchall category of *other organizations*. One component of this category is the intergovernmental organization—the Advisory Commission on Intergovernmental Relations, for example, or any one of the various regional commissions. Other organizations, including various claims commissions and the Administrative Conference of the United States, operate on the fringe of the judicial process. Finally, organizations such as the Smithsonian Institution, the National Academy of Sciences, and the American Red Cross are mentioned in federal legislation and receive subsidies but are far removed from the mainstream of government.[12]

In addition to the diversity and complexity of organization, we must note several other points. One is the redundancy that has been built into the system of organization. First, both Congress (through the Congressional Budget Office) and the Executive Office of the President (through the Office of Management and Budget) have expert budgetary analysis bodies. Given the doctrine of the separation of powers, such duplication makes a great deal of sense, but this still conflicts with some managerial thinking concerning duplicative functions. Second, within the the federal executive branch itself, we have seen that some units within the Executive Office of the President duplicate activities of the executive departments. Most notably, Presidents appear to demand foreign policy advice beyond that provided by the Departments of State and Defense. This may be justified, as those departments have existing policy commitments and ideas that may limit their ability to respond to presidential initiatives in foreign policy. But, during at least every administration since Richard Nixon, conflicts have arisen between the two sets of institutions, and the management of foreign policy may suffer as a result. In most instances, this conflict has been perceived as a conflict between the experienced professionals in the Department of State and committed amateurs in the National Security Council. Some redundancy can be rationalized as a means of limiting error and providing alternative means for accomplishing the same tasks. If the redundant institutions are occupied by ambitious men and women, however, the potential for conflict and inaction is great.[13]

It is also interesting to note that not all central management functions for the federal government are located in the Executive Office of the President. Several important central functions—monetary policy, personnel policy, debt management, and taxation—are managed by agencies outside the President's office and in one instance by an organization in the twilight zone. This is a definite limitation on the ability of the President to implement his policy priorities and consequently to control the federal establishment for which he is responsible.

Third, we have mentioned the variations in the "publicness" of organizations in the federal government. Some organizations are clearly public: They receive their funds from allocations in the federal budget; their employees are hired through public personnel systems; and they are subject to legislation such as the Freedom of Information Act, which attempts to differentiate public from private programs.[14] Other organizations described appear tied to the private sector as much as to government: They receive some or all of their funds as fees for service or interest, they have their own personnel policies, and they are only slightly more subject to normal restrictions on public organizations than is General Motors. Again, for a President—who will be held accountable to voters and to Congress for the performance of the federal government—this presents an immense and perhaps insoluble problem. This is but one of many difficulties a President encounters when he attempts to put his policies into effect; it also serves as a bridge to our discussion of implementation.

Implementation

All the organizations described above are established to assist in some way in the execution of legislation or in the monitoring of that execution. Once enacted, laws do not go into effect by themselves, as was assumed by those in the tradition of Woodrow Wilson who discussed "mere administration."[15] In fact, one of the most important things to understand is that it is a minor miracle that implementation is ever accomplished. There are so many more ways of blocking intended actions than there are of making results materialize that all legislators should be pleased if they live to see their pet projects not only passed into law but actually put into effect. Although this is perhaps an excessively negative attitude toward the implementation process, it should underline the extreme difficulties of administering and implementing public programs.

Policies do not fail on their own, however, and a number of factors may limit the ability of a political system to put policies into effect. Rarely will all these factors affect any single policy, but all must be considered in designing a policy and in attempting to translate that policy choice into real services for citizens.

The Legislation

The first factor that will affect the ability of a policy to be effectively implemented is the nature of the legislation itself. Laws vary according to their specificity, clarity, and the policy areas they attempt to influence. They also differ in the extent to which they bind the individuals and organizations that are charged with implementing them in the way the writers intended. Unfortunately both legislators and analysts sometimes overlook the importance of the legislation.

POLICY ISSUES

Legislators frequently choose to legislate in policy areas where there is not enough information about causal processes to enable them to make good policy choices. Although they may have the best intentions, their efforts are unlikely to succeed if they make only stabs in the dark in attempting to solve problems. If we refer to the table used in discussing policy formulation (table 3.1), we can estimate the likelihood of effective implementation. We anticipate that the highest probability of effective implementation will occur when we have both sufficient information and a good knowledge of the causes of the problems. In such situations, we can design legislation to solve, or at least ameliorate, the problem under attack. Likewise, we would expect little likelihood of effective implementation in policy areas where we have inadequate information and little knowledge of the causes of the problem. The other two possible combinations of knowledge of causation and information may differ very little in their likelihood of effective implementation, although we would expect a somewhat better probability of implementation where there is a knowledge of the patterns of causation as opposed to more basic information. If the underlying process is understood, it would appear possible to formulate policy responses based on poor information, even if those responses involve a certain amount of over-kill and excessive reaction. If the underlying process is misunderstood or not understood at all, however, there is little hope of effectively implementing a policy choice, except by pure luck.

Perhaps the best example of a large-scale policy formulation and implementation in spite of inadequate knowledge of patterns of causation was the war on poverty in the United States. There were (and are) as many theories about the causes of poverty as there were theorists, but there was little real understanding even of the basics of the economic and social dynamics. Thus, war was declared on an enemy that was poorly understood. Daniel P. Moynihan put it this way:

> This is the essential fact: The Government did not know what it was doing. It had a theory. Or rather a set of theories. Nothing more. The U.S. Government at this time was no more in possession of a confident knowledge as to how to prevent delinquency, cure anomie, or overcome that midmorning sense of power-lessness than it was the possessor of a dependable formula for motivating Viet-namese villagers to fight Communism.[16]

Not only was it a war, but it was a war that appeared to be based on something approaching a dogma about the plan of attack—for example, the use of large-scale and rather expensive programs involving direct services to clients. Arguably, these programs were doomed to fail as soon as they were adopted because they were based on dubious assumptions about the operations of society and the mechanisms for approaching such problems.

An even more extreme example of a policy that was made without adequate knowledge was the Clean Air Act of 1970 (see chapter 12).[17] The sponsors of this legislation were, in fact, quite sure that they did not understand the processes and that the technology for producing the environmental cleanup they legislated did not exist. This legislation was designed to force the development of the technology for improving the environment. To some extent the same was true of the space program, which did not have a sure technology for accomplishing its goals when President John Kennedy pledged to be on the moon by the end of the decade. This is an interesting if somewhat novel approach to designing public programs, but not one that can be recommended as the usual strategy. All this should not be taken to mean that governments should just keep to their well-worn paths and do what they have always done in the ways they have always done it. Rather, it is intended to demonstrate that if one expects significant results from programs based on insufficient understanding of the subject matter of the legislation, one's hopes are likely to be dashed frequently.

POLITICAL SETTING

Legislation is adopted through political action, and the political process may plant in legislation the seeds of its own destruction. The very actions necessary to pass legislation may ultimately make it impossible to implement. This is especially true when the construction of a necessary coalition forces logrolling and tradeoffs among competing interests and competing purposes in the legislation.

The effects of the political process of legislation are manifested in different ways. One is the vagueness of the language in which the legislation is written. This lack of clarity may be essential to develop a coalition for the passage of legislation, as every time a vague term is made specific, potential coalition members are excluded. But by phrasing legislation in vague and inoffensive language, legislators run the risk of making their intent unclear to those who must implement the laws and of allowing those who implement to alter the entire meaning of the program substantially. Terms such as "maximum feasible participation," "equality of educational opportunity," "special needs of educationally deprived students," and "full employment" are all subject to a number of different interpretations, any of which could betray the intent of the legislators. For example, the rather vague language of Social Security legislation from 1962 to 1972 provided for open-ended grants for "improved services" for citizens.[18] The assumption was that additional services would be provided with this money.

Rather, quite contrary to the intent of the drafters of the legislation, the money was used to subsidize existing programs and to provide fiscal relief for state budgets. These grants also grew much more rapidly than had been anticipated when states found ways of using them to shift a substantial portion of their social service expenditures to the federal government. Even words about which most citizens can agree may be sufficiently vague to produce problems during implementation, as when the Reagan administration attempted to include ketchup as a "vegetable" under the School Lunch Program.[19]

In addition to coalitions formed for the passage of a single piece of legislation, other coalitions may have to be formed across several pieces of legislation: the classic approach to logrolling. In order to gain support for one favored piece of legislation a coalition-building legislator may have to trade his or her support on other pieces of legislation. In some instances this may simply increase the overall volume of legislation enacted. In others, it may involve the passage of legislation that negates or decreases the effects of desired legislation. Some coalitions that must be formed are regional, so it may become virtually impossible to give one region an advantage, which may be justified by economic circumstances, without making commensurate concessions to other regions, thereby nullifying the intended advantages. It is also difficult to make legislative decisions that are redistributive across economic classes; either the legislation will be watered down to be distributive (giving everyone a piece of the pie) or additional legislation will be passed to spread the benefits more broadly. Both General Revenue Sharing and the Elementary and Secondary Education Act are examples of this tendency.

Similar problems of vagueness and even logrolling can occur when other institutions make rulings that must be implemented. In a number of instances a judicial decision, intended to mandate a certain action, has been so vague as to be difficult or impossible to implement. One of the best examples of this lack of clarity is the famous decision of *Brown* v. *Board of Education,* which ordered schools to desegregate with "all deliberate speed." Two of those three words—"deliberate" and "speed"—are somewhat contradictory, and the decision did not specify just what the phrase meant. The result was that school districts could deliberate for some time. Not until fifteen or twenty years after the beginning of the litigation did effective desegregation begin to occur. And the regulatory process, intended to clarify and specify legislation, can itself create ambiguities that require more regulations to clarify and more delay in implementing the decisions.

In summary, politics is central to the formulation of legislation, but the results are such that the legislation cannot be implemented effectively. The compromises necessitated by political feasibility may result in just the reductions

87

in clarity and purpose that make laws too diffuse to be implemented so as to have a real effect on society.

INTEREST-GROUP LIBERALISM

Related to the problem of vagueness and the problem of the involvement of government in policy areas about which it lacks knowledge of causation is Theodore J. Lowi's concern about government involvement in abstract aspects of human behavior.[20] Lowi's argument is that the United States has progressed from concerted and specific legislation such as the Interstate Commerce Act of 1887, which established clear standards of practice for the Interstate Commerce Commission, to abstract and general standards, such as "unfair competition" in the Clayton Act of 1914. This tendency has been extended through even more general and diffuse aspects of human behavior, in the attempts of social legislation in the 1960s to regulate what Lowi refers to as the "environment of conduct." It is simply more difficult to show that a person has discriminated against another person on the basis of race, color, or sex than it is to show that a railroad has violated prohibitions against discriminatory freight rates.

Lowi believes that the problems in these vague laws arise, not from their commendable intentions, but from the difficulty of implementing them. The diffuseness of the targets specified and the difficulty of defining standards open policies attempting to regulate those kinds of behaviors to errors in interpretation during the implementation process. Further, it becomes more difficult to hold government accountable when it administers ambiguous legislation. The interest-group liberalism inherent in American politics, in which the public interest tends to be defined in terms of many private interests, means that the implementation of legislation will generally differ greatly from the intentions of those who framed the legislation. Implementation will be undertaken by agencies that are themselves tied to clients and to particular definitions of the public interest and that will not want to be swayed from their position by a piece of legislation. The difficulties in accountability and the deviations of policies in practice from the intentions of their framers can only alienate the clients and frustrate the legislator, and perhaps the administrators.

The Organizational Setting

As noted above, most implementation is undertaken by organizations, especially organizations in the public bureaucracy. Given the nature of public organizations, and organizations in general, the probability that such an organization will effectively implement a program is not particularly high—not because of any venality on the part of the bureaucracy or the bureaucrats but simply because the internal dynamics of large organizations often limit their ability to respond to policy changes and to implement new or altered programs.

To begin to understand what goes wrong when organizations attempt to implement programs, a model of "perfect" administration may be useful. Chris Hood points to five characteristics a "perfect" administration would have:

1. Administration would be unitary; it would be one vast army all marching to the same drummer.
2. The norms and rules of administration would be uniform throughout the organization.
3. There would be no resistance to commands.
4. There would be perfect information and communication within the organization.
5. There would be adequate time to implement the program.[21]

Clearly very few of these conditions are present in organizations attempting to implement programs, and almost never are all of them present. Consequently, difficulties arise in administration and implementation. These difficulties need not be insurmountable, but they do need to be understood and planned for, if implementation is to occur. Just what characteristics and difficulties in organizations do lead to difficulties in implementation?

Organizational Disunity

Organizations are rarely unitary administrations. Instead, a number of points of disunity are almost inherent in organizational structures.

One feature of organizational disunity that affects implementation is the disjunction between central organizations and their field staffs. Decisions may be made by politicians and administrators sitting in national capitals, but those decisions must be implemented by field staff members who may not share the same values and goals as the administrators in the home office. This disjunction of values may take several forms. A change in central values and programs may occur, perhaps as a result of a change in Presidents or in Congress, and the field staff may remain loyal to the older policies. For example, the field staff, and indeed much of the central staff, of the Department of Health, Education, and Welfare, regarded the Nixon administration as a temporary phenomenon and remained loyal to the more liberal social values of previous Democratic Presidents.[22] This was true despite pressures from above for changes in policies. Much the same has been true of the staffs of the Environmental Protection Agency and the Department of the Interior under the Reagan administration's apparent retreat on environmental issues. Such problems with field staffs over policy changes produce frustration for politicians and make the implementation of certain policies extremely difficult.

A more common disparity between the goals of field staffs and those of the home office may occur as the field staff is "captured" by clients. Field staff members are frequently close to their clients, and they may adopt the perspective of their clients in their relationships with the remainder of the organization.[23] This is especially true when the clients are relatively disadvantaged and the organization is attempting to exercise some control over them. The identification of staff members with their clients is fostered by frequent contact, sympathy, empathy, and quite commonly by genuine devotion to a perceived mission that is in contrast to the mission fostered by the central office. For whatever reason, this identification does make the implementation of centrally determined policy difficult.

In many ways, government in recent years has promoted its own difficulties when using field staffs to implement policy. The requirement for community participation in decision making in many urban social service programs further lessens the control of central organizations over the implementation of programs. The development of community organizations that fulfill the requirements for participation is a major focus for pressures to divert the program away from centrally determined priorities toward more locally determined priorities.[24] Arguably, community participation has been less effective than was intended and at worst has been a facade for control by bureaucracies, but to the extent that it has been successful, it may well have made implementation less successful. Further, even in policy areas where community participation has not been so directly fostered by government, either the lessons learned from community participation elsewhere or the general climate favoring participation has produced greater activity by individuals and communities affected by policies. A whole range of programs—including decisions by the Army Corps of Engineers about project siting and the construction of portions of the interstate highway system—have been seriously affected by local participation.[25]

Also, field staffs may find that, if they are to perform their tasks effectively, they cannot follow all the directives coming to them from the center of the organization. In such instances, in order to get substantive compliance the organization members may not comply with procedural directives. For example, in a classic study of the FBI, Blau noted that field agents frequently did not comply with directives requiring them to report the offering of a bribe by a suspect.[26] The agents had found that they could use the offer of a bribe to gain greater cooperation from the subject, because at any time they could have the person prosecuted just for offering the bribe. Their performance of the task of prosecuting criminals was probably enhanced, but it was done so at the expense of the directive from the central office. More recently, Bardach and Kagan have argued that regulatory enforcement could be improved if the field staff were given greater latitude.[27] They believe that rigidities resulting from strict central controls actually produce less compliance with the spirit of the regulations than would a more flexible approach.

Standard Operating Procedures

Organizations develop standard operating procedures (SOPs) to respond to policy problems. When a prospective client walks into a social service agency, the agency follows a standard pattern of response: Certain forms must be filled out, certain personnel will interview the prospective client, specific criteria will be used to determine the person's eligibility for benefits. Likewise, if a "blip" appears on the radar screen of a defense installation, a certain set of procedures will be followed to determine if the blip is real and, if so, whether it is friendly or hostile. If it is hostile, specific actions will be taken.

Standard operating procedures are important for organizations. They reduce the amount of time spent processing each new situation and developing a response. The SOPs are the learned response of the organization to certain problems; they represent to some extent the organizational memory in action. SOPs may also be important for clients, as they are adopted at least in part to ensure equality and fairness for clients. Without SOPs, organizations might respond more slowly to each situation, they might respond less effectively, and they would probably respond more erratically.

Although SOPs are certainly important and generally beneficial, they can act as barriers to good implementation. This is most obvious when a new policy or a new approach to an existing policy is being considered. Organizations are likely to persist in defining policies and problems in their standard manner, even when the old definition or procedure no longer helps to fulfill the mission of the agency. For example, when the Medicare program was added to the responsibilities of the Social Security Administration, the agency was faced with an entirely new set of concerns in addition to its traditional task of making payments to individuals. In particular, it was responsible for limiting the costs of medical care. It chose, however, to undertake this responsibility in much the same way that it would have attempted to manage problems arising from pensions—by examining individual claims and denying those that appeared to be unjustified. It took the Social Security Administration some time to focus attention on more fundamental problems of medical cost inflation.

Thus there is a need for designing programs and organizations that will more consistently reassess their goals and the methods that they use to reach those goals. In some cases, for example the number of births and the need for schools, the response should be programmed to be almost automatic; other situations will require more thought and greater political involvement.

Standard operating procedures also tend to produce inappropriate or delayed responses to crises. Many stories about the slowness or apparent stupidity of the military came from the Cuban missile crisis, and similar stories probably would have come from other military encounters, if others had been as well documented. The military, perhaps more than any other organization, tends to employ SOPs and to train its members to carry through with those procedures in the absence of commands to the contrary. John Kennedy found that, although he was nominally in charge of the armed forces of the United States, many things occurred that he had not ordered, and he realized that they were happening simply because they were standard procedures. In several instances these things that "just happened" threatened to cause conflict when the President was doing everything possible to bring about a peaceful resolution of the crisis.

One standard means of avoiding the effects of SOPs in a new program is to create a new organization. When the Small Business Administration was created in 1953, it was purposely not placed in the Department of Commerce, whose SOPs tended to favor big business. Likewise, when the Office of Economic Opportunity was created as part of the war on poverty, it was deliberately located outside the Department of Health, Education, and Welfare, which was perceived as too closely tied to social insurance and too willing to accept less creative solutions than those proposed for OEO. There are, of course, limits to the number of new organizations that can be set up, for the more we create, the more chance there will be of interorganizational barriers to implementation.

Paradoxically, standard operating procedures aid in the implementation of established programs, whereas they are likely to be barriers to change and to the establishment of new programs. Likewise, they may be too standard to allow response to nonstandard situations, or to nonstandard clients, thereby creating rigidity and extremely inappropriate responses to novel situations.

Organizational Communication
Another barrier to effective implementation is the improper flow of information within organizations. Because government organizations depend heavily on the flow of information — just as manufacturers rely on the flow of raw materials — accurate information and the prevention of blockages of information are extremely important to the success of these public organizations. Unfortunately, organizations, particularly public organizations, are subject to inaccurate and blocked communication.

In general, information in bureaucracies tends to be concentrated at the bottom.[28] The field staffs of organizations are in closer contact with the environment of the organization, and technical experts tend to be clustered at the bottom of organizations, with more general managers concentrated at the top. This means, then, that if the organization is to be guided by changes in its environment and if it is to make good technical decisions, the information at the bottom must be transmitted to the top and then directions must be passed back down to the bottom for implementation. Unfortunately, the more levels through which information has to be transmitted, the greater the probability that the information will be distorted. This distortion may result from random error or from selective distortion. Selective distortion results when officials at each stage attempt to transmit only the information they believe their superiors wish to hear or the information they think will make them look good to their superiors. And the superiors, in turn, may attempt to estimate what sort of distortion their subordinates may have passed on and at least try to correct for that distortion.[29] The result of this transmitting of messages through a hierarchical organization frequently is rampant distortion and misinformation that limits the ability of the organization to effect implementation decisions.

Certain characteristics of the organization may improve the transmission of information through the hierarchy. Clearly, if all members of an organization "speak the same language," less distortion of communication should occur. In other words, if organization members share common technical or professional backgrounds, their communication with one another should be less distorted. Their ability to communicate with other organizations, however, may be diminished. In addition, attempts on the part of the organization to create internal unity through training and socialization should also improve patterns of communication. Finally, the "flatter" the organization (i.e., the fewer levels through which communication must go before being acted on), the less distortion is likely to occur.

Another way to improve communication in organizations is to create more, and redundant, channels. For example, President Franklin Roosevelt developed personal ties to lower-level members of organizations and placed his own people in organizations to be sure that he would receive direct and unvarnished reports from the operating levels of government. Alternatively, a President or manager might build in several channels of communication in order to receive messages and to serve as checks on one another. Again, Franklin Roosevelt's development of parallel organizations (e.g., the Works Progress Administration and the Public Works Administration) provided him with alternative channels of information about the progress of his New Deal programs.

One particular threat to effective organizational communication is secrecy.[30] While a certain level of secrecy is understood to be important for certain organizations, secrecy also may inhibit both communication and implementation. Secrecy frequently means that a communication might not be transmitted because it has been classified; other parts of the organization or other organizations are consequently denied needed information. Again, the Cuban missile crisis offered numerous examples of how the military's penchant for secrecy prevented a rapid response to situations. Also, secrecy may produce inefficiency, as when FBI agents must spend a great deal of time reporting on one another when they infiltrate subversive organizations. Of course, to make themselves more acceptable to the organizations they have infiltrated, the agents tend to be among the most vociferous members and consequently are the subjects of a disproportionate share of reports from other agents. Finally, secrecy may be counterproductive even where it is justified. For example, one argument holds that the interests of deterrence are best served by fully informing an adversary of the full extent of one's arsenal rather than masking its strength. This may prevent war. This logic may be particularly applicable in a nuclear age when every major power has the ability to destroy the world several times over.

In modern organizations knowledge is power, and the inability of an organization to gather and process information from its environment will certainly be a serious detriment to its performance. Clearly the management of communication flows within the organization is an important component of taking raw information and putting it into action. Most organizations, however, face massive problems in performing even this simple — or apparently simple — task and as a consequence do not implement their programs effectively.

Time Problems

Related to the problem of information management in the implementation of policies is the problem of time. Hood points to two time problems that inhibit the ability of public organizations to respond to situations in their policy environments. One is a linear time problem in which the reponses of implementing organizations tend to lag behind the need for the response.[31] This often happens in organizations that have learned their lessons too well and that base their responses on previous learning rather than on current conditions. This problem is somewhat similar to the problem of standard operating procedures, but it has less to do with processing individual cases and more to do with designing the mechanisms for putting new programs into effect. Organizations frequently implement programs to deal with a crisis that has just passed, rather than with the crisis they currently face or might soon face. To some degree the American armed forces in Vietnam used the lessons they had learned, or thought they had learned, in World War II and the Korean war. Unfortunately for them, a highly mechanized, technologically sophisticated, and logistically dependent fighting force broke down in a tropical, guerrilla war. Another example of this problem is the slow response of American elementary and secondary school systems to the baby booms that followed World War II and the Korean war. Virtually everyone knew that the children had indeed been born and would have to be educated, but few educators attempted to prepare for their arrival in the school systems or to construct the physical facilities or to train the teachers they would require.

Other time problems are cyclical, and delayed implementation, instead of solving problems, may actually contribute to them. This is especially important in making and implementing macroeconomic policy in which, even if the information available to a decision maker is timely and accurate, a delay in response may exaggerate economic fluctuations. If a decision maker responds to a threatened increase in inflation by reducing money supplies or reducing expenditures, and if that response is delayed for a year, or even for only a few months, it may only increase an economic slowdown resulting basically from other causes. Thus, it is not sufficient just to be right; an effective policy must be both correct and on time if it is to have the desired effect.

Horse-Shoe-Nail Problems and Public Planning

The final organizational problem in implementation arises when organizations plan their activities incompletely or inaccurately. Hood calls these "horse-shoe-nail" problems because the failure to provide the nail results in the eventual loss of the horse and, eventually, the battle.[32] And because government organizations often must plan for implementation with no access to information and no cues to the necessary choices, problems of this kind are likely to arise in the public sector. Examples of this problem abound: passing requirements to inspect coal mines but failing to hire inspectors; requiring clients to fill out certain forms but neglecting to have the forms printed; forgetting to stop construction of a $160 million tunnel leading to nowhere. There are countless examples of this political version of Murphy's law.[33]

To ensure effective management and implementation, planners must identify the crucial potential blockages, or "nails," in their organization and allow for them in their planning. Clearly, with a new program or policy this planning may be extremely difficult, as the problems that will arise are almost impossible to anticipate. Some planners use these difficulties to justify incrementalism or experimentation when introducing new policies. Instead of undertaking large projects with the possibility of equally large failures, they may undertake smaller projects for which any failures or unanticipated difficulties would impose minimal costs, but would help prepare the organization to implement full-scale projects.

Some programs, however, will be effective only if they are on a large scale and comprehensive. Schulman's analysis of the National Aeronautics and Space Administration points out that a program like the space program — designed to reach a major goal within a limited amount of time and with an engineering as opposed to a pure research focus — must be large scale in order to be effective.[34] Similarly, it has been argued that the war on poverty, instead of being the failure portrayed in the conventional wisdom, actually was never tried on a scale that might have made it effective. On the other hand, the so-called war on cancer required a more decentralized structure to allow scientific research to pursue as many avenues as possible.[35] Those who design programs and organizations must be very careful to develop programs to match the characteristics of the problem and the state of knowledge concerning the subject.

Interorganizational Politics

Few if any policies are designed and implemented by a "single lonely organization" in the 1980s.[36] Certainly individual organizations do have their problems, but many more problems are encountered in the design of implementation structures or the pattern of interactions among organizations as they attempt to implement a policy. The problems of organizational disunity and communication become exaggerated when the individuals involved are not bound even by a presumed loyalty to a single organization, but have competing loyalties to different organizations, not all of which may be interested in the effective implementation of a particular program.

Pressman and Wildavsky, who popularized the concern for implementation, speak of the problems of implementing policies through a number of organizations (or even within a single organization) as problems of "clearance points," the number of individual decision points that must be agreed to before any policy intentions can be translated into action.[37] Even if the decision makers at each "clearance point" are favorably disposed toward the program in question, there may still be impediments to their agreement. Some problems may be legal, some may be budgetary, and others may involve building coalitions with other organizations or interests in the society. Statistically, one would expect that if each decision point is independent of the others and if the probability of any individual decision maker's agreeing to the program is 90 percent (0.9), then the probability of any two agreeing is 81 percent (0.9 × 0.9); and for three points the probability would be 73 percent (0.9 × 0.9 × 0.9), and so forth. Pressman and Wildavsky determined that there were seventy clearance points in the implementation of the Economic Development Administration's decision to become involved in public works projects in Oakland, California.[38]

With this number of clearance points, the probability of all of them agreeing, given an average probability of 90 percent for each point, is less than one in a thousand. Only if there were a probability greater than 99 percent at each clearance point would the odds in favor of implementation be greater than 50-50. Of course, implementation is not just a problem in statistics, and the political and administrative leaders involved in the process can vastly alter the probabilities at each stage. With so many independent clearance points and limited political resources, however, a leader may well be tempted to succumb to the inertia inherent in the implementation system.

Judith Bowen has argued that the simple statistical model proposed by Pressman and Wildavsky may understate the probabilities of successful implementation.[39] She points out that if *persistence* is permitted, and each clearance point can be assaulted a number of times, the chances for a successful implementation increase significantly. She also explains that the clearance points *may not be independent* as assumed, and that success at one clearance may produce an increased probability of success at subsequent steps. Similarly, the clever implementer can make *strategic choices* about which clearance points to try first, and how to package the points so that some success can be gained even if the whole campaign is not won. Thus, while successful implementation is still not perceived as a simple task, it is subject to manipulation, as are other stages of the policy process, and the clever analyst can improve his or her probabilities of success.

Vertical Implementation Structures

One problem in implementation occurs vertically within the hierarchical structures of government. I have already described some problems of intergovernmental relations in the United States with the several levels of governments, all of which may well be involved in the implementation of a single piece of legislation. This is especially evident for federal social and urban legislation in which all three levels of government may be involved in putting a single piece of federal legislation into effect. For example, Title xx of the Social Security Amendments of 1972 called for the availability of day-care services for poor working mothers. These services were to be funded through the Social Security Administration in Washington but implemented through state and local governments. For the typical poor child to receive day care, supported by the federal government, the Social Security Administration must agree to give a grant for the proposed program to a local government. But this money will be channeled through the state government, which will issue regulations to carry out the intentions of the program within the structure of the particular state government. The grant money is then transferred to the local government. But the local government itself can rarely provide the day care; instead, it contracts with day-care providers (usually private) to provide the services. The local government will have to monitor the standards and contract compliance of the private-service providers and ensure that no federal policy guidelines are violated.

Such a vertical implementation structure can give rise to several possibilities for inadequate implementation, or no implementation. One problem could result from simple partisan politics, when the local government and the federal government are controlled by different political parties and consequently have different policy priorities. Or localities may, for other reasons, have different policy priorities than does the federal government. Two good examples of these differences can be seen in the resistance of local governments to federally mandated scattering of public housing projects in middle-class neighborhoods and in the resistance of local governments to court-mandated busing for the purpose of desegregating public schools. Even if local governments want to do what the federal government would have them do, they sometimes lack the resources to do so. For example, local governments have attempted to resist various federal mandates, such as the Water Pollution Control Act of 1972, claiming they lacked the funds to meet the standards imposed.[40] Also, the states and localities may have few incentives to comply with federal directives. For example, in the Elementary and Secondary Education Act of 1965 the states were to receive their grants merely for participating in the program, without having to do anything in particular to improve education.[41] When easy money is available, there is little or no reason, other than good faith and a desire to encourage good government, to comply with federal regulations.

Horizontal Implementation Structures

In addition to difficulties in producing compliance across several levels of government, difficulties may occur in coordinating activities and organizations horizontally. That is, the success of one agency's program may require the cooperation of other organizations, or at least the coordination of their activities. One classic example of the difficulties in bringing about this kind of coordination was the Model Cities Program of the war on poverty. A major purpose of the Model Cities Program was to coordinate the activities of the numerous social service agencies serving the model neighborhoods. Even with the existence of an umbrella organization such as the Model Cities agency in each city, coordination was difficult to achieve. And in the absence of such a coordinating mechanism, effective coordination may be virtually impossible.

The breakdown of coordination can come about in several ways. One is through language and coding difficulties. Individual agencies hire certain kinds of professionals and train their employees in a certain manner. As a result, the housing experts in the Model Cities Program decided that the problems of residents resulted from substandard housing, whereas employment experts thought that the problems arose from unemployment. Psychiatric social workers, however, perceived the problems as resulting from personality problems. Each group of professionals, in other words, found it difficult to understand the perspectives of the other groups and, consequently, found it difficult to cooperate in treating the "whole client"– one of the stated objectives of the program. This was strongly demonstrated in the pattern of referrals among agencies. The vast majority of referrals of clients from one agency to another occurred within policy areas rather than across policy areas.[42] A client who visited an agency seeking health-care services would frequently be referred to another agency, most commonly another health-care agency. Clients would much less frequently be referred to social welfare agencies for assistance in receiving funds to provide better nutrition, which might have been as effective as medical care in improving clients' health. Agencies tend to label and classify clients as belonging in their own policy areas; they often do not refer clients broadly or provide services for the client's whole range of needs. The perceptual blinders of organizations and their members prevent them from seeing all the client's needs, and their training as professionals makes it difficult for service providers to shake off their blinders.

The lack of control among agencies and the consequent deficiencies in the implementation of programs may also occur because the objectives of one organization conflict with those of another organization. Agencies have to live, and to live they require money and personnel. Thus, at a basic level an organization may not be willing to cooperate in the implementation of a program simply because the success of another agency may threaten its own future prospects. On a somewhat higher plane, organizations may disagree about the purposes of government and about the best ways to achieve the goals about which they do agree. Or an agency may simply want to receive credit for providing a service that inevitably involves the cooperation of many organizations and, by insisting on receiving credit, may prevent anything from happening. For example, several law enforcement agencies knew about a major drug shipment, but they allowed it to slip through their fingers simply because they could not agree about which of the "cooperating" agencies would make the actual arrest and receive the media attention.

Finally, a simple failure to coordinate may prevent effective implementation. This is the result of oversight and failure to understand the linkages among programs; it is not a result of language problems or of an attempt to protect an organization's turf. Even if a program can be implemented without ade-

99

quate coordination with other agencies, its effectiveness may be limited, or substantial duplication of efforts may result. Most citizens have heard their share of horror stories about the same streets being dug up and repaired in successive weeks by different city departments and by private utilities. Equally horrific stories are told of requirements for reporting for a variety of federal agencies that require contradictory definitions of terms or that involve excessive duplication of effort. Venality is rarely at the root of these problems, but that does not prevent the loss of efficiency or make citizens any happier about the management of their government.

Summary

American government is a massive, complex, and often confusing set of institutions. It has many organizations but lacks any central organizing principle. Much of the structure of American government was developed on an ad hoc basis to address particular problems at particular times. Even with a more coherent structure, many of the same problems might still arise. Many problems are inherent in any government, although they are certainly exacerbated by the complexity and diffusion of the structure of American government. For public policy, implementation is a vital step in the process of governing because it involves putting programs into action and producing effects for citizens. The difficulty in producing desired effects, or indeed any effects, then, means that policy is a much more difficult commodity to deliver to citizens than is commonly believed. The barriers to effective implementation commonly discourage individuals and organizations from engaging in the activities that were devised for their benefit. Public management then becomes a matter of threatening or cajoling organizations into complying with stated objectives, or a matter of convincing those organizations that what they want to accomplish can best be accomplished through the programs that have been authorized.

Notes

1. B. Guy Peters, *The Politics of Bureaucracy*, 2d ed. (New York: Longman, 1984).

2. Kenneth Culp Davis, *Discretionary Justice in Europe and America* (Urbana: University of Illinois Press, 1976).

3. See U.S. Senate, Committee on Governmental Affairs, *The Federal Executive Establishment: Evolution and Trends* (Washington, D.C.: Government Printing Office, 1980), 23-63.

4. See Richard F. Fenno, *The President's Cabinet* (Cambridge, Mass.: Harvard University Press, 1959), 224-34; and Harold Seidman and Robert S. Gilmour, *Politics, Postition, and Power*, 4th ed. (New York: Oxford University Press, 1986).

5. See Stephen Hess, *Organizing the Presidency* (Washington, D.C.: Brookings Institution, 1976).

6. Richard Rose and Ezra Suleiman, eds., *Presidents and Prime Ministers* (Washington, D.C.: American Enterprise Institute, 1980), 336-38.

7. Frederick C. Mosher, *The GAO* (Boulder, Colo.: Westview, 1979).

8. Samuel P. Huntington, "The Marasmus of the ICC," *Yale Law Review,* April 1952, 467-509; but see James Q. Wilson, *The Politics of Regulation* (New York: Basic Books, 1980).

9. Annmarie Hauck Walsh, *The Public's Business: The Politics and Practices of Government Corporations* (Cambridge, Mass.: MIT Press, 1980), 41-44.

10. See Richard Rose et al., *Public Employment in Western Democracies* (Cambridge: Cambridge University Press, 1985).

11. Herman Schwartz, "Governmentally Appointed Directors in a Private Corporation—The Communications Satellite Act of 1962," *Harvard Law Review,* December 1961, 341-65.

12. See Harold Seidman and Robert S. Gilmour, *Politics, Position, and Power,* 4th ed. (New York: Oxford University Press, 1986), 274.

13. Martin Landau, "The Rationality of Redundancy," *Public Administration Review,* 1969, 346-58.

14. Committee on Governmental Affairs, *Federal Executive Establishment,* 27-30.

15. Woodrow Wilson, "The Study of Administration," *Political Science Quarterly,* June 1887, 197-222.

16. Daniel P. Moynihan, *The Politics of Guaranteed Income* (New York: Vintage, 1973), 240.

17. See chapter 10.

18. Robert B. Stevens, ed., *Income Security: Statutory History of the United States* (New York: McGraw-Hill, 1970), 639-59.

19. The order to do so was eventually rescinded.

20. Theodore J. Lowi, *The End of Liberalism,* 2d ed. (New York: Norton, 1979), 42-63.

21. Chris Hood, *The Limits of Administration* (New York: Wiley, 1976), 6-8.

22. Ronald Randall, "Presidential Power Versus Bureaucratic Intransigence: The Influence of the Nixon Administration on Welfare Policy," *American Political Science Review* 73 (September 1979): 795-810; and Joel D. Aberbach and Bert A. Rockman, "Clashing Beliefs within the Executive Branch: The Nixon Administration Bureaucracy," *American Political Science Review* 70 (June 1976): 456-68.

23. The classic description of this danger may be found in Herbert Kaufman, *The Forest Ranger* (Baltimore: Johns Hopkins University Press, 1960).

24. Daniel P. Moynihan, *Maximum Feasible Misunderstanding: Community Action in the War on Poverty* (New York: Free Press, 1969).

25. Advisory Commission on Intergovernmental Relations, *Citizen Participation in the Federal System,* A-73 (Washington, D.C.: ACIR, 1979).

26. Peter M. Blau, *The Dynamics of Bureaucracy* (Chicago: University of Chicago Press, 1955), 184-93.

27. Graham Allison, *Essence of Decision* (Boston: Little, Brown, 1971); and Eugene Bardach and Robert A. Kagan, *Going by the Book: The Problem of Regulatory Unreasonableness* (Philadelphia: Temple University Press, 1982).

28. This is seen by some as a fundamental characteristic of bureaucracies. See Victor Thompson, *Modern Organizations* (New York: Knopf, 1961).

29. See Gordon Tullock, *The Politics of Bureaucracy* (Washington, D.C.: Public Affairs Press, 1965).

30. Harold L. Wilensky, *Organizational Intelligence* (New York: Basic Books, 1967), 130-45.

31. Hood, *Limits of Administration,* 25-26.

32. Ibid., 192-97.

33. A good compilation appears in Peter Hall, *Great Planning Disasters* (London: Weidenfeld and Nicolson, 1980).

34. Paul R. Schulman, *Large-Scale Policymaking* (New York: Elsevier, 1980).

35. Richard A. Rettig, *Cancer Crusade* (Princeton: Princeton University Press, 1977).

36. Benny Hjern and David O. Porter, "Implementation Structures: A New Unit of Administrative Analysis" (paper presented to the American Political Science Association, annual convention, September 1979).

37. Jeffrey L. Pressman and Aaron Wildavsky, *Implementation* (Berkeley: University of California Press, 1973), xxii.

38. Ibid., 102-10.

39. Judith Bowen, "The Pressman-Wildavsky Paradox," *Journal of Public Policy* 2, no. 1 (February 1982): 1-22.

40. Joel F. Handler, *Social Movements and the Legal System: A Theory of Reform and Change* (New York: Academic Press, 1978), 180-81.

41. Stephen K. Bailey and Edith K. Mosher, *ESEA: The Office of Education Administers a Law* (Syracuse: Syracuse University Press, 1968), 103-9.

42. R. Lewis Bowman, Eleanor C. Main, and B. Guy Peters, "Coordination in the Atlanta Model Cities Program." Emory University, December 1971. Mimeographed.

6. Budgeting: Allocation and Public Policy

To implement policies, government requires money as well as institutional structure. The budgetary process provides a means of allocating the available resources among the competing interests to which they could be applied. In principle, all resources in the society are available to government, although in the United States a politician who advocated such a policy would not last a day. Likewise, all the purposes for which politicians and administrators wish to use the money have some merit. The question is whether those purposes are sufficiently worthwhile to justify using the resources in the public sector instead of putting them to other possible uses. Finding answers to questions requires economic and analytical judgment, as well as political estimates of the feasibility of the actions being approved.

Two different aspects of budgeting sometimes merge. One is the question of system-level allocation between the public and private sectors: How many activities or problems justify government intervention into the economy for the purpose of taxing and spending?[1] Could the best interest of society as a whole be served by keeping the money in private hands for investment decisions and allowing some possible beneficial programs in government to go unfunded? Or do the equity, equality, and economic growth produced by a public project justify the use of political capital by officials to pass and collect an additional tax or to increase an existing tax?

The second major budgeting question is this: How should available resources be allocated? When they devise a budget, decision makers function within definite resource constraints and must base their decisions on the assumption that no more revenue will come in. They must therefore allot the available amount of money for the greatest social, economic, and political benefit. This is not an easy task, of course, because of differing opinions as to what uses would be best. In addition, decision makers are often constrained by a commitment to fund existing commitments, such as Social Security, before they can begin to allocate the rest of the funds to other worthy programs.

But, because money can be divided almost infinitely, it offers a medium for resolving social conflicts that other forms of public benefit, such as rights, do not.

Characteristics of the Federal Budget

Before we discuss the budget cycle through which the federal budget is constructed each year, several fundamental features of that budget must be explained.

An Executive Budget

The federal budget is an executive budget, prepared by the President and his staff, approved by Congress, and then executed by the President and the executive branch. This has not always been the case; before 1921, the budget was a legislative budget, prepared almost entirely by Congress and then executed by the President. One tenet of the reform movement in the early twentieth century was that an executive budget was a necessity for more effective management in government. No executive should have to manage a budget that he had no part in planning.

The passage of the Budget and Accounting Act of 1921 marked the beginning of a conflict between the executive and legislative branches over their respective powers in the budgetary process.[2] In general, power has accumulated in the executive branch and in the Executive Office of the President, in large part because of the analytical dominance of the Office of Management and Budget (which was called the Bureau of the Budget until 1971). The excesses of the Nixon administration, and to some degree those of the Johnson administration during the Vietnam war, led to the development of the Congressional Budget Office as a part of the Congressional Budget and Impoundment Control Act of 1974. This office gives Congress some of the analytical capability of the executive branch, just as the development of the budget committees in both houses gives Congress greater control over budgeting than it had before the passage of the act in 1974. Congress, however, is still very much in the position of responding to presidential initiatives.

Line Item

Despite several attempts at reform, the federal budget remains a line-item budget. That is, the final budget document appropriating funds allocates those funds into categories—wages and salaries, supplies, travel, equipment, and so forth. These traditional categories are extremely useful in that they give Congress some control over the executive branch. Moneys are appropriated for agencies and are allocated for specific purposes within the agency. It is then rather easy for the legislature, through the General Accounting Office, to make sure that the money is spent under legal authority.[3] It is, however, difficult to determine if the money was spent efficiently and effectively. Also, the line-item budget may prevent good managers in government from managing by limiting how they can spend the money.

An Annual Budget

The federal budget is primarily an annual budget. Agencies are now required to submit five-year expenditure forecasts associated with each of their expenditure plans, but this is primarily for management purposes within the Office of Management and Budget (OMB). The budget presented to Congress and eventually the appropriations bills of Congress together constitute an annual expenditure plan. The absence of a more complete multiyear budget makes planning difficult for federal managers and does not necessarily alert Congress to the long-term implications of expenditure decisions made in any one year.[4] A small expenditure in one year may result in much larger expenditures in subsequent years and create clientele who cannot be eliminated without significant political repercussions.

The Budget Cycle

Each year there must be a new budget, and an annual cycle has evolved for the appropriation and expenditure of available public moneys. The repetitive nature of the budget cycle is important, for those involved might behave differently if they did not know that they have to come back year after year to get more money from the same OMB officials and the same congressmen.

Setting the Parameters: The President and His Friends

Most of this chapter discusses the allocation of resources among programs, rather than the setting of broad expenditure and economic management policy. It is necessary, however, to begin with a brief discussion of decisions concerning overall levels of expenditure and revenue. The budget process is initiated by a number of decisions about total spending levels, and those decisions about parameters influence subsequent decisions.[5]

One of the first official acts of the budget cycle is the development, each spring, of estimates of the total size of the federal budget being prepared for the fiscal year. Although the agencies and the OMB will already have begun to discuss and prepare expenditure plans, the letter from the President through the OMB (usually in June) is an important first step in the formal process. This letter is a statement of overall budgetary strategy and of the limits within which the agencies will have to prepare their budgets. In addition to setting the overall parameters, this letter will present more detailed information on how those parameters apply to individual agencies. Also, the past experience of budgeting officials in each agency should give them some idea of how to interpret the general parameters. Defense agencies, for example, know that they are not necessarily bound by those parameters, whereas planners of domestic programs with little client support and few friends on Capitol Hill may hope they do as well as the letter leads them to believe they will.

The overall estimates for spending are prepared some sixteen months before the budget is to go into effect. For example, the fiscal year 1987 budget went into effect on 1 October 1986, but the planning for that budget began in June 1985 or earlier. For any budget, this means that the economic forecasts on which the expenditure estimates are based may be far from the economic reality that will prevail when the budget is actually executed. Those expenditure forecasts are important. A recession, for example, will mean a reduction in revenues; people who are out of work do not pay income and Social Security taxes. As well as being important, these forecasts are not entirely the product of technical considerations; they are also influenced by political and ideological considerations. For example, during the first years of the Reagan administration the belief that "supply-side" economics would produce larger revenues through an upswing in economic activity led to a serious overestimation of the amount of revenue and the beginning of the large federal deficits that have come to be a continuing feature of American public finance.[6]

The preparation of expenditure estimates is the result of the interaction of three principal actors: the Council of Economic Advisers (CEA), the OMB, and the Treasury. Collectively, these three are referred to as the "troika."[7] The CEA is, as the name implies, a group of economists who advise the President. Organizationally, they are located in the Executive Office of the President. The role of the CEA is largely technical, forecasting the state of the economy and advising the President on the basis of these forecasts. They also mathematically model the probable effects of certain budgetary choices on the economy. Of course, the economics of the CEA must be tempered with political judgment, for mathematical models and economists do not run for office, but Presidents must.

The OMB, despite its image, comes as close to a representative of the expenditure community as exists in the troika. Although the agencies whose budgets OMB supervises cannot perceive it as a kindly benefactor, its members may be favorably disposed toward expenditures. They see the huge volume of agency requests coming forward, and are aware of the large volume of "uncontrollable" expenditures (e.g., Social Security benefits) that will have to be appropriated regardless of changes in economic circumstances. These considerations have been less important under the Reagan administration than during previous administrations, in part because of the commitment of David Stockman, then director of the OMB, to the cause of reducing federal expenditures.

Finally, the Treasury represents the financial community, and to some extent it is the major advocate of a balanced budget in the troika. The Treasury, by issuing government bonds, must cover any debts created by a deficit. The principal interest of the Treasury may be to preserve the confidence of the financial community at home and abroad in the soundness of the U.S. economy and the government's management of that economy. Some particular concerns of the Treasury may be relationships with international financial organizations such as the International Monetary Fund.

Even at this first step in the budgetary process, a great deal of hard political and economic bargaining occurs. Each member of the troika must compete for the attention of the President as well as protect the interests of the particular community it represents. But this is just the beginning of a long series of bargains as agencies attempt to get the money they want and need from the budgetary process.

Agency Requests

As in so much American policymaking, the agency is a central actor in the budgetary process.[8] Whether working independently or in a cabinet-level department, the agency is primarily responsible for the preparation of estimates and requests for funding. The agency makes these preparations in conjunction with the OMB and, if applicable, with the agency's executive department. During the preparation of estimates, OMB provides guidance and advice concerning total levels of expenditure and particular aspects of the agency's budget. Likewise, the agency may have to coordinate its activities with those of the executive department in which it is located. It would do this through a departmental budget committee and the secretary's staff. This coordination is necessary to ensure that the agency is operating within the priorities of the President and the cabinet secretary and also to ensure support from the secretary in defending the budget to OMB and the Congress.

The task of the agency in the budgetary process is to be aggressive in seeking to expand its expenditure base but at the same time recognize that it is only one part of a larger organization. In other words, the agency must be aggressive but reasonable, seeking more money but realizing that it operates within the constraints of what government as a whole can afford. Likewise, the executive department must recognize its responsibilities to the President and his program and to the agencies under its umbrella. The cabinet secretary must be a major spokesman for his or her agencies in the higher levels of government, but at the same time agencies often have more direct support from interest groups and perhaps from Congress than does the department as a whole. Thus, a cabinet secretary may not be able to go far in following the President's program if that would seriously jeopardize ongoing programs in the department. This is reflective of the general fragmentation of American government, with much of the real power and the operational connections between government and the interest groups being at the agency, rather than department, level.

An agency may employ a number of strategies in seeking to expand its level of funding, but the use of these strategies is restrained by the knowledge that budgeting is an annual cycle and that any strategic choice in a single year may preclude the use of that strategy in later years and, perhaps more important, may destroy any confidence that OMB and Congress had in the agency.[9] For example, an agency may employ the "camel's nose" or "thin wedge" strategy to get a program funded at a modest level in its first year with the knowledge that the program will have rapidly increasing expenditure requirements. Then that agency may be assured that any future requests for new spending authority will be carefully scrutinized.

Executive Review

After the agency has decided on its requests, it passes them on to the OMB for review. The OMB is a presidential agency, and one of its principal tasks is to amass all the agency requests and make them conform to presidential policy priorities and to the overall levels of expenditure desired. This may make for a tight fit, as some programs are difficult or impossible to control, leaving little space for any new programs that the President may consider important.

After OMB receives the estimates, it passes them on to the budget examiners for review. In the rare case in which an agency has actually requested the amount, or less than the amount, that OMB had planned to give it, there is no problem. In most cases, however, the examiners must depend on their experience with the agency in question, as well as whatever information about programs and projected expenditures they can collect, to make a judgment concerning the necessity and priority of any requested expenditure. And, as with so many decisions about public finance, much depends on the trust that has developed among individuals across time. In this case, the examiners spend a great deal of their time in the agencies they supervise and may adopt a stance more favorable to the agency than might be expected, given the image of OMB as a tough budget-cutting organization.

On the basis of agency requests and the information developed by the examiner, OMB holds hearings, usually in October or November. At these hearings the agency must defend its requests before the examiner and other members of the staff. Although OMB sometimes seems to be committed to cutting expenditures, several factors prevent it from wielding too large an ax. First, it is frequently not difficult for the agency to pull an "end run" on the hearing board and to appeal to the director of OMB, the President, or ultimately to friends in Congress. Also, some budget examiners tend, over time, to favor the agencies they are supposed to control, so at times they may be advocates of an agency's requests rather than the fiscal conservatives they are expected to be.

The results of the hearing are forwarded to the director of OMB for the "director's review," which involves all the top staff of the bureau. At this stage, through additional trimming and negotiation, the staff tries to pare the final budget down to the amount desired by the President. After each portion of the budget goes through the director's review it is then forwarded to the President for final review and then for compilation into the final budget document. This stage necessarily involves final appeals from agency and department personnel to OMB and the President as well as last-minute adjustments to take into account unanticipated changes in economic forecasts and desired changes in the total size of the budget. The presidential budget is then prepared for delivery to Congress within fifteen days after it convenes in January.

In this way the presidential budget is made ready to be reviewed for appropriations by Congress. By 10 November of each year, however, the President must submit to Congress the "current services budget," which includes "proposed budget authority and estimated outlays that would be included in the budget for the ensuing fiscal year . . . if all programs and activities were carried on at the same level as the fiscal year in progress."[10] This is a form of "volume budgeting," for it budgets for a constant volume of public services.[11] Given the rate of inflation in the 1970s and early 1980s, this constant service gives Congress an early warning of the anticipated size of current expenditure commitments if they are extended. It is, however, subject to substantial inaccuracy, either purposive or accidental. It gives Congress a rough estimate for planning purposes, but only that.

Congressional Action

Although Congress is specifically granted the powers of the purse in the Constitution, by the 1960s and 1970s it had clearly ceased to be the dominant actor in making budgetary decisions. Congress has attempted a counterattack, largely through the Congressional Budget and Impoundment Control Act of 1974. Among other provisions, this act established in each house of Congress a budget committee to be responsible for developing two concurrent resolutions each year outlining fiscal policy constraints on expenditures, much as does the troika in the executive branch. The act also established the Congressional Budget Office to provide the budget committees a staff capacity analogous to that which OMB provides the President.[12]

Decisions on how to allocate total spending among agencies and programs are made by the appropriations committees in both houses.[13] These are extremely prestigious and powerful committees, and those serving on them are veteran members of Congress. Also, members tend to remain on these committees for long periods, thereby developing both expertise and political ties with the agencies they supervise. The two committees, and especially the House Appropriations Committee, do most of their work in subcommittees. These subcommittees may cover one executive department, such as Defense, or a number of agencies, such as Housing and Urban Development and independent executive agencies, or a function, such as public works. Most important, the whole committee does not closely scrutinize the decisions of its subcommittees, nor does the House of Representatives as a whole frequently reverse the decisions of its appropriations committee. Scrutiny has increased, in large part because of the general opening of congressional deliberations to more "sunshine," but once an agency's budget has been agreed to in a subcommittee, that budget has, in all probability, been largely decided.

That subcommittee must decide on the budget. On the basis of presidential recommendations, each subcommittee develops an appropriations bill, or occasionally two, for a total of thirteen or fourteen each year. Hearings are held, and agency personnel are summoned to testify and to justify the size of their desired appropriation. After those hearings, the subcommittee will "mark up" the bill—make such changes as it feels are necessary—and then submit it, first to the entire committee and then to the House of Representatives. In accordance with the Congressional Budget Act, the appropriations committees are expected to have a completed mark-up of all appropriations bills before submitting the first for final passage, so as to have a better overall idea of the level of expenditure that would be approved. The Senate follows a similar procedure, and any differences between the two houses are resolved in a conference committee. This procedure should be finished by 15 September, in order to be ready to go into effect by 1 October, but the Congressional Budget Act also requires the passage of a second and concurrent resolution setting forth the budget ceilings, revenue floors, and overall fiscal policy considerations governing the passage of the appropriations bills. As there will undoubtedly be differences in the ways in which the two houses make their appropriations figures correspond with the figures in the concurrent resolution, a reconciliation bill, in which both houses agree on the spending totals, must be passed by 25 September. The budget is then ready to go to the President for his signature and execution.

Budget Execution

After the executive branch has been appropriated money, the agencies must develop mechanisms for spending that money. An appropriations warrant, drawn by the Treasury and countersigned by the General Accounting Office, is sent to each agency. The agency then makes plans for its expenditures for the year, on the basis of this warrant, and submits a plan to OMB for apportionment of the funds. The funds appropriated by Congress are usually made available to the agencies on a quarterly basis, but for some agencies there may be great differences in the amounts made available each quarter. For example, the U.S. Park Service spends a very large proportion of its annual appropriation during the summer because of the demands on the national parks at that time. Two principal reasons for allowing agencies access to only a quarter of their funds at a time are to provide greater control over spending and to prevent an agency from spending everything early in the year and then requiring a supplemental appropriation. This still happens, but apportionment helps to control any potential profligacy.

The procedures for executing the budget are relatively simple when the executive branch actually wants to spend the money it has appropriated. Procedures become more complex when the President decides he does not want to spend the appropriated funds. Prior to the Congressional Budget Act of 1974, a President had at least a customary right to impound funds, that is, to refuse to spend them. The numerous impoundments during the Nixon administration (e.g., half the money appropriated for implementing the Federal Water Pollution Control Act Amendments of 1972 was impounded from the 1973 to 1975 budgets) forced Congress to take action to control executive actions.

The Congressional Budget and Impoundment Control Act of 1974 was designed to limit the ability of the President to use impoundment as an indirect means of overruling Congress, even when this could not be done through the normal legislative process (the water-pollution-control legislation had been passed over a presidential veto). The 1974 act defined two kinds of impoundment. First, recisions are cancellations of budgetary authority to spend money. A President may decide that a program could reach its goals with less money or simply that there were good reasons not to spend the money. The President must then send a message to Congress requesting the recision. Congress must act positively on this request within forty-five days; if it does not, the money is made available to the agency for obligation. Deferrals, on the other hand, are requests merely to delay making the obligational authority available to the agency. In this case, if either house of Congress does not exercise its veto power, the deferral is granted. The Comptroller General is given the power to classify specific presidential actions, and at times the difference between a deferral and a recision is not clear. For example, attempting to defer funds for programs scheduled to be phased out is, in practice, a recision. These reforms in the impoundment powers of the President have substantially increased the powers of Congress in determining how much money will indeed be spent by the federal government each year.

Budget Control

After the President and the executive branch spend the money appropriated by Congress, the Congress must check to be sure that the money was spent legally and properly. The General Accounting Office (GAO) and its head, the Comptroller General, are responsible for the postaudit of federal expenditures. Each year the Comptroller General's report to Congress outlines deviations from congressional intent.

The GAO has undergone a major transformation from a simple accounting organization into a policy-analytic organization for the legislative branch.[14] It has become concerned not only with the legality of expenditures but also with the efficiency with which the money is spent. Although the reports of the GAO on the efficiency of expenditures have no legal authority, any agency that wishes to maintain its good relations with Congress would be well advised to take those findings into account. And Congress will certainly by cognizant of those recommendations when it reviews an agency's budget the following year and will expect to see some changes. The problem with GAO controls—whether of an accounting or a more policy-analytic nature—is that they are largely ex post facto, so the money may well have been spent long before the decision that it is being spent either illegally or unwisely is made.

Summary

A long and complex process is required to perform the difficult tasks of allocating federal budget money among competing agencies. The process takes almost eighteen months and involves many bargains and decisions. From this process of bargaining and analysis emerges a plan for spending billions of dollars. But even this complex process, now made more complex by reforms of congressional budgeting procedures, cannot control all federal expenditures as completely as some would desire, nor can it provide the level of fiscal management that may be necessary for a smoothly functioning economic system. Let us now turn to a few problems that Presidents and congressmen alike face in making the budgetary process an effective allocative process. It may never be as "rational" as some would like because it is inherently a political as well as an economic process, but there are identifiable problems that cause particular difficulty.

Problems in the Budgetary Process

The major problems arising in the budgetary process of the federal government affect the fiscal management function of budgeting as well as the allocation of resources among agencies. It is difficult, if not impossible, for any President or Congress to make binding decisions as to how much money will be spent in any year, or even as to who will spend it for what, and this absence of basic controls makes the entire process subject to error. Those elected to make policy and control spending frequently find themselves incapable of producing the kinds of change they campaigned for, and this can result in disillusionment for both leaders and citizens.

Uncontrollable Expenditures

Many expenditure programs in the federal government in any year cannot be controlled without major policy changes that may be politically unpalatable.[15] For example, a President or the Congress can do very little to control the level of expenditure for Social Security in any year without either changing the criteria for eligibility or altering the formula for indexation (adjustment of the benefits for changes in consumer prices or workers' earnings) of the program. Either choice may produce a major political conflict and might well be impossible. Some minor changes, such as changing the tax treatment of Social Security benefits for beneficiaries with other income, may be entertained, but this category of expenditure is essentially uncontrollable.

TABLE 6.I

EXECUTIVE CONTROLLABILITY OF FEDERAL EXPENDITURES

(in percent)

	1970	1975	1980	1984
Relatively uncontrollable	62.2	69.4	72.7	74.1
Relatively controllable	37.8	30.6	27.3	25.9

SOURCE: *Budget of the United States,* annual.

Much of the federal budget is uncontrollable in any one year (see table 6.1). The most important uncontrollable expenditures are the large entitlement programs of social welfare spending such as Social Security, Medicare, and unemployment benefits. These expenditures are uncontrollable both because they cannot be readily cut by a government and because the government cannot accurately estimate, while planning a budget, just how much money will be needed for the programs. The final level of expenditures will depend on levels of inflation, illness, and unemployment, as well as on the number of eligible citizens who actually take advantage of the programs. In addition, outstanding contracts and obligations constitute a significant share of the uncontrollable portion of the budget, although these can be altered over a number of years, if not in any single year. The major controllable component of the federal budget is the defense budget. Given the political climate of the early 1980s, however, it is unlikely that the defense budget would be a target for any additional cuts. This has meant that even a President as committed to the goals of reducing federal expenditures and producing a balanced budget as President Reagan has found it difficult to determine where the expenditure reductions will come from. Some discretionary social expenditures have been reduced, but the bulk of federal expenditures has continued to increase (see table 6.2). Thus, any President coming into office with a desire to balance the budget or reduce federal spending may soon find it difficult to determine where those expenditure reductions will come from.

TABLE 6.2

FEDERAL SPENDING, FISCAL YEARS 1980-86

(*$ billion*)

	1980	1981	1982	1983	1984	1985[a]	1986[a]
Social Security	153.0	177.1	200.7	223.3	235.8	257.4	269.4
Defense	135.9	159.8	187.4	210.5	227.4	253.8	285.7
Other	290.7	320.3	340.3	362.2	388.6	447.9	418.6
TOTAL	579.6	657.2	728.4	796.0	851.8	959.1	973.7
(in percent)							
Social Security	26.4	26.9	27.6	28.1	27.7	26.8	27.7
Defense	23.4	24.3	25.7	26.4	26.7	26.5	27.7
Other	50.2	48.8	46.7	45.5	45.6	46.7	44.6
TOTAL	100.0	100.0	100.0	100.0	100.0	100.0	100.0

SOURCE: *Budget of the United States*, annual.

a. Estimated.

Back-Door Spending

Linked to the problem of uncontrollable expenditures is "back-door spending" — expenditure decisions that are not actually made through the formal appropriations process. These expenditures to some degree reflect an institutional conflict within Congress, between the appropriations committees and the substantive policy committees. There are three principal kinds of back-door spending.

BORROWING AUTHORITY

Agencies may be allowed to spend public money not appropriated by Congress if they borrow that money from the Treasury—for student-loan guarantees, for instance. It has been argued that this is not actually public expenditures, as the money will presumably be repaid eventually. In many instances, however, federal loans have been written off, and, even if the loans are repaid, the ability of government to control expenditure levels for purposes of economic management is seriously impaired when the authority to make spending decisions is so diffused.

CONTRACT AUTHORITY

Agencies also may enter into contracts that bind the federal government to pay a certain amount for specified goods and services without going through the appropriations process. Then, after the contract is let, the appropriations committees are placed in the awkward position of either appropriating the money to pay off the debt or forcing the agency to renege on its debts. While this kind of spending is uncontrollable in the short run, any agency attempting to engage in this circumvention of the appropriations committees probably soon will face the ire of those committees when attempting to have its annual budget approved.

PERMANENT APPROPRIATIONS

Certain programs have authorizing legislation that requires the spending of certain amounts of money. The largest expenditure of this kind is payment of interest on the public debt; this expense constituted over 13 percent of total federal expenditures in 1985 and is projected to increase as a result of continuing large federal deficits. Likewise, federal support of land-grant colleges is a permanent appropriation that began during the administration of Abraham Lincoln. In the case of a permanent appropriation, the appropriations committees have little discretion, unless they choose to renege on these standing commitments of the government.

The Overhang

Not all the money appropriated by Congress for a fiscal year need actually be spent during that fiscal year; it must only be obligated. That is, the agency must contract to spend the money, with the actual outlay of funds coming perhaps some years later. In 1987 there was a total budget authority of about $2.2 trillion (see figure 6.1) with only $1.1 trillion being appropriated during that year.[16] Thus, in 1987 the "overhang" was almost as large as the amount of money appropriated by Congress during that fiscal year. The President could not actually spend all that overhang in the single fiscal year (a good deal of it is

$ Billions

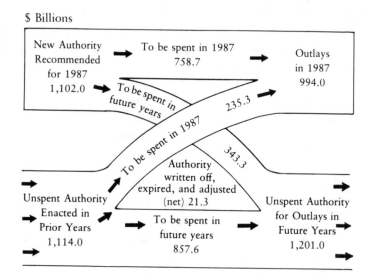

<figure>FIGURE 6.1
RELATION OF BUDGET AUTHORITY TO OUTLAYS — 1987 BUDGET</figure>

SOURCE: *Budget of the United States,* FY 1987 (Washington, D.C.: Government Printing Office, 1986).

in long-term contracts), but it represents a substantial amount in unspent obligations for the agencies and the government as a whole.

The major problem is that the overhang makes it difficult for a President to use the budget as an instrument of economic management. One principal component of economic management is the amount of public expenditure, and, with the overhang, the President and Congress cannot always control the actual outlay of funds. The agencies may have sufficient budget authority, convertible into actual outlays, to damage forecasts of outlays. They would do this, not out of malice, but out of perceived needs, especially if the President was seeking to restrict the creation of new obligational authority.

Intergovernmental Budget Control

Although it does not specifically affect the federal budgetary process, the lack of overall fiscal control in the public sector of the United States makes it impossible for the federal government to control total public expenditures and hence to exercise the kind of fiscal management it might like.

The federal government itself spends only about two-thirds (1985) of the total amount of money spent by government in the United States. It has the capacity to stimulate state and local government expenditures through matching grants, but reducing expenditures is more difficult. It has even less control over revenue collection. For example, in 1963 the Kennedy administration pushed through a tax cut for the federal government, only to have almost the entire effect of that cut negated by state and local tax increases.[17]

The principles of federalism would appear to give state and local governments a perfect right to decide on their own levels of revenues and expenditures. However, in an era in which the public budget is important for economic management as well as for the distribution of funds among organizations, there may be a need for greater overall control of expenditures. This need not be decided unilaterally by the federal government, but could perhaps be decided by "diplomacy" among representatives of the several levels of government. These potential effects on economic conditions are to some degree reflected by the presence of large state and local government surpluses in the mid-1980s, at the same time that the federal government is running large deficits.[18] Depending on one's point of view, this is either a good thing (helping to reduce total public borrowing) or a bad thing (counteracting the economic stimulus of the deficit). In either case, it represents the lack of an integrated fiscal policy within the United States.

Reprogramming and Transfers

The first four problems in the federal budgetary process affect primarily the total level of expenditures. The next two problems, reprogramming and transfers, affect levels of spending by individual agencies and the purposes for which the agencies spend their money.

Reprogramming is the shifting of funds within a specific appropriation account. When Congress passes an appropriations bill, that bill contains a number of appropriations accounts, which in turn contain a number of program elements. For example, the appropriations bill for the Department of Agriculture contains an appropriations account for crop supports, with separate program elements for cotton, corn, wheat, and so on. Reprogramming involves shifting obligational authority from one program element to another. The procedures for making reprogramming decisions has been thoroughly developed only in the Department of Defense. In general, there is a threshold (variable by agency) below which agencies are relatively free to reprogram funds, but above which they require approval from appropriations committee personnel, although not from the entire Congress. There are also requirements for reporting reprogramming decisions to the appropriations committees.

Transfers are more serious actions, for they involve transferring funds from one appropriations account to another. In our Department of Agriculture example above, this might involve shifting funds from crop supports to the Farmers

Home Administration or to rural electrification. Transfer funds have been subject to significant abuse and circumvention of congressional authority, especially during the Nixon administration and the Vietnam war. And, as with reprogramming—outside the Department of Defense—few established procedures exist for controlling the use of transfer funds other than those that specifically forbid the use of such funds for certain functions.

Both reprogramming and transfer funds are important in providing the executive branch with some flexibility in implementing its programs and in using public funds more effectively. These opportunities have been the subject of many abuses, however, and are ripe for reform and improvement. In particular, they frequently allow an agency to circumvent the judgment of the entire Congress through an appeal to the appropriations committee, or perhaps even to its chairman.

Supplemental Appropriations

Even with the apportionment of funds mentioned earlier, agencies may require supplemental appropriations—those made outside the normal budget cycle—to cover shortfalls during the fiscal year.[19] Agencies sometimes simply run out of money. This can result from improper management, but more often it happens because of changes in the demand for services or because of a poor estimate of the demand for a new service. For example, during a recession, the demand for unemployment assistance will naturally increase, and supplemental funding will be required. Likewise, a year of poor weather may force additional funding for crop supports in the Department of Agriculture. Or a new program, such as food stamps, may acquire more clients than anyone anticipated during the early years of its existence. When we are talking about supplemental appropriations, we are not talking about insignificant amounts of money. In 1984 a net of some $6.1 billion was appropriated through supplementals. While some of the supplemental actions were to reduce the amounts appropriated, the additions to agency obligational authority ranged from $500,000 for international agricultural programs to over $5 billion for unemployment compensation.

The request for supplemental appropriations may be a useful strategy for agencies attempting to expand their funding. The agency may be able to initiate a program with minimal appropriations, anticipating a wide acceptance of its program by prospective clients, and then return to Congress for a supplemental appropriation when clients do indeed materialize and demand benefits. Supplemental appropriations frequently are not scrutinized as carefully as are regular appropriations, and this may allow a friendly congressman to hide an expanding program. But obvious and frequent abuse of the supplemental appropriations process will almost certainly damage the relationship between the agency and the Congress and may hurt more than help the agency, in the long run, in expanding its expenditure base.

Assessing the Outcomes: Incrementalism or What?

One standard word used to describe changes in budgetary allocations in the United States is *incremental*. Any number of meanings have been attached to this word. Broadly, incrementalism means that changes which appear in an agency's budget from year to year tend to be predictable.[20] More specifically, incrementalism has taken on several additional interpretations. First, incremental decision making is described as *process* that is not "synoptic," or fully "rational."[21] That is, incremental decision making does not involve examining sweeping alternatives to the status quo and then making a decision about the optimal use of budgetary resources. Rather, incremental decision making involves "successive limited comparisons," or the sequential examination of marginal changes from the status quo and decisions about whether to make these marginal adjustments to existing policies.[22] The decision-making process tends to build on earlier decisions and then seek means to improve the situation rather than alter existing policies or budgetary priorities completely. In budgetary terms this means an agency can expect to receive this year approximately what it received last year, plus a little bit more to adjust for inflation or expanded services.

Advocates of incremental decision making argue that this method of making policy choices is actually more rational than the synoptic method. Because it provides an experiential base from which to work, the incremental method offers a greater opportunity to make good policy choices than does the synoptic method. In addition, any errors that are made in an incremental decision-making process can be more easily reversed than can major changes made in a synoptic process. In many ways incremental decision making is a cost-minimizing form of rationality rather than a benefit-maximizing approach. It reduces costs, first, by limiting the range of alternatives and thereby limiting the research and calculation costs for decision makers; and, second, by reducing the costs of change, particularly of error correction. Because few policy choices involve significant deviations from existing policies, or appropriations, there is little need to make major adjustments either in the actual programs or in the thought patterns about the policies. Given the limited calculative capacity of human beings, even with the aid of modern technology, and the resistance of most individuals and organizations to change, incrementalism can be argued to be a rational means for making choices.

Incrementalism has also been used to describe the pattern of *outcomes* of the budgetary process. In particular, Davis, Dempster, and Wildavsky found a great deal of stability in the increases in appropriations granted to agencies from year to year by the President and the Congress.[23] The changes in budgets are not only small but also quite stable and predictable, so the best estimate of an agency's budget in one year would be the previous year's budget plus a stable percentage increase. Some agencies grow more rapidly than do others, but each will exhibit a stable pattern of growth.

Several factors contribute to the pattern of incremental budgeting found in the United States. One is the large percentage of the budget that is uncontrollable, so few significant changes in appropriations can be made from year to year. Also, most empirical examinations of incremental budgeting have been done during periods of relative economic stability and high rates of economic growth, so, as less favorable economic conditions become more common in the United States, the level of incrementalism is appropriate for rich and predictable budgeting systems, but not for those that are less stable.[24]

Most important, the repetitive and sequential nature of the budgeting process tends to produce incremental outcomes in budgeting. A budget must be passed each year, so minor adjustments can be made from year to year as the need arises, thus avoiding the need to correct all the problems of the policy area at once. Also, the annual cycle prevents an agency from trying to "shoot the moon" in any one year—trying, in other words, to expand its budget greatly, perhaps with flimsy evidence. Agency leaders know that they will have to return for more money next year, and any attempt to deceive only invites future punishment. The sequential nature of the process, in which several different actors make several different decisions one after another, also tends to produce incremental outcomes. Many decisions have to be made, and many bargains must be struck. The incremental solution not only provides a "natural" choice but also helps to minimize bargaining costs among institutions. Once a decision rule of a certain percentage increase for a particular agency each year has been established, it is far simpler to honor that rule than to seek a "better" decision for one year.

Criticism of Incrementalism

A number of criticisms have been leveled at incrementalism, both in its prescriptive capacity (decisions *should* be made incrementally) and in its descriptive capacity (decisions *are* made incrementally). The basic argument against incrementalism as a prescription for policymaking is that it is excessively conservative, so the status quo is perpetuated long after better solutions are available. This is true for certain kinds of program decisions as well as for expenditure decisions. Incrementalism may be a perfectly rational means of policymaking so long as all parties agree that a policy or program is functioning well and is well managed. But how many policies fall in that happy category?

In addition, even the incrementalist might agree that at times (e.g., during periods of crisis) nonincremental decisions are required, but the method provides no means of identifying when and how those nonincremental decisions should be made. If one uses the approach to provide a prescriptive model of governmental decision making, then one must be able to specify what a "big" change would be, when it would be appropriate, and how it might be made.

Several problems also relate to incrementalism as a description of budgetary decision making. In the first place, the majority of empirical examinations of incremental budgeting have been performed at the agency level. This is certainly justifiable, given the importance of those organizations in American public policy, but it is perhaps too high a level of aggregation for examining incremental budgeting.[25] When other researchers have disaggregated agency budgets into program-level budgets, they have found a great deal of nonincremental change, although, as pointed out, it is sometimes difficult to define just what an incremental change is or is not. Thus, while organizations may have a stable pattern of expenditure change, the managers of these organizations may drastically alter priorities among the operating programs within the agency.

In addition, when the uncontrollable elements of public expenditures are removed from the analysis, the pattern of expenditure change for the controllable portion is anything but incremental.[26] As budgets have been squeezed by inflation and citizen resistance to taxation, increments have not been granted as usual, and at times the base has also been cut—that is, there have been real reductions in the amount of new obligational authority for the agency as compared with the preceding year. Incrementalism may therefore be descriptive of only certain kinds of expenditures, and not of the budget process as a whole. Of course, since uncontrollable expenditures account for approximately 75 percent of total federal expenditures, the incrementalist approach may still be useful.

Also, incrementalism may apply only to certain kinds of agencies and programs, such as those whose existence has been fully accepted as a part of the realm of government activity; it may not apply to newer or more marginal programs. For example, the budgets of programs such as Aid to Families with Dependent Children (AFDC, "welfare") are always more subject to change than are more legitimated programs, such as those that control veterans' benefits, although both would be broadly classified as social service expenditures.

In addition, incrementalist theory does not explain how and when programs make big gains—or big losses—in their appropriations. Even if the approach is successful in explaining a great deal of the variance in normal times, it seems incapable of explaining the most interesting and most important aspects of budgeting—who wins and who loses.[27]

Finally, the prescriptive appeal of incrementalism is based in part on the reversibility of small changes. In the real world of policymaking, many changes may not be reversible.[28] Once a commitment is made to a client, or a benefit is indexed, it is difficult to go back and take away the benefit. This is especially true of programs that have a "stock" component, that is, involve the development of a capital infrastructure or the development of a financial base. Once a program such as Social Security is introduced, those covered under the program take the benefits under the program into account when making their financial plans; thus, any reduction or elimination of benefits may create a hardship.

Whether incrementalism accurately describes the budgeting process in the United States or its results, it has certainly become the conventional wisdom. And, in turn, it has prompted a number of proposals for reform of the budgetary process to make it more "rational" and to try to reduce the tendency of a program, once authorized, to remain in existence forever. It is to those attempts at reform that we now turn our attention.

Reforming Budgeting

Numerous criticisms have been directed at the budgetary process in the United States. In general, these criticisms have focused on the incremental, "irrational," and fragmented nature of the process. Several methods have sought to make the consideration of expenditure priorities more comprehensive and to allow governments to make the best possible use of their limited resources. The two most important budgeting reforms have been program budgeting and zero-base budgeting.

Program Budgeting

Program budgeting was largely a product of the Johnson administration, although in some agencies it had been tried previously. Whereas traditional budgeting allocates personnel costs, supplies, equipment, and so forth, among organizations, program budgeting allocates resources on the basis of the activities of government and the services that government supplies to society.[29] It also places a pronounced emphasis on the analysis of programmatic expenditures and the most efficient use of resources.

Underlying program budgeting, or more specifically the planning, programming, budgeting system (PPBS), is a systems concept. That is, it is assumed that the elements of government policy are closely intertwined, so that a change in one type of policy may affect all others. For example, if one wants to improve the quality of health for citizens in the United States, it may be more efficient to improve nutrition and housing than to invest money in medical care.

Program budgeting is always looking for interactions among policy areas and for means of producing desired effects in the most efficient manner.

There are six basic characteristics of program budgeting as it is practiced in the federal government. First, *the major goals and objectives of government must be identified.* We must be able to specify what government is attempting to do, but this identification is made high in the hierarchy of government, usually by the President and Congress. Whereas traditional line-item budgeting is initiated by the agencies, program budgeting must begin with a specification of the central goals and priorities of government, which can be supplied only by the principal political leaders.

Second, *programs must be developed according to the goals that have been specified.* How will government attempt to attain the goals that have been set for it? These programs are analytically defined and may not exist as organizational entities. For example, when Robert McNamara—who with his "whiz kids" was largely responsible for introducing program budgeting into the Defense Department and thence into the federal government as a whole—developed the program structure for the Department of Defense, one of the programs developed was "strategic deterrence." This program was actually spread among all three services. The air force had its manned bombers and some missiles, the navy had Polaris submarines, and the army had Intermediate Range Ballistic Missiles located in Europe. Strategic deterrence certainly did describe one set of activities of the defense establishment, but no organization was specifically responsible for that program.

Third, *resources must be allocated among programs.* Although many traditional line items were used in developing the program budget, the final budget document was presented in terms of overall costs for the achievement of certain objectives. These costs would then be justified as being an efficient and effective means of reaching the desired goals. Program budgeting then places its emphasis on the costs of reaching certain objectives, whereas line-item budgeting tends to emphasize the costs of keeping organizations or programs in operation.

Fourth, *organizations are not sacrosanct* in program budgeting, and there is no assumption that each program is housed within a single agency or that each agency provides only a single program. As with the defense example mentioned above, program budgeting attempts to expand the framework of budgeting and planning to include all actors who contribute to the achievement of the goals. This is obviously a realistic attitude toward the interaction of several activities and organizations in producing the final effects on the society, but it does make budgeting more difficult in an environment perhaps best regarded as composed of many organizations, each of which is attempting to sustain its own interests.

Fifth, *program budgeting extends the time limit beyond the single year* common in line-item budgeting. It attempts to ask and answer questions about the medium and long-term implications of the programs decided on. Some programs that appear efficient in the short run may actually be less desirable when their long-term implications are considered. For example, most publicly supported health programs concentrate on curative medicine, whereas it may be more efficient in the long run to emphasize preventive medicine. Curative medicine, however, may be more popular politically, as ill people are obviously being aided, while the benefits of preventive medicine are more diffuse and less likely to be identifiable by the average citizen.

Sixth, *alternative programs are systematically analyzed.* Agencies examine alternatives to existing program structures in hope of finding more effective and efficient programs. Agencies are expected to present their justifications for programs — to show, in other words, that the chosen program is superior to the other programs investigated. Also, this aspect of program budgeting relates to our previous discussion of policy formulation, for agencies are expected to develop alternatives and to examine their relative merits, using techniques such as cost-benefit analysis.

CRITICISM OF PROGRAM BUDGETING

Advocates of program budgeting point with pride to the enhanced rationality and analytic rigor associated with this form of budgeting and to the way that it breaks down organizational control over budgetary outcomes. Despite these apparent advantages, program budgeting has not been especially successful in most of its applications. There are some technical reasons for these apparent failures, but the most severe problems in the implementation of program budgeting are political.

Technically, applying program budgeting successfully requires a great deal of time and effort; it also requires an almost certain knowledge of unknown relationships of spending to program success. The systems concept built into the method implies that if one aspect of the system is altered, the entire system must be rethought. This in turn may mean that program budgeting may actually institutionalize the rigidity that it was designed to eliminate. Also, it is difficult if not impossible to define programs, measure their results, and evaluate the contributions of individual agencies and activities to the achievement of those results. One major problem in public policy analysis and budgeting is the difficulty, or impossibility, of measuring the effects of government, and such measurement occupies a central place in program budgeting.

Program budgeting also has several political disadvantages. First, as we have mentioned, the method tends to force decisions onto a high level of government.[30] Agencies dislike this centralizing tendency, as do congressmen who have invested a considerable amount of effort in developing a relationship with clientele groups allied with the agency. Likewise, the assumption that organizations are not the most appropriate objects of allocation runs counter to all the theories of government in the United States. Finally, the need to analyze systematically all alternative strategies for achieving ends forces the agency to expose its program to possible attack, as it may develop and eliminate alternative programs that others might prefer, and the explicit nature of the process brings those alternatives to the front for active consideration. In addition, the discussion of alternative policies reduces the maneuverability of the agency, as it must justify its policy choice in writing and consequently cannot play games with OMB, or even with Congress if the information developed from the planning, programming, budgeting system is passed on to the legislative branch. In short, PPBS was a dagger pointed toward the central role of the agency in policymaking in the federal government, and as such it could not really have been expected to be successful, except perhaps in organizations such as the Department of Defense under Robert McNamara. That organization had a strong leader committed to the concept of program budgeting, and it had extremely nebulous results, which could be tested only against simulations or scenario-building exercises; it also had few political enemies. For other agencies, with considerably greater political opposition and real clients demanding services, PPBS was apparently doomed to failure from the beginning.

Zero-Base Budgeting

If program budgeting required an almost superhuman analytical capability and rafts of data, the conceptual underpinnings of zero-base budgeting are extremely simple. The idea is that, whereas traditional incremental budgeting operates from the assumption that the previous year's budget was justified (the "base") and it is principally the increments that need examination, a more comprehensive examination of all expenditures should be made.[31] That is, there should be no base, and the entire spending plan should be justified. By so doing, it was assumed that weaker programs, which were being extended largely because of inertia, would be terminated, or at least severely cut, and more meritorious programs would be fully funded. This form of budgeting came to Washington with the Carter administration, after having been tried by President Carter when he was governor of Georgia.

Zero-base budgeting is done on the basis of decision units, which may be agencies but which frequently are smaller components such as operating programs within an agency. Each budget manager is expected to prepare a number of *decision packages* to reflect his or her priorities for funding. These packages are presented in rank order, with a "survival package" being presented first. This package is the lowest level of funding on which the unit can continue to exist. On top of the survival package are additional decision packages, reflecting, first, the continuation of existing programs at existing levels of service and then expansions of services. Each decision package is justified in terms of the services it would provide at an acceptable cost.

Decision packages prepared by lower-level budget managers are then passed on up the organizational hierarchy to higher-level managers who prepare *consolidated decision packages* that reflect a ranking of priorities among the several decision units that he or she may supervise. These rankings are then passed along and consolidated further, ending up in the Office of Management and Budget. All the rankings from the lower levels are passed along with the consolidated packages so that higher levels can examine the preferences of lower-level managers and their justifications of those preferences. Like program budgeting, zero-base budgeting is geared toward multiyear budgeting to better understand the implications of budget choices made during any one budget cycle.

Zero-base budgeting, again like program budgeting, has several apparent advantages. Obviously, the method is intended to eliminate incremental budgeting. The agency's base is no longer protected but must be defended—although in practice the survival level may function as a base. Also, the method focuses on cost effectiveness in the justification of the rankings of decision packages and even of the survival level of funding. One principal advantage of zero-base budgeting appears to be the involvement of managers at relatively low levels of the organization in the consideration of priorities and goals for the organization. Also, this method considers the allocation of resources in package terms, whereas the incremental budget tends to assume that any additional amount of money can be effectively used. It makes substantially greater sense to think of adding meaningful amounts of money that can produce additional services, rather than simply add more money without regard for the threshold values for service provision and efficiency.

Nevertheless, there are a number of glaring difficulties with zero-base budgeting. For example, this form of budgeting is an obvious threat to the existence of some agencies. In practice, however, a number of factors, such as clientele groups and uncontrollable expenditures, may negate the concern that many administrators may have about the method. It is nevertheless clear that the intent of the method is to bring the existence of each program into question each year.

To some degree the enormity of the task of examining each program carefully each year is a major weakness of this method. There is no means by which OMB, held to a reasonable size, or a Congress with a number of other commitments, can carefully consider the entire budget each year. Therefore, either there is a superficial analysis of each program under the guise of a zero-base review—probably with incremental results—or there is a selective review of a number of more controversial programs. Either is an acceptable means of reducing the work load, but neither would constitute a significant departure from the incremental budget or justify the massive outlay of effort required to prepare the necessary documents.

In addition, zero-base budgeting threatens established programs by allowing the reopening of political conflicts during each budget cycle. One virtue of traditional incremental budgeting is that, once a program is agreed to, it is accepted and is not subject to significant scrutiny unless there are major changes in the environment or serious administrative problems in the programs of the agency. With zero-base budgeting, however, the existence of the program is subject to question each year, and the political fights that authorized the existence of the agency may have to be fought again and again. This is, of course, no problem for well-established and popular programs, but it is certainly a problem for newer and more controversial programs. Also, zero-base budgeting tends to combine financial decisions with program decisions and to place perhaps an excessive burden on budgetary decision makers.

More than the analytic methodologies proposed in program budgeting and (to some degree) zero-base budgeting, the fundamental incrementalist patterns have been more challenged by the continuing fiscal problems of government. These problems have spawned "solutions" such as the balanced-budget amendment and across-the-board cuts.[32] In their own way, these reforms are incrementalism turned around. As with incrementalism, there is a tendency to substitute minimization of decision-making costs for maximization of benefits resulting from expenditures. They are, for the most part, "no-think solutions," just as incrementalism has been a nonanalytic means for making budgetary decisions. But, even as incrementalism has been successful and acceptable, so too these methods for dealing with complex problems have been acceptable to some because of their simplicity. Simple policies are not always, and perhaps only rarely, the best solutions, but they are usually the most acceptable.

The Balanced-Budget Amendment
The size of the federal budget deficit has become a paramount concern in government circles and has produced a number of proposed solutions. The most commonly discussed solution has been the balanced-budget amendment. This amendment to the Constitution would require Congress to pass a balanced budget each year, unless an extraordinary majority of Congress declared that a sufficient economic emergency existed to justify running a deficit.[33] Unlike

the situation under the current budgetary process, the amendment would force a more explicit comparison of revenue and expenditure figures, and would further require those involved in the budgetary process to be responsible for the amount of money that they appropriate.

The balanced-budget amendment has appeal and has gained some support, but like so many simple "solutions" to complex problems, it has some major difficulties. First, as already noted, the planning for a budget begins over a year before the start of its execution, and over two years before the completion of the budget year. Further, both revenue and expenditure projections in a budget are to some degree influenced by the condition of the economy and the projected state of the economy during the time the budget is to be executed. It is easy to get the projections wrong—over the past thirteen years, the official figures have missed revenues by an average of 2.9 percent and expenditures by an average of 3.5 percent.[34] Even if Congress acts in good faith and attempts to comply with the spirit of the amendment, it could miss badly. As well as the potential economic problems caused by such an unplanned deficit, the deficit may seem to some to be a violation of the Constitution and may further undermine already weakened public respect for Congress. A more cynical scenario would have Congress passing a budget that, although it balanced on paper, would be known to have little chance of balancing when executed. In either case, there could be substantial political damage to the legitimacy of Congress and to the government as a whole. The implementation of the Gramm-Rudman-Hollings plan by Congress to limit spending may give some idea of how such an agreement would work.

In addition, deficits are not necessarily a public evil. When adopted for economic reasons, as opposed to the political unwillingness to impose the true costs of government on citizens, budget deficits can be an important tool for economic management, following the Keynesian tradition. Passing a balanced-budget amendment would only remove one tool of economic management from the federal government, without any certainty that economic benefits sufficient to justify that loss would be generated.

The Line-Item Veto

In his 1985 budget submission, President Reagan proposed that the line-item veto be adopted for the President, especially for appropriations bills. Similar to the powers that governors in forty-three states already have, the line-item veto would allow the President to veto a portion of a bill and allow the rest to be put into effect.[35] This is seen as a weapon for the President in dealing with the tendency of congressmen to add their pet projects to appropriations bills, placing the President in the awkward position of having to refuse money for a large segment of the federal government in order to prevent one or two small projects from being funded. Also, as noted above, the majority of appropriations for the federal government are contained in a dozen or so appropriations acts. Again, in order to eliminate a few items, the President would have to veto the entire act and create potential disruption and hardships.

One of the justifications for this change in the budgetary process (it would have to be a constitutional amendment) is that it would attack the problem of growing federal deficits. This may be so, but as proposed, the veto could not be applied to many uncontrollable programs, such as debt interest and Social Security. In addition, at least in the present administration, there is a tendency not to want to reduce defense expenditures. This leaves only nondefense discretionary expenditures (approximately 17 percent of the federal budget in 1984) that would be subject to the line-item veto. This is a sizable amount of money (over $150 billion) but a small part of the total problem.

The line-item veto might actually encourage Congress to add *more* pet projects onto appropriations acts, and place the onus of removing those projects on the President. It might also give the President independent powers not intended by the framers of the Constitution nor desired by the public. Thus, as with the balanced-budget amendment, there are few magic solutions for solving the deficit problems, but there is a need for political will and fortitude.

Decrementalism

The preceding discussion of the balanced-budget amendment and the line-item veto is indicative of the general problem facing American government and the governments of other industrialized countries: the control of public expenditures. While incrementalism has become the conventional wisdom for describing budgeting, large numbers of politicians are looking for means of enforcing decrementalism, or the gradual reduction of expenditures, on government. The majority of these political leaders are from the political right—as exemplified by President Reagan and Margaret Thatcher in the United Kingdom—but even some on the political left are seeking to reduce expenditures while maintaining levels of service.

In addition to the rationalistic approaches discussed above, somewhat more blunt instruments have been employed to try to reduce expenditures. One of these has been the President's Private Sector Survey on Cost Control (the Grace Commission). This survey brought to Washington some 2000 volunteers from business and other private-sector organizations to examine the management of the federal government. The volunteers prepared 2478 distinct recommendations projected to save the government $424 billion a year if they were all implemented.[36] Many of these proposals for cost reduction have been criticized as being politically naive or simply impossible, given the political realities of Washington and the connection of the agencies with powerful clientele groups. The survey did, however, give those in Washington something to think about.

Other efforts at controlling costs have been even more crude. These have included across-the-board reductions in staffing levels and budgets and moratoria on the implementation of new programs and regulations. In addition, President Reagan and his advisers decided to try to reduce the pay of public employees to a level of 94 percent of comparable employees in the private sector — the 6 percent difference was to be made up by the greater job security and fringe benefits associated with federal employment.[37] Reaction to these efforts has been almost opposite that of proposals such as program budgeting and zero-base budgeting. The more recent across-the-board exercises have been criticized as mindless, as simply attacking government without regard to the real benefits created by some agencies and the real waste created by others. This contrasts with the large-scale analytic exercises that would have been required to implement program or zero-base budgeting.

Is Budget Change Its Own Reward?

Both program budgeting and zero-base budgeting have been significant efforts at reforming the budgetary process. Although both methods have a great deal to commend them, neither has been particularly successful in producing changes in the behavior of budgetary decision makers, and the major effect appears to be the death of countless trees to make the reams of paper required by both methods. Despite the real problems in both the budget process and budget outcomes, why does the traditional line-item incremental budget persist?[38]

There appear to be several reasons. One is that it gives the legislature an excellent means of controlling the executive. The traditional budget allocates funds to identifiable organizations for identifiable purposes (personnel, equipment, etc.) rather than to nebulous "programs" or "decision units." Those who manage the real organizations can then be held accountable for the expenditure of the money appropriated to them.

More important, while the benefits promised by both program and zero-base budgeting are significant, so too are the costs. These costs are in terms of both the calculations required to reach decisions and the political turmoil created by nonincremental changes. Incremental budgeting provides ready guidelines for those who must make budget decisions, minimizing the necessity for them to engage in costly analysis and calculation. In addition, as most political interests are manifested through organizations, the absence of threats to those organizations in incremental budgeting means that political conflicts can be confined to marginal conflicts rather than conflicts over the very existence of those organizations.

In short, although incremental budgeting does nothing very well, neither does it do anything very poorly. It is a convenient means of allocating resources for public purposes. It is not an optimal means, but it is a means that works and a means in which those who must use it have confidence. This in itself is enough to explain its perpetuation in the face of so many challenges.

Notes

1. Charles Wolf, Jr., "A Theory of Nonmarket Failure: Framework for Implementation Analysis," *Journal of Law and Economics,* April 1979, 107-40.

2. Louis C. Fischer, *Presidential Spending Power* (Princeton: Princeton University Press, 1975).

3. Frederick C. Mosher, *The GAO: The Quest for Accountability in American Government* (Boulder, Colo.: Westview, 1979), 65-96.

4. This is especially true for capital programs, which require multiple-year commitments.

5. The zero-base budgeting process and, to some degree, program budgeting have included medium-range forecasts. But these are rarely included in appropriations decisions.

6. Barry P. Bosworth, *Tax Incentives and Economic Growth* (Washington, D.C.: Brookings Institution, 1984).

7. Lawrence C. Pierce, *The Politics of Fiscal Policy Formation* (Pacific Palisades, Calif.: Goodyear, 1974), 48-52.

8. Aaron Wildavsky, *The Politics of the Budgetary Process,* 4th ed. (Boston: Little, Brown, 1984).

9. Ibid., 74-84.

10. U.S. Office of Managment and Budget, *Preparation and Submission of "Current Services" Budget Estimates,* Bulletin 76-4 (Washington, D.C.: OMB, 13 August 1975), 2-4.

11. Maurice Wright explains volume budgeting in "From Planning to Control: PESC in the 1970s," in *Public Spending Decisions,* ed. Maurice Wright (London: Allen and Unwin, 1980s), 88-119.

12. John W. Ellwood and James A. Thurber, "The Politics of the Congressional Budget Process Reexamined," in *Congress Reconsidered,* ed. Lawrence C. Dodd and Bruce Oppenheimer, 2d ed. (Washington, D.C.: Congressional Quarterly Press, 1981), 246-71.

13. Richard Fenno, *The Power of the Purse: Appropriations Politics in Congress* (Boston: Little, Brown, 1966); and Ellwood and Thurber, "Politics of the Congressional Budget Process."

14. Mosher, *The GAO,* 169-200.

15. See Barry M. Blechman, Edward M. Gramlich, and Robert W. Hartman, *Setting National Priorities, The 1976 Budget* (Washington, D.C.: Brookings Institution, 1975), 192-202.

16. Executive Office of the President, *Budget of the United States Government,* FY 1987 (Washington, D.C.: Government Printing Office, 1986).

17. Other federal systems, such as that of West Germany, allow the central government greater control over aggregate expenditures and revenues, especially in times of economic difficulty.

18. Taken on balance, the *operating* budgets of the public sector in the United States have been very close to being in balance.

19. In 1979 these appropriations constituted 2.3 percent of total federal expenditures.

20. See M.A.H. Dempster and Aaron Wildavsky, "On Change: Or, There Is No Magic Size for an Increment," *Political Studies,* June 1980, 371-89.

21. Ibid., 374-76.

22. See David Braybrooke and Charles E. Lindblom, *A Strategy for Decision* (New York: Free Press, 1963).

23. Otto A. Davis, M.A.H. Dempster, and Aaron Wildavsky, "A Theory of the Budgetary Process," *American Political Science Review* 60 (1969): 529-47.

24. Aaron Wildavsky, *Budgeting: A Comparative Theory of Budgetary Processes* (Boston: Little, Brown, 1975), 9-19.

25. Peter B. Natchez and Irvin C. Bupp, "Policy and Priority in the Budgetary Process," *American Political Science Review,* September 1973, 951-63.

26. John R. Gist, " 'Increment' and 'Base' in the Congressional Appropriations Process," *American Journal of Political Science,* May 1977, 341-52.

27. Daniel Tarschys, "Rational Decremental Budgeting: Elements of an Expenditure Policy for the 1980s," *Policy Sciences* 14 (1982): 49-58.

28. Robert E. Goodin, *Political Theory and Public Policy* (Chicago: University of Chicago Press, 1982), 22-38.

29. David Novick, ed., *Program Budgeting: Program Analysis and the Federal Budget* (Cambridge, Mass.: Harvard University Press, 1967).

30. Aaron Wildavsky, "Political Implications of Budgetary Reform," *Public Administration Review,* Autumn 1961, 183-90.

31. U.S. Office of Management and Budget, *Bulletin,* no. 77-9, 19 April 1977.

32. Tarschys, "Rational Decremental Budgeting."

33. Alvin Rabushka, "Fiscal Responsibility: Will Anything Less Than a Constitutional Amendment Do?" in *The Federal Budget,* ed. Michael J. Boskin and Aaron Wildavsky (San Francisco: Institute for Contemporary Studies, 1982), 333-50.

34. Rudolph G. Penner, "Forecasting Budget Totals: Why We Can't Get It Right," in Boskin and Wildavsky, *The Federal Budget,* 89-110.

35. U.S. House, Committee on the Budget, *The Line-Item Veto: An Appraisal* (Washington, D.C.: Government Printing Office, 1984).

36. J. Peter Grace, *War on Waste* (Washington, D.C.: President's Private Sector Survey on Cost Control, 1984).

37. Sar A. Levitan and Alexandra B. Noden, *Working for the Sovereign* (Baltimore: Johns Hopkins Univesity Press, 1983), 85.

38. Aaron Wildavsky, "A Budget for All Seasons: Why the Traditional Budget Lasts," *Public Administration Review,* November/December 1978, 501-9.

7. Evaluation and Policy Change

The final state of the policy process is the assessment of what has occurred as a result of the selection and implementation of a policy and, if it is found necessary, a change in the current policies of government. Critics of government tend to think that these activities are rather mechanical and that inefficiencies and maladministration can be corrected easily, if only government really wanted to do so. As this chapter points out, however, producing a valid evaluation of government actions is a difficult and highly political process in itself. And, if change is found to be necessary, the policymaking process involved in making the change is perhaps even more difficult to follow through successfully than the process of policy initiation—the adoption of a policy. Government organizations have several weapons to protect themselves against change, so any attempts to alter existing policies and organizations are almost certain to engender conflict.

Problems in Evaluating Public Programs

In its simplest form, evaluating a public program involves cataloging the goals of the program, measuring the degree to which these goals have been achieved, and perhaps suggesting changes that might bring the performance of the organization more in line with the stated purposes of the program. Although these seem to be simple things to do, it is actually difficult to produce unambiguous measurements of the performance of a public organization. Several barriers stand in the way of those who try to produce such evaluations.

Goal Specification

The first step is to identify the goals of the program, but even this seemingly simple task may be difficult, if not impossible.[1] The legislation that establishes programs or organizations should be the source of goal statements, but we have already seen that legislation is frequently written in vague language to avoid offending potential members of a coalition necessary to pass that legislation. As a result, it is difficult to attach any readily quantifiable goals to programs or organizations. In addition, the goals specified may be impossible or contradictory. For example, one program had as its goal to raise all students to the mean reading level (think about it), while the aim of a foreign aid program was to assist those nations in greatest need as well as those that would most likely use the money to produce significant developmental effects. When an organization is faced merely with impossible goals, it can still do something positive, but when it is faced with contradictory goals, its own internal political dynamics will become more important than any legislative statement of purpose. And as organizations do not function alone in the world, the contradictions existing across organizations—as when the government subsidizes tobacco production and simultaneously discourages tobacco consumption—make the identification of government's goals that much more difficult.

Of course, internal political dynamics are important in organizations with clear and unambiguous goals. An initial statement of goals may be important in initiating a program, but, once that program is in operation, the goals may be modified. This may be positive, as when programs adapt to changing environmental conditions in order to meet real societal needs. These positive changes in goals most often have been noted in the private sector, as when the March of Dimes shifted its goal from serving victims of polio to helping children with birth defects, but they also occur in the public sector.[2] For example, the Bureau of Indian Affairs has been transformed from an organization that exercised control over Native Americans into one that now frequently serves as an advocate of the rights and interests of those people. Also, the Army Corps of Engineers transformed its image from one of environmental disregard to environmental sensitivity.[3]

Goal transformations are, of course, also negative at times. The capture of regulatory bodies by their regulated industries is a commonly cited example of negative goal change.[4] A more common example is the "displacement of goals" among the members of an organization.[5] Although members may have been recruited on the basis of service goals, over time the individuals' goals may become more focused on personal survival. Likewise, the goals of the organization as a whole may shift toward maintenance and survival. Downs describes organizations going through a life cycle beginning as zealots or advocates of certain social causes, but over time becoming more interested in surviving and maintaining their budgets than in doing anything for clients.[6] In these instances the operating goals of the program deteriorate, even if the stated goals remain the same. The organization may not even realize that the change has occurred, but the clients almost certainly will.

Even when the goals are clearly expressed, they may not be practical. The Preamble to the Constitution, for instance, expresses a number of goals for the American government but few, if any, are expressed in concrete language that would enable a researcher to verify that these lofty goals are or are not being achieved. Specifying such goals and putting them into operation would require further political action within the organization or the imposition of the values of the research in order to make it possible to compare performance with aspiration. For example, the Employment Act of 1946 pledged the government of the United States to maintain "full employment." At the time the act was passed, full employment was declared to be 4 percent unemployment. Over time the official definition crept upward to 4.5 percent and then to 5 percent unemployed. Obviously, it is to the advantage of political leaders to declare that full employment has been achieved; thus pressure is applied to change the definition of "full employment." In this case, an admirable goal has been modified in practice, although the basic concept has remained part of national policy.

In addition, most public organizations are serving multiple constituencies and therefore may have different goals with respect to those different groups in society. For example, the Comprehensive Employment and Training Act (CETA) performed a number of different functions for different segments of the society and was differentially successful at serving those constituencies. For example, for those employed by the program, it was a source of employment and potentially of training for a better job. For those concerned about unemployment and whose political careers may have depended on reducing unemployment, it was a means of reducing unemployment without the more difficult task of stimulating the entire economy or altering the economic structure to supply more jobs for unskilled and semiskilled workers. Finally, for mayors and other local government officials, the program served as a source of cheap labor that enabled them either to balance their city budgets or to prevent even more rapid tax increases than otherwise would have been necessary. To the extent that the program kept the mayors happy by providing cheap labor in unskilled jobs such as garbage collection, it could never fulfill the goals of training those in the program for better jobs in the private sector. Thus, when programs are being evaluated, it is important to ask *whose* goals as well as *what* goals.

Finally, it should be noted that goals may be either straitjackets or opportunities. In addition to telling an organization what it should be doing, specific goals tell it what it is not supposed to be doing. This may limit the creativity of the organization and may serve as a powerful conservative force within the organization. And the specification of goals may limit the overall efficiency of government as a whole. It may divide responsibilities in ways that are less meaningful, given an expansion of knowledge and information. Giving one program or organization a goal may mean that other, more efficient means of delivering the same service will not be explored or that duplication of services will not be eliminated.

Measurement

Once goals have been identified and expressed in clear, concrete language, the next task is to devise a means to measure the extent to which those goals have been attained. In the public sector, measuring results or production is frequently difficult. In fact, one fundamental problem that limits the efficiency and effectiveness of government is the absence of any ready means of judging the value of what is being produced. One of the best examples of this problem is also one of government's oldest functions: national defense. The product called "defense" is in many ways the failure of real or potential enemies to take certain actions. Logically, the best defense would never do anything, for there would be no threats; in fact, to some degree, if a defense force is called into action, it has already failed. But measuring nonevents and counterfactual occurrences is difficult, so defense is frequently measured by surrogate measures, and, as a result, the megatonnage of nuclear weapons available and capable of being launched in fifteen minutes or the number of plane-hours of flight time logged by the Strategic Air Command become measures of defense.

The illustrations from defense policy help to make the point that frequently *activity* measures are substituted for *output* measures when attempting to evaluate performance in the public sector. Some scholars and some politicians despair of finding adequate means to measure the benefits of many public-sector programs. For example, Byatt argues that "it is not possible to measure benefits from defense by any known techniques, nor is it easy to even begin to see how one might be developed." He goes on to say that "it is quite impossible to allocate costs to the final objectives of education."[7] Scholarly pessimism aside, the perpetuation of activity measures serves the interests of existing organizations. First, it can shield them from stringent evaluations on nonprocedural criteria. Perhaps more important, action becomes equated with success. This may have an obvious effect on levels of government expenditure. It may have the less obvious effect of giving program personnel incentives to keep people on programs when they might be able to survive without the benefits.

Several factors inhibit the adequate measurement of government performance. One is the time span over which the benefits of many public programs are created. For example, although the short-term goal of education is to improve reading, writing, and computation, the long-term and perhaps ultimate goals of education are to be achieved in the future, not in the time during which the child is going to school. Among other things, education is supposed to improve the earning potential of individuals, make society more stable, and simply improve the quality of life for those who receive it. These are elusive qualities to measure when an evaluation must be done quickly. This problem is also illustrated by Lester Salamon's analysis of the effects of the New Deal programs in the rural South, where it was widely thought these programs were ineffective but where significant results were apparent thirty years after the programs were terminated.[8]

The other side of the time problem is that any effects produced by a program should be durable.[9] Some programs, for example, produce effects only after they have been in existence for years, whereas other programs produce demonstrable results in the short term but have no significant effects in the long run. It has been argued that the latter is true of the Head Start program. Beneficiaries of the program tend to enter school with skills superior to those of non-Head Start children. After several years, however, no significant differences can be seen between those who were in the program and those who were not. It seems that without reinforcement in later years, the effects of Head Start decay. The program per se therefore is not unsuccessful; it does not persist long enough.[10]

The time problem also produces significant political difficulties. Many individuals responsible for making policy decisions are short of time, and they must produce results quickly if their programs are to be successful. Congressmen, for example, have a tenure of two years before facing reelection, and any program they advocate should show some "profit" before those two years have passed. Thus, the policy process may favor short-term gains, even if they are not durable, over long-term success. Some actors in the policy process, most notably the permanent public bureaucracy, can afford to take a longer time, but many cannot and do not. Thus, time itself can be crucial in evaluation. The cycle of policymaking is largely determined by the political calendar, but the effects of policies have their own timetables. Part of the job of the analyst and evaluator is to try to make the two coincide.

The evaluation of public programs is also confounded by the many factors affecting the population. If we are to evaluate the effectiveness of a health program on a poor population, for example, we may find it difficult to isolate the effects of that health program from those of a nutrition program or those of a housing program. All these programs may have the effect of improving the health of the population, and we may find it difficult to determine which program caused the observed changes. In fact, all the programs may be related to those changes, in which case it becomes difficult to determine which program is the most efficient means of affecting the health of that community. We may be able to isolate the effects of an individual program with a more controlled social experiment, but few people want to be the subjects of such an experiment. Further, it is difficult to hold constant all the factors that might affect the success of a program. All these problems point out that measurement in policy analysis is not as simple as the measurement that a scientist can make of a passive molecule or an ameba.

In addition, measurement of the effects of public programs can be confounded by the history of the program and of the individuals involved.[11] Few new policies are initiated in industrialized countries such as the United States, and programs that have existed all along may jeopardize the success of a new program. Clients may well become cynical when program after program promises to "solve" their problems. Likewise, administrators may become cynical and frustrated after changing the direction of their activities several times. Any number of policy areas have gone through cycles of change and contradiction, with inevitable effects on the morale and cooperation of clients and administrators alike. The numerous attempts to "solve" the problems of the poor are the best example of endless change and confusion. In addition to creating frustration over the ability of government to make up its collective mind, one policy may not be successful after another policy has failed. For example, if a policy of lenient treatment and rehabilitation has been tried in a prison, it may be difficult to return to more punitive methods without disruption. Interestingly, the reverse may also be true.

Another problem in measurement is that the organizational basis of much evaluation limits excessively the scope of the inquiry, and many unintended consequences of the program are not included in the evaluation. For example, highway engineers probably regard the interstate highway system as a great success. Many miles of highways have been built in a relatively short period, and these highways have saved many lives and many gallons of gasoline, assuming that Americans would have driven the same number of miles if these superhighways had not been built. The mayor of a large city or members of the Department of Energy, however, may regard the program as a crashing failure. They realize that the building of highways in urban areas has facilitated sprawl and the flight of whites to the suburbs. They also know that this in turn reduced the tax base of the city and resulted in social and economic problems in the city while the surrounding suburbs grew affluent. Likewise, the rapid automobile transportation promised by the highways encouraged people to move to the suburbs and consequently to use millions of gallons of gasoline each year in commuting. This one program and its effects show that measures used by any single agency to evaluate its programs may be too narrow and will frequently ignore many important unintended social effects of the programs.

Finally, if experimentation is used as a means of attempting to ascertain the possible utility of a program, the danger that the "reactive effects of testing" will influence the results is evident.[12] If citizens know that a certain policy is being tried "as an experiment," they may well behave differently from the way they would if the policy was declared to be "the policy." In other words, those who favor the policy may work especially hard to make the program appear effective, whereas those who do not support the program may attempt to make it appear ineffective. Even those who have no definite opinions on the policy may not behave as they would otherwise. For example, if a voucher plan for educational financing is being experimented with, neither parents nor educational providers are likely to behave as they would if a voucher plan were actually in operation. Parents may be reluctant to place their children in private schools for fear the program will be terminated, and providers are unlikely to enter the marketplace if the number of parents capable of paying for their services is apt to decrease soon. The simple knowledge that something is a test will alter the behavior of those involved and consequently influence the results of the experiment. As with other problems in measuring the effects of policy, the problems with experiments simply reduce the analysts' ability to make definitive statements about the real worth of public programs.

Targets
Related to the problem of goals is the problem of targets. It is important to know not only what you intend to do but also to whom you intend to do it. Programs that have significant effects on the population as a whole may not have the desired effects on a target population. For example, the Medicare program was intended, among other things, to benefit less affluent older people, although all the elderly were declared eligible for the program. However, although the health of the elderly population in general has improved, probably at least in part as a result of Medicare, the health of the neediest portion of the elderly population has not improved commensurately.[13] As the program has been implemented, substantial coinsurance has been required along with substantial deductibles if the insured enters a hospital. As a consequence, it is difficult for the neediest elderly citizens to participate in the program. Likewise, the principal intention of the Elementary and Secondary Education Act of 1965 (ESEA) was to improve the educational attainment of underprivileged children. The evidence of the success of this legislation is mixed, but the access of all children to educational materials and facilities has increased substantially, whether or not their educational attainment has improved. In both instances, the general population has benefited, while the target population most in need has not particularly benefited. In one instance, the target group

benefited very little, while in the other it has not benefited differentially compared to the total population.

One problem in defining a target population and the program's success in reaching that population is that many programs are voluntary and depend on individuals who are potential beneficiaries to "take up" the benefit. Voluntary programs directed at the poor and the less educated frequently face difficulties in making the availability of the program widely known among the target population. Even if it is widely known, pride, perceived administrative barriers and real difficulties in consuming the benefits produced may make the program less effective than intended. An extreme example may be taken from the United Kingdom and its experience with National Health Service. One ostensible purpose of the National Health Service was to equalize access to medical care for all social classes. The evidence after three decades of the National Health Service does not indicate that such equalization has taken place.[14] Instead, the disparities in health status that existed before the adoption of the NHS and that in fact existed in the early twentieth century have not been narrowed by an almost completely free system of medical care. Noneconomic barriers such as education, transportation, free time, and simple belief in the efficacy of medical care have served to ensure that although there has been a general improvement in health status among the British population, little or no narrowing of class differentials has occurred. The less affluent simply have not availed themselves of the services to the extent that they might, especially given their relatively greater need for medical services.[15]

Programs may create a false sense of success by "creaming" the segment of the population they serve.[16] Programs that have stringent criteria for admission may select clients who actually need little help, rather than those who have the greatest need. This can make them seem successful, although those being served did not need the program in the first place, and a large segment of the neediest go unserved. Such programs are successes of a limited nature. Further, it would be a mistake to generalize from the "success" of such programs and assume that similar programs would work if applied to a larger population.

As with so much of policy evaluation, defining the target population is a political exercise as much as an exercise in rational policy analysis. As we noted when discussing legitimation, one tendency in formulating and adopting policies is to broaden the definition of the possible beneficiaries and loosen eligibility requirements for the program. This broadening frequently makes the target of the program more diffuse and consequently more difficult to evaluate. It is unfair to blame program managers for failing to serve the target population when those who constructed the legislation provided broad and unworkable definitions of that target.

Efficiency and Effectiveness

A related problem is the search for the philosopher's stone of efficiency in government, a search that often leads to a dead-end street. Measuring efficiency requires relating efforts to results and assessing the ratio of the two. As noted, measuring results is difficult in many policy areas; it is often equally difficult to assign costs to particular results, even if those results are measurable. For the same reason, equal difficulties may arise in measuring effectiveness. Surrogate measures of the intended results are frequently developed for public programs and policies, but all require the suspension of disbelief to be accepted as valid and reliable descriptions of what is occurring in the public sector.

As a consequence of these difficulties, much of the assessment of performance in government depends on the evaluation of procedural efficiency. That is, what is assessed is not so much what is produced as how the agencies go about producing it. Some of this depends on legal requirements for personnel management, budgeting, and accounting; but attempts to assess procedural efficiency go beyond these requirements. The efficiency of public agencies may be assessed by determining the speed with which certain actions occur or by going through all the appropriate procedural stages specified for a process. The important point here is that goals may be displaced when evaluations are made on such a basis so that the process itself, rather than the services that the process is intended to produce, becomes the measure of all things.[17] The concern with efficiency in procedures may, in fact, reduce the efficiency of the process in producing results for citizens because of the proliferation of procedural stages and red tape.

Values and Evaluation

Finally, the analyst who performs an evaluation requires a value system to enable him or her to assign valuations to outcomes. But value systems are by no means constant across the population, and even the analyst who is administering a single program may perceive different purposes and priorities within that policy area. Thus, there may be no simple means of determining the proper valuation of the outcomes of a program. This is especially true when the program has significant unintended effects that must be weighed against the intended consequences.

One point for consideration is that the analyst brings his or her own values to the evaluation process. Despite their rational and neutral stance, most analysts involved in policymaking have proceeded beyond the "baby analyst" stage to the point at which they have values they wish to see manifested in the policy process.[18] And as the analyst is in a central position in evaluation, he or she may have a substantial influence over the final evaluation of outcomes. But the analyst's values will be but one of several sets of values involved in making that final assessment. The organizations involved will have their own collective values to guide them in evaluating outcomes, or at least activities. The professions with which members of the organization or external service providers identify will also provide sets of well-articulated values that may affect the assessment of policies.[19] Frequently, all these different sets of values conflict with one another or with the values of clients or of the general public. Thus, assessing a policy is not a simple matter of relating a set of known facts to a given set of values. As in almost all aspects of the policy process, the values themselves may be the major source of conflict, while rational argumentation and policy analysis are merely the ammunition.

Summary

Policy evaluation is a central political process and although it is also an analytic procedure, the central place of politics and value conflict cannot be ignored. As increasing pressures are brought to bear on the public sector to perform its role more effectively and efficiently, evaluation will probably become even more a center of conflict. Negative evaluations of the effectiveness and efficiency now will be more likely to lead to the termination of the program than would have been true in more affluent times. The content of an evaluation, the values that are contained in it, and even the organization performing the evaluation will all affect the final assessment. The latter point is accentuated by the evaluation of a CETA program performed by both the John F. Kennedy School of Government at Harvard University and the School of Public Policy at the University of California, Berkeley. These two schools stressed different factors in their evaluations of the program, with the JFK researchers concentrating on the costs and benefits of the program in economic terms, while the Berkeley researchers stressed the political and participatory aspects of the program.[20] The difficulty is, of course, that they were both right.

Policy Change

After evaluation, the next stage of the policy process is policy change. Rarely are policies maintained in exactly the same form over time; instead, they are constantly evolving. This may be the direct result of evaluation, but more often it is the result of changes in the environment, learning on the part of those administering the program, or simple elaboration of existing structures and ideas. Further, a great deal of policymaking in industrialized countries such as the United States is the result of attempts at policy change rather than the result of new issues coming to the public sector for the first round of resolution.[21] Policy succession, or the replacement of one policy by another, is therefore an important way of examining the changes that have been occurring in contemporary public policies.

When a policy or program is reconsidered or evaluated, three outcomes are possible: policy maintenance, policy termination, or policy succession.[22] Policy maintenance occurs rarely as a conscious choice, but it happens as a result of simple failure to make decisions. It is unlikely, however, that a policy will be seriously considered and then maintained in exactly the same form. In the first place, politicians make names for themselves by advocating new legislation, not by advocating the maintenance of existing programs. Less cynically, few policies or programs are so well designed initially that they require no changes after they begin operation. The implementation of programs frequently demonstrates the weaknesses in the design of programs that then require modification. Through this almost continuous experimentation, programs can be made to match changes in society, in the economy, and in knowledge, and can thus be made to work.

It is unlikely that many public programs will be terminated. Once begun, programs have a life of their own. They develop organizations, and those organizations hire personnel. Programs also develop a clientele, who come to depend on the program for certain services. Once clients use the services of a program, they may find it difficult ever to return to the market provision of goods or services. This is especially true for programs that create a "stock" of benefits, as opposed to those that are merely a flow of resources. For example, Social Security created a stock of future benefits for its recipients, so once the program was initiated, future recipients began to plan differently for their future. Any reduction in benefits would thus create a severe hardship that they could not have anticipated. Programs such as AFDC or food stamps, which involve no planning by recipients, create hardships if they are reduced, but the planning element is not involved, and so it may be possible to move clients back into the market system. Public programs, policies, and organizations may not be immortal, but relatively few are ever fully terminated.[23] Even the Reagan administration, which came into office with promises to terminate organizations like the Department of Education, has found those promises difficult to keep as the support for existing programs tends to keep them running.[24]

Dismissing the other two options leaves policy succession as the most probable fate of an existing policy or program. Policy succession may take several forms:[25]

1. *Linear.* Linear successions involve the direct replacement of one program, policy, or organization by another, or the simple change of

location of an existing program. For example, the replacement of earlier manpower programs by the Comprehensive Employment and Training Act is an example of a linear succession.

2. *Consolidation*. Some successions involve placing several programs that have existed independently into a single program. The rolling together of a number of categorical health and welfare programs into a few block grants in the Reagan administration, as well as reflecting a change in the delivery system, was a consolidation.

3. *Splitting*. Some programs are split into two or more individual components. For example, the Atomic Energy Commission was split in 1974 into the Nuclear Regulatory Agency and the Energy Research Development Agency, reflecting the contradictory programs of regulation and support of nuclear energy that had existed in the earlier organization.

4. *Nonlinear*. Some policy and organizational successions are complex and involve elements of other kinds of successions. The complex changes involved in creating the Department of Energy from existing programs (including the two nuclear agencies mentioned above) is an example of nonlinear succession.

Although they entail much of the process described, policy successions are processed in a distinctive manner. First, the agenda-setting stage is not so difficult for policy succession as it is for policy initiation. The broad issue at question has already been accepted as part of the agenda and therefore needs only to be returned to a particular institutional agenda. Some issues, such as debt ceilings and annual reauthorizations of existing programs, automatically return to an agenda every year or even more frequently. More commonly, dissatisfaction with the existing programs returns an issue for further consideration. But returning the issue to the institutional agenda is easier than introducing it, because there are organizational manifestations of the program and identified clients who are in a better position to bring about the consideration. Furthermore, once organizations exist, it is more likely that program administrators will learn from other similar programs and will find opportunities for improving the program, or that they will simply think of better "solutions" to the problems.

The legitimation and formulation processes will also be different from those used in policy initiation. But instead of fewer obstacles, as in agenda setting, there are likely to be more barriers. As noted, the existence of a program produces a set of client and producer interests that may be threatened by any policy change. This is especially true if the proposed succession involves a "policy consolidation" (combining several programs) or a change in the policy instrument delivering the program in a direction that will demand less direct administration.[26] For example, using policy consolidation to combine a number of categorical grants into block grants during the Nixon administration provoked outcries from both clients (primarily big-city mayors) and producers (administrators who had managed the categorical programs). And part of the conflict over the negative income tax proposed in President Nixon's Family Assistance Plan concerned the change in the instruments used to deliver the benefits, as well as ideological conflicts over the level of benefits.[27] Thus, once a policy change of one of these kinds enters an institutional arena, it is quite likely to encounter severe resistance from the affected interests. This may be true even if the threat to those interests is not real. The mere threat of upsetting established patterns of delivering services may be sufficient to provoke resistance.

Of course, some policy successions may be generated within the organization administering the program rather than imposed from the outside. An array of external political forces may be strong enough to effect the change, and the organization and the clientele will "gladly" accede. They may even publicly co-sponsor the change. Also, some program managers may be risk takers, rather than risk averse like most public bureaucrats. They may be willing to gamble that the proposed change will produce greater benefits for the organization, so they need not attempt to hang on to what they have. Finally, some programs may have expanded too far, and their personnel may wish to pare off some of the peripheral programs to target their clientele more clearly and to protect the "heartlands."[28] This does not necessarily imply that the pared-off programs will be terminated, only that they will change their organizational locations.

Clientele groups may seek to split a program from a larger organization in order to develop a clearer target for their activities. Pressures from the National Educational Association and other educational groups to divide the Department of Health, Education, and Welfare and establish an independent Department of Education illustrate this point. It was argued that HEW did not give educational interests the direct attention they deserved. In addition, since the education budget had the greatest flexibility of all the budgets in HEW (the remainder being primarily entitlement programs), any cutting that was done was likely to be in education.[29] Although there has been pressure on the Reagan administration to eliminate the Department of Education, once established it may be difficult to alter its independent status.

Forming a coalition for policy change requires careful attention to the commitments of individual congressmen to particular interests and to ongoing programs. As with the initial formulation and legitimation of a policy, an attempt at policy succession requires the use of the mechanisms of partisan analysis, logrolling and the pork barrel, in order to deliver that change (see chapter 4). Again, this may be more difficult than in policy initiation, for while the implications of a new policy are at times vague, those of a policy change may be more readily identifiable. It may be easy to persuade legislators of the benefits of a new policy on the basis of limited information, but once the program has been running, information will become available to the legislator, making the task that much more difficult. There may, however, still be many who are dissatisfied with the program as it is being implemented, and those individuals can be mobilized to make the change. A coalition of this kind may involve those from the right and left who oppose the existing policy. Although it was not specifically concerned with a policy succession, the coalition that defeated President Carter's hospital cost-control proposal clearly demonstates such a coalition.[30] The group was composed of those who did not think the proposed legislation went far enough in controlling costs as well as those who wanted no controls. But, in managing a policy succession, organizing such a coalition runs the risk that termination of the policy may be the only thing on which the coalition can agree as an alternative to the status quo. Therefore, before beginning the process, it is crucial for the analyst to have in mind the particular policy succession that he or she would like to have implemented. Otherwise, allowing political forces to follow their own lead may threaten the existence of the program.

Finally, implementing a policy succession may be the most difficult choice of all. That is, of course, much the same as with the original initiation of the policy, for putting a policy into effect in the intended manner is problematic at best. Several features of policy succession as a process may, however, make it that much more difficult. First, it is important to remember that organizations exist in the field as well as at headquarters.[31] People working in the field may have policy preferences as strong as do those in the home office, but they may not be consulted about proposed changes. Yet those field workers must put the policy change into effect and must ultimately decide who will get what as a result of the change. Thus, if policy change does not involve significant and clear changes, then the field staffs may well be able to continue doing what they were doing prior to the nominal change and subvert the intention of the legislation. This subversion need not be intentional; it may be only the result of inertia or inadequate understanding of the intentions of headquarters and the legislation.

In addition, it is important to remember that organizations do not exist alone in the world, nor do policies.[32] Rather, each organization exists within a complicated network of other organizations, all of which must cooperate in order for any of them to be successful. Any change in the policies of one organization may reduce the ability of other organizations to fulfill their goals. This is perhaps especially true in the field of social policy where a variety of policies are necessary to meet the needs of poor families and in which changes in any one may influence the success of all the programs. Terminating food stamps, for example, would mean that AFDC payments would not be sufficient for families to buy the amounts of food they used to buy. As a consequence, housing and even employment programs would be adversely affected.

Finally, implementing policy succession is almost certain to be disappointing. The massive political effort required to bring about a policy succession is unlikely to be rewarded the first month, or even the first year, after the change. This is almost certain to create disappointment in the new policy and perhaps cynicism about the entire policy area. As a consequence, one policy succession may create sufficient disruption to engender a rapid series of changes. Further, once a stable set of policies and organizations has been disturbed, there will no longer be a single set of entrenched interests with which to contend, so forming a new coalition in favor of policy change or termination may be easier.

Since we now understand that implementing policy succession will be difficult, we should address the problem of designing a policy change that will be easier to implement. The ease with which this can be accomplished results in part from the design of previous organizations and programs. In an era of increased skepticism concerning government and bureaucracy, policies are being designed with built-in triggers for evaluation and termination. The interest in "sunset laws" means that any administrator joining such an organization or any client becoming dependent on its services should have reason to question the stability of those arrangements.[33] If the declining conception of entitlement to either employment or benefits from an organization can make future policy successions more palatable to those already connected with the program, then one major hurdle to policy change will have been overcome.

It is not possible to reverse history and redesign programs and organizations that are already functioning without such built-in terminators. The analyst or practitioner of policy change must therefore be prepared to intervene in existing organizations in order to produce the smooth transition from one set of policies to another. One obvious trigger for such change would be a change in the party in office, especially in the Presidency. Until the Reagan Presidency, however, the alternation of parties in office has produced little significant policy change. Rapid change in demand and in environmental conditions may also trigger attempts at policy succession, but organizations have proved to be remarkably effective in deflecting attempts at change and in using change for their own purposes. At present it is fair to say that there is no available technology for implementing policy succession, just as there is no reliable technology for implementation in general.

Summary

Policies must be evaluated and must frequently be changed. But neither task is as easy as some politicians and even some academicians make it appear. Identifying goals of policies, determining the results of programs, and isolating the effects of policies as compared with the effects of other social and economic forces all make evaluating public policies tricky, and at times impossible. The surrogate measures that must be used at times may be worse than no measures at all, for they emphasize activity of any sort rather than actions performed well and efficiently. The method of evaluation then places pressure on agencies merely to spend their money rather than always to spend it wisely.

Evaluation frequently leads to policy change, and the process of producing desired changes and of implementing those changes will tax the abilities of the analyst and the politician. All the usual steps in policymaking must be gone through, but they must be gone through in relation to established organizations and clients. The implications of the proposed changes may be all too obvious to those actors, and they may therefore strenuously oppose the changes. Government may be a great machine that will proceed onward in its established direction without the application of significant and skillful political force.

Notes

1. J.N. Noy et al., "If You Don't Care Where You Get To, Then It Doesn't Matter Which Way You Go," in *The Evolution of Social Programs,* ed. C.C. Abt (Beverly Hills, Calif.: Sage, 1976), 97-120.

2. David L. Sills, *The Volunteers* (Glencoe, Ill.: Free Press, 1957), 253-68.

3. Daniel A. Mazmanian and Jeanne Nienaber, *Can Organizations Change?* (Washington, D.C.: Brookings Institution, 1979).

4. Samuel P. Huntington, "The Marasmus of the ICC," *Yale Law Review,* April 1952, 467-509.

5. Robert K. Merton, "Bureaucratic Structure and Personality," *Social Forces,* April 1940, 560-68.

6. Anthony Downs, *Inside Bureaucracy* (Boston: Little, Brown, 1967), 92-111.

7. I.C.R. Byatt, "Theoretical Issues in Expenditure Decision," in *Public Expenditure: Allocation among Competing Ends,* ed. Michael V. Posner (Cambridge: Cambridge University Press, 1977), 22-27.

8. Lester M. Salamon, "The Time Dimension in Policy Evaluation: The Case of New Deal Land Relief Programs," *Public Policy,* Spring 1979, 129-83.

9. Robert E. Goodin, *Political Theory and Public Policy* (Chicago: University of Chicago Press, 1983), 26-29.

10. For a detailed discussion, see Henry J. Aaron, *Politics and the Professors* (Washington, D.C.: Brookings Institution, 1978), 84-85.

11. For a general discussion of this and other threats to validity, see Donald T. Campbell and Julian C. Stanley, *Experimental and Quasi-Experimental Designs for Research* (Chicago: Rand McNally, 1963).

12. Ibid., 5-19, passim.

13. Karen Davis, "Equal Treatment and Unequal Benefits," *Milbank Memorial Fund Quarterly,* Fall 1975, 449-88.

14. Rudolf Klein, *The Politics of the National Health Service* (London: Longman, 1983).

15. Anne Cartwright and Maureen O'Brien, "Social Class Variations in Health Care and in the Nature of General Practitioner Consultation," *Sociological Review Monograph,* no. 22 (1976).

16. B. Guy Peters and Brian W. Hogwood, *The Pathology of Policy* (Oxford: Oxford University Press, 1985).

17. The domination of form over substance is one of the commonly cited dysfunctions of bureaucracy. See, for example, Donald P. Warwick, *A Theory of Public Bureaucracy* (Cambridge, Mass.: Harvard University Press, 1975); and Douglas Yates, *Bureaucratic Democracy* (Cambridge, Mass.: Harvard University Press, 1983).

18. Arnold Meltsner, *Policy Analysts in the Bureaucracy* (Berkeley: University of California Press, 1976).

19. See, for example, Frederick C. Mosher, "Professions in the Public Service," *Public Administration Review,* March/April 1978, 141-47; and B. Guy Peters, "A Low Cost Civil Service: At What Cost?" *Dialogues* (Washington, D.C.: Brookings Institution, 1985).

20. Michael Nelson, "What's Wrong with Policy Analysis?" *Washington Monthly,* September 1979, 53-60.

21. Brian W. Hogwood and B. Guy Peters, *Policy Dynamics* (New York: St. Martin's, 1983).

22. Ibid.

23. Peter de Leon, "A Theory of Policy Termination," in *The Policy Cycle*, ed. Judith V. May and Aaron B. Wildavsky (Beverly Hills, Calif.: Sage, 1978), 279-300.

24. In this instance, the attempt at termination was a result of ideological considerations rather than evaluation.

25. Hogwood and Peters, *Policy Dynamics*.

26. Ibid.

27. Laurence E. Lynn, Jr., and David deF. Whitman, *The President as Policymaker: Jimmy Carter and Welfare Reform* (Philadelphia: Temple University Press, 1981).

28. Downs, *Inside Bureaucracy,* 212-13.

29. Rufus E. Miles, Jr., "Considerations for a President Bent on Reorganization," *Public Administration Review,* March/April 1977, 157.

30. Linda E. Demkovich, "Can We Do a Better Job of Controlling Hospital Costs?" *National Journal,* 10 February 1979, 219-23.

31. Jean-Claude Thoenig and Eduard Friedberg, "The Power of the Field Staff," in *The Management of Change in Government,* ed. Arne F. Leemans (The Hague: Nijhoff, 1976), 304-37.

32. Kenneth Hanf and Fritz W. Scharpf, *Interorganizational Policy-Making* (Beverly Hills, Calif.: Sage, 1978).

33. R.E. Cohen, "Taking Up the Tools to Tame the Bureaucracy: Sunset Legislation," *National Journal,* 2 April 1977, 514-20.

PART THREE

Substantive Policy Issues

Introduction

In addition to having a firm understanding of the processes through which policies are made in the American political system, it is important to understand some of the substantive policy choices that have been made. These policy areas illustrate the way in which the policy process functions and the kinds of decisions that emerge from the constellation of interests and institutions that make policies. Each issue area is unique, but each also demonstrates some common features of American policymaking, especially the importance of interest groups and public bureaucracies in the development of policy alternatives.

All policy areas are important to some segments of American society, but part 3 attempts to concentrate on a set of issues that touch a large number of citizens and that are candidates for significant changes during the 1980s. In each issue area, I have attempted to illustrate problems faced by the society relevant to that issue area, the responses of governments to those problems, and the range of possible alternative responses. So, for example, in the area of health policy, I discuss the major health issues of access, cost, and quality that are central to any system of health care. They are particularly important in the United States because of the dominance of the private sector in medical care. I then discuss government responses, such as Medicare, Medicaid, and health-care planning. Finally, I discuss major alternative strategies for meeting the problems, primarily nationalized health insurance.

Although they have not directly followed through the policymaking cycle outlined previously in each of these policy areas, the issue-area chapters illustrate a good deal about processes. Most of all, they illustrate the extent to which any policymaking in industrialized societies replaces existing policies with different policies, instead of initiating an entirely new policy. Even an "innovation" such as national health insurance would merely bring all Americans under public medical care, as opposed to the 26 percent who already receive medical care from that source. Thus, one major task in understanding the options to the existing policies discussed is to understand how those options may be coordinated with the existing policies.

8. Making Economic Policy

The performance of the economy in Western societies was once considered something like the weather: Everyone talked about it, but no one did anything about it. Economic cycles and fluctuations were considered natural, acts of God, beyond the control of governments or human beings. That concept of the economy was altered forever during the depression in the 1930s and the postwar economic boom.[1] The magnitude and duration of the depression were such that even conservative governments were forced to pay some attention to its effects.[2] Perhaps more important, the work of John Maynard Keynes and other economists gave governments the economic tools, and the intellectual justification for using those tools, to control an economy. The confidence of governments in their ability to manage economies is perhaps best exemplified in the postwar full-employment acts in both the United States and the United Kingdom, pledging the governments of the two nations never again to allow mass unemployment. This confidence was bolstered during the economic miracles of the 1950s and 1960s in which most Western nations experienced rapid and consistent economic growth, very low levels of unemployment (the United States being a notable exception), and relatively stable price levels. In the early 1960s advisers to President Kennedy spoke of their ability to "fine tune" the economy and to manipulate economic outcomes by pulling a few simple economic levers.[3]

Anyone reading the above paragraph today must regard it as a curious piece of history. The economic circumstances of the late 1970s and early 1980s were characterized by slow and unreliable growth, high unemployment, and high rates of inflation (see table 8.1). This "stagflation" resulted in little or no abiding faith in the ability of governments effectively to manage their national economies, and politicians who promised a bright economic future were regarded with some skepticism. Governments cannot escape the need for economic policies, and they must attempt to ameliorate economic miseries as much as possible.

Economic policy is both a central concern of government and a by-product of other policies. One important step that a government must take is to form a set of policies intended to manage the economy. Factors important in that

TABLE 8.I

MAJOR ECONOMIC INDICATORS, SELECTED COUNTRIES

(in percent)

	Inflation[a]	Unemployment[b]	Economic Growth[c]
United States	4.6	9.5	3.4
United Kingdom	5.9	13.2	3.1
France	9.3	8.1	0.7
West Germany	3.1	7.5	1.3
Italy	11.4	9.7	− 1.2
Japan	1.7	2.6	3.0
Sweden	7.9	3.5	1.3

SOURCE: Organization for Economic Cooperation and Development, *Economic Outlook,* June 1984 (Paris: OECD, 1984).

a. Change in retail prices, 1982-83.
b. Average rates, 1983.
c. GDP growth, 1982-83.

policy are the results of decisions about matters such as spending for public programs, patterns of taxation, and prices charged by public enterprises. Economic policy also depends heavily on the actions of people over which governments have little or no control. In the basic Keynesian concept an excess of public expenditures above revenues is supposed to stimulate the economy because citizens will spend the additional money, creating additional demand. But if citizens choose instead to save all their money, then the intended stimulative effect is not created. Only when governments choose directly to regulate the economy through instruments such as wage and price controls can they be reasonably confident of the behavior their actions will generate. Even then, policing compliance with a full-scale wage-and-price control policy presents administrative difficulties of its own (see pp. 167-69).

The Goals of Economic Policy

Economic policy has a number of goals, all of which are socially desirable, but some of which are not always compatible. Political leaders frequently must make decisions that benefit some citizens while they deprive others. For example, although it is by no means as clear as it once was, there is a tradeoff between inflation and unemployment.[4] To the extent that governments attempt to reduce unemployment, they may increase the rate of inflation. The results of such a decision may benefit the worker about to be laid off, but deprive the senior citizen living on a fixed income. In general, economic policy has four fundamental goals, which German political economists have labeled "the golden quadrangle." These goals are economic growth, full employment, stable prices, and a positive balance of payments from international trade. To these may be added an additional intermediate goal: structural change.

Economic Growth

Economic growth has been a boon both to citizens and to governments. Although it is popular in the 1980s to question the benefits of economic growth and to praise smaller and less technologically complex economic systems, most American citizens still want more of everything.[5] They became accustomed to receiving more each year during the postwar period. All this economic growth translated into massive increases in the availability of consumer goods, and items such as television sets and automobiles, which were not widely available in 1950, are owned almost universally today. In material terms, economic growth has produced a much higher standard of living than was true in 1950 or even 1970.

Economic growth has also been important in the political history of the postwar era. It has acted as a political "solvent" to ease the transition from the "warfare state" to the "welfare state." Economic growth was so great that virtually every segment of the society could be given its own government programs without exhausting all the new wealth. Public programs grew along with private affluence, so individuals did not feel particularly disadvantaged by the benefits granted to others.[6] And economic growth aided in the redistribution of income to the less advantaged. One calculation is that 90 percent of the improvement in the economic status of American blacks was the result of economic growth rather than redistributive public programs.

Yet American economic growth has not compared well with the majority of our major trading partners during the postwar period. In addition, American economic growth has been falling (although it has improved relative to that of most industrialized countries); average economic growth in the 1980s is less than half what it was during the 1950s. The United States may be entering a "zero-sum society" in which the gains from one segment of the society must come from some other segment.[7] Increased benefits for the elderly through Social Security may mean a direct loss in the income of working-age citizens, and programs for the poor may mean a reduction in the income of the middle and upper classes. Perhaps, then, the decline and uncertainty of economic growth will make politics more contentious and more difficult.

Full Employment

The benefits of full employment are obvious. Most adults want to work and use their talents. The welfare state has provided a floor for those who are made unemployable so that they and their families are unlikely to starve or do without medical care, but these benefits cannot match the income that can be earned by working, nor can they replace the pride and psychological satisfaction of earning one's own way. These psychological benefits are perhaps especially pronounced in the United States, where the social and political culture attaches great importance to work and self-reliance. This is reflected partly in rates of family problems, suicides, and alcoholism, which are higher among the unemployed than among the employed.

In addition to its effects on individuals, unemployment has some influence on government budgets. When individuals are not working, they do not contribute to Social Security or pay income taxes. Also, they cost the government money in unemployment benefits, Medicaid payments, food stamps, and the services of other social programs. Thus, unemployment may upset the government's best plans to produce a balanced budget. Even if the level of unemployment is accurately anticipated, revenues are still lost and expenditures required. Also, other important programs may be underfunded because of the need to assist the unemployed through public programs. Again, compared to many of its major trading partners, the United States has high rates of unemployment, although these became somewhat lower relative to the other countries as the U.S. economic recovery began in the early 1980s. But for most time periods, unemployment in the United States has been high. The reasons behind our higher rate of unemployment are multiple and complex.[8] What is perhaps more important than the aggregate performance of the United States on this indicator is the concentration of unemployment by race and age. Blacks and young Americans bear by far the highest rates of unemployment; among young blacks, the rate of unemployment is almost 50 percent.

Unemployment in the United States became especially high during the early 1980s. It also was concentrated in the older industrial states of the Northeast and in the Great Lakes area (see table 8.2). Once at the heart of American industrial might, these areas have become depressed as older industries such as steel and automobile manufacturing have succumbed to the combination of old factories, high labor costs, and strong foreign competition. Thus, in addition to managing the economy as a whole, government must be concerned about the particular plight of some industries and some sections of the country.

The decline of the northern industrial states to some degree reflects changes in the structure of the U.S. economy. The whole economy is shifting toward a service base. This poses a very great problem for some regions of the country, and for the traditional industrial labor force. New jobs are being created in the United States every day, but they tend to be either for those with tech-

TABLE 8.2
UNEMPLOYMENT IN THE UNITED STATES
(in percent)

Across Time

1965	1970	1975	1980	1982	1983	1984
4.4	4.8	8.5	7.1	9.7	9.6	7.4

By State (May 1985)

High		Low	
West Virginia	11.6	Massachusetts	3.4
Louisiana	11.1	New Hampshire	4.0
Michigan	9.8	Kansas	4.3
Oregon	9.6	Maryland	4.4
Illinois	9.4	Delaware	4.6

SOURCE: U.S. Department of Labor, *Employment and Earnings,* monthly.

nical skills (computer programmers) or to be relatively low paying (workers in fast-food restaurants). Industrial workers accustomed to earning high wages in unskilled or semiskilled occupations have found the structural change in the economy very disturbing, but they are almost powerless to change it.

Stable Prices

Unlike unemployment, inflation affects all citizens through price increases.[9] Inflation affects different portions of the community differently, however, and may even benefit some people. On the one hand, it is clear that inflation particularly hurts those living on fixed incomes, such as the elderly who live on pensions. It also adversely affects those (such as college professors) who are not sufficiently well organized to gain increases in wages equal to increases in price levels. On the other hand, inflation benefits those who owe money. The real importance of a debt is reduced as inflation eats away at the value of the currency.

As the biggest debtor in the society, government is perhaps particularly benefited by inflation. Governments with progressive tax structures also benefit from inflation as people whose real incomes (i.e., adjusted for changes in purchasing power) have not increased see their money incomes increase. These people move into higher tax brackets and pay a larger proportion of their income in taxes; as a consequence, government receives a relatively painless (politically) increase in its revenues. But inflation is by no means an undivided benefit for governments. Many benefits paid out by governments are indexed, or adjusted for changes in the price level. As a consequence, much of the increase in revenues is paid out directly as increased benefits. The other things that a government must buy, most notably the labor of its employees, also goes up in price during inflation. And government work tends to be so labor intensive that its cost will in fact increase more rapidly than other costs in the society. Consequently, government revenues must indeed increase more rapidly than those of the rest of the economy in order for the government to be able to supply the same quantity of goods and services.[10]

The performance of the American economy in maintaining a stable price level has been better than that of most of its major trading partners (see table 8.1). Only Germany and Japan have been more successful in the postwar period in holding down price increases, and countries such as Italy have had more than double the rate of inflation of the United States. The relatively superior performance of the U.S. economy in this area can be explained by a number of factors, including its relatively poorer performance on unemployment. It is also argued that the Federal Reserve Board's independence from political interference has allowed it to use various monetary instruments to better regulate the price level.[11] And the relative weakness of the labor movement in the United States has meant fewer strong pressures to push wages upward than have been brought to bear in other Western countries, although the power of large corporations might have been expected to be related to increasing prices. For whatever reason, even though we as U.S. citizens may be far from pleased, compared with other nations we have been a low-inflation country for most of the postwar period. Even in the late 1970s and early 1980s when inflation was increasing rapidly, it was still less than that occurring in other industrial countries.

A Positive Balance of Payments

The economy of the United States is relatively autarkic, and the U.S. economy is relatively less involved in international trade than are the economies of most other industrialized countries.[12] It is still important for the United States to regulate the balance of payments from that trade. The balance of payments is the net result of the cost of imports and the cost of exports. If a country spends more money abroad than it receives from abroad, it will have a negative balance of payments. Naturally, a country that spends less overseas than it receives will have a positive balance of payments. The final figure for the balance of payments is composed of the balance of trade (payment for real goods traded) and the balance on "invisibles," such as insurance, banking, and shipping fees. Over the past decade, the United States has generally had a negative balance of trade but a positive balance on invisibles, and these have added up to a negative balance of payments. During the 1970s, the negative balance of payments was to a great degree a function of the demand for imported oil and the increasing price of that oil. Oil prices stabilized and then declined in the early 1980s, as did the demand for energy. However, America's demand for foreign products, such as Japanese automobiles, has continued to increase. In addition, the artificially strong dollar (in part a result of high interest rates, which attracted foreign money into the United States) has made American products very expensive overseas. For example, in 1980 the British pound was worth $2.33 at one point, and in 1986 it was worth $1.40; the German mark went from 1.9 to the dollar to 2.9 to the dollar. These exchange rates were wonderful for American tourists, but very difficult for American businessmen.

The effects of a net negative balance of payments are generally detrimental to a country's economy. In the first place, a negative balance of payments indicates that the country's products are not competitive with those from other countries. This may occur because of price, because of quality, or because a country cannot produce a commodity, such as oil. More important, a negative balance of payments tends to reduce the value of the country's currency in proportion to that of other nations. If a country continues to trade its money for commodities overseas, the laws of supply and demand dictate that the value of the country's currency will decline, as more money goes abroad than is returned. This effect has been especially difficult for the United States, because the dollar has been the top currency in international trade for some years and because so many dollars are held overseas and used in international transactions.[13] Finally, as in the case of trading for raw materials, a negative balance of payments may indicate a country's dependence on the products of other nations, with the potential for international "blackmail." And holding a great deal of a country's currency abroad may mean that the value of that currency is especially vulnerable to the actions of others.

Structural Change
The final goal of economic policy is structural change, or the changing of the industrial and regional composition of production. Some regions of a country may be more depressed than others; the South traditionally has been the depressed section of the United States, but it is now relatively prosperous compared to the Great Lakes states. In addition, the composition of production makes some regions extremely vulnerable to economic fluctuations. The experience of Michigan during the slump in automobile production in 1980 is graphic evidence of the danger of relying too heavily on a single product. And a government may want to alter the composition of production of the entire economy. The most common manifestation of this is the effort of Third World countries to industrialize their agricultural economies. This was, of course, also true of the United States in the nineteenth century.

In the United States, the federal government has been relatively little involved in promoting structural change. The major exceptions have been the Tennessee Valley Authority and the Appalachian Regional Commission. But state and local governments have been very active in trying to promote economic development and structural change, particularly through their tax systems. States will allow industries moving in to receive tax credits for their investments and to write off a certain percentage of their profits for some years. New industries may also be exempted from property taxation for a number of years. Local governments have fewer tax options, but they can give grants for industrial sites and other infrastructural developments to make themselves attractive to industries. Southern states have been especially active in promoting economic development through tax incentives; these, combined with favorable climate, more available energy, and low rates of unionization, have tended to reverse the traditional imbalance in economic growth between the North and the South.[14] The Frostbelt states are now becoming depressed, while many Sunbelt states are growing rapidly. The northern industrial states have appealed to the federal government for assistance but have yet to receive any solid help. It may be that they will have to use their own incentives to lure industries to remain where they are instead of moving south.

The Instruments of Economic Policy

Governments have a number of weapons at their disposal to try to influence the performance of their economies. Analysts often speak of a dichotomy between monetary policy and fiscal policy.[15] These are certainly two of the more important options, but other options are available. This chapter discusses fiscal policy, monetary policy, regulations and control, financial support, public ownership, incentives, and moral suasion as instruments of economic management.

Fiscal Policy

We have discussed the importance of the budgetary process as a means of allocating resources among government agencies and between the public and private sectors of the economy. The budgetary process is also important for management of the economy. This is true under the Keynesian approach to economic management, which stresses the importance of the budget in regulating effective demand. Simply stated, if government wants to stimulate the economy (i.e., to increase economic growth and to reduce unemployment), it should run a budget deficit. Such a deficit would place in circulation more money than the government had removed from circulation, thereby generating more demand for goods and services as citizens found more money to spend. This additional money, as it is circulated through the economy, multiplies in magnitude to an extent that depends on the propensity of citizens to spend their additional income rather than save it. Likewise, if a government seeks to reduce inflation in an "overheated" economy, it would run a budget surplus, removing more money from circulation in taxes than it put back in through expenditures. This would leave citizens with less money than they had before the government's action and should lessen total demand.

The theory of fiscal policy is rather straightforward, but the practice presents some difficulties. Perhaps the most important of these is that deficits and surpluses are not politically neutral. It is a reasonable hypothesis that citizens like to receive benefits from government but do not like to pay taxes. Consequently, despite the rhetoric in American politics lauding the balanced budget, there have been twenty-eight deficits in the thirty-one years from 1950 to 1980. Many deficits occurred even in the 1950s and 1960s when the economy was performing well. Politicians have practiced "one-eyed Keynesianism," reading the passages Keynes wrote about running deficits, but not reading the passages about running surpluses.[16]

Also, as noted, estimating the magnitude of revenue received or the outlays of public programs is not a simple task. Even with the best budget planning it is not possible to adjust finely the level of a deficit or surplus. To some extent there are automatic stabilizers built into the revenue and expenditure programs of government. For example, when the economy begins to turn downward, revenues will decline as workers become unemployed and cease paying income and Social Security taxes. Also, these unemployed will begin to place demands on a variety of social programs. The decline in revenue and the increase in expenditures will automatically push the budget toward a deficit without political leaders making any conscious choices about fiscal policy. Of course, if the recession is very deep or continues for a very long time, government may have to act with new programs.

To aid in making decisions about the right-size budget deficit or surplus to aim for, the "full-employment budget" has been suggested, and to some extent used, as a decision-making aid.[17] The idea here is that the budget should be in balance during periods of full employment, defined as 5 percent unemployed. Naturally, during times of higher unemployment there would be a deficit, given the fundamental Keynesian paradigm. A budget is calculated that would be in balance at full employment, and then the added costs of unemployment in both social expenditures and lost revenues are added to determine the full-employment deficit. Such a deficit is deemed justifiable, as it results not from the profligacy of governments but from difficulties in the economy. Any deficit higher than that can be seen as a political decision to spend money that will not be raised as taxes and that gives the incumbent government a decided political advantage. Of course, in an overheated economy, there would be a full-employment surplus, with the additional revenues being taken out of circulation.

MAKING FISCAL POLICY

Most fiscal policy decisions are made through the budgetary process outlined in chapter 6. When the President and his advisers set the limits under which expenditure decisions of the individual agencies must be made, they make these decisions with a particular budget deficit or surplus in mind. Given the rhetoric and conventional wisdom of American politics, it appears that most Presidents initiate the process with the intention of producing a balanced budget, but few if any actually do. They are overwhelmed by the complexity of the calculations and, more important, by political pressures to spend but not to tax.

Fiscal policy is primarily a presidential concern, and it is a primary one. Only at the level of the entire budget can global decisions about economic management be made and somewhat shielded from special interests. But the decisions cannot be purely presidential. Within the executive branch the President is subject to advice and pressures—largely in the direction of spending more. Although he can attempt to rise above special interests, his cabinet secretaries certainly cannot, and they may press appeals on him. And the President cannot make expenditure and taxation decisions alone. Congress is involved in these decisions, and its involvement has been increasing in importance. The formation of the Congressional Budget Office and the increasing vigor of the Joint Economic Committee have given Congress a greatly enhanced capacity to compete with the President over fiscal policy decisions.

Despite the competition of Congress, the budget is labeled a presidential budget, and the economic success or failure it produces (or at least with which it is coincident) is laid at the President's doorstep, politically.[18] As a consequence, even if the budget is not the global influence on economic performance it is sometimes made out to be, a President will want to have his ideas implemented in the budget and at least be justified on the effects of his policies, not those of Congress.

SUPPLY-SIDE ECONOMICS

With the election of President Reagan in 1980 there came something of a revolution in fiscal policy, usually referred to as "supply-side economics." Basically, this approach states that, instead of inadequate demand in the American economy (the standard Keynesian critique), there is a dearth of supply, especially a dearth of investment. The fundamental idea of supply-side economics is to increase the supply of both labor and capital so that economic growth will take place.

The major instrument for implementing supply-side economics was the Economic Recovery Tax Act of 1981, which, over four years, reduced the average income tax by 23 percent. The reductions were not across the board, but especially advantaged those in higher income brackets, presumably those most likely to invest if they have additional after-tax income. The assumption of the act was that if individuals had increased incentives to work and invest, they would do so, and economic growth would occur. Thus, while Keynesian economics believed in providing people (usually the less affluent) with increased income through government expenditures, with the expectation that they would spend the money and create more demand for goods and services, the supply-side solution provided people with a greater incentive to work and invest because they could retain more of what they earned.

The immediate impact of the Economic Recovery Tax Act was a massive increase in the federal deficit. Taxes were reduced significantly, but despite the best efforts of some members of the administration, expenditures were not reduced nearly as much. The deficit was largely ignored at first by the Reagan administration, despite protests by administration members such as David Stockman (who later left the administration at least in part because of questions about the deficit). This absence of concern by a fiscally conservative administration was justified by the belief that the reduction in taxes would so stimulate economic growth that, over time, *more* revenue would be generated by lower tax rates; this is known as the "Laffer curve," after the economist Arthur Laffer.[19]

Although the deficits have continued at historically high levels, the Reagan administration has done little to increase revenues, while expenditures have proven more difficult to reduce than expected. The Tax Equity and Financial Responsibility Act of 1982 was directed at increasing revenues by closing some tax loopholes and increasing some indirect taxes, but the problem of the deficit persists. Many economists fear that the deficit will choke off any economic recovery that may have been stimulated by the tax cuts. The deficit places the federal government in competition with private firms for funds in the capital market, and resulting high interest rates may make it difficult for firms to invest.

Monetary Policy
Whereas the basic fiscal policy paradigm stresses the importance of demand management through levels of revenues and expenditures, the monetary solution to economic management stresses the importance of the money supply in controlling economic fluctuations. Like the presence of additional expenditures, increasing the amount of money in circulation is presumed to stimulate

the economy. The extra money makes it easier for citizens to borrow for investments or for purchases, and this encourages economic activity. Likewise, reducing the availability of money makes it more difficult to borrow and to spend, thus slowing down an inflationary economy.

In the United States, the Federal Reserve Board and the Federal Reserve banks are the primary makers of monetary policy. The Federal Reserve Board and the banks are intentionally independent from the executive authority of the President, and, because their budget is only appended to the federal budget, it is also independent from congressional control through the budgetary process.[20] The Federal Reserve is independent intentionally, so its members exercise their judgment as bankers rather than submit to the control of political officials who might want to manipulate the money supply for political gain. And the Federal Reserve has exercised its independence and has refused several times to accede to presidential requests. For example, during the Johnson administration, Federal Reserve Chairman William McC. Martin turned down the President's request to increase the money supply more rapidly to ease the financial pressures created by the simultaneous expansion of domestic social programs and the Vietnam war.

The Federal Reserve has a variety of tools at its disposal. The three principal tools are open-market operations, the discount rate, and reserve requirements. Open-market operations are the most commonly used mechanisms for control. These involve the Federal Reserve going into the money markets to buy or sell securities issued by the Federal Reserve Board. If it wishes to reduce the supply of money, the Federal Reserve attempts to sell securities, exchanging the bond for a quantity of cash that was in circulation prior to the purchase. If it wants to expand the money supply, it will buy securities, exchanging money for the bonds. The success or failure of these operations depends, of course, on the willingness of citizens to buy and sell the securities at the time and at the rate of return the Federal Reserve offers.

The more drastic option available to the Federal Reserve is to change the discount rate. The discount rate is the rate of interest at which member banks can borrow money from the Federal Reserve bank. Obviously, this rate will affect interest rates in the economy as a whole, as member banks will have to increase their interest rates to compensate for the increased cost of borrowing money from the Federal Reserve. And with the basic monetary paradigm, making money more difficult (or at least more costly) to borrow will slow down economic activity and presumably inflation.

Finally, the Federal Reserve Board can change the reserve requirement. Member banks of the Federal Reserve system are required to keep reserves on deposit at the Federal Reserve banks to cover their outstanding loans. This is a percentage of the total amount they have out in loans, normally around 20 percent. If the Federal Reserve raises the reserve requirement from 20 to 25 percent, then for each dollar a bank had out in loans before the change, it can lend only 80 cents. The bank will have to deposit more money, call in some loans, or reduce the pace at which it grants new loans. Any of these measures will reduce the amount of money in circulation and should slow down economic activity. On the other hand, if the Federal Reserve reduces the reserve requirement, banks can make more money available for loans and increase economic activity.

The Federal Reserve has been a paragon of conservative economic policy. Its members traditionally have been bankers or businessmen who have tried to please a constituency composed of the same. The Federal Reserve's tight money policies have been criticized frequently for producing economic hardship and slow growth, but they have also been defended as proper, given threats of inflation. What is most important, however, is the possibility that a lack of coordination of fiscal and monetary policy will cause the two to cancel each other's effects and produce little or no real benefit, or the possibility that their coordination may produce an excessive amount of correction to the economy so that changes constantly overshoot the mark and the fluctuations of the economy are exaggerated rather than minimized.

Regulations and Control

In general, regulation has been used, not for the purpose of general economic management, but for the sake of achieving other economic and social goals—for example, a cleaner environment, a safer workplace, or consumer safety. Obviously such regulations have an effect on overall economic growth, for they make it more or less profitable to engage in certain economic activities. Also, some regulatory activities, such as antitrust regulation, have a pervasive impact on the economic structure of the society. (We treat those policy considerations in our discussion of business policy.)

One form of regulation that does have more pervasive effects on the economic goals outlined previously is wage and price control. American experience with this regulation is rather limited, although it has been used during wartime. But even in peacetime wage and price policies have been proposed and even adopted. The New Economic Policy of the Nixon adminstration was a wage and price policy (sometimes called an incomes policy) adopted during a time when there was no declared war, although Vietnam certainly did have some influence on the economy of the time. Later, Senator Edward Kennedy stressed wage and price controls as a part of his approach to solving America's economic problems during his primary campaign in 1980.

The fundamental idea behind wage and price controls is to mandate rates at which those two crucial factors in the economy can change. These policies are directed primarily at problems of inflation but have effects on a variety of economic indicators. Further, these controls can be administered in a number of ways. For example, Nixon's New Economic Policy had four stages.[21] In the first stage, wages, prices, and rents were frozen for ninety days. After that, changes in wages and prices had to be reported to federal government boards that had the authority to block increases deemed inflationary. This was followed by a voluntary Phase III and by the reinstitution of the mandatory controls of Phase II in Phase IV. One option that was not employed during those months was a flat-rate ceiling, such as 7 or 10 percent, to limit increases.

Wage and price policies are dramatic steps, especially in countries such as the United States with dominant free-market ideologies, and they are even more dramatic when adopted by Presidents with conservative images. At least in the short run, these policies can buy time to allow other policies to work in an attempt to slow down inflation. For any extended period, wage and price controls present significant management and economic difficulties.

Perhaps most important is the sheer magnitude of the task. Freezes or flat-rate ceilings require enforcement and monitoring, but if the government attempts to make judgments as to whether or not different levels of increases are justified in different industries, the task becomes enormous. The Nixon administration made these determinations through the Cost-of-Living Council with a separate Pay Board and Price Commission. These organizations were composed of labor, business, and "public interest" members, whose differences of opinion often produced rancor and slowed down the decision-making process. But even without disagreements, an attempt to supervise prices and wages in a large and complex economy is a heroic undertaking.

A wage and price policy may present other administrative and economic problems. For example, if some price increases are allowed because of excess demand or for other good reasons, many citizens will not accept those increases without commensurate increases in their own income. They may believe themselves to be at a disadvantage in comparison with powerful corporations or other producers, and their faith in the fairness of the system may be undermined. Also, in some situations controls may be instituted so that the mandated ceilings on wages and prices become the floors as well, and no increases under that figure are adopted. In fact, it was argued that the actions of the Nixon administration actually increased inflation in some industries, and may have made later inflation worse.

Perhaps the most remarkable thing about the limited experience of the United States with wage and price controls is that they have been very popular, especially given the prevailing economic ideology of the country.[22] Citizens apparently believed that at last the government was attempting to do something to control inflation and was attempting to make equitable decisions about price increases. And there is some evidence that citizens would have welcomed a more direct effort at price control during the more rapid inflation of the late 1970s and early 1980s. Wage and price controls involve massive administrative efforts, but as inflation is built as much on psychology as it is on economics, the very act of attempting to control inflation may be more important than the accuracy of the determinations made in implementing the policy.

Public Support for Business
In addition to regulating the conduct of business and providing support through tax incentives, governments provide a number of more direct subsidies to industry. In the United States the federal government has a share of the actions in providing such subsidies, but a great deal of support also comes from state and even local governments. The majority of the direct expenditures benefiting business and industry are for research and development, and for the subsidization of credit. Other forms of support for industry include providing support for inland water transportation by making use of locks and dams on rivers free, and a variety of grants and loans for small business. Federal credit facilities are available for a host of business projects, including the facilitation of international trade through the Export-Import Bank and a variety of supports for agriculture and housing. Taken together, the federal government in 1984 supplied over $60 billion in support for business and industry.[23]

State and local governments tend to provide supports for business and industry in a competitive environment. Just as they compete with one another with tax incentives in order to attract industries into locating in their localities, so too direct services and credits can be used to attract industry.[24] In fact, there is some evidence that government services are more important than tax breaks in attracting industries. The services of state and local governments need not be anything extraordinary; they may mean only that the state and local governments do the things that they usually do, such as supplying transportation, water, sewers, and similar services, and supply them well. Of course, some expenditures of subnational governments are more extraordinary; they may even include the building of plants for industries that agree to come to the locality.

All these supports for business must be examined in the context of the "industrial policy debate" in the United States. As the United States has fallen behind Japan, West Germany, and even smaller countries (e.g., South Korea) in the production of basic commodities such as steel and finished products such as automobiles, the question, "What is wrong with American industry?" has arisen.[25] There are numerous answers to that question, including inept management, avaricious unions, and meddlesome government. Another answer is that government does not do enough to support American industry; a more comprehensive approach to the problems of industry should be adopted. Such a program might include some or all of the following elements:

1. *Direct government grants for the modernization and expansion of industry.* Much of the machinery of American industry is outdated in comparison with our competitors. Government could help by supplying grants, loans, or both.

2. *Trade policy.* American government has followed free-trade policies during most of the postwar period, and has used tariffs and other restrictions on imports infrequently. Another option for government would be to impose tariffs and other trade barriers until American industry "gets back on its feet." There are voluntary arrangements with Japan over the import of automobiles, but some advocate broader use of these powers.

3. *Deregulation.* Some sections of the business community argue that the numerous safety and environmental regulations of the federal government make it difficult for American industry to produce products at a price that is competitive on the world market. They believe that deregulation would improve the competitiveness of business. In addition, the United States tends to pursue regulatory policies such as antitrust with much greater vigor than is true for most of the rest of the world. This also may inhibit the competitiveness of American industry in world markets.

4. *Research and development.* American industry has a tradition of being the most advanced technologically in the world. Unfortunately, this has become more of a tradition than a reality; except for a few industries, such as computers, American industry appears to be falling behind many countries. Government could make a major contribution to American industry by making more funds available for research.

5. *Regional policy.* The effects of the declining industrial fortunes of the United States have not been spread evenly over the country but have been concentrated in the older industrial regions, especially in the Great Lakes area. Thus, as well as dealing with the direct problems of industry, there is a need to address some of the human problems created by a changing industrial base in many states and localities. In turn, these efforts may make those localities more attractive to industries considering relocation.

Government has been involved in supporting industry for most of the history of the United States. Many of the great industrial ventures in this country, for example the spread of the railroad westward, were done with the direct or indirect support of government. There may now be an even greater need for government support for business and industry than in the past, given the declining industrial position of the United States. However, too much dependence on government to "bail out losers" may mean that American industry ceases to be responsible for its actions.[26]

Public Ownership

Although it is not common in the United States, public ownership of certain kinds of industries may be important for economic management, especially influencing the location of certain industries. Even in the United States a number of public and quasi-public corporations are involved in the economy. In 1976 there were twenty wholly publicly owned and seven partly owned corporations in the federal government. At the state and local levels many enterprises are organized to carry out economic functions. These range from publicly owned utilities, such as electricity, gas, and transportation, to functions usually associated with the private sector, such as insurance and banking.

These public corporations perform a variety of functions for government. One is to provide revenue for government. For example, local government utilities can buy electricity at commercial rates and then distribute it at rates that yield a profit. Also, public corporations can be used to regulate prices and certain essential services. Although many publicly owned transportation corporations run with a deficit, they maintain relatively low costs and provide greater service than could be given by a private firm, and local government considers those objectives important. At the federal level, corporate structures have been used for regional development in the Tennessee Valley Authority in an attempt to transform the economy of a backward region through public action and public ownership of electrical power production. Also, federal corporations have been active in promoting U.S. foreign trade through the Import-Export Bank and the Overseas Private Investors Corporation (related to the goals of having a positive balance of payments) and in providing transportation to promote economic growth through the St. Lawrence Seaway, Amtrak, and Conrail.

One interesting variation on public ownership is the use of loan guarantees as a means of attempting to guarantee continuing employment and economic growth. The most notable example of this policy option is the Loan Guarantee Board, which is charged with developing financing to keep the Chrysler Corporation in business and its workers in jobs. The federal government did not buy one share of Chrysler stock, but used its economic powers to keep the company alive. It might be argued that public involvement in a moribund corporation simply to keep unemployment from increasing is actually a disguised social program and may actually slow economic growth. At least for the short-term, however, it does represent an important economic policy instrument.

Incentives

Governments can also attempt to influence economic change through incentives. Most incentives come through the tax system and are directed primarily at encouraging investment and change. We have already mentioned the role that state government tax policies play in encouraging structural change in their individual state economies. The federal government also provides special incentives for certain industries and general incentives to invest.

The major incentives for structural change in the U.S. economy have been the oil depletion allowance and similar allowances for other depletable natural resources. The allowances permit investors to write off against profits a portion of the investments they made in searching for oil. The decontrol of "new oil" under President Carter's energy program was another means of encouraging exploration for domestic energy supplies. A variety of provisions of the federal tax code also serve to encourage investment in general by both corporations and individuals. The capital gains provisions of the tax laws permit profits made on investments held for over six months to be taxed at half the individual's normal tax rate, and in no case at higher than 25 percent. Likewise, industries are given extensive tax credits for new investments and allowed higher-than-average depreciation on investments during the first year. All these policies make it easier and more profitable for industries to invest and for economic growth to follow that investment, but none mandates that the industry make the investments. The administrative costs of incentive programs are comparatively small when subsidy programs are considered as an alternative, and the programs are perceived as less intrusive into the free-market economy.[27] But the dollar an industry saves from taxes is worth exactly the same as the dollar given as a subsidy, and perhaps even more, since there are fewer restrictions on how the dollar saved from taxes can be spent.

Moral Suasion

When all else fails, or perhaps before anything else is tried, governments can attempt to use persuasion to influence the behavior of citizens and industries. Persuasion works best in times of national emergency, but economic circumstances may be sufficiently dire to create the perception of such an emergency. Presidents, using their power as spokesmen for the nation, are central to the use of suasion to control economic behavior. They can use a variety of symbols to try to influence the citizens. A number of recent examples illustrate the appeals that Presidents can make. President Lyndon Johnson attempted to exert the power of his office in "jawboning" industries into restraining price increases. He attempted to speak for the nation as President, and he appealed to patriotism to get what he wanted. President Gerald Ford used more subtle methods in trying to influence citizens through his WIN (Whip Inflation Now) program, complete with buttons and other advertising. And most Presidents have personally appealed to labor leaders and industrialists to moderate their demands for wage and price increases.

The effects of persuasion depend on the nature of the problem being addressed and the character of the political leader attempting to use the persuasion. Industrialists are unlikely to continue to provide jobs for workers in an unprofitable factory simply because they are asked to, but citizens may well try to "buy American" in order to improve the balance of payments. Political leaders who are trusted and respected may find it fairly easy to influence their fellow citizens, whereas those who are less popular may find more direct mechanisms for economic management more effective.

Tax Policy

Another major component of economic policy is tax policy. The process of public budgeting involves decisions about raising enough revenues to meet expenditure demands; here we are more concerned with the choice of revenue instruments used to collect the needed money. Raising the same amount of tax revenues by different means may have very different economic and political effects, and those effects should be understood when discussing tax policies.

Table 8.3 shows the tax profile of the United States in comparison with other major Western countries. The table shows the proportion of total tax revenue in each country derived from a number of possible revenue sources. The United States stands out from its major trading partners in several ways. First, there is much less reliance on taxes on goods and services in the United States than in the other countries. Although most states and many localities have sales and excise taxes, there is no national sales tax comparable to the value-added tax (VAT) used in most European countries. Fiscal pressures, especially on the Social Security system (see chapter 10), may one day make such a tax necessary, but it has been delayed longer in this country than elsewhere.

Second, the United States derives substantially more of its total tax revenue from property tax than most other countries do. Property taxes are collected by state and local governments and are the principal revenue source for those governments. This seems to reflect an Anglo-Saxon tradition in revenue col-

TABLE 8.3
SOURCES OF REVENUE, 1983
(in percent)

	Income	Social Security	VAT and Sales	Excise	Corporation	Customs	Property	Other
United States	37.6	26.5	6.3	10.4	8.6	0.9	8.5	1.2
United Kingdom	29.3	16.2	12.6	14.7	9.2	1.2	11.5	5.3
France	13.4	42.7	21.1	8.1	5.0	0.5	1.7	7.5
Germany	29.0	35.5	17.0	9.1	5.0	1.1	1.0	2.3
Canada	34.8	11.5	11.0	18.9	10.5	3.6	7.7	2.0
Italy	26.4	35.9	14.9	9.4	9.0	0.4	0.0	4.0
Sweden	39.9	29.6	13.5	9.4	2.9	0.9	0.0	3.8

lection, for both the United Kingdom and Canada use the property tax heavily.[28]

Third, there is a relatively high reliance on corporate taxes in the United States. Given the characterization of American politics as dominated by special interests (especially business interests) corporate taxation may require more explanation. Corporations rarely bear the full burden of corporate taxation: The real tax burden falls on consumers of the firms' products or on the companies' workers. Under many economic circumstances, firms can add taxes as a cost of doing business on to the price of their products. A more political explanation involves the tradition of populism in many states in the United States; these states place a relatively heavier burden of taxation on corporations than on individuals.

One thing that table 8.3 cannot show is the complexity of the tax system in the United States. As the tax system has evolved, numerous deductions, exemptions, and other special treatments ("loopholes") have been written into the tax laws (see table 8.4).[29] While many of these exclusions came about for good economic and social reasons (e.g., the deductibility of mortgage interest stimulates homeownership as well as the construction industry), numerous loopholes seem to benefit only the wealthy and the well organized. The apparent unfairness of many aspects of the tax system has produced a number of efforts at tax simplification, including a major initiative by the Reagan administration.

TABLE 8.4

TAX EXEMPTIONS AND DEDUCTIONS, 1982

(in millions)

Exclusion of employers' pension contributions	$25,765
Home mortgage interest	23,030
State and local taxes (other than property tax)	20,395
Investment credits	20,038
Capital gains	18,315
Exclusion of Social Security and other benefits	18,300
Exclusion of employers' health insurance contributions	15,330
Property tax	10,065
Charitable contributions	8,345
Oil and gas exploration and depletion	6,500
Other	39,960

Choices in Tax Policy

The United States has obviously made a number of choices about taxation that are different from choices made in other industrialized countries. The aggregate figures presented above represent taxation decisions made by many thousands of individual governments. What criteria might these governments be employing when they make their decisions about taxes?

COLLECTIBILITY

One criterion that must be considered is the ability of government to collect a tax, and even more the ability of that tax to yield large amounts of revenue. Collecting taxes is expensive and has political costs. Therefore, a government should be sure that it can generate enough revenue from a tax to justify it.

The two major tax "handles" for modern, industrialized governments are income and expenditure. By definition, almost all money in an economy is both income *and* expenditure, and governments can raise revenue by tapping either or both streams of economic transactions. Further, given that in modern economies most income is earned as salaries and wages in relatively large organizations, and most purchases are made from relatively large and identifiable organizations, governments can employ private bodies to do much of the tax collection for them. Employers typically withhold a portion of their employees' incomes for taxes, and are required to submit detailed accountings of sales and value-added taxes. These procedures impose a cost on the private sector, but they make the collection of revenue easier and less expensive for government.

FISCAL NEUTRALITY

As well as being collectible, a "good" tax is one that does not produce any significant distortions in the economy.[30] That is, the tax system should not give preference to one kind of revenue or expenditure, unless there is a very good reason to do so.

Unfortunately, the existing tax system in the United States is not fiscally neutral because of the large number of special-interest provisions that have been written into the law. These provide citizens and corporations alike with incentives to use their money in ways that may be unproductive on economic grounds but that are quite lucrative from the perspective of the tax system. Attempts at tax reform hope to make the tax system more fiscally neutral, but run counter to the tradition of providing tax benefits to organized interest groups.

BUOYANCY

Raising revenue is unpopular politically, so any tax that can produce additional revenue without any political activity is a valuable tax. A buoyant tax is one for which the yield keeps pace with, or exceeds, the pace of either economic growth or inflation. In principle, the progressive income tax is a buoyant tax. As individuals earn more income, they pay not only higher taxes but higher *rates* of tax, so there is a fiscal dividend from the tax, with government automatically receiving a higher proportion of national income. Taxes that require reassessment or adjustments in rates in order to keep pace with inflation (e.g., the property tax) are not buoyant and hence may generate political difficulties if their relative yield is to be maintained.

The fiscal dividend associated with the progressive income tax during inflationary periods has led to legislation indexing tax brackets. That is, as inflation increases the money income of citizens without increasing their real income, the income level at which tax rates change are increased so that rates change at the same *real* income. Everything else being equal, the amount of real income for government would therefore remain constant without legislative action to increase rates. This kind of change was a major part of tax reform during the first Reagan administration.

DISTRIBUTIVE EFFECTS

Another thing that taxes can do for government is to alter the income distribution in society. This is usually thought of as benefiting the less affluent at the expense of the more affluent. However, many taxes used by governments may be regressive, that is, they may take a larger proportion of income from the poor than from the rich. These regressive taxes (e.g., the Social Security tax) must be justified on other grounds.

Analyses of the net impacts of taxes on income distribution are difficult to calculate, especially as some attention must be given to the effects of expenditures that the taxes finance. Nevertheless, there does seem to be a general finding in the United States that both the poor—especially the working poor—and the rich pay a higher rate of tax than the majority of citizens do, while the large majority of citizens pay approximately the same rate of tax.[31] This is true when federal, state, and local taxes are added together; the federal tax structure is at least moderately progressive, and state and local taxes tend to be moderately regressive. It is especially interesting that the working poor pay such a high rate of tax. This is explained by their higher propensity to consume, rather than save their income, so almost all their income is subject to sales and excise taxes. All their income also is covered by Social Security taxation, whereas the more affluent can earn substantial amounts of money over the threshold rate of Social Security income. Finally, the working poor may be unable to take advantage of many of the "loopholes" in the tax system that the more affluent can use.

VISIBILITY

Finally, those making political decisions about taxes must be concerned about the political acceptability of taxes. To some degree this is crucial for taxes related to the historical traditions of a country or even a state: The property tax is regarded as a threat to the "little man" who owns a house in many states with populist political cultures. The political acceptability of taxes may also be a function of the visibility of the taxes. Everything else being equal, the less visible a tax is, the more acceptable it will be.[32] Even though income tax is withheld from employees' checks at each pay period, the citizen is still required to file a statement each year on which he or she can can see a total tax account for the year. Similarly, property-tax bills are typically sent to homeowners each year; in states with high property taxes, the bill may seem huge. Both taxes are obvious to the taxpayer and therefore may be resisted. The Social Security tax is less visible. Even though it is deducted from paychecks along with the income tax, there is no annual reckoning that might bring the total tax bill to the citizen's attention.

The lack of a total tax bill is a very important element in a country (such as the United States) with several layers of government, all of which levy taxes. These taxes are levied at different times and in different ways, so only the better informed are likely to know their total tax bills.[33] Even though the United States is a low-tax country, the division among taxes and taxing units may make the total bill seem even lower.

The problem of tax visibility is one reason for considering a value-added tax (VAT) for the United States. Unlike a sales tax, which is levied as the consumer pays for the commodity and is added on as a separate item, the VAT is levied at each stage of the process of production and is included in the price of the product when sold. Thus the actual amount of the tax—and even the fact that a tax is being levied—may be hidden from the consumer; consequently, there may be less political mobilization to oppose the tax. It is just such an invisible feature, however, that makes many fiscal conservatives extremely concerned about the VAT, fearing that government could expand its activities without citizens understanding what the real increases in their tax bills had been.

The Politics of Tax Reform

Taxation is different from other kinds of policy in that it is essentially something that no one really wants and everyone seeks to avoid when possible. Senator Russell Long of Louisiana, long a power on the Senate Finance Committee, which is responsible for tax legislation, encapsulated the nature of taxation in this little ditty: "Don't tax you, don't tax me, tax that fellow behind the tree."

The nature of tax politics is to try to divert the burden of taxation on to others and to build in special privileges for oneself.

Tax policymaking also has been relatively technical and legalistic compared with other forms of policymaking. The tax code is an extremely complex set of laws, and it is made even more complex by rulings made by the Internal Revenue Service and tax courts concerning just what the tax code really means. In Congress, tax policymaking has been the preserve of a relatively few powerful and knowledgeable congressmen and senators (e.g., Senator Long and former Congressman Wilbur Mills).[34] The perceived complexity of tax policymaking has allowed many special interests to have desired provisions written into the tax code with little awareness on the part of the general public. The many special interests are also represented by members of Congress whose constituencies may contain large concentrations of one kind of industry or another. Adding loopholes to a tax law may be an exercise in coalition building through logrolling, with every congressman capable of adding in his or her provision in return for support of the legislation as a whole. All this has resulted in a federal tax system, especially an income tax, perceived as highly unfair by many citizens. Harris surveys have indicated that an average 90 percent of respondents thought the federal income tax was unfair.[35]

A major attempt to rectify the complexity and the perceived unfairness of the tax system is the flat-rate tax, which, as the name implies, recommends that most income *from whatever source* should be taxed at the same rate. Rather than a host of special breaks for investment income or income from oil wells, income would be income — and all taxpayers would be treated equally.

Flat-rate tax proposals have not been totally flat rate. Most would retain the provision for the deductibility of interest on home (usually only first home) mortgages; any attempts to remove that tax break could ensure the defeat of the proposal. Most other "loopholes" would be closed, and even a number of other widely used benefits (e.g., the deductibility of state and local taxes) would be ended. In addition, there would not be a single flat rate but there would be some moderate progressivity to the rate of tax. Under the Reagan plan, for example, the first $29,000 of taxable income on joint returns would be taxed at 15 percent, the next $41,000 would be taxed at 25 percent, and all remaining income would be taxed at 35 percent. This contrasts with the current top rate of 50 percent on income over $85,000.

Naturally, those whose particular benefits are affected by tax simplification oppose the legislation. Among the first to question the efficacy of the legislation were mayors and governors. Not only would the ending of the deductibility of state and local taxes make it more difficult for subnational governments to increase taxes, but the legislation would make the interest on state and local bonds taxable (rather than tax exempt as under existing law). This would force the governments to increase interest rates on their bonds and thereby increase their debt costs. Mayors and governors were followed closely by business interests, which argued that the repeal of special investment credits, accelerated depreciation, and other benefits going to investment would further slow the rate of capital formation in the United States and thereby slow economic growth. A standard place to begin political analysis is to ask "whose ox is gored," and a large number of oxen would be gored by this legislation.

Despite the public discontent with many aspects of the current tax system, tax reform is a difficult undertaking. Making tax policy has traditionally been the preserve of the special interests, and it may be difficult to prevent them from continuing their role in the process. In addition, many of the arguments advanced by the interests may have social and economic validity. For example, making state and local bonds taxable would impose a great deal of cost on governments that are financially troubled already. In short, tax reform may be a desirable but unattainable goal.

Summary

The management of the economy is a central concern of government. It is one area of policymaking on which governments are frequently judged by citizens. This is true not only because of the central importance of the issues for citizens but also because of the frequent reporting of such indicators as the inflation rate and the unemployment rate. Even if an individual has a job and an income that keeps pace with the cost of living, he or she may believe the President is not doing a good job because of the numbers that regularly appear in the newspapers. It is interesting to notice the extent to which the performance of the economy is laid at the feet of government, especially the President. This is in marked contrast to the era before the depression, when the economy was not believed to be controllable by government. The President clearly plays a crucial role in economic management. This is true in part because of his role as spokesman for government. It is also true because of the central role of the President's budget in controlling the economy and because of his importance in other areas of economic policy such as taxation and the management of any direct controls that may be required.

It is also important to understand that the state of the economy is not totally a presidential responsibility. Congress is involved in setting even the budget, which is the central instrument of presidential intervention in the economy. And the Federal Reserve Board is almost totally beyond the control of the President. Furthermore, the federal structure of the United States is such that state and local governments have a significant impact not only on the overall stimulative or depressive effects of public expenditures but also on attempts to move industries and labor geographically.

Finally, we citizens have a substantial impact on the state of the economy. Many presidential decisions on fiscal policy and some Federal Reserve decisions on monetary policy depend on citizens responding in the predicted fashion. Even major aggregates such as economic growth depend to a great extent on the perceptions and behavior of citizens. If citizens and businesses believe that prosperity is coming, they will be willing to invest and thus may make their belief a self-fulfilling prophecy. Government can do everything in its power to try to influence the behavior of citizens, but ultimately most decisions are beyond its control. Nevertheless, the success of an economic policy is a major factor in determining whether citizens believe that government is doing a good job.

Notes

1. See Michael Stewart, *Keynes and After* (Harmondsworth, England: Penguin, 1972); and John Kenneth Galbraith, *The Great Crash* (London: Hamish Hamilton, 1955).

2. See Robert J. Skidelsky, *Politicians and the Slump* (London: Macmillan, 1967).

3. Walter Heller, *New Dimensions of Political Economy* (Cambridge, Mass.: Harvard University Press, 1966).

4. See A.W. Phillips, "The Relation between Unemployment and the Rate of Change in Money Wage Rates in the United Kingdom, 1861-1957," *Economica,* November 1958, 283-99.

5. E.C. Schumacher, *Small Is Beautiful* (New York: Harper & Row, 1973); and E.J. Mishan, *Growth: The Price We Pay* (London: Staples, 1969).

6. Richard Rose and Guy Peters, *Can Government Go Bankrupt?* (New York: Basic Books, 1979), 42-64.

7. Lester Thurow, *The Zero-Sum Society* (New York: Basic Books, 1979).

8. Doreen B. Massey, *The Anatomy of Job Loss: The How, Why and Where of Employment Decline* (New York: Methuen, 1982).

9. See Fred Hirsch and John H. Goldthorpe, *The Political Economy of Inflation* (Cambridge, Mass.: Harvard University Press, 1978).

10. W.J. Baumol, "Macroeconomics of Unbalanced Growth: The Anatomy of Urban Crisis," in *Is Economics Relevant?* ed. R.L. Heilbroner and A.M. Ford (Pacific Palisades, Calif.: Goodyear, 1971), 194-213.

11. John T. Woolley, "Monetary Policy Instrumentation and the Relationship of Central Banks and Governments," *The Annals,* November 1977, 151-73.

12. Rose and Peters, *Can Government Go Bankrupt?* 192-99.

13. C. Fred Bergsten, *The Dilemmas of the Dollar* (New York: New York University Press, 1975).

14. For example, personal income in the United States grew by 39 percent from 1970 to 1980. In the South-Atlantic states it grew by 51 percent, in the East-South-Central states by 49 percent and in the West-South-Central by 72 percent. In the Mid-Atlantic

states it grew by only 16 percent. U.S. Bureau of the Census, *Statistical Abstract of the United States, 1982-83* (Washington, D.C.: Government Printing Office, 1983), table 42.6.

15. Henry C. Wallich, "The Interface between Monetary and Fiscal Policy," *Policy Studies Journal*, Fall 1980, 68-74.

16. Rose and Peters, *Can Government Go Bankrupt?* 135-41; and James M. Buchanan and Richard Wagner, *Democracy in Deficit: The Political Legacy of Lord Keynes* (New York: Academic Press, 1977), 38-48.

17. This concept has been set forth in a number of publications of the Brookings Institution, e.g., Henry Aaron et al., *Setting National Priorities: The 1980 Budget* (Washington, D.C.: Brookings Institution, 1979).

18. Roger B. Porter, "The President and Economic Policy: Problems, Patterns and Alternatives," in *The Illusion of Presidential Government*, ed. Hugh Heclo and Lester M. Salamon (Boulder, Colo.: Westview, 1981), 203-27.

19. See the articles in *The Supply-Side Solution*, ed. Bruce Bartlett and Timothy P. Roth (Chatham, N.J.: Chatham House, 1983).

20. Michael D. Reagan, "The Political Structure of the Federal Reserve System," *American Political Science Review*, March 1961, 64-76.

21. Lawrence C. Pierce, "Wage and Price Controls: Economic Necessity or Political Expediency," in *What Government Does*, ed. Matthew Holden, Jr., and Dennis L. Dresang (Beverly Hills, Calif.: Sage, 1977), 51-83.

22. Ibid., 77-78.

23. Congressional Budget Office, *Federal Support of U.S. Business* (Washington, D.C.: Government Printing Office, January 1984).

24. Robert J. Reinshuttle, *Economic Development: A Survey of State Activities* (Lexington, Ky.: Council of State Governments, 1983).

25. Robert Z. Lawrence, *Can America Compete?* (Washington, D.C.: Brookings Institution, 1984).

26. See, for example, David McKay, "Industrial Policy and Nonpolicy in the United States," *Journal of Public Policy*, May 1983, 29-48.

27. See Charles L. Schultze, *The Public Use of Private Interest* (Washington, D.C.: Brookings Institution, 1977).

28. B. Guy Peters, "Variations in Tax Policy," in *The Crisis of the Welfare State*, ed. Douglas E. Ashford (Oxford: Basil Blackwell, 1986).

29. Benjamin I. Page, *Who Gets What from Government* (Berkeley: University of California Press, 1983), 41ff.

30. Bernard P. Herber, *Modern Public Finance*, 3d ed. (Homewood, Ill.: Irwin, 1975), 111-15.

31. See Benjamin A. Okner, "Total U.S. Taxes and Their Effects on the Distribution of Family Incomes in 1966 and 1970," in *The Economics of Taxation*, ed. Henry J. Aaron and Michael J. Boskin (Washington, D.C.: Brookings Institution, 1980).

32. Harold L. Wilensky, *The New Corporatism: Centralization and the Welfare State* (Beverly Hills, Calif.: Sage, 1976).

33. R.J. Bennett, *The Geography of Public Finance* (New York: Methuen, 1980).

34. John F. Manley, *The Politics of Finance: The House Committee on Ways and Means* (Boston: Little, Brown, 1970).

35. Cited in Karyl A. Kinsey, *Survey Data on Tax Compliance: A Compendium and Review* (Chicago: American Bar Foundation, 1984), 4.

9. Health-Care Policies

One of the great myths about American life and public policy is that we have a private health-care system. In fact, in 1980, over 43 percent of all health-care expenditures in the United States were made by government agencies of some sort, and many physicians who so loudly proclaim the virtues of private medical care receive a substantial portion of their income from public medical programs such as Medicare and Medicaid. The public sector makes a much smaller proportion of total health expenditures than in most other industrialized countries, but there is a significant involvement of government in the provision of health care.

The extent of involvement of American government in health care can be seen in part in the health-care programs listed in table 9.1. All three levels of government are to some degree involved in health care, and at the federal level a wide variety of public agencies are involved. Almost all cabinet-level departments of the federal government are to some degree involved with health care, as are a number of independent executive agencies. Their involvement ranges from directly providing medical care to some segments of the population (e.g., through the Department of Defense, the Department of the Interior, or the Veterans Administration), through regulating some aspects of medical care, to subsidizing medical research. Without public involvement, American health care would certainly be very different and probably would not be as good as it is. It certainly would not be accessible to the poor and the elderly, and the overall quality would probably not be as high as it currently is for those who nominally pay all their medical expenses. For one thing, the federal government is a major source of funds for medical research, without which many of the advances in medicine with which the average citizen is now familiar would not have happened or would have been delayed.

Rather than go in the direction of greater involvement in medical care, the Reagan administration has tried to cut back on the federal role. Attempts have included cutting back on federal health funding and converting former categorical programs into block-grant programs. These programs depend much more on the priorities of state governments for implementation, and there is

TABLE 9.1

MAJOR HEALTH PROGRAMS

Federal	State	Local
Department of Agriculture	State hospitals	City hospitals
Meat inspection	State mental	Sanitation and
	hospitals	public health
Department of Health and Human Services	Substance abuse	
Food and Drug Administration	Medicaid	
Community Health Services		
Indian Health Services		
National Institutes of Health		
Substance-abuse programs		
Health education		
HMO loan funds		
U.S. Public Health Service		
Medicare		
Medicaid		
Department of the Interior		
Territorial health programs		
Veterans Administration		
VA hospitals		

some evidence that health care for the very poor has been significantly reduced in quantity and quality.[1]

Problems in Health Care

The United States is one of the richest countries in the world, and it spends a larger proportion of its economic resources (as measured by gross national product) on health care than does any other industrialized nation. The results of all those expenditures, however, are not so impressive. In infant mortality, a commonly used indicator of the quality of medical care, the United States is tied for thirteenth in the world, behind most Western European countries, East Germany, and Japan.[2] Depending on one's perspective, these figures are made better or worse if the total figure is disaggregated by race. For the white population in the United States, the infant mortality rate is as low as that of almost any Western European country, but for minority populations, the infant mortality rate is perhaps closer to that of a Third World country (see table 9.2). Health care of the finest kind is available in the United States, but it may be available only to a limited portion of the population. Vast disparities exist among racial, economic, and geographical groups in the United States, and

TABLE 9.2

INFANT MORTALITY

Country	Rate (deaths per 1000 live births)
Sweden	7
Netherlands	8
Finland	8
Japan	8
Switzerland	9
Norway	9
Denmark	9
France	10
Iceland	11
United States (whites only)	11
Canada	12
Belgium	12
Australia	12
Spain	13
Singapore	13
Luxembourg	13
United Kingdom	13
East Germany	13
United States (total)	13
New Zealand	14
Italy	15
West Germany	15
Jamaica	16
Malta	16
Cyprus	16
Israel	16
Cuba	19
Greece	19
Czechoslovakia	19
Brunei	20
United States (blacks only)	21
Costa Rica	22
Bulgaria	22
Poland	22

even with Medicare, Medicaid, and other public programs, the poor, the elderly, and those living in rural areas get less medical care than do white middle-class urban citizens.[3] And an increasing number of middle-class citizens are beginning to be squeezed out of the medical-care market by rapidly increasing prices. The problems that Americans now face in medical care are basically three: access, quality, and cost.

Access to Medical Care

For any medical-care system to function effectively, prospective patients must have access to the system. A number of factors can deter citizens from becoming patients, and one purpose of public involvement in the medical marketplace must be to attempt to equalize access for all citizens.

The most commonly cited barrier to access is economics. As the majority of medical care in the United States is still paid for privately, those who lack the income or insurance to pay for medical care may not have such medical care. Even with several public medical-care programs, medicine is still not as available to the poor as it is to the more affluent. As of 1980 some 30 percent of all the poor (those with incomes below the official poverty line) were not eligible to receive Medicaid benefits. They were poor, but not poor enough to qualify under the means-testing criteria of Medicaid. Only 20 percent of the poor have any privately financed health insurance, and only 10 percent of the poor have any nonhospital coverage.[4] The elderly poor, who have access to Medicare as a result of their age, must still pay for parts of their insurance, and at a rate that may well deter some from taking full advantage of the program. Even the middle class may find that the rising cost of medical care and the possibility of catastrophic illness may make all but the very wealthy medically indigent.

Even if direct economic barriers to access to medical care were removed, there might still be significant economic barriers to equal access. Interestingly, even with the almost entirely free medical-care system of the United Kingdom, the differences in health status by social or economic class have not been narrowed significantly.[5] Each social class is on average healthier, but the disparities between the wealthy and the poor have been maintained, indicating that there are other barriers to consuming health care and, perhaps more important, barriers to creating health, which cannot be removed simply by providing free access. Members of the poor and working classes tend to lose hourly wages if they go to the doctor, whereas salaried employees either do not lose pay or have personal-business leaves. Transportation is generally easier for the more affluent, whereas the poor must rely on public transportation. Perhaps most important, the more affluent and educated know better how to get what they want from professional and bureaucratic organizations than do the poor, and they are more likely to be well treated by individuals and institutions than are the less well off. A doctor is more likely to pay serious attention to the description of symptoms of a middle-class person than to those of a poor person, and the middle-class person is more likely to demand extra diagnostic and curative procedures. So even if all direct economic barriers were removed, there might still be serious barriers to gaining equality in medical care, especially as the poor are generally not as healthy to begin with as the more affluent and as a consequence may require greater medical care.

In addition to economic conditions, geography plays a significant dual role in defining access to medical care. First, urban areas are generally better served with doctors and especially with hospitals than are rural areas. For example, in Standard Metropolitan Statistical Areas in the United States, the average number of physicians per 100,000 population is 215, and the average number of hospital beds per 100,000 is 459. This contrasts with 97 physicians per 100,000 and 425 hospital beds per 100,000 in the non-SMSA regions of the country.[6] The disparity in medical services would be even more pronounced if the areas of specialization of physicians and the standards and equipment of the hospitals were also considered.

Second, there are marked regional imbalances in access to medical care. These can be related in part, but not entirely, to the urban-rural differences. Places in the United States best served by physicians and hospitals are the Middle Atlantic states and the states of the Far West. The worst are the Upper Midwest and the Deep South. There are, for example, 272 physicians per 100,000 population in Massachusetts and 268 per 100,000 in Maryland, but only 107 per 100,000 in Idaho and Mississippi.[7]

Thus, in some parts of the United States, high-quality medical care may not be available, even for someone who can afford it, without a substantial investment in travel. For any serious emergency, this puts the affected individual at even greater risk. Several pilot programs to encourage young doctors to practice in rural, "underdoctored" areas have been tried, and more are being advocated, but there are still pronounced inequalities. These must be addressed if there is to be greater equality in access to health care.

Cost

The second fundamental problem that has troubled health-care consumers and health policymakers is the rising cost of medical care. Table 9.3 shows changes in prices for some components of medical care compared with the overall consumer price index, and the composite medical-care price index. It is clear from these data that medical costs as a whole have increased more rapidly than have total consumer costs and that, among the components of medical costs, hospital costs have increased most rapidly. These costs have increased 105 percent more over a twenty-three-year period than have total consumer prices, while those for total medical care have increased "only" 19 percent more rapidly than the consumer price index.

The importance of these data on costs is that medical care is becoming more difficult for the average person to afford. Even if an individual's income

TABLE 9.3

CHANGES IN MEDICAL-CARE COSTS COMPARED WITH CONSUMER PRICE INDEX

(1967 = 100)

Year	CPI	Total Medicine	Hospital	Physicians	Commodities
1960	88.7	79.1	57.3	77.0	104.5
1965	94.5	89.5	75.9	88.3	100.2
1970	116.3	120.6	145.4	121.4	103.6
1975	161.2	168.6	236.1	169.4	118.8
1976	170.5	184.7	268.8	188.5	126.0
1977	181.5	202.4	299.5	206.0	134.1
1978	195.4	219.4	332.4	223.1	143.5
1979	214.1	239.7	370.3	243.6	153.8
1980	246.8	265.9	418.9	269.3	168.1
1981	272.4	294.5	481.1	299.0	186.5
1982	289.1	328.7	556.7	327.1	205.7
1983	298.4	357.3	619.7	352.3	223.3
1984	310.7	378.0	662.0	377.1	238.7
1985	326.6	413.0	722.5	407.9	262.7

SOURCE: U.S. Bureau of the Census, *Statistical Abstract of the United States, 1985* (Washington, D.C.: Government Printing Office, 1985); U.S. Bureau of Labor Statistics, *CPI Detailed Report,* monthly.

keeps pace with the consumer price index, it will still fall behind the increase in the costs of even general medical care. With these rapidly increasing prices, few people can afford to pay for a catastrophic illness requiring long-term hospitalization and extensive treatment. Even the best medical insurance available will frequently be exhausted by such an illness. Thus it has become increasingly possible that even those with substantial incomes will be financially destroyed by a major illness. There is an additional problem that all the concern about the cost of medicine will undermine the quality of medical care, something that may be especially problematic with "prospective reimbursement" and diagnostic related groupings (DRGs, see below).

Medical-care costs are a problem for government as well as for private citizens, as almost half the total medical-care bill in the United States is paid by governments. But even such a large share of the medical marketplace has not enabled government to exercise any significant control over health costs, perhaps because decisions about health-care spending are made, not by one government, but by several. And within each government are several agencies. Government's attempts to control medical costs have been diffuse, but later we discuss the possibility of more extensive public involvement to assist citizens —both as taxpayers and as patients.

To be able to control costs, we must understand why medical costs have been increasing so rapidly. A number of factors have been identified as causing at least a part of the increase in medical-care costs.[8] For hospitals, one factor has been a rapid increase in the cost of supplies and equipment. This has been true of large capital investments such as X-ray machines, as well as more mundane items such as dressings and surgical gloves. In addition, labor costs for hospitals have been increasing rapidly, as many professional and nonprofessional employees unionize to bargain for higher wages. And there may be too many hospital beds for the number of available patients. Empty hospital beds have capital costs and even some running costs that must be met, and these are spread among the patients who occupy beds through increases in the room rates.

Physician costs also have been rising, although not as rapidly as hospital costs. In addition to the general pressures of inflation in the economy as a whole, increases in equipment and supply costs, the increasing cost of medical malpractice insurance, and the practice of "defensive medicine" to protect against malpractice suits by ordering every possible diagnostic procedure have all produced increases in doctor's fees.[9] In part as a reaction to public pressures, and to reduce the possibility of controls being mandated by government, the American Medical Association (AMA) proposed to its member physicians that they impose a one-year moratorium on new price increases. Somewhat surprisingly, a large majority of physicians surveyed supported such a cost-reducing (or cost-maintaining) action.

Finally, the method of payment for most medical care, especially hospital care, may influence increasing costs. Over 90 percent of all hospital costs and 69 percent of all medical expenses are paid by third-party payers.[10] These third-party payers may be private (e.g., Blue Cross) or public (Medicaid or Medicare). As a result, neither doctors nor patients have an incentive to restrict their consumption of medical care; it is perceived as "free." Individuals may, in fact, want to use their insurance benefits to recover the amount they have paid as premiums over the years. Of course, the increased consumption of medical care will be reflected in higher insurance premiums for all consumers in the future. This is a "tragedy of the commons" in which the rational behavior of individuals creates a pattern of irrationality for the society as a whole. To rectify some of the problems with third-party payment, the Reagan administration proposed in the 1985 budget to tax employer-financed health insurance above a certain value. This would make it more expensive to have so-called first-dollar coverage (i.e., coverage from the first dollar spent for treatment and all subsequent dollars). The change is intended to make the consumer of medical care more conscious of the costs of medicine, something that third-party payment does not do.

Quality

Finally, both citizens and government must be concerned with the quality of medical care being provided. Citizens' obvious expressions of concern about quality have been the increased number of malpractice suits and complaints against physicians and hospitals. Governments' concerns about quality extend from the general social responsibility for regulating the safety and effectiveness of medicines and medical devices on the market, to the quality of care provided to Medicare and Medicaid patients, to perhaps a more philosophical concern with the efficacy of modern medical care as a remedy for the health problems of American citizens.[11]

When a patient—regardless of whether the resulting bill will be paid by Blue Cross-Blue Shield, by Medicaid, or out of pocket—enters a physician's office, he or she has the right to expect, at a minimum, competent medical care that meets current standards. Unfortunately, many patients do not receive such care. Many patients complain about receiving poor-quality care or medical treatment that they believe is delivered without any genuine humanity. On the other side of the medical-care coin, a number of studies have documented excessive use of medical technology and drugs as a means of earning more money for the physician and the hospital. For the public sector, complaints of this kind mean increased costs for Medicare and Medicaid patients.

A more important philosophical question has been injected into the discussion of the quality of care. This was done in part by the comment of Colorado Governor Richard Lamm that ". . . we all have the duty to die," meaning that the terminally ill perhaps should not be kept alive by heroic means when that intervention only "prolongs dying" rather than saves life.[12] Is it high-technology medicine that sustains a semblance of life that has lost most human qualities, or is it a high-technology ego trip for the physician? The physicians' first commandment, *primum non nocere* (first, do no harm), has always been taken to mean preserving life at all costs; modern technology has made that an expensive and possibly inhumane interpretation.

Public Programs in Health Care

As we have demonstrated, government is deeply involved in health services, despite the rhetoric concerning a free-enterprise medical-care system in the United States. Existing public programs provide direct medical services for some segments of the population, offer medical-care insurance for others, and support the health of the entire population through public health programs, regulation, and medical research. Many citizens question the efficacy of these programs, especially the regulatory programs, but they are evidence of the large and important role the government plays in medicine. We now proceed to discuss several major government programs in medical care, with some attention to the policy issues involved in each, and the possibilities of improving the quality of health through public action.

Medicare

The government medical-care program with which most citizens are familiar is almost certainly Medicare, adopted as part of the Social Security Amendments of 1965. The program is essentially one of medical insurance for the elderly and the disabled who are eligible for Social Security or Railroad Retirement benefits. The program has two parts. Part A, financed principally through payroll taxation, is a hospitalization plan. It covers the first sixty days of hospitalization, but requires the patient to pay the first $356 and $89 for each day of hospitalization during the sixty-first to ninetieth days (1985). This portion of the plan also covers up to one hundred days in a nursing-care facility after release from the hospital, with this coverage being subject to a $44.50 copayment by the insured after the first twenty days (1985).

Part B of Medicare is a supplementary insurance program covering doctors' fees and other outpatient services. These expenses are also subject to deductibles and to coinsurance, with the insured paying the first $60 each year, plus 20 percent of the allowable costs. This portion of the Medicare program is financed by the insured, who pay a monthly premium of $15.50 (1985). Insured persons bear a rather high proportion of their own medical expenses under Medicare, given that it is a publicly provided insurance program. The program is certainly subsidized, however, and is still a bargain for the average retired person, who might not be able to purchase anything like the coverage provided, given that the elderly have significantly higher medical expenses than the population as a whole.

Medicare is a better program than would be available to the elderly under many private insurance programs; it requires no physical examination for coverage, covers preexisting health conditions, and is uniformly available throughout the country. The plan does have some problems. Perhaps the greatest difficulty is that the program requires those insured to pay a significant amount out of their own pockets for coverage, even when they are hospitalized. Purchasing Part B of the plan requires an annual outlay of $186 (1985), which, although it is not much money for health insurance, may be a relatively large share of a pensioner's income. In addition, the costs of deductibles and coinsurance may place a burden on less affluent beneficiaries of the program.

In addition to the costs to the recipient of covered expenses, Medicare does not cover all the medical expenses a beneficiary may incur. For example, it does not pay for prescription drugs, eye or dental examinations, eyeglasses or dentures, preventive examinations, or immunizations. Nor does the program cover very extended care. In short, Medicare does not cover many medical problems that plague the elderly population the program was intended to serve, and as a result it does not really meet the needs of the elderly poor, who are most in need of services. In fact, one study shows that the gap between the health status of rich and poor elderly people has widened since the introduction of Medicare.[13] The more affluent can use the program as a supplement to their own assets or private health insurance programs, while the less affluent are still incapable of providing adequately for their medical needs, even with Medicare.

One attempt to solve the "medigap" problem has been the introduction of a number of private health insurance programs to fill in the lacunae of Medicare coverage. Unfortunately, most existing policies of this type do not cover the most glaring deficiencies of Medicare—for example, the absence of coverage for extended nursing home care. In addition, the policies do not cover preexisting health problems and frequently have long waiting periods for eligibility. In short, these policies often cost more money without providing the protection required. The Ninety-sixth Congress passed legislation in 1980 imposing some standards on such insurance policies, but the law was directed more at outright fraud than at providing a means of making useful policies available to cover the gaps in Medicare coverage.

On the government's side of the Medicare program, the costs of funding medical insurance for the elderly impose a burden on the working-age population and on government resources. The basic hospitalization coverage under Medicare is financed by a payroll tax collected as a part of the Social Security tax, amounting in 1986 to 1.45 percent of the first $42,000 of each worker's salary. With increasing opposition to the Social Security tax have come suggestions to shift the financing of Medicare to general tax revenues such as the income tax, leaving the entire payroll tax to fund Social Security pensions.[14] But with the increasing costs of medical care and the growing number of Americans eligible for Medicare, difficulties are likely to arise in financing the program for some years to come.

Finally, problems of quality and fair pricing for Medicare patients are also likely to persist. Medicare regulations allow the Health Care Financing Administration to pay "reasonable" costs to physicians and hospitals for services rendered to beneficiaries and, of course, also require that the providers give adequate and "standard" treatment. In some instances physicians have charged more than the amount designated as "reasonable," thereby imposing additional costs on the patient. In other instances physicians have employed tests and procedures generally considered unnecessary, knowing that the costs would be largely covered by Medicare. In 1972 Congress established Professional Standards Review Organizations to police the quality and pricing of the services rendered to Medicare and Medicaid patients. These PSROs are composed primarily of physicians, and the results of their efforts have been mixed. Some have reported substantial savings as a result of their efforts, while others have been almost totally ineffective in enforcing any discipline on physicians or hospitals.[15] But with the increasing costs of all medical care, the need for effective cost control for these programs is likely to remain an important issue for some time to come.

One move to control costs for public medical programs is called Diagnostic Related Groups (DRGs). This program, adopted 1 October 1983, has hospitals reimbursed for Medicare and Medicaid patients according to one of over 400 specific diagnostic groups (e.g., appendicitis). The hospital is guaranteed a fixed amount for each patient according to the DRG he or she is assigned to. A hospital that is able to treat a patient for less can retain the difference, but if the hospital stay costs more than allowed under the DRG, the hospital must absorb the loss. This is a new program, and a number of questions remain about how it will function. For example, the doctor, more than the hospital, determines how much a course of treatment will cost, and there may be increased conflict between hospital administrators and physicians about how patients are to be treated. Also, this program may tend to reduce the quality of care provided to Medicaid and Medicare patients, or cause too-early dismissals of patients with associated cost shifting onto home medical-care programs and community medicine. Nevertheless, the DRG program is an interesting attempt to impose greater cost consciousness on hospitals and physicians.

Medicaid

While Medicare is directed toward the elderly and disabled, Medicaid, the second major public health-care program, is directed toward the indigent. Medicaid was passed at the same time as Medicare, to provide federal matching funds to state and local governments for medical care of welfare recipients and the "medically indigent," a category intended to include those who do not qualify for public assistance but whose income is not sufficient to cover necessary medical expenses. Unlike Medicare, which is a uniform national program, Medicaid is administered by the states, and as a consequence the benefits, eligibility requirements, and administration vary considerably. However, if a state chooses to have a Medicaid program (only Arizona does not), it must provide benefits for all welfare recipients and for those who receive Supplemental Security Income because of categorical problems—age, blindness, and disability.

Medicaid regulations require states to provide a range of services: hospitalization, laboratory and other diagnostic services, X rays, nursing home services, screening for a range of diseases, and physicians' services. The states may also extend benefits to cover prescription drugs and other services. For each service, the states may set limitations on the amount of care covered and on the rate of reimbursement.

In addition to the problems of variance in the coverage and benefits across the country, Medicaid has other policy problems. The ones most commonly cited are fraud and abuse. It is sometimes estimated that up to 7 percent of total federal outlays for Medicaid are accounted for by abuse.[16] Most instances of fraud and abuse have been on the part of the service providers rather than the recipients, in part because of the complex eligibility requirements and procedures for reimbursement. With a strain on public resources, any program that has a reputation for fraud is likely to encounter difficulties in receiving its funding.

The general strain on fiscal resources at all levels of government and increased medical costs have also produced problems for the Medicaid program. States have been forced to cut back on optional services under the program and to reduce coverage of primary (physician) care in order to be able to finance hospital care for recipients. Also, some states have set limitations on physicians' reimbursements. These limits are significantly lower than the rates doctors would receive from private or Medicare patients; the result is that many physicians refuse to accept Medicaid patients. In part because of these trends, Medicaid has increasingly become a program of institutional medical care—paradoxically, the most expensive way of delivering medical services. As with Medicare, however, institutional care is the one kind of medical care almost sure to be covered under the program. So, in 1984 only 1.8 percent of all Medicaid spending went to home health services, while 42.8 percent of all expenditures went to extended-care facilities, many of which did not meet federal standards.

Like Medicare, the Medicaid program has done a great deal of good in making medical care available to people who might not otherwise receive it. Nevertheless, some significant Medicaid problems will be political issues for years. Proposals for solution range from the abolition of both programs to the establishment of national health insurance, with a number of proposals for internal readjustments of the programs in between the more radical alternatives.

Health Maintenance Organizations

A fundamental criticism is sometimes made of American medical care: It is a fee-for-service medicine. Medical practitioners are paid for each service they perform, and as a consequence they have an incentive to practice their skills on patients; surgeons make money by wielding their knives, and internists make money by ordering diagnostic procedures. Furthermore, critics charge that American medical care is primarily acute care. The system is oriented toward treating the ill rather than toward preventing illness.[17] The money is to be made in illness, not in health.

The Health Maintenance Organization (HMO) is at least a partial attack on these two characteristics of the health-care system.[18] First, the HMO provides prepaid medical care. Members of an HMO pay an annual fee in return for which they receive virtually all their medical care. They may have to pay ancillary costs (e.g., a small set fee for each prescription), but the vast majority of medical expenses are covered through HMO by the annual fee. Under this payment scheme, doctors working for the HMO have no incentive to prescribe additional treatments. If anything, given that the doctors commonly share in the profits of the organization or frequently own the HMO themselves, they have an incentive *not* to prescribe treatments. Any surgery or treatment that would cost the organization money without providing additional income reduces profits. With the same reasoning, doctors in an HMO have an incentive to keep the members healthy and to encourage preventive medicine. A healthy member is all profit, while a sick member is all loss. It is argued that, by reversing the incentives usually presented to physicians, HMOs can significantly improve the quality of health care and reduce the rapid escalation of medical-care costs. Critics argue that the incentives have been altered too far and that members of HMOs may not receive the treatment they need because of the owners' desire to maintain levels of profit. At a minimum, the HMO is an interesting and potentially significant innovation in American health care.

The formation of HMOs is supported by the federal government. In 1973 President Nixon signed into law a bill directed at improving choice in the health marketplace.[19] The legislation provided for planning and development grants for prospective HMOs, but at the same time placed a number of restrictions on any HMO using federal funding. Most important, all HMOs had to offer an extensive array of services including psychiatric care. Any employer offering group insurance to employees had to make the same amount of money available to any employee who wanted to join an HMO. The federal involvement in HMOs was reauthorized in 1978 for another three years, with additional support for the development of outpatient care facilities—important in eliminating expensive hospitalization. The HMO movement has also been assisted by federal efforts restricting the actions of physicians and private insurers who sought to reduce the competition offered by HMOs.

Several successful HMOs now operate in the United States, the most successful being the Kaiser-Permanente organization with over 3 million members and 3000 physicians. The American Medical Association has resisted these organizations as unfair competition because HMOs are subsidized by the federal government, and as not providing adequate medical care. Although they appeal to many people, HMOs must overcome several obstacles if they are to make a significant impact on American health care. One important obstacle is the capital required to start a large-scale medical-care facility. The federal government has yet to underwrite these expenses; it provides funds only for planning. A good deal of skepticism continues about the quality of medical care provided by HMOs, and some citizens seem unwilling to adopt this rather significant departure from the traditional means of delivering health services.

Although the concept does have critics—most of them members of the medical profession—it also has supporters. HMO plans have been supported by organized labor as one means of reducing medical inflation, and they appear to be increasingly acceptable to businesses as a means of reducing costs, a mechanism that is more palatable than direct government regulation. In one vote of confidence, the Reagan administration in 1984 allowed Medicare and Medicaid patients to opt to join HMOs for their medical care, believing that this option could reduce the government's costs for these programs with no loss of medical quality.[20]

Health-Care Regulation

Perhaps the most pervasive impact of government on the delivery of health-care services in the United States has been through regulation. There are many kinds of health-care regulations, and this chapter now briefly discusses four: facilities, costs, quality, and pharmaceuticals.

FACILITIES AND PLANNING

In addition to attempting to influence health-care delivery indirectly by providing financial support for certain activities, government is involved in more direct attempts to move resources around in the health industry. One such attempt is through the regulation of health-care facilities and more comprehensive planning for the health needs of communities. Another basic criticism that has been made of American medicine is that it overuses and overpurchases high technology. The symbol of this medical technology is the CAT scanner, a sophisticated, computer-assisted X-ray machine.[21] One hears many stories of these extremely expensive machines being used only a few hours a day, and of several hospitals in the same area having the same expensive and underused equipment. But why would presumably rational hospital administrators purchase such a machine when they know that one exists just down the street? The answer is that hospitals do not have patients; doctors do. Hospitals must compete among themselves to attract doctors who have patients so that the hospital can fill its beds and meet its budget. One common means of competing for doctors is making sure that your hospital has the most up-to-date equipment available. Costs are rarely a consideration for the doctors or even the patients, as the majority of expenses are paid by a third party, such as Blue Cross or Medicare or Medicaid. Therefore, the hospital can afford to purchase a CAT scanner or any other piece of equipment and then simply pass the cost along to patients through the room rate and other charges.

The 1974 Health Planning Act was an attempt on the part of the federal government to address this cause of medical-care inflation, as well as the more fundamental question of the underuse of resources in the health-care industry. The money used to purchase the CAT scanner not only drives up the costs of medical care but also means that the money cannot be used for another program, such as a broad-scale screening for hypertension or diabetes, which might benefit a much larger number of people. The 1974 act created a series of local planning agencies to monitor the development of medical-care facilities. Each of these Health Systems Agencies (HSAs) covers between 1 million and 3 million people, with statewide agencies coordinating the activities of local agencies. Associated with the federal regulations are state certificate-of-need laws, which establish guidelines on what needs must be manifest before the local HSA can allow the construction of a new health-care facility. As of 1980, all states except Louisiana passed certificate-of-need legislation. These laws must cover new hospital facilities and all capital equipment with a value of $150,000 or more. Interestingly, the new facilities of an HMO are exempt from these certificate-of-need regulations, as a means of ensuring that these rules will not prevent new HMOs from being established.

A number of issues arise in health planning and in the implementation of certificate-of-need legislation. The reauthorization of the health-planning system in 1979 brought some of these issues to the attention of Congress and the public. One is the basic issue of the role of government in health care. Interestingly, the coalition that passed the 1979 bill was composed of liberals who desired continued regulation and conservatives who feared even more extensive regulation such as that in President Carter's hospital cost-control act. The evidence to date is that health planning has not been particularly intrusive, nor has it had great success in controlling the development of medical facilities. The fundamental philosophical point remains, however, and many individuals would like to get government out of this activity entirely.

At the other end of the ideological spectrum are those who would like to see the certificate-of-need laws have more power, including the right to decertify facilities found to be redundant. Some states, such as Wisconsin, have moved in this direction, but there is no national movement to strengthen health planning to this extent. The 1979 legislation does provide some financial support for closing facilities as an incentive for eliminating excess hospital capacity. Also, the existing legislation allows groups of physicians to escape requirements for a certificate of need and to purchase expensive medical equipment without any review. These purchases will probably have the same effect on the overall health bill for the nation and on the utilization of resources. The 1979 legislation allowed this loophole in the laws to continue.

Finally, some have questioned the composition of local HSAs and their ties to the medical profession. Critics argue that instead of being strict regulators of medical care, the HSAs have come to be too closely tied to the regulated interests—in the classic pattern of capture of a regulatory body—and that the HSAs overlook the needs of the poor.[22] Partly as a response to these claims, the 1979 bill strengthened the role of local elective officials and state governors in reviewing state and local planning decisions. In practice, however, it appears that granting this more important role to elected officials has increased the power of health providers rather than the power of consumers and their advocates. As with all the health-care issues we have been discussing, the importance and cost of health care will mean that these concerns about planning are likely to remain political issues for some time.

The health-planning legislation has been extended until 1986, at which time it may be more closely related to the whole DRG approach to reimbursement of hospitals. The idea would be that capital as well as operating costs of hospitals would be reimbursed based on their patient mix, classified by the DRGs.[23] Thus, a hospital with relatively few complex surgical cases might have little justification for purchasing, and little federal money to support purchasing, capital equipment such as CAT scanners. As with much of the thrust of the Reagan administration, such a program would substitute a market incentive for a direct regulation. The program would be beneficial to some hospitals (e.g., inner-city hospitals) that have relatively low capital costs but would handicap the growth of new and especially new proprietary hospitals. Although it is essentially a market incentive, many in the industry would like to have even that degree of control removed from their capital decisions.

HOSPITAL COSTS

Cost increases are a major consideration in health care in the 1980s, and hospital costs have been the most rapidly increasing component of medical costs. Further, as hospitals constitute a major component of the total health-care bill (40 percent in 1981) and are readily identifiable institutions with better record-keeping than the average physician, it seems sensible to concentrate on them as a locus for controlling medical-care costs.[24] The approaches to controlling hospital costs have been varied. The Carter administration proposed direct regulation of hospital costs. This was not passed, but it seemed to frighten the hospital industry sufficiently to introduce their own voluntary effort (VE) program to slow increases in costs. Spokesmen for the industry claimed that this program reduced the rate of inflation to 12.8 percent per year, below the target figure of 13.6 percent. Yet these figures were significantly higher than the 9 percent proposed by the Carter administration.

Another major approach to controlling hospital costs, begun in New Jersey, has been prospective reimbursement. The federal version of this approach for Medicare patients is the Diagnostic Related Groupings mentioned previously. In essence it is a market approach to cost containment, for it allows hospitals that are efficient to make a profit, while those that are not well run can sustain losses. As such, it is more in line with the thinking of the Reagan administration than the direct price controls proposed by the Carter administration.

Although both the Carter program and DRGs attack the problem of hospital costs, neither attempts to attack some fundamental problems causing prices to escalate. One problem is the fundamental principle of fee-for-service medicine, which gives hospitals and doctors an incentive to provide more services. Related to that is the tendency of the medical profession to use high-cost hospital treatment when lower-cost options would be as effective. This is done for the convenience of the physician and because many health insurance policies will pay for hospital treatments but not for the same treatments performed on an outpatient basis. Finally, it is important to remember that hospitals do not have patients, doctors do; and hospitals must compete for doctors in order to fill hospital beds. This competition takes place largely through the acquisition of high-cost technology (CAT scanners, etc.), which must be amortized through the price of hospital care.

HEALTH QUALITY

The regulation of health-care quality is one of the most controversial areas of government intervention in the health field. First, it comes up directly against long-established canons of clinical freedom and the right of members of the medical profession to regulate their conduct. The medical profession, and probably most of the public, assumes that the only person qualified to judge the professional conduct of a physican is another physician.

In addition, private mechanisms have been established for rectifying any harm done by a physician in the conduct of his or her profession. There are, of course, tort and malpractice lawsuits. These legal proceedings have themselves generated problems for medicine, however, and have been cited as one of the factors causing the rapid increases in medical-care costs. Some effects of malpractice litigation are direct, as physicians pass the doubled or tripled malpractice insurance costs on to patients in higher fees. But one important effect of increasing malpractice settlement is more indirect: the practice of "defensive medicine."[25] A doctor, fearing a malpractice suit, will prescribe additional diagnostic procedures, extra days in the hospital, or extra treatments to lessen his or her chances of being declared legally negligent. The costs of these extra procedures are passed on to all consumers through increased medical insurance premiums or higher taxes.

As we mentioned when discussing Medicare, the major public instruments for regulating the quality of medical care are the Professional Services Review Organizations (PSROs). These organizations are designed in part to monitor costs of services provided to Medicare patients, but they necessarily become involved in the issue of appropriate and effective treatment as well. Treatments that are ineffective or dangerous can be costly as well. Some PSROs have gone so far as to establish standard profiles of treatment for certain rather common conditions and then to question physicians whose treatment differs significantly from those patterns. Physicians who are using more extensive treatments may be imposing additional costs on the program, while those who are using unusual or less extensive treatments may be threatening the health of the patient.

Most PSROs are not so diligent, however; the standard complaint against PSROs has been that they are not sufficiently aggressive in monitoring the practice of Medicare and Medicaid physicians. This is generally said to result from the domination of PSROs by physicians and from doctors' tendency to protect one another from outsiders' attempts to impose any regulations on their practice of medicine. The growth of malpractice litigation and its attendant costs, however, may produce pressures on the profession to adopt more stringent internal policing of professional practices, as well as the development of administrative rather than legal mechanisms for redressing grievances.

DRUG REGULATION

The federal government is also deeply involved in the regulation of the pharmaceutical industry and in the control of substances in food and water that are potentially harmful to health. The federal government began to regulate food and drugs in 1902, with extensive increases in its powers in 1938 and again in 1962. The issues surrounding drug regulation have been more heated in the late 1970s and early 1980s than at any time since the initial passage of the legislation. The Food and Drug Administration (FDA), which is responsible for most drug regulation, has been under attack from all sides. Some argue that its regulations have been excessively stringent and have prevented useful drugs from coming to the market. Others believe that its regulations have been too lax and excessively dominated by the pharmaceutical industry and that, as a result, potentially dangerous drugs have been certified for sale.

The basic regulatory doctrine applied to pharmaceuticals is that a drug must be shown to be both safe and effective before it can be approved for sale. Several problems arise from this doctrine. First, almost any drug will have some side effects, so that proving its safety is difficult, and some criteria must be established for weighing the benefits of an individual drug against the side effects it may produce. The example commonly cited here is that, because of a range of known side effects, common aspirin might have considerable difficulty being certified for use under the standards prevailing in the 1970s and 1980s. The safety and effectiveness of a drug must be demonstrated by clinical trials that are often time-consuming and expensive, and potentially important drugs are thereby delayed in coming to the public.

Critics of the drug industry point to other problems in drug regulation and in the pharmaceutical industry as a whole. For example, there are the problems of look-alike drugs and the use of brand names as opposed to generic drugs.[26] It is argued that a great deal of the attention in drug research is directed toward finding combinations of drugs that can be marketed under a brand name or in reproducing findings of already proven drugs so that they can be marketed with a different brand name. The brand-name drugs are invariably more expensive than generic drugs, and critics argue that the licensing of brand names actually aids the pharmaceutical industry by promoting the sale of higher-priced drugs. They also argue that drugs are sold and prescribed without adequate dissemination of information about the possible side effects of the drugs. Some states have intervened to reduce the problem of generic drug costs. These states now allow pharmacists to substitute a generic drug for a brand-name drug unless the physician specifically forbids such substitution. Many drugstores attempt to make their customers aware of this opportunity, so unless physicians believe that the generic drug would not be effective (some would argue for other, less noble reasons as well), citizens can get generic drugs.

A major attempt to modify drug regulations was made in 1979 in a Senate bill proposed by Senator Edward Kennedy. Among the most important issues in the proposed legislation was the shortening of the review periods required prior to marketing new drugs, especially so-called breakthrough drugs that offer great promise for serious illnesses and seem greatly superior to existing drugs. The proposed legislation also mandated that more information on drugs be disseminated to physicians and patients so that more informed decisions could be made about the drugs' use, and it attempted to limit certain drug-company promotion practices. Through skilled political management, the bill passed the Senate easily but did not pass the House of Representatives. The legislation represents, however, some possible directions for future drug regulation.

Associated with drug regulation in the Food and Drug Administration has been food regulation, especially the prohibition of carcinogenic substances in food. The Delaney Amendment requires the Food and Drug Administration to remove from the market foods containing any substance that "induces" cancer in human beings or animals. An issue developed over this amendment during the late 1970s in regard to the attempt to ban the sale of the artificial sweetener saccharin. In April 1977 studies in Canada showed that large amounts of saccharin tended to produce bladder cancer. Under the Delaney Amendment (passed in 1958), the FDA was then required to propose a ban on saccharin. The ban would have removed saccharin from the market as a general food additive but would have allowed its sales as an over-the-counter drug with a warning label. The proposed regulations aroused the interest of diabetics, the food and soft drink industries, and weight watchers, among others. The outcry was sufficient to cause Congress to pass a bill in 1977 delaying for eighteen months the removal of saccharin from the market, requiring the labeling of items containing saccharin, and demanding more testing of the effects of saccharin, both as a carcinogen and as an aid in weight control.

The studies during the eighteen-month period did not provide any conclusive evidence on the safety of saccharin, but they did point to possible changes in the regulation of possibly carcinogenic or otherwise harmful substances. The reports of the National Academy of Science recommended that the government, instead of prohibiting all such substances, establish categories of risk with attached regulations ranging from complete prohibition to warning labels to no action at all. It suggested also that such decisions take into consideration the possible benefits from the continued sale of the substance. Because many believed that saccharin was highly beneficial for some people and was only a low risk, they suggested that it be allowed to remain on sale. These risk-benefit or cost-benefit considerations are a common aid to decision making (see chapter 14) in the public sector, although they are perhaps less valid when applied to risks of the occurrence of a disease such as cancer. For whatever reasons, Congress reauthorized the continuing sale of saccharin.

SUMMARY

Regulation is a common and pervasive form of public intervention into the health-care industry. It is not without controversy, and almost all forms of regulation are under review and reconsideration. With the reelection of a Republican President and a Republican Senate in 1984, it is possible that there will be even more pressure for deregulation. The existing regulations may be replaced by competitive mechanisms using market forces to produce desired changes in the health-service industry or perhaps by no public attempts to control this industry at all.

The Pursuit of National Health Insurance

The United States is the only Western industrialized nation without a significant program of national health insurance or direct health-service delivery. As we have seen, this does not mean that the government has no role in medicine. In fact, approximately 14 percent of the American people depend on government for their health care. What the absence of national health insurance does mean is that citizens who do not fit into a particular category—for example, the aged, veterans, the medically indigent—must rely on private health care. With rising medical expenses and the ever-present possibility of catastrophic illnesses with equally catastrophic economic consequences, there have been pressures to extend the public role in medicine to the entire population.

The idea of a national health insurance program for the United States goes back at least to the Truman administration. When President Truman proposed a comprehensive national health insurance program in 1945 as a part of the Social Security program, it met with severe opposition from the American Medical Association and conservative business organizations, who called the plan "socialized medicine." The AMA spent millions of dollars in its campaign against national health insurance. The adoption of Medicare in 1965 represented a partial success for those who wanted a national health insurance program, but pressures continued for a plan that would insure the entire population. Interestingly, public opinion has also changed. Although the AMA's arguments against socialized medicine were persuasive in the 1940s and 1950s, by 1973 a majority of Americans polled favored some system of public health insurance.

Three basic forms of health insurance were proposed in the late 1970s. The most comprehensive was the Kennedy/Waxman plan, which was supported by organized labor. This plan relied heavily on existing insurance carriers such as Blue Cross-Blue Shield and did not suggest the establishment of separate publicly funded insurance. However, as the insurance was to be offered through employers, the elderly, unemployed, and some other citizens would be covered by publicly funded programs.

Although it would use private insurance carriers, the Kennedy program would differ from the status quo in several important ways. First, all citizens would be required to have medical insurance (in 1977 some 15 percent of the American population had no coverage for basic hospital room and board costs, and almost 30 percent had no major medical or catastrophic disease coverage). Also, the health insurance would have to be comprehensive; there would be no deductibles and no coinsurance provisions, so the insured would be able to use the insurance without additional charges. The costs of the insurance would be met by premiums from employers and employees (with employees being liable for up to 35 percent of the costs). Finally, there was an emphasis on cost containment in the program, which had several provisions. First, the annual health budget under the plan would have to be approved by Congress and would be planned to increase at the same rate as the gross national product. Second, the plan would use "prospective reimbursement" as a means of controlling hospital costs. Each hospital's budget would be set in advance each year, and the hospital would be at risk for any expenses over that budget. A National Health Board would review the costs and procedures being performed in hospitals and restrict them or refuse reimubursement if they did not conform to national standards.

The Carter administration also proposed a program of national health insurance, directed primarily at catastrophic coverage. It would have required coverage for catastrophic expenses for all Americans, and most citizens would have paid for some portion of their coverage. Individuals who lack "first dollar" coverage for medical expenses under a private insurance plan would be liable for $2500 in medical expenses each year, plus a portion of their medical insurance premiums. This deductible was intended to prevent the overuse of the medical-care system. The coverage of this insurance would be written by existing insurance companies, with employers absorbing most additional expenses. The cost-control provisions of the legislation were the Carter administration's plans for placing a "cap" of 9 percent on rising hospital costs.

Finally, the third proposal for national health insurance was made by a group of Republican senators and was directed at only the most catastrophic medical expenses. This plan would have covered medical expenses only after the sum of $5000 in medical expenses had been incurred and after sixty days of hospitalization had been required. This coverage would be provided by existing insurance companies and would be financed jointly by employers and employees with federal subsidies for smaller employers. Associated with this insurance program was a plan to improve coverage under Medicare, reducing the coinsurance and deductibles required under the present program. Little or no provision for cost control was built into this program, other than the requirement of the Medicare legislation that the program pay only "reasonable" costs for treatment.

The three major programs for national health insurance under consideration in the late 1970s were in some ways similar. They all depended on existing health insurance providers for most coverage. They all required the insured and the insured's employer to pay for part of the coverage. The programs obviously differ in the extent to which they ask government to involve itself in medicine. The Kennedy program is the most pervasive, both in terms of expenses covered and in the regulation of the delivery of medical services. The plan proposed by the Republican senators is a safety net for catastrophic illnesses and involves little or no additional regulatory intervention. And the Kennedy program has the strongest emphasis on cost containment, introducing the concept of prospective reimbursement on an extensive scale, whereas the Republican plan does little or nothing to attempt to control growing medical costs.

The Reagan administration and a Republican-dominated Senate have put any form of national health insurance on the political back burner. Nevertheless, public opinion polls still show concern about the availability and costs of medical care in the United States and support for some form of public involvement in meeting the health needs of the nation. Market-oriented solutions are receiving an even more thorough examination in the second Reagan administration, and if they fail, then political mobilization for a public role may be increased.

The Reagan Administration and Health Expenditures

In general, public expenditures for medical care have been reduced under the Reagan administration. In addition, the manner in which the money is made available to state and local governments has changed. In fiscal year 1984 the federal government spent approximately $13 billion less than was projected under the policies in place before that administration took office. More than half of the reduction in expenditures took place in programs such as health research and family planning, although some reductions did occur in Medicare and Medicaid funding.

In addition to reductions in federal money available for health services, the mechanism for delivering money to states and localities, which deliver the majority of the services, has changed. As a part of its general strategy for revitalizing federalism (or at least one version of federalism) the Reagan administration has rolled together a number of categorical grant programs into block grants. Unlike the categorical grants, all the block grants are channeled through the states, and the money contained in them is relatively fungible; that is, the states have a good deal of latitude in how they will spend the money. This allows state legislatures to make a number of allocative decisions about the use of federal money that they could not have made about the categorical grants. This raises the possibility that areas in dire need of the money—inner cities and poor rural districts—will lose out in the politics of state governments.

Summary

Changing and reforming policy is always difficult, and health is perhaps a particularly difficult field in which to produce change. Although restoring or encouraging competition in the medical-care industry is appealing as an ideal, there may be difficulties in implementing it. The health industry differs from other industries in important ways that may reduce the usefulness of competition as a remedy for its problems.

First, very little information on the price or quality of medical care is available to the consumer. Prices for health services are rarely advertised; frequently the consumer does not even consider them. In fact, in a perverse way, consumers might choose a higher-priced rather than a lower-priced service in the belief that the more expensive service will be superior. And, beyond hearsay, little information is available about the quality of services provided by individual physicians or hospitals.

In addition, the provision of health care is, in many ways, a monopoly or cartel. Entry into the marketplace for potential suppliers is limited by licensing requirements and further controlled by the professions themselves, which limit the number of places available in medical schools. Thus, unlike other industries, the health-care field makes it difficult for competition to develop among suppliers. One possible means of promoting competition would be to break down the monopoly held by the medical profession by giving nurse practitioners and other paraprofessionals greater opportunity to practice. The medical professions, however, rather vigorously resist such changes.

Bringing about any significant reforms in the delivery of health services in the United States will be difficult because of the powers of the professions and of large medical organizations such as hospitals. Their strongest incentives are in the direction of preserving the status quo, and with a control over the technology of medicine they are in a position to control the actual delivery of service. It may well be that only a large-scale program such as national health insurance will be sufficient to break the hold the professions have on medical care and to provide better and more equitable medicine to most Americans. Such a program should not be expected from an administration that is strongly committed to competition in health care.

Notes

1. Evidence is that most states have *not* replaced money lost from block grants. See George E. Peterson et al., *Block Grants* (Washington, D.C.: Urban Institute, 1984).

2. U.S. Bureau of the Census, *Demographic Estimates, 1982* (Washington, D.C.: Government Printing Office, 1982).

3. Lynn Poringer et al., *Health Status and Use of Medical Services: Evidence on the Poor, Black and Rural Elderly* (Washington, D.C.: Urban Institute, 1979).

4. Karen Davis, *National Health Insurance: Benefits, Costs and Consequences* (Washington, D.C.: Brookings Institution, 1975), 34-37; and *Source Book on Health Insurance Data, 1983-84* (Washington, D.C.: Health Insurance Association of America, 1984).

5. Rudolf Klein, *Politics of the National Health Service* (London: Longman, 1983).

6. American Medical Association, *Physician Distribution and Medical Licensure in the United States, 1978* (Chicago: American Medical Association, 1979); and Karen Davis and Diane Rowland, "Uninsured and Underserved: Inequities in Health Care in the United States," *Health and Society* 61, no. 2 (1983): 149-76.

7. Programs such as the National Health Service Corps have done little to equalize access to medical care.

8. Theodore Marmor et al., "The Politics of Medical Inflation," *Journal of Health Politics, Policy and Law,* Spring 1976, 69-84.

9. See Michael Zubkoff, *Health: A Victim or a Cause of Inflation* (New York: Milbank Memorial Fund, 1976), 3-6.

10. *Source Book of Health Insurance Data,* table 5.5.

11. Ivan Illich, *Medical Nemesis* (New York: Pantheon, 1972).

12. The issues have become even more prominent with the development of medical technologies such as artificial hearts. See "One Miracle, Many Doubts," *Time,* 10 December 1984, 70ff.

13. Karen Davis, "Equal Treatment and Unequal Benefits," *Milbank Memorial Fund Quarterly,* Fall 1975, 449-88.

14. Ibid.

15. Congressional Budget Office, *The Impact of PSROs on Health Care Costs* (Washington, D.C.: U.S. Congress, 1981); and Frank J. Thompson, *Health Policy and the Bureaucracy* (Cambridge, Mass.: MIT Press, 1981), 153-54.

16. *Health Policy: The Legislative Agenda* (Washington, D.C.: Congressional Quarterly Press, 1980), 80.

17. See Steven Jones, *Medical Mystery: The Training of Doctors in the United States* (New York: Norton, 1979).

18. Patricia Bauman, "The Formulation and Evolution of Health Maintenance Organization Policy, 1970-73," *Social Science and Medicine,* 1976, 129-42.

19. See ibid., 134-37, for the legislative history.

20. This conforms to the tendency of the Reagan administration to use vouchers and other means to create quasi markets where public or professional monopolies have existed. See pages 244-45 for education examples.

21. The CAT scanner, the most commonly cited example, is only one of a number of expensive technologies whose costs are amortized through increases in room prices and other charges. See Henry Aaron, *Painful Prescription* (Washington, D.C.: Brookings Institution, 1984).

22. Bruce Vladeck, "Interest Group Representation and the HSAs: Health Planning and Political Theory," *American Journal of Public Health,* 1977, 23-29.

23. Linda E. Demkovich, "When Medicare Tears Up the Blank Check, Who Will Lend Hospitals Capital?" *National Journal,* 21 January 1984, 113-16.

24. Ronald Greenspan, "Hospital Cost Control: Single-Edged Initiative for a Two-sided Problem," *Harvard Journal of Legislation,* 1978, 603-68.

25. Jane Stein, "The High Cost of Suing," *National Journal,* 25 February 1984, 382.

26. Henry J. Grabowski and John M. Vernon, *The Regulation of Pharmaceuticals: Balancing the Benefits and Risks* (Washington, D.C.: American Enterprise Institute, 1983).

10. Income Maintenance: Social Security and Welfare

The United States has frequently been described as a welfare state "laggard" because its levels of expenditures on social policies are low compared with those of other industrialized nations and because it has not adopted certain programs (e.g., a child benefit) that are common in other countries.[1] Although this is true, the gap between the United States and other Western democracies narrowed as American expenditures for social programs increased dramatically during the 1960s and 1970s. The increased level of expenditures reflected both new programs, especially during the Johnson administration's war on poverty, and increasing expenditures for established programs, particularly Social Security. U.S. social programs, broadly defined, in 1981 cost $319 billion and provided services to millions of clients. These expenditures accounted for 34 percent of all federal expenditures. The Reagan administration has reduced the rate at which social expenditures have expanded at the federal level. The amount spent on social programs in 1984 is at least as great as when that administration took office, although the amount is approximately 10-12 percent less than would have been spent under pre-1981 law. Despite their apparent vulnerability, some characteristics of social programs, especially social insurance programs like Social Security, make it difficult to cut them. Social programs are perhaps the major battleground for forces of the political right and left in the United States.

What are these social programs that cost so much and touch the lives of so many citizens? Leaving aside programs such as public housing, education (see chapter 11), and health care (see chapter 9), all of which have obvious social importance, we are left with a broad array of programs that provide an equally broad range of services and benefits. The largest programs, in terms of costs and numbers of beneficiaries, are the social insurance programs such as Social Security (pensions and disability), unemployment, and workmen's compensation (see table 10.1). Also significant in terms of expenditure are means-tested benefits such as Aid to Families with Dependent Children (AFDC—"welfare"),

TABLE 10.1

COSTS OF INCOME MAINTENANCE PROGRAMS, 1960–82

(in billions)

	1960	1970	1975	1980	1982	Percent Increase
Social Security	$11,032	29,686	$63,649	$117,118	$155,619	1,315
Unemployment	2,830	3,819	13,836	18,327	20,735	631
Public aid	3,609	4,864	15,166	20,001	22,019	510
Food stamps	0	577	4,694	9,083	11,989	1,978[c]
Public housing	177	702	3,172	7,209	9,511	5,274
Other[a]	6,591	19,660	37,694	73,151	92,500[b]	1,301
TOTAL	$24,239	$59,308	$138,211	$255,889	$312,373	1,188
Percentage of Public Expenditure	18.0	19.8	26.5	27.8	28.3	—
Percentage of GNP	4.8	6.0	8.9	9.3	10.2	—

a. Includes public employee retirement, workmen's compensation, and a number of other, smaller programs.
b. Estimated.
c. 1970-82.

food stamps, and Supplemental Security Income. These programs are available only to individuals who are willing to demonstrate that their earnings fall below the level of need designated by the program. Finally, there are the personal social services directed toward improving the quality of life for individuals through services such as counseling, adoption, foster care, and rehabilitation. These three major kinds of programs address different social needs and benefit different clients. Likewise, each has its own particular programs and political problems, which we address in this chapter.

Social Insurance

The largest single federal program is Social Security. Although generally thought of as providing pensions for retired workers, the program actually offers other protections to its clients. It provides benefits, for example, for the survivors of workers who die before retirement. Thus the program provides benefits for children of a deceased worker until they reach the age of eighteen, if they are not employed. The program also offers disability protection so that, if a worker becomes incapable of earning a living, he or she and any dependents can receive benefits. Finally, Medicare is linked with Social Security for financing purposes, as discussed in chapter 9. In addition to Social Security, there are two other significant social insurance programs in the United States. One, unemployment insurance, is managed by the states with a federal subsidy. The other, workmen's compensation, is managed by the states with employers bearing the major financial burden for the program.

Table 10.2 provides information on the recipients of social insurance benefits. By far the largest number of recipients were retired workers, although significant numbers of citizens received benefits under other social insurance programs. Likewise, the largest share of social insurance goes to retired persons, although the highest average benefit paid was for the unemployed, followed closely by disabled workers.

We must understand several important characteristics of social insurance programs, especially Social Security, if we are to comprehend the programs and the political debates that sometimes surround them.

First, social insurance programs do little to redistribute income across economic classes.[2] Rather, they redistribute income across time and across generations. Unlike a private annuity, in which an individual pays in money that accumulates in a personal account, Social Security is not an actuarially sound insurance program. Social Security is a direct transfer that taxes working people and their employers and pays out that money to program beneficiaries. The major purpose of Social Security is to distribute income across time; workers

TABLE IO.2

SOCIAL INSURANCE BENEFICIARIES,

1984

Program	N
Social Security	
Retired workers	25,412,000
Disabled workers	3,826,000
Survivors	7,119,000
Railroad retirement	
Workers	663,000
Survivors	316,000
Unemployment insurance	1,893,000
TOTAL	39,229,000

and their employers pay into the fund while employed, thereby reducing their income at that time, but receive benefits when they retire or if they become disabled; also, any surviving family members receive benefits if the worker dies.

Second, despite the absence of actuarial soundness, these programs are conceived as social insurance rather than government giveaway programs. Citizens regard themselves as purchasing an insurance policy by paying their payroll taxes during their working life. Defining the programs as social insurance has been crucial in legitimating them, as many citizens would not have been willing to accept a public pension to which they had not contributed, and most congressmen in 1935 (when the programs were enacted) would not have been willing to vote for the programs if they had not been defined as insurance. The insurance element is also important because of the contractual arrangement between the citizen and the government. More than any other public program, Social Security is an entitlement program; citizens believe themselves entitled to benefits and believe they have a legal and moral claim to receive those benefits.

The insurance nature of the programs also helps explain their financing. Social Security is financed by payroll contributions, paid equally by employers and employees.[3] These payroll taxes are paid, not on all earnings, but on only the first $42,000 (in 1986) of earnings each year. As shown in table 10.3, rates of tax and the threshold at which individuals stop paying taxes are expected to increase during the 1980s in order to pay for the rising costs of the program. Thus, instead of being a general tax, Social Security "contributions" are limited in much the same way that the premiums for a private insurance policy are fixed, although not all workers will pay the same amount for social insurance

TABLE 10.3
INCREASING RATES OF SOCIAL SECURITY TAXATION

| | Tax Rate | | On Earnings | Maximum |
	OASDI[a]	HI[b]	to ($)	Tax ($)
1960	3.00	NA	4,800	144
1965	3.625	0.35	4,800	174
1970	4.20	0.60	7,800	374
1975	4.95	0.90	14,100	825
1980	5.08	1.05	25,900	1,588
1981	5.35	1.30	29,700	1,975
1982	5.40	1.30	32,400	2,171
1983	5.40	1.30	35,700	2,392
1984	5.70	1.30	37,800	2,533
1985	5.70	1.35	39,600	2,792
1986	5.70	1.45	42,000	3,003

a. Old age, Survivors, and Disability Insurance.
b. Heatlh insurance (Medicare).

if they earn below the threshold. For the same reasons, the Social Security tax has been a flat-rate tax rather than one that progressively increases, like the income tax. Finally, Social Security is an earmarked tax: All the money collected is devoted to Social Security benefits, and only Social Security taxes are available for financing the benefits. The restrictiveness of the financial system makes the tax, and the program in general, more palatable to many citizens, but it also severely constrains the financial base for the program.

Another important element of the Social Security system is that it includes almost all working people. In 1980 about 90 percent of all employed Americans were covered by the program. This figure includes a large number of self-employed individuals, who pay a self-employment tax instead of having their contributions matched by an employer. The principal groups now excluded from the program are federal government employees hired before 1984, employees of many state and local governments, and some farm workers. Despite these exclusions, made for reasons of administrative convenience or because of the constitutional inability of the federal government to levy a tax on a state or local government, Social Security is a national program and perhaps more than any other program unites all citizens as participants in a single government program.

Finally, the benefits of the program are only partly related to earnings.[4] Those who pay more into the program during their working lifetime receive greater benefits when they retire, although those at the bottom of the income ladder receive a larger rate of return on their contributions and have a higher

TABLE 10.4

REPLACEMENT RATIOS OF EARNINGS IN SOCIAL SECURITY BY INCOME GROUPS

(in percent)

	Monthly Earnings					
	$100	$500	$1000	$1387	$1800	$2033
Worker alone	167	74	60	51	44	41
Worker with spouse (aged 65 +)	250	112	89	77	66	62

replacement of their earnings on retirement than do those with higher earnings (see table 10.4). Social Security is not intended to be a welfare program; at the same time it is slightly redistributive in that it attempts to ensure that those at the bottom of the earnings ladder have something approximating an adequate retirement income, although it is difficult to argue that anyone living entirely on Social Security, even at the full benefit level, really receives enough money to live on.

Problems in Social Security

Although the Social Security program is widely accepted and generally popular, a number of problems must be considered. These are generally policy issues that arise when the program is considered for renewal or modification.

THE RETIREMENT TEST

One problem is the retirement test—the penalty imposed on recipients of Social Security who wish to supplement their benefits by working. As the program is currently run, if a recipient earns a certain amount of money (excluding income from private retirement funds or investments), a penalty is imposed on the benefits paid to him or her. In 1986 a recipient of Social Security up to the age of sixty-four could earn $5760 a year and from age sixty-five to seventy could earn $7800 a year; above those amounts, the beneficiary would forfeit $1 in benefits for every $2 earned. This is, in effect, a 50 percent tax on earnings over the income allowed Social Security recipients, a tax rate that ordinarily would not be imposed on an individual who earned less than $80,000 a year in taxable income.[5]

There are several good reasons for removing or at least relaxing this retirement test. First, if the program is conceived of as social insurance rather than a means-tested benefit, then recipients should receive their benefits as a matter of right, much as would the recipient of a private annuity. The imposition of the retirement test in many ways gives the lie to the conception of Social Security as purely a social insurance program.

Additionally, the imposition of the retirement test may make the program more expensive and more of a donation from the young to the old. As it becomes unrewarding for retirees to work, they will stop working and cease paying Social Security taxes, whereas if they continued to work they could, in some ways, pay their own benefits through taxation. This means that those who are working—in other words, the younger generations—must bear a higher tax cost for the program than would otherwise be necessary. Finally, there are humane reasons for eliminating or modifying the retirement test. With the increase in life expectancy of American citizens, many individuals are capable of continuing to work after the usual retirement age. In a society that frequently defines an individual's worth on the basis of his or her work, retirement and the inability to work may impose severe psychological as well as economic burdens on the retiree. More flexible or unlimited earnings would allow Social Security recipients to participate in the labor market, perhaps not to the extent they did previously, and would permit a phasing out of work rather than a sudden and often traumatic retirement.

On the other side of the argument, we must realize that allowing retirees to continue working would have significant effects on other potential employees, especially those just entering the labor market. Every retiree who continues to work means one less job for a young person. And as unemployment among the young is already a significant public problem, the needs of the elderly must be balanced against the needs of younger people. Additionally, allowing the retiree to continue working while still receiving benefits would amount to a direct transfer of income from the young to the old, based simply on age.

FIXED RETIREMENT AGE

Related to the problem of the retirement test is the question of a fixed retirement age. Under existing laws, the standard retirement age is sixty-five. After this age, individuals receive little additional benefit for working under the Social Security system, although they have to continue to pay Social Security taxes. In addition, if individuals choose to retire before reaching sixty-five, even if they have been paying into the system for years, their benefits will be reduced. These rules provide a great incentive for workers to retire at the official age, and under this system all individuals are expected to retire at that age regardless of health or financial situation.

Good reasons can be found for both raising and lowering the retirement age. Some are based on reasons of cost containment in a system that is facing severe financial problems, and others are based on humane considerations. By raising the retirement age, the total costs of the program will be reduced, for people will not be living on the program as long. When Social Security was adopted in 1935, the life expectancy for males was less than sixty-five years, so relatively few men could expect to live on Social Security for long. In 1986, however, the average male worker lives to slightly over age seventy and can expect to be on the program for five years. Thus, on average, a retiree costs more today, and total program costs are increased. In addition, the health status, the nature of work, and the educational levels of workers have all been improving. As we approach the twenty-first century, the average retiree will be in better health, have a relatively nonstrenuous and more intellectually challenging job, and may simply not want to retire. Finally, the absence of private pension plans for some workers may mean that they cannot maintain their life styles if they retire.

On the other side of the argument are reasons to lower the retirement age. Many people who have retirement incomes in addition to Social Security may want to retire while they are still in good health and capable of enjoying some years of leisure. And at the systemic level the lowering of the retirement age may create job openings for unemployed youths. In addition, the availability of a flexible retirement age may make it easier to modernize the nation's work force. Workers with obsolete skills may move to Social Security more readily, and as a consequence some human costs of modernization and economic change may be reduced.

Clearly some policies for determining benefits and appropriate retirement ages will have to be retained, but there are good reasons for making this determination more flexible and for balancing a number of needs. This flexibility could benefit individuals as well as the economy and society as a whole.

THE TREATMENT OF WOMEN AND FAMILIES

A continuing issue is the treatment of women under the Social Security system. The system was designed in an era when the vast majority of women were housewives who did not work outside the home and who remained married to the same men for their entire lives. This would hardly describe the average woman today, and as a consequence the treatment of women under Social Security now appears outdated and blatantly discriminatory.

Several aspects of Social Security substantiate these claims. For example, if a woman is married to a covered employee for fewer than ten years (it was twenty years until the 1977 amendments were added), a divorce takes all the husband's benefits away from her, and for Social Security purposes it is as if they had never been married. And, as we have noted, the benefits an individual receives are roughly based on contributions so that, even if a woman returns to work or begins to work after the divorce, she will find it difficult to accumulate sufficient credits to earn a significant retirement benefit.

Also, if both husband and wife work, the pair receive little additional benefit, even though they may pay twice as much in Social Security contributions as a couple with only one covered worker. Benefits are based on each partner's individual work record, and there is no spousal benefit unless one worker (usually the wife) would receive more from a spousal benefit than from her (or his) own work record.

An even broader question arises as to whether a woman who chooses not to work outside the home should not in fact receive some Social Security protection based on her contributions to the household and to society through her work in the home. The idea of a "homemaker's credit" in Social Security has been advanced so that these women would have their own protection as a part of Social Security. This protection may be especially important for disability insurance, for if the wife should become disabled, especially with children still in the home, this would impose additional burdens on the rest of the family, who would have to do work she had once performed in the home. With the current financial pressures on Social Security, however, there is little likelihood of women's benefits being expanded; if anything, the treatment of women may be even less generous. For example, the Reagan administration has reduced extra spouses' benefits and surviving spouses' benefits over a number of years. The major beneficiaries of these spouses' benefits are women.

THE DISABILITY TEST

One important issue that arises under the disability insurance program is the "substantial gainful employment" test. The test, as administered, is rather harsh and requires that a person be totally disabled before he or she can receive benefits.[6] The individual must be disqualified from any "substantial gainful employment," if such employment is available in the geographical area of the potential beneficiary and if that applicant has the requisite skills. These standards are much more stringent than those applied in private disability programs, which require only the inability to engage in one's customary occupation, or for other public programs such as the Black Lung program. At present, fewer than 50 percent of all applicants for disability receive benefits.

The stringency of the disability test requires workers who have any disability to absent themselves from the work force entirely (the top limit of substantial gainful employment is $240 per year) and thereby attempt to receive disability benefits. A situation may well arise in which an individual is too unhealthy to earn an adequate income but too healthy to receive benefits under the disability program. For both social and financial reasons it would appear beneficial to have a more graduated disability test to assist those who have a partial disability but who wish to continue to be as productive in the labor market as they can. Such a test is already in use in the Veterans Administration, and it would seem possible to implement a similar arrangement for civilian disability benefits.

SOCIAL SECURITY AND THE ECONOMY

Social Security is also believed to affect the economy of the United States. The most commonly cited effect is the reduction of individual savings and the consequent absence of as much capital available for investment as would be available if there were no public insurance program. Because individuals know that their retirement will be partly financed by Social Security, they do not save as much during their working lives as they might otherwise. And because Social Security, as it is currently managed, does not itself accumulate large reserves but tends to be a direct intergenerational transfer program, there is an absence of capital accumulation. Estimates of the magnitude of savings lost as a result of the Social Security program vary widely, ranging from $3.6 billion to $38 billion in 1969, but there is some general agreement that this effect has been produced.[7]

The second major effect of Social Security on the economy is the lessened participation of older workers in the labor force. As noted, the retirement test and the fixing of a standard retirement age tend to provide disincentives for potential workers over sixty-five to continue working. As with the economic effect of reduced savings, it is difficult to estimate the magnitude of this effect, but several empirical studies have documented its existence.

Financing Social Security

We now come to the most frequently discussed question concerning Social Security: How can the program be financed? Periodically since the 1960s there have been reports that Social Security was going bankrupt, raising the specter that many elderly people would be left with no income from their contributions. In 1984 President Reagan said that he did not believe that those currently making contributions to the system would ever receive that much back in benefits.[8] Given the entitlement nature of the program, such dire outcomes are extremely unlikely. But the Social Security system as a program financed entirely by payroll taxes may be in severe difficulty, and the trust fund created to back the program will be in danger of being exhausted as the number of retirees increase relative to the number of workers.

There are several reasons for the financial difficulties of the Social Security program. The most obvious problem is the increasing number of aging Americans, a trend that began in the 1960s and is projected to continue if the birth rate continues to be low. In 1960 only 9 percent of the American population was over sixty-five. By 1984 that figure had increased to almost 12 percent, and it is expected to increase to almost 20 percent by 2025. Phrased differently, in 1984 each Social Security beneficiary was supported by the taxes of approximately three active workers. By 2025, each beneficiary will be supported by only 2.0 workers, and by 2040, by 1.8 active workers.[9] This obviously implies either an increasing burden on active workers or a modification of the existing financial structure of the program.

Another factor increasing the difficulties in financing Social Security has been the indexing of benefits to match increases in prices and wages. Under existing arrangements, the initial benefit levels paid retirees are adjusted annually to reflect changes in the average wages paid in the economy. In addition, in every twelve-month period during which prices increase more than 3 percent, benefits are adjusted so that retirees have approximately constant purchasing power from their pensions.

This indexing of benefits (a cost-of-living adjustment, or COLA, as it is sometimes called) is an obvious target for those seeking to control the costs of social programs. As Social Security faced one more crisis in 1983, legislation was passed that imposed a one-time delay of six months in the COLA. Another suggestion, by a group of economists at the usually moderate to liberal Brookings Institution, would be to eliminate the COLA in a year in which inflation was less than 5 percent; if inflation were greater than 5 percent, the correction would be the rate of inflation less 5 percent. Another suggestion would have the COLA pegged several percentage points lower than the rate of inflation.[10]

The reasons for attacking the indexing of benefits as a means of reducing some of the financial problems in Social Security are twofold. First, it is a relatively simple change to make. Second, it has the potential to save significant amounts of money.[11] For example, it is estimated that the six-month COLA delay in the 1983 legislation saved $40 billion from fiscal 1983-88. Similarly, pegging the COLA rate at two percentage points below the rate of inflation would save $52.9 billion from 1984-89. On the other hand, such measures may well be serious hardships on some of the elderly. One study has estimated that a COLA three percentage points below inflation would put over a million elderly below the official poverty line within several years; many wonder why the federal budget and the Social Security system have to be made solvent on the backs of the elderly.[12] Even President Reagan, who has been openly skeptical about the future of Social Security, agreed in July 1984 that even if inflation fell below the 3 percent figure, the COLA adjustment would still be made. Congress rapidly agreed with the President.

With the financial pressures on Social Security, there is a question whether the system can afford to continue financing itself entirely through payroll taxes.

There are also questions about the payroll tax, perhaps the most important being that the tax is basically regressive, exacting a higher percentage tax from low-paid workers than from the more affluent. This regressivity is the result of the threshold above which individuals earning additional income do not pay additional tax. In 1986 individuals paid a payroll tax of 7.15 percent on the first $42,000 of covered employment for a maximum tax of $3003; after that amount, they paid no more Social Security taxes. Thus, everyone who earns the threshold amount or less paid the same 7.15 percent of their income, while some earning $100,000 paid only 3 percent of their income as Social Security taxes. But because the system is conceptualized as providing insurance and not as providing benefits directly proportional to earnings, this disparity is justified; once you have paid your annual "premium" on the insurance policy, there is no need to pay more. The payroll tax for Social Security is regressive in another way as well. Most economists argue that workers actually bear the burden of the employers' contributions (the same 7.15 percent of salaries and wages up to the threshold) to Social Security. Employers count their contributions as part of the costs of employing a worker, and reduce wages accordingly.[13]

The payroll tax also has the disadvantage of being relatively visible to employees.[14] They see the amount of money deducted from each paycheck for Social Security, and they have some idea of how much money they are paying into the system. This in turn means that the level of payroll taxation may be limited by real or potential taxpayer resistance.

The earmarked payroll tax does have one advantage that some people believe is worth retaining. Because the receipts from this tax are relatively limited, politicians are prevented from using the Social Security system for political gains. That is, as general tax revenue does not go into the system, it is difficult for a President or the Congress to increase rates of benefits just before an election in order to attempt to win votes from the elderly. The COLA adjustment of benefits, however, may have some of the same effects, as in the 1984 election when benefits were improved just before the election.

Several proposals have been made to alleviate some of the financial problems of Social Security. One would be to remove the financing of Medicare from the payroll tax and finance that program through general revenues. This would give Social Security more money while retaining the existing rates of payroll taxation. Another mechanism, already mentioned, is to change the COLA adjustment and timing, although in a period of high inflation, such a change might work a considerable hardship on the elderly. We have also mentioned that raising the retirement age, or at least making it more flexible, is another possible solution to the costs of Social Security, as would be a reduction of some of the welfare-like benefits attached to the program (e.g., the spouses' benefits). One such minor benefit—the burial allowance—has in some cases already been eliminated.

These proposals represent rather minor tinkering with the program, but more significant modifications have been proposed. One would be to make the program truly comprehensive so that it would include all workers, even federal government employees. This would provide a larger financial base of workers who earn better-than-average incomes. This might also have certain psychological benefits: It would point out that the people who administer Social Security have sufficient confidence in the system to be a part of it.

Finally, others have suggested that we change the entire basis of Social Security financing from payroll contributions to general revenue, either through the income tax or through a value-added tax (VAT) like the one commonly used in Europe.[15] The VAT is a tax levied on businesses at each stage of the production process, based on the value that the business added to the raw materials it used to create the product it sells. The VAT has the advantage of being virtually invisible, its cost reflected only in the price of a product. It also has the advantage of being somewhat less regressive than the payroll tax, especially if some commodities (food, prescription drugs, etc.) are not taxed. The invisibility of the VAT would be an advantage for those managing the Social Security system, although many citizens might not regard it as such. The VAT would allow the income of the Social Security system to expand with less restraint than the present system of finances.

Social Security finance is likely to remain an important policy issue for years. The average age of the population continues to increase, and the costs of the program keep growing. In fact, these costs will probably increase more rapidly than will the yield from the payroll tax. Unfortunately for the managers of the program, the form of finance has become rather entrenched, and it may be difficult to modify without changing the insurance concept of the system and perhaps thereby reducing the general support for the program.

It has also been suggested that Social Security benefits should be counted as taxable income. The 1983 amendments to the Social Security Act permitted the taxation of benefits received by retirees with incomes at the higher end of the scale: $25,000 for individuals, $32,000 for a couple. Given that many of the elderly have very little income anyway (fewer than 10 percent were subject to the tax in 1984), and already find it difficult to exist on Social Security, such a program could produce substantial hardship if it was extended lower down the income ladder. But the passage of any provision to tax benefits indicates the perceived crisis in Social Security financing, and would in effect make Social Security a means-tested program.

Summary

Social Security is a large, complex, and expensive program. As a result, several important policy issues exist concerning its effects on citizens and on the economy. What is more fundamental, however, is that the program will persist, albeit in modified form. Some way must be found to finance the program so that it will provide an adequate or at least minimal income for pensioners without bankrupting the working-age population. Likewise, there are increasing demands that we remove some of the rigidities and discrimination from the system and make it more humane and responsive. The system, in all probability, will continue to be a major success story in public policy but one that will remain on the policymaking agenda.

Means-Tested Programs

The second major kind of social program is the means-tested program. To qualify for benefits under such a program an individual must satisfy a means test, or more accurately an absence-of-means test. Individuals cannot earn more than a specified amount or have any major assets if they are to qualify for a means-test program. Rather obviously, then, these programs benefit groups of people, defined by economic criteria, that are generally neither the most influential in society nor the easiest to mobilize politically. Also, the means testing involved in the program tends to stigmatize and to some extent degrade individuals who must apply for the benefits. And these programs are regarded as handouts or giveaways by many citizens, who also describe recipients of such benefits as "lazy welfare cheaters" and sing songs about "welfare Cadillacs." Racial issues are also involved in the management of means-tested benefits, for although the majority of welfare recipients are white, a disproportionate share of blacks and Hispanics receive welfare benefits.[16] These means-tested benefits—Aid to Families with Dependent Children (AFDC), food stamps, Supplemental Security Income, and a variety of other programs—are important to many citizens, and they raise several important political issues.

AFDC—Welfare

The largest means-tested program, and the one that generates the most political controversy, is AFDC, or "welfare." This program benefited more than 11 million Americans, including approximately 8 million children, in 1982. The program cost over $12 billion, or less than 1 percent of all public expenditures and 2 percent of all "social expenditures," broadly defined to include education. It is an expensive program, although perhaps not so expensive as some believe, and because the program provides benefits on the basis of need rather than contributions, it is a controversial program. It is especially interesting that the controversy over AFDC arose in the 1960s and 1970s rather than in the 1930s when it was adopted. The program was adopted as a part of the package that produced Social Security, but at that time the major controversy was over Social Security rather than AFDC.[17] It was assumed that AFDC would be used by a relatively small number of widows with children, rather than by women who were remarried, divorced, or separated. Social Security has now become an accepted part of American life, while AFDC is perceived as a problem by the taxpayers who fund the program and by recipients of the benefits.

To qualify for AFDC a woman must have children and virtually no income ($3200), and there must be no one living in the household who is capable of providing support for the children. Actually, some males also qualify for AFDC. Table 10.5 provides a profile of the recipients of AFDC payments. In 1981 fewer than 15 percent of the recipients were widows, wives of disabled men, or unemployed, those for whom the program was intended. Most recipients are now fatherless families; the largest single category is made up of families in which the mother and father are not married. The image of the "welfare mother" having illegitimate children in order to qualify for benefits is one that gives supporters of the program difficulties when they attempt to improve funding and benefits.

TABLE 10.5

CHARACTERISTICS OF AFDC RECIPIENTS

(in percent)

Race		Sex (of adults)		Age	
White	53	Male	13	Adults	31
Black	43	Female	87	Children	69
Other	4				

AFDC, though a national program, is administered by states and localities. Despite several attempts at reform and "nationalization" of the program, its administration is still decentralized. The federal government provides a small subsidy to the states for the program, with the remainder of the benefit coming from state and local funds. The benefits are not uniform across the nation and vary widely.

In 1983 the highest average monthly benefit for a family was $516 in Alaska, while the lowest was $89 in Mississippi; the average was $303 per month. None of the levels of benefits is particularly munificent, and substantial differences exist, even taking into account differences in the cost of living in the various localities.

Problems with AFDC

As mentioned, both taxpayers and the recipients of AFDC see problems in the program. Naturally, these problems are rarely the same, although to some extent they may be different ways of saying the same thing about certain aspects of the program.

MEANS TESTING

Programs that require recipients to prove that they are indigent create problems for the recipients, who become stigmatized, especially in a society that places a high value on success and income as symbols of personal worth. Most recipients are relatively powerless anyway, and the stigma attached to being on programs such as AFDC tends to lessen their feelings of self-worth and power, which in turn may help to perpetuate the problems that caused them to go on AFDC in the first place. Unfortunately, the program as designed tends to perpetuate indigence rather than allow people to work their way out of poverty.

PUNISHMENT FOR WORKING

As a part of the means testing of the program, individuals who attempt to work their way out of poverty are severely penalized. An individual can work no more than 100 hours per month, no matter what rate of pay is received. After a certain amount is earned each year (the sum varies by state), the AFDC recipient is required to return $2 in benefits for every $3 earned. This is in effect a tax higher than *any* income tax rate in the regular income tax system. Rather obviously, such a high rate of "tax" on earnings provides little incentive for individuals to work their way out of poverty. And given the relatively poor job skills of the typical AFDC recipient, along with the obvious problems of working when there are small children at home, the program presents a strong disincentive even to try hard. Thus, once people go on AFDC they find it difficult to get off, and the system perpetuates itself and poverty. In addition, because other benefits, such as food stamps and Medicaid, may be tied to receiving AFDC, going out to take a job may mean the loss of a great deal more than the AFDC check. Finally, if an individual on "welfare" takes a job and then leaves that job, it may take several weeks or months to get back on the program, with the associated difficulties in supporting a family.

FAMILY STRUCTURE

The AFDC program also has severe effects on family structure. As noted, a woman with children cannot receive benefits if an ablebodied male lives in the home. This means that the traditional family—husband, wife, and children—is not eligible for AFDC. This requirement makes it more difficult for a woman on AFDC to work, since she must either care for the children herself or find suitable day-care facilities. It may also have a deleterious effect on children, who grow up in a fatherless household. Especially for male children, such an arrangement has been shown to produce difficulties in adjustment in later life. These problems in the program may be lessening, however, as single-parent families become more common in the United States.

COSTS AND BENEFITS

Depending on whom you ask, the benefits of AFDC are either too high or too low. Those concerned about the costs of the program argue that the generous benefits encourage people to stay on welfare rather than find a job, and they simply do not want to pay taxes so that other people can refuse to work.

On the other side of the argument, most recipients of AFDC benefits would point out that even the highest average monthly state benefit of $516 is hardly sufficient for a life of leisure and that the average benefit across the country is only $303. They would argue that in fact the benefits are too low to provide a decent living for the recipients and their children. These children inherit poverty along with substandard housing, low-quality education, and a poor diet.

Alternatives to AFDC

With all the problems associated with AFDC, why is the program maintained? Perhaps because of inertia and general resistance to reform. It can also be argued that although they may oppose the program in principle, conservatives have been major obstacles to change because the existing, rather punitive program is a means of regulating the poor and ensuring that their lives are so impoverished that they want to get off AFDC. There are alternatives to the existing program, some of which have been seriously proposed in the United States and some of which are in operation in Europe. These programs might provide benefits for poor citizens without the stigma or the administrative complexity of the existing program.

FAMILY ALLOWANCES

One alternative, in operation in virtually all other democratic, industrialized societies, is the family allowance.[18] Under this program all families are given a monthly benefit check from the government. For the more affluent, this is simply taxable income, while for the poor it is the major source of income. But the most important aspect of the program is that it includes everyone, or at least all households with children. The stigma is therefore removed, and the program is substantially easier to administer than AFDC. The level of benefit for each child would have to be sufficient to match the current level of AFDC benefit, which would mean that a great deal of money would have to pass through the public sector as taxes and expenditures, but the effects would perhaps justify that decision, given the current difficulties with AFDC.

THE NEGATIVE INCOME TAX

A second alternative to AFDC is the negative income tax.[19] Under such an arrangement, a minimal level of income would be determined, based on family size. Each family would then file its tax statement, with those earning below the established minimal level receiving a rebate or subsidy, while those above that minimal level would pay taxes much as usual. Such a program would establish a guaranteed annual income for all citizens and would be administratively simpler than AFDC. The recipients themselves would provide a good deal of the information necessary to calculate benefits, instead of having to rely on numerous state and local welfare offices. In addition, this would establish equality in benefits across the United States, with perhaps some adjustments for different costs of living in different parts of the country. The negative income tax, as usually proposed, also makes it somewhat easier to work one's way out of poverty because it imposes only one-third or one-half reduction of benefits for any money earned, so even the working poor would benefit from the program.

The negative income tax was seriously proposed for the United States. Interestingly, President Nixon's 1969 proposal for a family assistance plan was much like a negative income tax.[20] If this program had been enacted, it would certainly have been the most sweeping reform of the welfare system ever made. The program was not adopted by Congress, however. It was defeated by a coalition of liberals, who thought its benefits were too meager, and of conservatives, who were ideologically opposed to the concept of a guaranteed minimum income. In addition, social workers and other professionals felt their jobs threatened by a program that placed the major burden of proving eligibility on the individual citizen.

WORKFARE

One proposal that has been partially implemented by the Reagan administration is referred to as "workfare." The idea here is that those receiving welfare benefits should be made to work for the benefits. This typically means that the participants have to work enough hours to "earn" their benefits if paid at the minimum wage; they also receive a small allowance to cover the costs of going to work. This usually means working in some sort of public-service capacity (e.g., picking up trash in the parks). Such a program, while emphasizing the traditional work ethic, may further stigmatize AFDC recipients and is based on a preconception of malingering by the recipients. To the extent that it may be a substitute for real public-service jobs it may have the effect of substituting pay at well below minimum wage for at least the minimum wage. In addition, implementing "workfare" would actually *increase* welfare costs, as the costs of finding jobs and administering the program would increase and the participants would have to be paid a daily expense allowance.[21]

FULL EMPLOYMENT

Perhaps the simplest means of eliminating many of the problems of AFDC is to guarantee jobs rather than benefits. The federal government has been involved in several programs of job training and subsidized employment, the most prominent being the Comprehensive Employment and Training Act (CETA) in the 1970s and early 1980s. The purpose of CETA was to enable people to acquire job skills by working with local private contractors and then to subsidize the employment of those trainees for several years until they had improved their productivity sufficiently to be able to earn a decent wage in the labor market. Although CETA continued in operation until 1981, it was severely criticized on several grounds—using inefficient and corrupt prime contractors, for example, and training people to do nonexistent jobs. Some charge that the CETA program placed too many trainees in the public rather than the private sector. Critics say this swelled the size of many local governments and created problems when the trainees' eligibility expired after the local governments had become dependent on their relatively cheap labor.

An even more far-ranging proposal to use employment as an alternative to welfare or unemployment benefits was the Humphrey-Hawkins bill, named for the late Senator Hubert Humphrey and Congressman Augustus F. Hawkins. The idea behind the bill was that the government should renew the pledge of full employment it made in 1946, and the federal government should become the employer of last resort for any person who wanted a job. It was argued that the money ordinarily spent for benefits could be better used to provide jobs for the same people. On the other side of the political fence, the specter of make-work jobs was raised, along with the argument that once they had been employed by the government, these workers would never find their way into private jobs and that both a permanent obligation and a slowdown in economic growth would result. In the end, despite active support from the AFL-CIO, the Humphrey-Hawkins bill was soundly defeated, although it does still represent one option for handling the problem of poverty in the United States.

THE WAR ON POVERTY

Finally, we come to the Johnson administration's war on poverty. During the administration of John F. Kennedy, poverty was "rediscovered" in the United

States and became a popular political issue, especially among liberals. With Kennedy's death, Lyndon Johnson used his formidable political talents and the memory of John Kennedy to create a series of legislative proposals to attempt to break the cycle of poverty, which, as we have seen, tends to be perpetuated by most existing social programs. The war on poverty differed from other social programs of the time in that it was less directed toward the short-term amelioration of deprivations than toward changing long-standing patterns and conditions of the very poor.[22] War-on-poverty programs did more than just hand out money, although they certainly did a good deal of that, by attempting to attack the cultural and social conditions associated with poverty. The programs also sought to involve the poor in the design and implementation of the programs more directly than had the more paternalistic programs common at the time.

The umbrella organization for the programs of the war on poverty was the Office of Economic Opportunity, created as a separate agency outside the Department of Health, Education, and Welfare. It was feared that the bureaucratic nature of HEW and its commitment to social insurance programs would hinder the activism envisioned for the war on poverty, and consequently an independent organization was established.

One of the aims of the war on poverty was to attack poverty by educating the children of the poor to a level at which they could compete in school and in the economy. One of the most popular programs for children was Head Start, which attempted to prepare poor children to compete with other children when they entered school. The program tried to provide the skills that middle-class children generally have when they enter kindergarten but that children from economically deprived households frequently lack. But despite the popularity of Head Start, its demonstrable effects were rather modest. Children who participated in the program were indeed better prepared to enter kindergarten than children who had not been in the program, but their lead rapidly vanished, and after several years the Head Start children were not significantly different from children who had not participated in the program.[23] Of course, depending on one's point of view, this could be an argument that the program had failed or that it needed much more follow-up after the children reached elementary school.

The war on poverty also provided programs such as the Neighborhood Youth Corps and the Job Corps to attempt to prepare older children for jobs, or at least to provide temporary employment in public-service jobs. Additionally, a college work-study program was initiated to try to make it possible for students from low-income families to attend college, a program that has been expanded and continues after the demise of the war on poverty.

For adults, the war on poverty initiated a variety of programs primarily intended to provide employment or to prepare people from poor households for productive employment. These programs commonly involved cooperation between the federal government and either state and local governments or private businesses. In addition to the employment-related projects, many of the smaller programs provided counseling, loans for small businesses, family planning, and a whole range of other social services. In general, the war on poverty provided something for almost everyone who needed and wanted work or help.

By the early 1980s most of the programs of the war on poverty had been dismantled, reduced, or modified. What happened? Several events reduced the emphasis that government originally placed on the programs. One was the escalation of the Vietnam war to the point that it diverted both attention and money from domestic programs, especially those lacking a solid political base and an institutionalized bureaucracy. Also, the goals of the war on poverty were so lofty, and perhaps so unrealistic, that it was easy for critics to point out that the programs had not been successful and to question the reasons for continuing to fund them.

On the other hand, it would be difficult to say that many of the programs were really seriously tried. So many programs were started that some were funded only as pilot programs and others, such as Head Start, may have lacked the funds to pursue their goals to a successful achievement. And to say that a set of programs intended to change generations of poverty and deprivation could actually work miracles in a few years is unrealistic, so the "trial" given the programs may not have been a fair trial at all. Finally, with the election of Richard Nixon as President in 1968 the political climate that had spawned the programs changed, and since the impetus for the programs had so clearly been presidential, Congress had few strong advocates to defend the war-on-poverty programs.

But were the programs of the war on poverty, and the whole war itself, a massive failure or at best a noble experiment? As pointed out, it may be that instead of failing, they were never really tried. These programs did represent a major departure from the traditional means of attempting to solve, or at least ameliorate, the problems of poverty in the United States, and their impact may actually be more enduring than short-term evaluations indicate. Certainly the need to address the problems of poverty in the midst of affluence remains as pressing in 1986 as in 1965 when the programs were initiated. Whether it is to be through jobs in the private sector or through public programs, 30 million Americans are living beneath the poverty line and are waiting to be brought into the economic mainstream of American life.

The Persistence of Poverty in the United States

We began our discussion of agenda setting with a discussion of the impact of Michael Harrington's book *The Other America* on the development of a poverty program in the United States. Despite the attention brought to the problem and programs such as the war on poverty, the problem of poverty continues. In fact, poverty in the mid-1980s is actually *greater* than in the mid-1960s when the war on poverty was beginning. Poverty had been declining during the 1960s and 1970s (see table 10.6) but began to increase again under the Reagan administration. Further, the poverty rate is not uniform across the population, with female-headed households, blacks, and children being particularly likely to live in poverty. On the other hand, the poverty rate for the elderly has improved substantially over the decades since poverty became an issue; that rate is now less than half what it was in 1966, despite a growing elderly population. It seems that, in general, the social policies of the Reagan administration have forced more people to live in poverty than would have been true under the continuation of the social policies existing earlier.

TABLE 10.6
CHANGES IN POVERTY RATE, 1965-83[a]

	1965	1966	1970	1975	1980	1983
Total	17.3	14.7	12.6	12.3	13.0	15.2
Blacks	NA	41.8	33.5	31.3	32.5	32.7
Children under 6 years	NA	18.1	16.6	18.2	20.3	25.0
Female-headed households	NA	39.8	38.1	37.5	36.7	40.2
Over age 65	NA	28.5	24.5	15.3	15.7	14.1

SOURCE: *National Journal,* 8 September 1984, 1650.

a. Proportion of population living below official poverty rate.

Poverty is a symbolic issue, but it is also a matter of counting. How do we know who is poor and who is not? The official definition of poverty for 1983 was a family of four living on an income of $10,178 or less; adjustments are made for family size, urban versus rural areas, and so on. This definition does not include as income noncash public benefits, such as food stamps, Medicare or Medicaid, and housing subsidies. Because of the availability of those benefits and the relationship of poverty status for eligibility for other public programs, conservative economists have argued for a change in the definition of poverty. Such a change in the definition would show that many fewer people

TABLE 10.7
ALTERNATIVE DEFINITIONS OF POVERTY

	1979	1980	1981	1982	1983
Current	11.7	13.0	14.0	15.0	15.2
Market-value approach[a]	6.8	7.9	9.0	10.0	10.2
Recipient-value approach[b]	9.0	10.4	11.7	12.7	13.0
Poverty budget share approach[c]	9.1	10.4	11.5	12.5	12.9

SOURCE: *National Journal*, 18 August 1984, 1564.

a. Estimated value of in-kind benefits in the marketplace.
b. Estimated cash value that recipients would exchange for the benefits.
c. Based on Census Bureau estimate of value of benefits relative to consumption patterns of poor families.

were in poverty (see table 10.7) and would thereby benefit an administration that has consistently argued that their policies have not harmed the poor. In addition, such a change in definition might have the effect of a "reverse Harrington"; if the problem is defined out of existence, it may be easy to eliminate it from the public agenda.

Personal Social Services

The final category of social service programs delivered by the public sector receives less attention than either Social Security or AFDC, largely because these programs cost much less and deliver benefits that do not depend on either age or income. The term "personal social services" applies to a range of services, such as adoption, foster care, suicide prevention, counseling, and the like, that are definitely not for the poor alone. In fact, some services, such as adoption, are used primarily by middle-class families. Eligibility for most personal social services is determined by citizenship or by definition of need based on attributes other than lack of income rather than by means testing. Again, unlike many other social services, personal social services — adoptions, for example — are viewed positively and carry no stigma. Even for services that are not so positively regarded (e.g., suicide prevention or alcoholism counseling), there is greater sympathy for the client or victim than for the poor person who must accept AFDC benefits.

Personal social services, more so than even AFDC, are dominated by professional social workers. As a consequence, these programs can seem formidable to the uneducated potential client. It may, in fact, be virtually impossible for the poor or the poorly educated to use these programs. This in turn may mean that economic benefits may have to be provided when more personal counseling might have been sufficient. Then, in terms of a policy analysis, there may be a situation in which too much of one service (AFDC or other means-tested benefits) is being provided.

Summary

The social services are composed of a large number of rather diverse programs. What holds them together is an overriding concern with individual needs and conditions, some economic and some personal. The programs that have been tried and that are still in operation represent attempts on the part of government to improve the conditions of its citizens, although the programs in operation by no means represent entirely satisfactory solutions to the problems. This chapter pointed to some ways of modifying existing programs, as well as some more sweeping changes in program structure that may benefit both government and program clients. The problems will not go away; if anything, the mid- and late 1980s will bring increasing demands for services, especially for the elderly. What must be found is a means of providing adequate benefits through a humane mechanism that will not bankrupt the taxpayers. This is no easy task, but it is one that policymakers must address.

Notes

1. Harold L. Wilensky, *The Welfare State and Equality* (Berkeley: University of California Press, 1975), 32-36.

2. Donald O. Parsons and Douglas R. Munro, "Intergenerational Transfers in Social Security," in *The Crisis in Social Security,* ed. Michael J. Boskin (San Francisco: Institute for Contemporary Studies, 1977), 65-86.

3. The self-employed pay a higher rate that is almost the combined sum of the employee and the employer.

4. Alicia H. Munnell, *The Future of Social Security* (Washington, D.C.: Brookings Institution, 1977), 26-30.

5. Income from other sources (e.g., investments) does *not* reduce benefits.

6. Deborah Stone, *The Disabled State* (Philadelphia: Temple University Press, 1985).

7. Martin Feldstein, "Social Security, Induced Retirement, and Aggregate Capital Accumulation," *Journal of Political Economy,* September 1974, 905-26; and Alicia H. Munnell, *The Effect of Social Security on Personal Savings* (Cambridge, Mass.: Ballinger, 1976), 68-96.

8. Later in the campaign the President pledged to preserve and even strengthen the program.

9. Social Security Board of Trustees, *1982 Annual Report of the Board of Trustees of the Federal Old-Age and Survivors Insurance and Disability Insurance Trust Funds* (Washington, D.C.: April 1982).

10. Linda E. Demkovich, "Budget Cutters Think the Unthinkable — Social Security Cuts Would Stem Red Ink," *National Journal,* 23 June 1984.

11. Ibid.

12. Ibid.

13. See George F. Break, "The Economic Effects of Social Security Financing," in *Social Security Financing,* ed. Felicity Skidmore (Cambridge, Mass.: MIT Press, 1981), 45-80.

14. Harold L. Wilensky, *The New Corporatism: Centralization and the Welfare State* (Beverly Hills, Calif.: Sage, 1976).

15. Charles E. McClure, "VAT Versus the Payroll Tax," in Skidmore, *Social Security Financing,* 129-63.

16. U.S. Bureau of the Census, *Statistical Abstract of the United States, 1980* (Washington, D.C.: Government Printing Office, 1981), table 573.

17. Edwin W. Witte, *The Development of the Social Security Act* (Madison: University of Wisconsin Press, 1962), 5-39.

18. Anne Cordem, David Piachaud, and Jonathan Bradshaw, "How Europe Meets Family Costs," *New Society,* 23 October 1980, 159-61.

19. Laurence E. Lynn, Jr., and David deF. Whitman, *The President as Policymaker: Jimmy Carter and Welfare Reform* (Philadelphia: Temple University Press, 1981).

20. M. Kenneth Bowler, *The Nixon Guaranteed Income Proposal: Substance and Process in Policy Change* (Cambridge, Mass.: Ballinger, 1974).

21. U.S. General Accounting Office, *Workfare Programs,* GAO/PEMD-84-2, 2 April 1984.

22. Andrew W. Dobelstein, *Politics, Economics and Public Welfare* (Englewood Cliffs, N.J.: Prentice-Hall, 1980), 182-86.

23. Sar A. Levitan, *The Great Society's Poor Law: A New Approach to Poverty* (Baltimore: Johns Hopkins University Press, 1969).

11. Educational Policy in the United States

Education has traditionally had a central position in American public policies. Although we as a nation have been slow to adopt other social programs—pensions, unemployment insurance, health programs, and the like—we have always been among the world leaders in public education. It is true that most public involvement in education has been at the state and local levels and that the federal government has become directly involved in elementary and secondary education only recently.

The public role in education began very early in the United States, with the state of New York adopting free public education in 1834. And education was made compulsory until a student reached a certain age (this provision was temporarily revoked in some southern states as a means of avoiding integration). But the federal role in education should not be discounted. The Northwest Ordinance of 1787, in planning the organization of the Northwest Territories of the United States, divided the land into townships and the townships into sections. One of the sixteen sections in every township was to be set aside for supporting free common education. And in 1862 Congress passed the Morrill Act, granting land and a continuing appropriation of federal funds to establish and maintain in each state a college dedicated to teaching "agriculture and mechanical arts." From this act grew the system of land-grant colleges from which have grown such major educational institutions as Cornell and the Universities of Wisconsin, Illinois, and Minnesota. The research and extension activities of these institutions have also been important for the expansion of American agricultural productivity.

There have been several other important trends in American education and educational policy. First, the emphasis on education is indicative of the general attitude the United States has taken toward social mobility and social change, the belief that education is important in giving people "chances not checks."[1] The prevailing ethos is that government should attempt to create equal opportunity through education rather than equal outcomes through social expenditure programs. Individuals who have the ability are presumed to be able to better their circumstances through education and to succeed no matter what their backgrounds may have been. It is perhaps important to note here that, despite the evil of segregation, blacks in the South prior to *Brown* v. *Board of Education* were given access to public schools and public educational opportunities through the Ph.D. degree. One cannot realistically argue that the opportunities were equal, but education was more easily available than might be expected, given the social status of blacks in those states. The norms of educational opportunity covered even social groups that were systematically discriminated against.

Related to this is the importance of American public schools for social integration and assimilation. The United States has absorbed a huge number of immigrants, 8 million of whom arrived in the first decade of the twentieth century alone. The institution that was most important in bringing those new arrivals into the mainstream of American life was the public school system. This was certainly true for adults who learned English and civics in "Americanism" classes in the evenings. Also important in this regard is that the public schools in the United States traditionally taught all the children in a community. Only a very few wealthy families sent their children to private schools; everyone else in the community went to the same school, often all the way through their elementary and secondary years. The tradition of comprehensive schools that provided a variety of educational opportunities, from college preparatory through vocational, was important in reinforcing the ideology of a classless society and in at least promoting social homogeneity, if not achieving it.

But despite the centrality of public education, there has never been a state monopoly on education at the elementary and secondary levels. Existing alongside the state schools were religious schools (almost 10 percent of the elementary students in the United States in 1983 attended parochial schools) and other private schools. This diversity is especially evident in postsecondary education, with 24 percent of all college students in 1983 attending private institutions.[2] Almost anyone can open a school, provided it meets the standards set by government. If anything, the diversity in American education has been increasing over the past several decades.

Finally, the emphasis has always been on local and parental control in American education. Of all the major social functions of government, education is the one clearly retaining the greatest degree of local control and local funding. In fact, the largest single category of public employment in the United States is made up of public school teachers that are employed by local governments. And the control that government exercises over education is often local. There are 14,851 local school boards in the United States, almost as many

as the 22,000 counties and cities. And there have been pressures for even greater local control and parental involvement. These pressures have come from white
suburbanites and several other segments of society, all of whom think that the
public schools should be doing things differently. Although the local school
has traditionally been a positive symbol of local government and the community, there are now a number of doubts about education and pressures for change.
I discuss the perceived problems and the proposed reforms later in this chapter.

The Federal Government's Role in Education

It does not make a great deal of sense to discuss the public role in education,
since most education is public, but it is important to describe something of
the role of the federal government. The involvement of the federal government
in education has become controversial, and it was thought that the Reagan
administration might further reduce the federal involvement. Mr. Reagan's first
secretary of education, Terrell Bell, came into office pledging to dismantle the
newly created Department of Education. But the need for improved education
and educational funding became more apparent as the four years of the first
Reagan administration progressed, and not only was the Department of Education saved but some new initiatives to try to improve American education were
launched under its sponsorship.

We should discuss one aspect of local control in education because it influences some of the need for federal involvement. This is the funding of public
education through the local property tax, the traditional means of financing
education, which in the 1970s and 1980s has presented two significant problems. One is that property-tax revenues have not generally kept pace with inflation (see table 11.1). The administration of the property tax involves assessing
the value of property and applying some rate of tax to the assessed value. In
an inflationary period, assessments may not reflect the real value of the property, and certainly not the costs of goods and services, unless revaluation is
done very frequently. Thus, many local school boards find that their funding
is no longer adequate. Even if there were no inflation, the tax base available
to some school districts would be markedly different from that available to
others. To provide the same quality of education, parents living in poorer districts would have to tax themselves at higher rates than would those living in
more affluent areas. This is extremely regressive, as the poor have to pay a higher rate of tax to provide the same service. What usually happens is that the
education provided to poorer children is not as good as that provided to the
wealthier students. Thus, it is argued that the local property tax is an inequi-
table means of financing education and that some alternative, such as federal

TABLE II.I
PROPERTY-TAX REVENUES

	Local Property Tax (current prices; in millions)	Local Property Tax (constant prices; in millions)
1942	$4,273	$13,695.5
1952	8,282	17,509.5
1962	18,414	30,137.5
1972	41,620	41,620.0
1977	60,267	41,194.1
1981	72,020	34,725.1
1982	78,805	35,760.7

SOURCE: *Facts and Figures on Government Finance, 1983* (Washington, D.C.: Tax Foundation); *Statistical Abstract of the United States, 1985* (Washington, D.C.: Government Printing Office).

or state general revenues, should be used to equalize access to education. As I discuss later, the court system has already begun to bring about some changes in this direction, but the inadequacy of local taxation remains an important reason for federal involvement in education.

Higher Education

It has traditionally been more acceptable for the federal government to be involved with higher education—perhaps because the students are almost adults and are assumed to have formed their basic value systems before the central government could influence them, or perhaps simply because of the higher per student expense. At any rate, the federal government began somewhat earlier to assist institutions of higher education than elementary schools.

We have mentioned that during the Lincoln administration the federal government initiated the land-grant college system that continues to receive substantial federal support, especially for its agricultural extension activities. The federal government also runs several institutions of higher education of its own—the service academies, Gallaudet College (for the deaf), and Howard University. In addition to the direct funding of almost eighty colleges and universities, the federal government provides indirect support for almost every college in the United States.

The major form of indirect subsidy for colleges and universities is the funding of individual students. These funding programs obviously benefit students directly, but without the federal funds many students could not attend college and many colleges might have closed. A variety of federal programs can aid students. The largest is the GI Bill, enabling veterans of World War II, Korea, and, to a lesser extent, Vietnam to attend college with the government paying virtually all the costs. For nonveterans, one of the largest programs of student aid was also justified as a defense program—the National Defense Education Act. Passed in 1958 just after the Soviet Union launched Sputnik, this act was intended to help the United States catch up in science, although students in the social sciences and foreign languages benefited as well. Federal assistance reached beyond defense-related concerns during the 1960s and 1970s. The college work-study program was adopted as a part of the war on poverty but was moved from the Office of Economic Opportunity to the Office of Education. Likewise, the Education Amendments of 1972 instituted something approaching a minimum income for college students. The Basic Educational Opportunity Grant (or Pell grants), the centerpiece of the program, gave students $1800 minus what the student's family could be expected to contribute, a figure later increased slightly to account for inflation. While this is not much money if the student wants to attend Harvard or Yale, it does provide the means to attend at least some institution of higher education. Finally, the federal government also guarantees student loans and even provides some student loans. The guaranteed loans are particularly important because they allow government to use a great deal of private money as leverage for higher education with minimal direct outlays. The federal government agrees to guarantee a private lending institution that the money that institution lends a student will be repaid even if the student reneges. In turn, the money is offered at a lower interest rate than would otherwise be available.

All these programs benefit primarily students entering college just out of high school. One federal program, however, benefits more mature students. The provisions of the income tax code that provide students deductions if they go to school to maintain or improve their job skills support a variety of trade and technical schools as well as academic institutions. This tax expenditure for education amounted to over $300 million in 1983, and although the university never sees the money, this program stimulates attendance, especially among a segment of the population that might not otherwise attend college.

Finally, the federal government supports higher education in other ways— for example, by providing assistance to facilities through the Higher Education Facilities Act of 1963 and to dormitories through the Department of Housing and Urban Development. Federal research money also helps institutions of higher education meet both direct and indirect costs and offers specialized grant programs for such fields as public service and urban studies. In short, the federal government is central to the maintenance of higher education. But the large amounts of federal money invested in higher education also give the federal government a substantial amount of control over the policies of the universities. This has been manifested primarily through controls over the hiring of women and members of minority groups. In the *Grove City College* case, however, the Supreme Court diminished the influence of the federal government to some degree in ensuring greater equality in higher education programs. Before that decision, if a college was found to be discriminating, all its federal money could be withdrawn. In their 1984 ruling the Court found that only money directly supporting the activity in which the discrimination occurred could be withdrawn. So, for example, if discrimination was found in the programs covered by Title IX (athletics and student activities), the government could not withdraw money from student support or federal research grants. Given the conservative policies of the Reagan administration, it is unlikely that such discrimination will be pursued vigorously either by the Department of Education or the Department of Justice.

The Reagan administration has cut back on support for higher education. The base level of the Pell grant was cut by $80 and the income restrictions were tightened. This resulted in approximately 100,000 fewer Pell grant recipients in 1983 than in 1981. There was also a drop of some 460,000 in the number of new guaranteed student loans. There have also been attempts to cut back federal funding of social science and humanities research through cuts in the budgets of the National Science Foundation and the National Endowment for the Humanities.

Elementary and Secondary Education

The role of the federal government in secondary and elementary education has been less significant historically and is less significant today than its involvement in higher education. However, there is definitely a federal role. Other than the planning provisions of the Northwest Ordinance, the first involvement of the federal government in elementary and secondary education resulted from the passage of the Smith-Hughes Act (1917), which made funds available for vocational education. In the 1930s surplus commodities and money were provided to school districts for hot lunch programs, with those programs expanded during the war on poverty to include breakfasts for children from poor families. Then the Lanham Act of 1940 made federal funds available to schools in "federally impacted areas," meaning areas with large numbers of government employees and especially areas in which tax-exempt government properties reduced the tax base. In 1958 the National Defense Education Act authorized funds to improve science, mathematics, and foreign language teaching in the elementary and secondary schools as well as at the college level.

The major involvement of the federal government in elementary and secondary education currently is through the Elementary and Secondary Education Act of 1965. This act was the culmination of efforts of a number of education and labor groups to secure more extensive federal funding for education.[3] This legislation passed along with a number of other social and educational programs during the Johnson administration, and like so much of that legislation, it could not have been passed without the substantial legislative skills of Lyndon Johnson and the memory of John Kennedy. But before it could become law, legislators had to remove the barriers that had blocked previous attempts at federal aid to education.

One of these barriers was the general belief that education should be controlled locally. The federal aid that had already been given to schools had been peripheral to the principal teaching functions of the schools—the exception being the National Defense Education Act—in the belief that such aid could not influence what was taught in the classroom. The Elementary and Secondary Education Act (ESEA) involved direct, general subsidies for education, and it was feared that this would influence what was taught. However, as the federal government was already becoming increasingly involved in many aspects of education and social life through other mechanisms, such as the courts, this fear of federal control diminished.

Another issue that arose with respect to federal subsidies to education was the question of funds for parochial schools. Such aid involved constitutional questions about the separation of church and state. Most Protestant groups opposed aid to parochial schools as a violation of that separation, while Catholic groups opposed any aid program that did not provide assistance to parochial schools. ESEA funds eventually went to parochial as well as public schools, although the money cannot be spent for the teaching of religious subjects. The legislation specified that the money was to go to the students, not to the schools, which helped defuse any significant criticism based on separation of church and state.

Also, federal aid to education encountered opposition prior to the 1965 act because of the possibility that the money might be used by segregated school systems in the South. The passage of the Civil Rights Act of 1964 had already prohibited the use of federal funds in any program that discriminated on the basis of race. This meant that this issue was largely decided by the time the 1965 legislation was considered. On the other side, southern school systems had been afraid that federal subsidies would be used to enforce desegregation, using a carrot rather than a stick. However, these schools were under pressure from the courts to desegregate anyway, and so the acceptance of ESEA money was be a minor additional step toward eventual desegregation.

The 1965 ESEA legislation was passed as a component of the war on poverty, but it provided assistance to almost all school districts in the United States. Only 5 percent of all school districts received no ESEA money. The legislation provided funds for such purposes as hiring teachers' aides, stocking libraries, purchasing audiovisual materials, and developing compensatory programs. The basic intention of the program was to enable students from poor families to perform better in school and to learn to compete more effectively in the labor market.

Federal funds from ESEA were allocated to the states according to a formula, as is true of a number of federal programs, the most important of which is general revenue sharing. The formula adopted for ESEA in 1965 allocated each state federal funds equal to one-half of its annual per pupil educational expenditure multiplied by the number of low-income children. These funds were to be used for remedial programs (Title 1) and to purchase materials, but the principal policymaking and programming were to come from the federal government rather than from the local school boards. The 1965 formula aided the high-income states more than the low-income states, as it was based on the amount of money already being spent. This formula quickly came under attack and was amended in 1967 to provide greater assistance to the poorer states. Under the 1967 formula a state could receive half of its own per pupil expenditures or half of the mean national per pupil expenditure, whichever was higher. Also, the definition of low-income students was eased so that school districts could claim more students and receive more federal funding. These 1967 amendments had the effect of equalizing funding between richer and poorer states and of producing rapid increases in ESEA expenditures.

During the Nixon administration the categorical nature of the funds allocated through ESEA came under attack, as a part of the "new federalism."[4] Efforts to convert ESEA funding into another of the block grants that characterized that administration's approach to federal grants did not succeed, however, and the federal government retained nominal control over the ways in which money was to be spent. What did change was the formula for computing aid.

In 1974 a new formula was adopted that put both rich and poor states at a disadvantage, as measured by their per pupil expenditures. It narrowed the range of allowable per pupil grant funds from 80 to 120 percent of the national mean. In other words, the very wealthy states could claim only 120 percent of the national average per low-income pupil when computing aid, while the very poor states could claim only 80 percent of the national average (and not the national average). And instead of receiving 50 percent of the per pupil figure, the states could receive only 40 percent. These changes reduced the amount a state would probably receive from ESEA funding, although amendments to the legislation did specify that no state would receive less than 85 percent of what it had received under the previous formula.

As with so many public programs, the implementation was crucial to the success of the ESEA programs. And in many ways ESEA represents a classic example of a program being modified through implementation. The U.S. Office of Education, which was charged with implementing ESEA, was quite passive in ensuring the attainment of the stated goal of the program: the equalization of educational opportunity for economically deprived children. The tendency of those who implemented the program at the state and local levels was to pork-barrel the funds and to spread them around among all school districts regardless of the concentration of low-income students. As a result, wealthier suburban school districts used ESEA funds to purchase expensive "frills," while many inner-city and rural school districts still lacked basic materials and programs that might compensate for the backgrounds of the pupils.[5] This initial failure in implementation resulted in part from the close ties between the U.S. Office of Education and local school districts and in part from the misinterpretation of the intention of Congress, which had established the program, not as general assistance to education, but strictly as a compensatory program. With some changes in the Office of Education and greater concern about the use of the funds, the implementation of ESEA has been improved, although a number of questions remain about the ways in which the funds are being used. The Title I money, or that portion of the program that is most directly compensatory, is now targeted more clearly on the poorer districts, but the money available under other provisions of the act is still widely distributed and used by much wealthier schools and school districts to supplement their programs.

The Reagan administration has returned federal aid to education to a more compensatory focus. The Education Consolidation and Improvement Act (ECIA) of 1981 supports compensatory education for deprived students in virtually all school districts but is concentrated in school districts with the most poor children. This act also supports education for the handicapped, adult education, and aid for school districts heavily impacted by federal installations with large numbers of children to be educated. ECIA now accounts for about 80 percent of federal aid to elementary and secondary education, with the remainder primarily in a block grant to state and local governments for educational purposes.

Has all this federal aid to education really improved the quality of American education? There is some evidence that ESEA Title I reading programs were successful in raising the reading levels of low-income students.[6] Further, to the extent that additional funding can aid education in any number of ways, some of which are difficult to quantify, these programs have certainly produced benefits. It is ironic, however, that in spite of all the federal money being directed at improving the quality of education ($7 billion in 1984), the issue of the quality of American education is more prominent in the 1980s than at any time since the launching of *Sputnik I* in 1957.

Issues in Educational Policy

Even with the victory of those who wished to obtain federal funding for elementary and secondary education, a number of problems remain in public education, and some new ones are arising. In general, the public schools and their teachers have lost some of the respect with which they were traditionally regarded, and educational policy has been the subject of more heated discussion than was true during most of our history. In fact, it is not uncommon for politicians or analysts in the 1980s to charge that the public schools have failed and to call for significant change. Some would counter this argument by pointing out that it is perhaps not so much that the schools have failed but that too much has been demanded of them and that the schools cannot be expected to solve all of society's problems. These analysts would argue that the resources and tasks given the schools have not been equal and that too much has been expected for too little. Several specific issues illustrate both sides of this argument, but what may be most important is that education, which has been regarded as one of the great success stories of American public policy, is no longer considered quite that successful.

The Quality of Education

One common complaint against the schools that has continued since the 1950s is that "Johnny can't read"—that is, that the schools are failing in their fundamental task of teaching basic skills such as reading, writing, and computation. In addition to reading, this criticism has extended to progressive teaching techniques like the "new math." Substantial evidence that would appear to support this point includes the continuing decline of SAT scores since the early 1960s. It should be noted, however, that an increasing proportion of high school students were taking the SATs in the early 1980s, so the reduction in scores may reflect to some degree simply a number of students not intending to go to college but being required to take the test. Test scores in 1983 showed a modest upward turn after almost two decades of steady decline.

The complaint about the schools' failure to teach basic skills can be contrasted to the complaints of another group of critics who regard the existing educational system as excessively rigid and stultifying. These critics believe that public schools destroy the innate creativity of children; they would prefer more "open" education with fewer rigid requirements and greater emphasis on creativity and expression. Others believe that the public schools are excessively rigid in teaching a single class or racial perception of the world, instead of providing a broader perspective on the human experience.

While these complaints seem worlds apart, they have in common a desire to modify the existing composition of education offered in the public schools. One way to respond to these complaints is to decentralize the school system. This is in the tradition of local control over education but merely alters the definition of what the appropriate local area is. In New York City the conflict between parents in Ocean Hill-Brownsville and the city's public schools represented one of the most explosive events of this movement, but for most problems in public education decentralization may not be the answer.[7]

A more common policy option proposed to the problem of quality education is the use of educational vouchers.[8] The voucher plan would give each parent a "check" equal to some amount of money but good only for education. The parents could spend that voucher either in the public schools, where it would pay the entire cost of the child's education, or at some other school where the voucher might not cover the entire cost and the parents would have to spend some of their own money. Under the voucher plan, parents would have a significantly greater control over the kind of education their children would receive: They could choose an open school, a fundamental school stressing basic skills and discipline, a religiously oriented school, or any other school that met state standards.

Although the voucher plan is appealing as a means of improving choice in education and thereby improving education, a number of questions have been raised. Perhaps the most fundamental question about the voucher plan is whether it would increase stratification in education; one of the fundamental virtues and goals of American education has, after all, been social homogeneity and integration. If a voucher plan did not cover the full price of a child's education, many low-income parents would not be able to make up the difference between the value of the voucher and the tuition of private schools, especially the better private schools. The voucher plan might subsidize middle-class parents and not improve the quality of education for the poor, who need that improvement the most. In fact, the plan might well undo the racial integration that resulted from years of effort and policymaking. All these questions are reinforced by the Coleman report and other studies of education pointing out that the home background of children is crucial to educational success.[9] A voucher plan would tend to benefit children who would probably succeed anyway, and it would divert funds from children who need the most help.

Also, although the educational vouchers could be used only for schools that met established state standards, there are still questions about the propriety of spending public money for education over which the state has no control and about the possibility that the voucher system might actually lower the quality of education. It is not entirely clear where the capital—both human and physical—required to implement the system would come from. As a consequence, a full-scale voucher plan might result in the formation of a number of small and inadequate schools, none of them providing the quality of education that could be offered by a large, comprehensive public school.

Finally, the idea of the voucher plan is justified by the market ideology. Some analysts think that the introduction of competition into the education marketplace will improve the quality of education by increasing the choices available to consumers and by placing competitive pressures for improvement on existing public schools. For this education marketplace to function effectively, however, the consumer must have access to information about the "product" being produced. This may be difficult if a number of new schools are started in response to a voucher plan. After all, even in established systems of public and private education, it is difficult to assess quality, especially since much of the difference in educational success of students is accounted for by family backgrounds, and much of the effect of education may not be evident until far in the future.

Related to the voucher plan have been schemes to provide "tuition tax credits" for parents sending their children to private schools. These credits have been actively supported by the Reagan administration as a means of providing better education and education in line with the "cultural and moral values" of the parents. The credits would provide tax credits of 50 percent of tuition paid to a private school (up to some maximum amount). The political arguments, and educational arguments, for tuition tax credits are similar to those for vouchers. They would promote greater pluralism in education and allow parents greater choice. In addition, as many minority students have been shown to perform better in private (especially Catholic) schools, such a program could be of substantial benefit to minorities.

Those opposed to tuition tax credits, such as the National Education Association and the American Federation of Teachers (AFL-CIO), argue that these tax credits will only undermine public education and create a two-class educational system. Even though some minority students seem to do better in private schools, their parents must still have the means of paying anything over the $500 (or other) credit, so the students who benefit will be middle-class students, who may not need the benefit. Finally, programs such as this which would tend to benefit parochial and other religiously based schools and raise the question of the separation of church and state.

Thus, while few educators or policy analysts would claim that education is currently what most citizens want it to be, it is not entirely clear that a voucher plan would improve it all that much. The benefits of the voucher plan may be as much psychological as real: It would offer parents more choices and allow them more control over their children's education. However, the effects on the quality of education may be difficult to provide or discern.

Another means of addressing issues of educational quality is competency testing.[10] This plan is intended to address the claim that students are being promoted who have not mastered the material required at each grade level, that they are being promoted simply to get them through the school system, and that students who cannot read and write are graduating from high school. Competency testing would require a student to pass a test on basic educational skills — reading, writing, and computation — before being awarded a high school diploma. This program is intended to ensure that at least minimal standards of quality are enforced. Advocates of competency testing also argued that it would provide more incentives for students to learn and for teachers to teach.

The program has been attacked as racist, however, as a disproportionate share of the students who fail the tests in states where such programs are in operation (most notably Florida) are nonwhite. These tests, now being challenged in the courts, are claimed to be biased against nonwhites because the tests employ standard English and are based on values and concepts that are in keeping with white middle-class thinking. The tests are, at best, a minimal demonstration of educational quality. They are, however, indicative of the concern over the poor quality of education being offered some students.

The Reagan administration became alarmed about the problem of low-quality public education and offered a number of possible solutions. The two most commonly discussed were improving discipline in schools and improving the quality of instruction by improving teachers' salaries. Both proposals certainly have merit, but they also have problems. It has been argued that the schools are incapable of enforcing disciplinary standards without strong parental support and that students who present problems in school may have similar problems at home. Likewise, although it seems that higher teachers' salaries might attract better teachers to elementary and secondary education, local school districts lack adequate funds to provide such improved salaries, and the federal government, strapped with a huge deficit and with an ideological commitment to reduce federal involvement in the economy and society, might be unwilling to supply the funds. In addition, such an effort may take years to produce any tangible results. It takes at least four years to train a new teacher, plus some years of experience before that individual reaches his or her full potential. This concern about the quality of education must also be judged within the context of reductions in the amount of money available for education (e.g.,

20 percent reductions in compensatory education programs) and shifts away from need-based and compensatory programs.[11]

The Separation of Church and State
The First Amendment to the Constitution of the United States forbids the establishment of a religion and ensures the free exercise of religion. In public education, these two clauses have caused a number of controversies about education and government's role in education. The two clauses may, in fact, be interpreted as being in conflict. For example, if schools require a prayer, this is deemed an establishment of religion (*Engle* v. *Vitale,* 370 US. 421 [1962]). On the other hand, prohibiting prayer is seen by some as a limitation on the free exercise of religion.

Issues of church and state in education arise over two areas. The first is the school prayer issue. Since 1962, when the Supreme Court outlawed official school prayer, there have been attempts on the part of religious groups to have prayer returned to the schools, either through a constitutional amendment permitting prayer or through mechanisms such as silent meditation and voluntary attendance at prayers. The issue of prayer in school resurfaced in 1984 when a Reagan administration proposal directed at improving the quality of American education contained a provision allowing local school boards to permit a moment of silent meditation at the beginning of the school day. It is far from clear whether that proposal will be declared constitutional by the Supreme Court.

If the Supreme Court follows the election returns, the justices are likely to side with President Reagan and his fundamentalist supporters. Large majorities of the American population have expressed opinions in favor of prayer in schools. As with many other issues, elite groups tend to be more sensitive to the civil liberties issues involved in school prayer, and attempts at passing a school-prayer amendment in Congress have been killed, although usually by procedural mechanisms rather than by a vote that would make it clear to constituents how congressmen felt about the issue.

The second area of controversy concerning the separation of church and state is public support for religious schools. In deciding this issue, the Supreme Court has been forced to make a number of difficult decisions, but over the years it has been tending to allow greater public support for religious education. For example, in 1930 the Court upheld the right of states to provide textbooks to children in parochial schools on the same basis as books are provided to students in public schools.[12] In 1947 the Court upheld bus transportation for parochial school students at public expense. Both rulings were upheld on the grounds that these expenditures benefited the *students,* not the church.[13] On the other hand, in 1971 the Court struck down a Pennsylvania law that had the state pay a part of parochial school teachers' salaries, arguing that this was of direct benefit to the church and created excessive entanglement between church and state.[14] In a somewhat contradictory fashion, the Court in 1976 upheld general grants of public money to church-affiliated *colleges*. The reasoning behind all these decisions may seem tortuous, but two principles stand out. The first is that aid to students and their families is more acceptable than aid to institutions. Second, institutions of higher education are permitted more entanglement between church and state than are elementary schools.

Unionization and Management

The image of the American "schoolmarm" is ingrained in the popular mind. Leaving aside any sexist notions about all elementary and secondary school-teachers being female, the point here is that the image of the teacher has been a positive one. The image was that of a person dedicated to education and to students, even in the face of adverse circumstances. The teacher and the school were considered integral parts of the American community.

The image of the teacher is now changing, partly because of increasing unionization and a growing number of teachers' strikes. No longer the representatives of culture and learning in small towns, teachers are now more likely to be employed by large school districts and to be members of an organization that bargains collectively for improved wages and benefits. One of the two major teachers' organizations is the American Federation of Teachers, affiliated with the AFL-CIO. This organization is clearly a union and has been quite willing to employ the strike weapon in its dealings with school districts. The second major teachers' organization, the National Education Association, is a professional organization, but its local chapters operate as collective bargaining units. The NEA has been more reluctant to use the strike to gain its ends, although certainly a number of its local chapters have struck. As of 1980 approximately 70 percent of the teachers in the United States were members of these organizations or of local teachers' unions. In 1980 there were 225 strikes by public school teachers. The sight of teachers picketing and of children out of school until October and even November has changed the once-positive image of the teacher.

In addition to forcing parents to make arrangement for their children during strikes, the increasing labor unrest in education has other, more important consequences. We have mentioned that many Americans think that the quality of American education is not as high as it should be. The sight of educators on strike tends to erode their image even further. Of course, those who favor the more militant actions by teachers quite rightly point out that good teachers will not work for the salaries they are sometimes offered, but there are still important problems of symbolism and image when teachers go on the picket line.

Equalization of Resources

As mentioned earlier in this chapter, most public education is financed by local property taxes, and this basis of finance can produce substantial inequities in education. Local school districts with poor resource bases must either tax their poorer constituents more heavily or, more commonly, provide inferior education. And as poorer school districts frequently have concentrations of minority group families, this form of finance also affects racial and cultural integration and fairness.

The use of the local property tax to finance schools has been challenged successfully in the courts. In two cases the courts have entered this policy area, but they have not provided any definitive answers to the questions involved. In *Serrano* v. *Priest* (1971), the California Supreme Court ruled that the great disparity between richer and poorer school districts in the Los Angeles area violated provisions of both the state and the federal constitution. In particular, this disparity constituted a denial of equal protection for the residents of the poorer district. The court did not, however, make any direct recommendations on how this disparity could be ameliorated to meet constitutional standards. One common assumption was that the state might have to either take over educational finance entirely or alter the formula for distributing state equalization payments.

In a similar case, *San Antonio School District* v. *Rodriquez* (1973), the U.S. Supreme Court ruled that the differences between two school districts in Texas were not so great as to constitute a violation of the equal protection clause. The Court did not say how much of a difference would constitute such a violation. This leaves the constitutionality of the continuation of these disparities between school districts up in the air, but the problems of local school districts' attempting to provide decent education with low taxable property remain quite tangible. The states have a variety of mechanisms for equalizing the access to funding, and ESEA money can also be used. Disparities persist, however, and many children receive substandard education because of the neighborhood in which their parents happen to live.

Desegregation and Busing

Finally, we come to the question of desegregation and busing. The important educational question here is whether the school system can be expected to solve all of society's problems or whether it should concentrate more narrowly on educational considerations. This question is frequently raised with respect to desegregation, particularly in regard to busing. The argument is that little is being done to change the underlying causes of segregation, especially segregated housing, and that the only institution in society that encounters such stringent requirements for desegregation is the public school system. Frequently busing affects popular support for education. The decline of public education after desegregation becomes a self-fulfilling prophecy as white parents remove their children from the integrated school and send them to private school.

On the other side of the argument is the central importance of education in the formation of children's attitudes. Desegregation may benefit black children by improving not only the quality of their education but also their own self-image. It may also be important in reducing the isolation of white children from black children. Social integration has traditionally been one purpose of American public education, and it may be important to continue to serve that purpose through desegregation.

These issues can be, and have been, debated at length, but the issue of busing has become so emotionally charged that rational discourse is frequently impossible. The connection between educational quality and racial equality is an important one that must be pursued in both areas of policy. Education is too central to the formation of the social fabric of the United States to be allowed to become isolated from other social concerns. However, education also may be too important in a highly technological society to be torn apart in an attempt to solve other social problems.

Summary

Education has been and remains a central concern of Americn public policy. While traditionally a concern of state and local government, it is becoming increasingly influenced by federal policy But while education has been an important and highly respected public function, it is currently under attack. The quality of education, the competence of school personnel, and the place of education in social change are all topics of vital concern to many Americans. Several policy instruments have been proposed to attempt to rectify the perceived difficulties in these areas, the most commonly discussed being the voucher plan, but few statements on educational policy have gained wide acceptance. This is in part a result of the absence of a widely accepted theory of causation in education. Unlike health or science policy, educational policy is a subject about which reasonable people often disagree radically. Voucher plans are intended in part to allow people to make individual choices concerning education without having to pay too great an economic price. The role of government as the funding agent for these programs, however, may require greater attention to the real benefits of certain forms of education and a decision about just how far the use of vouchers can be allowed to extend. This is a task for rational policy analysts who recognize that such an analysis must be subjected to serious political and social scrutiny. This is especially true because education is an issue about which almost everyone has an opinion; and because the students involved are the children of those people, there will be controversy.

Notes

1. Richard Hofferbert, "Race, Space and the American Policy Paradox" (paper presented at the 1980 convention of the Southern Political Science Association).

2. U.S. Bureau of the Census, *Statistical Abstract of the United States, 1980* (Washington, D.C.: Government Printing Office, 1981), tables 254, 273.

3. Norman C. Thomas, *Education in National Politics* (New York: McKay, 1975).

4. Michael D. Reagan, *The New Federalism* (New York: Oxford University Press, 1972).

5. Jerome T. Murphy, "Title I of ESEA: The Politics of Implementing Federal Educational Reform," *Harvard Education Review,* February 1971, 35-63.

6. *Title I of ESEA: Is It Helping Poor Children?* (Washington, D.C.: NAACP Legal Defense Fund, 1969).

7. Mario Fantini and Marilyn Gittell, *Decentralization: Achieving Reform* (New York: Praeger, 1973), 53-55.

8. R.F. Butts, "Educational Vouchers: The Private Pursuit of the Public Purse," *Phil Delta Kappan,* September 1979, 7-9.

9. James S. Coleman et al., *Equality of Educational Opportunity* (Washington, D.C.: Government Printing Office, 1966). Coleman has since modified his views in directions that are less favorable to the busing that his report helped to initiate.

10. D.M. Lewis, "Certifying Functional Literacy: Competency Testing and the Implications for Due Process and Equal Educational Opportunity," *Journal of Law and Education,* April 1979, 145-83.

11. John L. Palmer and Isabel V. Sawhill, eds., *The Reagan Record* (Washington, D.C.: Urban Institute, 1984), 364-65.

12. *Cochran v. Board of Education,* 281 U.S. 370.

13. *Everson v. Board of Education,* 330 U.S. 1.

14. *Roemer v. Maryland,* 415 U.S. 382.

12. Energy and the Environment

In the latter half of the twentieth century the United States faces two significant problems that affect the relationship between its economy and the physical world. One is a demand for energy that has become virtually insatiable. The other is the need to manage the effluents of an industrialized society and to preserve the natural environment. These two problems interact in several ways. The high consumption of energy, especially the use of fossil fuels, produces huge quantities of pollution, and the shortage and high prices of petroleum and natural gas place pressures on industries to burn cheaper coal, at the cost of even higher levels of pollution. And some regulations issued by the Environmental Protection Agency to reduce pollution (e.g., emission controls on automobiles) have tended to use more energy. Both issues are also directly linked with problems in the American economy. Uncertainty about energy supplies and rising energy prices makes investment decisions more difficult and contributes to inflation. Likewise, environmental controls make economic projects more expensive and in some cases impossible. This chapter examines energy and environmental problems, the responses of governments to these problems, and some possible alternative policies.

Energy: Problems and Policies

Energy is a crucial component of the American way of life. We are accustomed to using, and squandering, energy to a degree unimaginable even in other industrialized societies. The large American automobile, now a dying if not extinct species, was a symbol of that attitude toward energy usage, as is the single person driving an automobile to work each day. The United States uses 23 percent of all the energy used in the world. This country uses 98 percent more energy per capita than does Sweden and 10 percent more per capita than does Canada. (Both countries have standards of living similar to that of the United States.)[1] While energy usage is related to industrialization and higher standards of living, the United States uses much more than is required to maintain the comfortable standard of living to which most citizens have been accustomed.

Until the 1970s, energy was not perceived as a problem for the United States. The OPEC (Organization of Petroleum Exporting Countries) embargo on exports of oil to the United States in 1973 demonstrated the dependence of the United States on imported oil.[2] The rapidly escalating price of oil that resulted from OPEC price-fixing, restricted production, and then a second embargo emphasized even more the dependence of the United States on foreign oil to supplement relatively large quantities of domestic oil, natural gas, and coal. On the basis of the experiences of the 1970s, it is clear that we need seriously to examine the energy policies of the United States and probably to alter some of those policies.

Energy Sources
In spite of the importance of foreign petroleum and the American love affair with the automobile, petroleum is not the only kind of energy used in the United States, and others could be more highly developed. Oil is, however, the major energy source for the United States, accounting for 43 percent of all energy consumed in 1983, a percentage that has tended to increase annually. Approximately 30 percent of our oil is imported. A little simple arithmetic reveals that approximately 13 percent of the total U.S. energy supply is imported oil.[3] Again, the total amount of oil we import has been increasing as domestic supplies have become more difficult to extract and as demands have continued to increase.

This reliance on imported oil produces a number of problems for the United States. First, it makes energy supplies for the United States extremely uncertain and places the American economy in the position of a hostage of foreign powers. Second, the money we pay for foreign oil goes out of the United States and is difficult to match with exports. The U.S. balance of payments has been negative during most of the 1970s and the 1980s, and this has negative consequences for the domestic economy (see chapter 8). Finally, oil is a finite resource, and proven reserves of oil are sufficient only for a limited number of years at current rates of consumption. This means that eventually the American economy will have to convert to some other form of energy, and a continued reliance on foreign oil may only delay the hard economic and social choices we will have to make when this particular energy resource is depleted.

NATURAL GAS
The United States has been more blessed with natural gas than with petroleum. Currently, almost all our natural gas comes from domestic sources. Natural gas is also a limited resource, though, with something between thirty-five and sixty years' worth of proven reserves available at current and predicted rates

of consumption.[4] Therefore, natural gas does not constitute a long-term alternative for the United States. In addition, natural gas is so valuable for its industrial uses—in the fabrication of plastics and synthetic fibers, for example—that it may be inefficient to use it to heat buildings and cook meals.

Alternatives to domestically produced natural gas include importing gas in liquid form from Algeria or the Soviet Union. This would extend the availability of natural gas supplies but would present the same problems that imported oil presents. In addition, the technology involved in transporting liquid natural gas is such that massive explosions can occur if great care is not exercised. Given the difficulties encountered with oil spills, the development of a new technology that may produce even greater difficulties simply to preserve an energy supply for a relatively short period may not be acceptable.

COAL

America's most abundant energy resource is coal. The United States has enough coal to last approximately 200 years, and it exports substantial quantities of coal to Japan and to parts of Europe. In addition to supplying relatively cheap energy, coal can be used for industrial purposes, as is natural gas. If coal was developed more fully, the demand for natural gas and petroleum might be reduced.

Coal has several disadvantages as an energy resource, however. First, there is the environmental problem. Coal does not burn as cleanly as does oil or natural gas, and a good deal of our coal is rather high in sulfur. When this coal is burned, it forms sulfur dioxide (SO_2), which then combines with water to form sulfuric acid (H_2SO_4). This is a major source of the "acid rain" that has threatened forests and wildlife in the northern United States and Canada. Also, the extraction of coal presents environmental difficulties, since much coal is most efficiently extracted by strip mining. This method may deeply scar the landscape and render land unusable for years. Improved methods for reclaiming strip-mined land have been developed, but the recovery of the land still takes time, and the original natural landscape is lost forever. In addition, no technology exists for using coal to power automobiles or trucks. The "synfuels" project that was one component of President Carter's energy plan was intended to find a way to extract a liquid fuel from coal, but at present no such technology exists.[5] Thus, coal can be used to generate electricity and heat, but not for transportation, which accounts for 26 percent of energy use in the United States. The development of other technologies (e.g., improved storage batteries and the electric car) may help, but at present the usefulness of coal is limited.

Finally, there are massive logistical problems in using coal as a major energy source. Coal is more difficult to transport than petroleum or natural gas, which are readily movable through pipelines. At present, American railroads do not have sufficient rolling stock and roadbeds to manage major shipments of coal, and a good deal of the coal is located a substantial distance from points of energy demand. There may be increased water transportation, especially if the Tennessee-Tombigbee waterway is completed, but even that possibility will require investment in barges to make the use of coal a more practical option than it is at present.

NUCLEAR POWER

As of 1984 the United States had eighty nuclear power plants that produced 3 percent of the total energy used in this country. At one time it was believed that nuclear power would meet future energy needs as, particularly with breeder reactors, the supply of energy appeared almost endless. But after the near disaster at the Three Mile Island nuclear plant, the possibility of a nuclear future seems less likely. In part this is true because, without the breeder reactor and its potential danger, we must deal with the limited supply of fissionable uranium. More important, safety and environmental problems have called nuclear power into question.[6]

The Three Mile Island incident pointed to the possibility that nuclear power plants present potential health and safety hazards for citizens living near them and possibly even for those living hundreds of miles away. If the "China syndrome" had occurred and the reactor core had melted, the extent of damage to the health of citizens is difficult to estimate. If a nuclear power plant has no incidents of this sort, the additional radioactivity in its vicinity is indeed negligible, but there is the possibility — although advocates of the technology argue that it is remote — of a serious accident.

Even if there was no danger of accidents, the environmental and health problems associated with nuclear waste disposal would present difficulties. Some nuclear wastes lose their radioactivity very slowly: The half life, or the time required for half the nuclear activity to be exhausted, of plutonium-239 is 24,000 years. This means that we must find a means of disposing of these wastes so as to prevent them from contaminating the environment. We must also find a means to prevent terrorists from gaining control of the material, for it would constitute a powerful instrument for blackmail. The disposal of nuclear wastes presents environmental problems and potential problems in guarding large areas against possible terrorist attacks and thefts.

Finally, the construction of nuclear power plants has been so slow that many utilities have become frustrated and abandoned the projects. The requirements for inspection and reinspection of the plants as they are built, because of the dangers of accidents and contamination, have slowed the construction of the plants significantly, as have the lawsuits filed by opponents of nuclear power. The operating costs of nuclear power plants will certainly be less than those of fossil-fuel plants, but the initial capital investment has caused many private utilities to cancel plans to build nuclear plants.

OTHER ENERGY SOURCES

Several other energy sources are currently being used in the United States, although none accounts for a significant percentage of capacity. These include hydroelectric power, wood, and some solar and geothermal power. To date, with the exception of hydroelectric power, these have not offered much hope for rapid development, although a great deal is promised for solar power. Wood is perhaps our oldest power source, but the constraints on the amount of wood available, its cost, and the pollution problems it presents limit its usefulness, in spite of a growing number of Franklin stoves and woodburning furnaces in the northern United States. We discuss solar power next, along with other unconventional sources of energy advocated as solutions to the energy crisis.

UNCONVENTIONAL ENERGY SOURCES

As the problem of America's energy future has become more apparent to citizens, politicians, and scientists, a number of alternatives to fossil fuels and nuclear power have been explored. The search has been for energy sources that are renewable, clean, safe, and compatible with the American life style. Of the four criteria, the last has appeared less important as some understanding of the uniqueness of that life style has begun to penetrate our collective consciousness. At present, there appear to be five major possible alternative energy sources, two of which are variations on existing power sources. These two variations are the extraction of oil from the shale found in Colorado and Wyoming and nuclear fusion (rather than fission). The oil-shale technology, if it were developed, would have an immense environmental impact, much like that of strip-mined coal. And the extraction process would produce a number of undesirable effluents in an area that is both beautiful and environmentally fragile. In addition, the extraction of oil from shale would require huge amounts of water in an area already short of water. And all of this is for a relatively small amount of oil, when compared with current levels of consumption.

The technology of fusion power is in the beginning stages. The idea of this power source is to approximate, in a laboratory or power station, the processes that produce the energy of the sun. This will require temperatures of tens of millions of degrees and the technology to create and then contain a superheated "plasma" of charged particles.[7] In other words, fusion will require massive technological developments, but it might someday produce cheap and virtually limitless supplies of energy, with much less radioactivity than is caused by nuclear fission.

Limited amounts of solar power are also in use in the United States, heating some houses and businesses and heating water for home use. But the use of solar power to produce electricity for mass distribution ("big solar") will require technological breakthroughs as well as answers to some environmental questions. Although we theoretically have a limitless source of solar power, many areas of the country may not receive the sunlight they need when they need it most. For example, northern cities need energy most during the winter, for heating, but they receive little sunlight then. Also the photovoltaic cell — the means of converting sunlight into electrical energy — is at present under-developed and inefficient. Thus, to make sufficient quantitites of electricity with solar power will require large areas devoted to solar panels, and some environmentalists may regard this as another form of pollution.

There has also been a great deal of discussion about using wind power to generate electricity. The windmill, which used to dominate rural landscapes, is to many people the symbol of the future. Again, like solar power, wind power is already in use in a small and decentralized way, but the unreliability of the source and the thought of thousands of windmills dotting the American plains and coasts have reduced the attractiveness of this alternative.[8] Possibly, with better means of storing electricity, wind power will become a more practical means of meeting some of America's future energy requirements.

Finally, there is the possibility of using the agricultural productivity of the United States as a means of addressing energy needs. Gasohol, a combination of gasoline and methyl (wood) alcohol produced from plants, is already sold in most areas of the United States. The same plant material could be converted to methane gas and used like natural gas. And there are a number of options for using the substantial forest reserves of the United States, and the by-products of timber, as alternative energy resources.

The production of energy from biomass has several advantages. One is that it is renewable. If rapidly growing plants are used — or agricultural by-products such as cornstalks — it will not disrupt the environment. But even then, massive amounts of land would have to be cultivated to produce the necessary amounts of organic material. This means of energy production has the additional advantage of producing a product that — unlike solar, wind, or fusion power — can be burned in automobiles. Of course, more efficient electric automobiles and storage batteries may be developed, and gasohol or even pure methanol can be burned in a modified internal combustion engine. The technology for burning methane gas is also being developed. Thus, biomass production may serve the American life style better than other alternative forms of energy production. At present, price is a major barrier to the production of significant quantities of methanol; the price of alcohol has been higher than the price of gasoline. However, with deregulation of petroleum prices and increased methanol production, methanol is becoming a more competitive energy source.

Policy Options

Broadly speaking, there are two ways of addressing the energy crisis in the United States. One is conservation, or discouraging energy consumption by citizens and industry. Conservation was the principal approach of the Carter administration to the energy problem. For example, there were orders specifying the range of temperatures in public buildings and tax incentives for insulation and other energy-saving modifications for homes. But more than anything else, the issue of conservation was highlighted by controversies over deregulation of oil and natural gas prices, especially for so-called new oil and gas. The idea was that any gas and oil discovered after the passage of the legislation would be priced at a rate determined by the market, rather than at the controlled price of domestic oil and gas, which was below world prices. This would allow the price of oil and gas to rise, thereby encouraging conservation. But it would also mean huge "windfall" profits for oil and gas companies.

To attempt to make the outcome of decontrol more equitable across the society, a windfall profits tax was part of the Carter energy package. This would have produced revenues of over $225 billion for the federal government during the 1980s. The tax on oil company profits was considered justifiable by a significant portion of the population, especially as each quarterly announcement of oil profits showed huge and growing profits for those companies, while many citizens felt squeezed by the prices of gasoline, natural gas, and home heating oil. And the income from the windfall profits tax would have been used for other projects directed toward increasing the energy independence of the United States and for compensating individuals for their increased expenditures for energy.[9] One-quarter of the tax revenue would have gone to welfare recipients to help them meet the increased costs of energy. Another 60 percent would have gone to the remainder of the population and to businesses through tax reductions, again to compensate for increased energy costs. Finally, 15 percent would have gone to energy development and to support mass transportation. Another important aspect of the Carter approach to energy problems was the Synthetic Fuels Corporation, intended to develop substitutes for petroleum from coal and other resources. Finally, there was to be a stockpile of petroleum—the Strategic Petroleum Reserve—which would delay the effects of any future oil embargoes on the United States.

The Reagan administration's approach to energy has been more market and production oriented. During his 1980 campaign, candidate Reagan stressed the need for the market to deal with energy problems and condemned the Department of Energy as a "wasteful bureaucracy."[10] Reagan's first administration assumed that the deregulation of prices would encourage the market to produce more energy and that price increases would make some energy sources (e.g., oil in old wells) profitable to exploit. Also, the administration—with the special attention of Interior Secretary James Watt—sought, largely unsuccessfully, to exploit energy resources on public lands, such as the Alaska lands "locked up" under the Carter administration. There was some leasing of federal lands for coal mining—some 16,000 acres in the Powder River Basin of Montana and Wyoming, for example—but the favorable prices offered to private coal companies when the coal market was glutted was condemned as poor resource management and as a national "fire sale." This sale was especially vulnerable to criticism because of the environmental sensitivity of the area leased. The stable and even declining price of petroleum on the international market, however, has made the planned exploitation of shale oils in equally sensitive areas of the West less attractive and that development has been slowed.

The price of oil has had other effects on national energy policy in the 1980s. First, it has made the development of the Strategic Petroleum Reserve more feasible, and by January 1984 it had reached 360 million barrels (almost a month's supply), which was a 300 percent increase over what was available in 1980. Further, as shale oils became less attractive, so too did synthetic fuels, and the Synthetic Fuels Corporation has had a difficult time in maintaining any interest in the private sector.[11] Stable energy prices have also made the continued deregulation of oil and natural gas feasible; the Reagan administration has pushed for complete deregulation, including the abrogation of existing pipeline contracts calling for the delivery of natural gas at a certain price.

In summary, during the Reagan administration energy policy has not been a major concern. Energy prices have been relatively stable, and the international market has had plentiful oil. Also, energy consumption in the United States has declined; existing supplies and sources have been more than adequate. At least for this policy area and at this time, the market-oriented strategies of the administration seem to have been largely successful.

Summary
It was once popular to talk about the energy "crisis" in the United States, and indeed in the 1970s a crisis seemed to loom as prices soared and supplies dwindled. Those fears now seem exaggerated, and energy is not an immediate problem. Yet there is reason to believe that this may only be a short respite to an

ongoing energy problem. Supplies of fossil fuels in the world are finite. The ending of the immediate problems in energy therefore provides a false sense of security and prevents the search for viable long-term energy sources. This is especially true in view of the fact that many citizens are suspicious of technological solutions (e.g., nuclear power) to energy problems. It may require yet another energy "crisis" for citizens and government to return to the active consideration of alternative energy futures for the United States.

One of the best presentations of the policy options facing the United States with respect to energy is Amory Lovins's discussion of "hard" versus "soft" energy paths.[12] Although there have been numerous criticisms of the apocalyptic conclusions reached by Lovins, his analysis of the alternative routes is important. The hard route is said to continue to increase energy consumption as fast or faster than national economic growth and to rely on fossil fuels, especially coal, or on nuclear power to supply that energy. This option is both production oriented and centralized in its use of large-scale energy production and distribution, primarily through existing electrical utilities. The soft route, on the other hand, would allow energy use to grow less rapidly than national economic growth and would stress conservation. The soft route would also stress decentralized production of energy, with each family or small community having its own power source, usually of a renewable variety.

Lovins's analysis is important for several reasons. First, economic growth is often linked with energy consumption. In fact the usual assumption has been that these two are inextricably linked, but they need not be in Lovins's decentralized vision of the future. Second, he stresses the connection between environmental issues (he is an environmental activist) and energy issues, as we have been doing here. Finally, he stresses the links between political decision making, political structures, and energy sources. He fears the centralization that might occur in politics as a result of large-scale use of nuclear power, with the attendant need to protect the waste storage sites and even the power plants themselves.

The energy "crisis" implies a need to change our life style so as to conserve energy, to live more frugally and with different forms of energy, or to find additional sources of petroleum, natural gas, and uranium. Or all three. There are few clear answers to the problems posed for the country by the need for energy and the exhaustion of our traditional sources. And it is important to discuss the political and social effects of the energy crisis and not just its technical aspects. As mentioned, the choices made about energy supplies may well affect the manner in which governments function, or in more extreme versions they may affect the level of government that citizens regard as most important. In a future characterized by highly decentralized energy, a centralized federal government may be less important than the community government. The community, as opposed to the large urban area, may become the appropriate unit of social organization. Like so many other policy areas, energy policy may be too important to be left to the experts, and there must be active citizen understanding and involvement to shape humane as well as technologically feasible politics.

Environmental Policies

Just as Harriet Beecher Stowe's *Uncle Tom's Cabin* is alleged to have helped initiate the Civil War and as Michael Harrington's *The Other America* is said to have helped initiate the war on poverty, so it is sometimes said that Rachel Carson's *The Silent Spring* helped to launch the environmental movement in the United States. Her description of the horror of a spring without the usual sounds of life associated with that time of the year helped to make citizens and policymakers understand the possible effects of the pollutants being poured into the air and water of the United States. This is no small problem. Even after a decade and a half of increased environmental awareness, tons of pollutants are still dumped into the air and water or stored in rusting barrels to poison the land for years. It is difficult to determine the amount of disease and the number of deaths that result from this pollution or to estimate the amount of property damage it causes, but the damage produced in each of these categories would be substantial. America does have a pollution problem, and although it is not solved, it has been addressed through a variety of statutes now enforced by the Environmental Protection Agency (EPA). But with the slowdown of the American economy in the late 1970s and early 1980s, many citizens began to question whether the nation could afford such stringent controls on pollution, and great concern was expressed for balancing environmental protection with economic growth. It was also argued that environmental controls contributed to the inflation that plagued the American economy by making some commodities, such as automobiles, more expensive than they would otherwise be.

Few people question the desirability of a clean environment, but some would like to see that value balanced more carefully with other equally important values, such as economic growth, jobs, and controlling inflation. The Reagan administration early in its tenure began to propose deregulation, especially with regard to the automobile industry, in an effort to promote greater economic growth.[13] Critics of these proposals point out that the net savings for consumers might be rather slight, as reductions in environmental controls on automobiles might be costly in the long run because of increased fuel consumption. However, the proposals are indicative of the battle being fought in the 1980s over the value of a clean environment and the point at which economic and environmental values come into conflict.

The Politics of Pollution

It would be difficult indeed to find a group that actively favors environmental degradation. Rather, the politics of pollution is generally phrased in terms of tradeoffs between environmental values and other values. There is sufficient public concern about the environment that it would be almost impossible to make wholesale retreats from existing environmental programs.

There are, however, tradeoffs that have to be made. As the U.S. economy slowed during the early 1980s, some of the blame for the slowdown was placed on more stringent environmental controls in the United States than in other countries. Similarly, a portion of inflation was blamed on regulations of all kinds, including environmental regulations; the cost of the average American automobile increased by several hundred dollars because of environmental controls.[14] Those same environmental controls made the automobile less energy efficient, so in this case energy conservation and environmental concerns constituted another tradeoff. A similar energy/environment tradeoff can be seen in coal mining. The cheapest means of mining coal—strip mining—is very destructive of the environment. Further, potential petroleum reserves have been found in environmentally sensitive areas. Even if all Americans are to some degree in favor of a clean environment, it will be difficult to find much agreement on how individual tradeoffs among values will be made.

Stakeholders in the environmental arena are obvious. Industry is a major actor, for many environmental regulations restrict the activities of businesses. Local governments are also the objects of environmental controls, for much water pollution is produced by poorly treated sewerage coming from local government sources. Again, most of those affected by pollution legislation have not opposed the legislation so much on ideological grounds as on technical grounds, arguing that many of the regulations are technologically infeasible or are so expensive that enforcing them would make the cost of doing business prohibitive.

On the other side of the debate are the environmental interest groups, such as the Sierra Club, the National Wildlife Federation, and the Friends of the Earth. A few of these organizations—most notably the Sierra Club—have been in existence for years, but the majority are the products of the environmental mobilization of the late 1960s and 1970s. In 1980 about 7 percent of the American population was affiliated with some environmental group.[15] Yet there are disagreements among members of these groups as to the tactics that they want to follow and their willingness to make tradeoffs with other values, such as economic growth.

Finally, government itself is an active participant in environmental politics. The major actor in government is the Environmental Protection Agency (EPA), organized in 1970 to take the lead in environmental regulation for the federal government. Given its mission and the time at which it was formed, many employees of the EPA were and are committed environmentalists. (This put them into conflict with political appointees of the Reagan administration who did not share those values.) The EPA is not, however, the only federal agency with environmental concerns; one enumeration found almost thirty federal organizations with some environmental regulatory responsibilities. The number of agencies involved in the environment has meant that there has been some lack of coordination and consequent attempts to produce greater uniformity in regulation.

Making environmental policy is in part a technical exercise. There are a huge number of complex technical questions about the nature of environmental problems and about the feasibility of solutions offered for problems. Making environmental policy is also an ideological exercise on the part of many of those involved, especially the environmental groups. Most fundamentally, making environmental policy means finding tradeoffs among environmental values, technical feasibility, and economic growth.

The Legislation

Except for some older pieces of legislation (e.g., the Refuse Act of 1899), environmental legislation was passed in the 1960s and 1970s. Most of this legislation had built into it specific guidelines so that authorization would expire after a certain number of years. Even among those very interested in environmental protection there is some interest in developing alternatives to direct regulation as a means of reducing pollution. We now discuss each area of legislation and the enforcement of environmental policy, as well as the alternatives to the existing system of regulation.

WATER POLLUTION

Federal interest in water pollution goes back to the Refuse Act of 1899, which was intended to prevent the dumping of refuse in navigable waters and was enforced by the Army Corps of Engineers. This legislation provided the principal federal means of attacking water pollution until more stringent legislation was passed in the 1970s. Another piece of relatively early federal legislation was the Water Pollution Control Act of 1956. This act allowed interested parties around a polluted body of water to call a conference concerning that pollution. Their recommendations would be passed on to enforcement officials in the states involved. If the states did not act within six months, the federal government (through the Department of the Interior) could intervene and seek an injunction to stop the polluting. Although there were possibilities of more stringent enforcement through the court system, only one injunction was issued during the fifteen years the law was in effect. But, by making federal matching funds available for the construction of sewerage treatment facilities, the act did encourage cities and towns to clean up their water.

The early legislation on water pollution proved ineffective, and the federal government took a major step forward in 1965 with the Water Quality Act. This act relied on the states, as had the 1956 act, but made the first steps toward establishing criteria for water quality. Each state submitted to the Department of Health, Education, and Welfare (after 1970 to the Environmental Protection Agency) standards for water quality. These standards were to be in measurable quantities (e.g., the number of bacteria per milliliter of water) so that they could be more readily enforced.[16] After HEW or the EPA approved these standards, they were to be translated into specific effluent standards (e.g., an industry could release only so many tons of pollutants each month). It was then anticipated that the states would enforce these standards; if they did not, the secretary of HEW was given the authority to apply the standards approved by the state within the state.

The state basis of the Water Quality Act proved to be its undoing. States compete with one another to attract industries, and states that adopted more stringent water-quality standards might scare industries away. Thus, water-quality standards tended to converge on the lowest common denominator. Even then, the states rarely if ever enforced the standards. And the federal government did little to encourage more vigorous enforcement. It became clear that the states had little incentive to enforce pollution standards and to clean up their own waters, and as a consequence more effective national standards would be required.

Those national standards were developed through the 1972 amendments to the Water Pollution Control Act. These amendments did establish national goals, with 1983 established as the deadline for all streams to be safe for fish and for human swimming, and 1985 as a date when all discharges into navigable streams must stop. To achieve these goals all private concerns were to adopt the "best practicable technology" by 1977 and the "best available technology" by 1983. Standards for public sewage treatment were less demanding, with all wastes to receive some treatment by 1977 and with the "best practicable technology" standard applied by 1983.[17] This legislation established a nationwide discharge permit system, enabling the Environmental Protection Agency to specify the amount of effluents that could be released and to monitor compliance with the technology requirements. As noted, this legislation set nationwide standards, although a good deal of the implementation was done at the state level. States could not use low water-quality standards as a means of competing for industry, but their implementation of the standards continued to differ substantially in severity.

AIR POLLUTION

Air pollution did not become a matter of federal concern as early as did water pollution, perhaps because of the lack of a clear constitutional peg on which to hang any attempt at enforcement. Federal control over navigable streams provided such a peg for water pollution legislation. In addition, the effects of air pollution failed to bring action—even though twenty people died during severe pollution in Donora, Pennsylvania, in 1948 and even though an obvious smog problem plagued the Los Angeles area.

The first federal legislation against air pollution was the Clean Air Act of 1963. This legislation was similar to the 1956 Water Pollution Act in that it relied on conferences, voluntary compliance, and possible HEW enforcement. Only once during the seven years in which the act was in effect did HEW attempt to force a firm to cease polluting. Also, in 1965 the act was amended to authorize the secretary of HEW to set standards for automobile emissions, using measurable standards like those of the Water Pollution Control Act Amendments of 1972.

The Clean Air Act was significantly amended in 1970, and the EPA was directed to establish ambient ("surrounding") air-quality standards. There were to be two sets of standards, primary and secondary. Primary standards were those necessary to protect public health and were to be attained by 1975. Secondary standards, those necessary to protect vegetation, paint, buildings, and so forth, were to be attained within "a reasonable time."[18] Also, the EPA was given the authority to establish emission standards for certain new plants, such as cement and sulfuric acid factories and electrical generating stations fired by fossil fuels, which had greater-than-average potential for significant air pollution.

The amendments also addressed emissions from automobiles. The 1970 standards superseded the weak hydrocarbon standards and carbon monoxide standards contained in the 1965 Motor Vehicle Air Pollution Control Act. The 1970 amendments mandated a 90 percent reduction in the level of hydrocarbons and carbon monoxide emissions by 1975, with similar reductions in oxides of nitrogen to be achieved by 1976. Although the standards set by the amendments were tough, a variety of factors slowed their implementation. Primarily, the technology for achieving these reductions was difficult and expensive to develop, and some of it, such as the catalytic converter, had side effects that are perhaps as dangerous as the emissions they were designed to eliminate. In addition, many pollution controls reduced gasoline mileage, and increasing energy shortages brought the conflict between environmental concerns and energy problems to the attention of citizens and policymakers alike.

GENERAL ENVIRONMENTAL LEGISLATION

In addition to the legislation addressing specific kinds of pollution described above, the National Environmental Policy Act (NEPA) of 1970 established guidelines for environmental controls for projects involving the federal government. The principal component of this legislation was the Environmental Impact Statement, which was required for any federally funded project that might have an effect on environmental quality. Before a project can be approved, the Environmental Impact Statement must be filed, detailing the environmental impact of the project, its potential negative consequences, and possible alternatives. These statements must be prepared well in advance of the proposed starting date of the project to allow citizen participation and review and then are filed with the Council on Environmental Quality in the Executive Office of the President.

The NEPA also allows citizens to challenge a project on environmental grounds, and over 400 court cases were filed during the first five years that the legislation was in effect. The legislation requires that environmental considerations be taken into account when a project is planned, but does not indicate the weight that is to be attached to these considerations as compared with other costs and benefits of the project. This ambiguity in the legislation has been the source of many court cases and has made decisions difficult for the judge involved. In the case of the Alaska pipeline, the court challenges required special legislation to allow the project to continue in the face of determined opposition by conservation groups. This case also pointed to the increasing conflict between energy needs and environmental protection.

TOXIC WASTE

Toxic wastes are one of the by-products of a society that has become dependent on synthetic products for its way of life. The Office of Technology Assessment has estimated that each year between 255 and 275 metric tons of hazardous wastes are created in the United States—over one ton per citizen in the United States.[19] In addition to their being hazardous, the problem with hazardous waste is that they tend to be persistent chemicals that have to be stored for years or even centuries and have to be kept away from people and their water and food supplies. Such storage is expensive, and before there was a full understanding of the dangers of these wastes, or proper regulation, industries disposed of these wastes in a very haphazard manner, thus endangering many citizens.

The issue of hazardous wastes first came to widescale attention in 1977 when the Love Canal dump near Buffalo, New York, spilled wastes into a nearby residential neighborhood. Eventually several hundred residents had to be moved out of their homes. Hazardous wastes again came to widespread attention in 1982 when it was found that the town of Times Beach, Missouri, had been contaminated with the extremely toxic chemical dioxin. The town had to be evacuated. Although these have been the most obvious manifestations of the toxic waste problem, there are approximatley 30,000 toxic waste dumps across the United States, and several thousands of them pose serious threats to the health of citizens. It is estimated that up to $50 billion would be required to clean up existing waste dumps and dispose of all the chemicals stored in them in an environmentally safe manner.

The federal government adopted two major pieces of legislation to address the problem of toxic wastes. The first was the Resource Conservation and Recovery Act (RCRA) of 1976, which was reauthorized in 1980. This act required the Environmental Protection Agency to determine what chemicals were hazardous and the appropriate means of disposing of those chemicals, and to establish a system of permits to ensure that hazardous chemicals were indeed disposed of properly. Because of the technical complexity of the task, and the low priority attached to the exercise during the Carter administration, the necessary regulations were not promulgated until 1980. The regulations were attacked by industry as being too stringent and by environmentalists as being too lenient. By the time President Carter was ready to leave office, toxic waste issues were beginning to be assigned a high priority in the EPA.

When the Reagan administration came into office in 1981, it began almost immediately to attack the "regulatory excess" believed to be characteristic of the RCRA. Specifically, using the authority of the Paperwork Reduction Act and an executive order promoting deregulation, the Office of Management and Budget sought to dismantle some of the reporting and permit regulations of the RCRA. The OMB also cut funding for the RCRA by almost 25 percent.[20] The attempts by the Reagan administration, under the leadership of the then head of the Environmental Protection Agency, Anne Gorsuch (Burford), met strong opposition from environmental groups and some congressmen, and the EPA did not achieve the degree of deregulation desired. When scandals within the EPA forced Gorsuch from office, the new EPA administrator, William Ruckelshaus, began to restore some teeth to a law that had become almost unenforced.

The second major program for dealing with toxic wastes is the Superfund. This is a program for cleaning up hazardous waste sites, with the funds for the program coming from a tax on oil and chemical companies. The program, as proposed by the Carter administration, contained regulations requiring industry to clean up its own sites, as well as providing funds to clean up particularly hazardous sites. The program was finally adopted just before the Reagan administration came into office, with substantially weaker penalties for industries violating the act than had been proposed, but the act did provide a means of addressing some of the worst hazardous waste sites in the United States.

The Reagan administration quickly moved away from the regulatory strategy and rapid timetable of the Carter administration and toward "negotiated settlements" between the industries and the Office of Waste Programs Enforcement in the EPA. There was a great deal of emphasis during this time on having industries clean up their own sites and on avoiding conflict with industries. Members of Congress grew increasingly impatient with what they regarded as a slowing of the planned cleanup schedule and a change in the intended mechanisms for achieving cleanups. They investigated the Superfund for alleged mismanagement and removed its head from office. The EPA under Ruckelshaus soon began to pursue cleaning up dumps more actively.

Both the RCRA and the Superfund are potentially important for addressing the problem of a massive amount of toxic waste threatening the environment. The implementation of these programs has been slowed by difficulties in writing the necessary regulations and by partisan and ideological opposition within the Reagan administration. This delay has only made the problem more serious. There is a need for a large-scale effort to identify existing waste sites, clean them, and devise regulatory mechanisms for the safe disposal of such wastes in the future.

Implementation of Environmental Controls

The principal organization charged with the implementation of environmental control legislation is the Environmental Protection Agency, organized in 1970 to administer the growing body of environmental legislation. It was conceived as an executive agency, responsible to the President but independent of any cabinet department. The agency was charged with implementing a variety of air, water, and toxic waste programs, but in so doing encountered a number of difficulties, some of which were political, involving the relationship between the EPA and other federal agencies and the states. The EPA was given a rather broad set of responsibilities and a wide field of action that inevitably brought it into conflict with other federal and state agencies. When the EPA sought to flex its environmental muscles, it almost inevitably ran into conflicts with agencies that wanted to build dams, roadways, or waterways. It also ran into difficulties with the heads of private industries who believed that the standards imposed on them by the EPA were too stringent and lessened their ability to compete in the marketplace, especially the world market. The EPA was given an unenviable task to perform, and since it was made up mostly of people committed to the environmental movement, it set out to accomplish that task with some zeal. The difficulties it encountered were intensified because many of the projects it sought to stop were pet projects of some congressman or senator, and the reputation the agency had on Capitol Hill was not the best.

The EPA was also given a difficult administrative task. Congress was relatively specific about the dates by which certain levels of pollution reduction were to be achieved. This gave the administration little latitude and little opportunity to bargain with polluting industries. Also, Congress, in attempting to specify so precisely the conditions for alleviating pollution, wrote into the legislation several contradictory paragraphs, which in turn created more implementation difficulties for the EPA. Finally, the strategy adopted for a good deal of the program — technology-forcing regulations — created substantial difficulties for implementors and for those seeking to comply with the legislation.[21] When standards were adopted to reduce air pollution by 1975 to 10 percent of what it was in 1970, the technology to produce that improvement in air quality simply did not exist. It was believed that passage of the legislation would result in the development of the technology, but the result was a delay in implementation rather than technological breakthrough. Certainly a number of improvements have been made, especially in the internal combustion engine, as a result of this legislation, but the major innovations anticipated have not materialized.

One major implementation problem associated with environmental policies has been standard setting. We noted that such terms as "primary and secondary standards of air quality" and "best available technology" were not clearly defined in the legislation. Even if they had been, it would still have been necessary to convert those standards into permissible levels of emissions from individual sources of pollution (e.g., for each factory and municipal waste treatment facility). Overall goals for pollution reduction are relatively easy to establish, but great difficulty is encountered in translating those goals into workable and enforceable criteria. And the criteria developed must be applicable to polluters, not just to pollution, if any significant improvements in environmental quality are to be achieved. But at times the difficulty of setting those standards has forced the EPA to adopt a "best practice" doctrine: If a plant is doing things like every other plant, then it must be doing things right.

The enforcement of established criteria has presented several interesting questions. First, should a mechanism exist for making tradeoffs between environmental protection and economic growth? For example, the Sierra Club succeeded in obtaining a court ruling that the air pollution legislation did not allow any degradation of existing air quality, an interpretation resisted by the EPA. This ruling meant that people living in an area with very clean air—probably an area with little or no industry—might be forbidden to bring in any industry. A related question is how to allocate any proposed reductions in effluents among industries or other polluters. For example, should there be across-the-board percentage reductions with each polluter reducing pollution by 20 percent or whatever, or should attention be given both to the level of emissions and the technological feasibility of reducing pollution at each source? For some industries even minor reductions in effluents might be very difficult to attain, while others might be able virtually to eliminate their effluents with only a limited investment. How should these considerations be taken into account?

Second, although environmental protection legislation is filled with legal weapons to force compliance from polluters, including the authority to close down an offending industry, in reality the enforcement of the legislation has been much less draconian. Politically, the EPA cannot afford to close an industry that provides a major source of employment, either nationally or in a single community. Thus, frequently the agency's hands are tied, and the level of compliance desired or mandated has not been achieved.

Finally, although the Environmental Protection Agency has been given a number of legal and administrative mechanisms for producing improved air and water quality, its hands are frequently tied by the complex systems of standard setting and implementation. State governments, for example, are essential in devising plans for reducing pollution, and local communities have to become involved in building new waste-treatment facilities. And the Environmental Protection Agency itself is not responsible for distributing matching federal funds for those treatment facilities, so instead of being distributed on the basis of the severity of the pollution being caused, the funds are allocated on a first-come, first-served basis. Consequently, instead of developing definitive standards and practices, the enforcement of environmental legislation is frequently only a by-product of compromise, negotiation, and bargaining. This does not, of course, distinguish environmental policy from most other policy, but it does run counter to some of the discussion of the Environmental Protection Agency running roughshod over the interests of industries and local communities.

Alternatives to Regulation
As we have been demonstrating, the principal means of addressing environmental problems has been through direct regulation—the mandating of certain ac-

tions or the attainment of certain standards—enforced through legal penalties or possible closings. It has been argued that a more efficient means of producing improvements in the environment would be to impose effluent charges or taxes.[22] In other words, instead of telling an industry that it could emit only a certain number of tons of effluents each year, government would allow it to emit as much as it desired. The effluents would, however, be taxed, and the more there were, the higher would be the tax. And possibly some means of graduating the tax could be devised so that the greater the volume of effluents, the higher the rate of taxation.

The presumed advantage of the effluent tax is that it would allow more efficient industries to pollute, while less efficient industries would either have to close down or improve their environmental standards. The more efficient industries could afford to pay the effluent tax and still make a profit, while less efficient industries could not. This market-oriented solution to the pollution problem would be compatible with economic growth and efficiency. It is argued that it would be a definite improvement over direct regulation as a means of forcing the tradeoff between those competing values, and it would give most industries a real incentive to improve their environmental performance.

Effluent taxation has also been criticized, however. It has been regarded by some critics as a means of buying the right to pollute, and even to kill. To those critics the value of a clean environment is greater than the value of economic growth in almost any circumstance, and they cannot accept the idea of balancing the two. In addition, enforcing a pollution tax might be even more difficult than enforcing existing regulatory standards. Effluents would have to be monitored almost continuously to determine the total amount of discharges, whereas under the present regulatory system more infrequent monitoring is sufficient, as is less exact measurement.

Summary

The air and water of the United States are much cleaner in the early 1980s than they were before the passage of the environmental legislation. Fish are returning to streams that were once biologically dead, and cities such as Pittsburgh, which were once shrouded in smoke and grit, now can be seen from a distance. Despite these successes, the EPA and its legislation have come under a great deal of criticism. The agency has been attacked from both sides—for being insensitive to the needs of industry and for being too soft on polluters. And questions about the role of the EPA are likely to become even more important as scarce resources and slow economic growth raise the average citizen's concern about national priorities. The Reagan administration began early during its term of office to question the efficacy of many standards and to soften environmental regulations, especially on automobile-caused pollution. This was intended to assist the depressed automobile industry and allow American automobiles to compete with imported automobiles, at least on price. Decisions in one policy area impinge on many other areas. Environmental policy cannot be discussed apart from energy policy, or from policies concerning economic growth. But the institutions of government frequently do not provide ways of rectifying conflicts of values. Each policy area is treated separately and has its own constellation of interests. As both national resources and government resources dwindle, however, decisions by "subgovernments" may be a luxury we can no longer afford.

The 1980s may be the decade during which some important questions about the relationship between Americans and their physical environment are decided. We as a nation must decide how much value to attach to a clean and relatively unspoiled environment, as compared with the amount of value we attach to the mastery of that environment through energy exploration and economic growth. Although renewable energy resources and some shifting of attitudes about the desirability of economic growth may soften these hard choices, there must still be choices. These choices will arise with respect to specific issues, such as the opening of more Alaskan lands to energy exploration, or how to manage the oil shale of the West. They may also arise over specific issues such as the disposal of increasing quantities of toxic industrial wastes and the need to develop cleaner means of producing the goods to which we have become accustomed. But the summation of the individual choices may say a good deal about the quality of life in the United States for years to come.

Notes

1. United Nations Statistical Office, *Yearbook of World Energy Statistics, 1981* (New York: United Nations, 1983), table 1.

2. Robin C. Landon and Michael W. Klass, *OPEC: Policy Implications for the United States* (New York: Praeger, 1980).

3. U.S. Congress, Office of Technology Assessment, *Analysis of Prepared National Energy Plan* (Washington, D.C.: Government Printing Office, 1979).

4. Ibid.

5. Library of Congress, Congressional Reference Service, *Coal Gasification and Liquefaction* (Washington, D.C.: Government Printing Office, 1978).

6. Walter A. Rosenbaum, *Energy, Politics and Public Policy* (Washington, D.C.: Congressional Quarterly Press, 1981), 107-17.

7. Library of Congress, Congressional Reference Service, *Fusion Power: Potential Energy Source* (Washington, D.C.: Government Printing Office, 1978).

8. As with "big solar," environment and land-use problems to some degree lessen the appeal of these renewable sources.

9. *New York Times,* 2 March 1980.

10. John L. Palmer and Isabel V. Sawhill, eds., *The Reagan Record* (Washington, D.C.: Urban Institute, 1984).

11. Regina S. Axelrod, "Energy Policy: Changing the Rules of the Game," in *Environmental Policy in the 1980s: Reagan's New Agenda,* ed. Norman J. Vig and Michael E. Kraft (Washington, D.C.: Congressional Quarterly Press, 1984), 207-9.

12. Amory B. Lovins, *Soft Energy Paths: Toward a Durable Peace* (New York: Harper & Row, 1979).

13. "OMB to Keep Its Regulatory Powers in Reserve in Case Agencies Lag," *National Journal,* 14 March 1981, 424-29.

14. Murray L. Weidenbaum, *Business, Government and the Public,* 2d ed. (Englewood Cliffs, N.J.: Prentice-Hall, 1981), 34.

15. Council on Environmental Quality, *Public Opinion on Environmental Issues* (Washington, D.C.: Government Printing Office, 1980), 44.

16. J. Clarence Davis III and Barbara S. Davis, "Federal Standards and Enforcement," in *Economics of the Environment,* ed. Robert Dorfman and Nancy S. Dorfman (New York: Norton, 1977), 83-87.

17. Larry E. Ruff, "Federal Environmental Regulation," in *Case Studies in Regulation: Revolution and Reform,* ed. Leonard W. Weiss and Michael W. Klass (Boston: Little, Brown, 1981), 253-54.

18. Clean Air Act, as amended, Secs. 190 (6) (1) and 190 (6) (2).

19. Office of Technology Assessment, *Technologies and Management Strategies for Hazardous Waste Control* (Washington, D.C.: Government Printing Office, 1983), 7.

20. Steven Cohen, "Federal Hazardous Waste Programs," in Vig and Kraft, *Environmental Policy in the 1980s,* 279-81.

21. John E. Bonine, "The Evolution of Technology—Forcing in the Clean Air Act," *Environmental Reporter,* 25 July 1975, 6-9; and Charles O. Jones, "Speculative Augmentation in Federal Air Pollution Policy-Making," *Journal of Politics,* May 1974, 438-64.

22. J. Clarence Davis III and Barbara S. Davis, *The Politics of Pollution,* 2d ed. (Indianapolis: Pegasus, 1975), 203-8.

13. Defense Policy

The Constitution of the United States lists "to provide for the common defense" as the second of the purposes of the government of the United States. Going back to Lexington and Concord and the Minutemen, military defense has been a visible and sometimes expensive function in a country favoring small government and few government employees.[1] The task of providing for the common defense is now a much more complex and expensive task than it was when an effective military force could be raised by each man in the community taking down the rifle from over the fireplace. Military spending accounted for 46 percent of federal spending in 1984, up from 35 percent in 1980 (see table 13.1). In 1985 military spending was 6.6 percent of gross national product; thus, $6.60 out of every $100 in the economy went for military defense. Military spending, and the whole defense posture of the United States, has become more controversial in the aftermath of the Vietnam war. Defense policy now demands choices that involve great complexity, great expense, and perhaps survival.

The Environment of Defense Policy

A number of factors condition the manner in which defense policy is made and the likely outcomes of the policy process. Unlike many other policy areas. defense policy factors are to a great extent beyond the control of those in government making the decisions. In part because of the uncertainty involved in making defense policy, there may be greater perceptual differences among individuals involved in the process than is true for other policy areas. For example, the degree of threat that any decision maker perceives in the international environment will affect his or her willingness to allocate resources to defense.

Adversaries and Potential Adversaries

The fundamental factor affecting the formulation of defense policy is the international climate and the relationship between the United States and the Soviet Union. Almost as soon as the two superpowers ceased being allies after World War II, they became adversaries on a global scale. Early stages of that adver-

TABLE 13.1
DEFENSE EXPENDITURES
(in billions)

	Current Dollars	Constant Dollars (1972)	Percent GNP
1960	$45.9	$73.1	7.9
1965	47.5	68.9	7.2
1970	78.6	90.1	8.1
1975	85.6	68.7	6.0
1980	135.9	72.7	6.1
1983	214.8	88.8	6.7
1984	227.4	89.2	6.4
1985	252.7	92.7	6.6

SOURCE: *Budget of the United States* (annual).

sarial relationship included the Berlin blockade and the Korean war, which were followed by the U-2 incident, the Cuban missile crisis, Vietnam, and Afghanistan, not to mention hundreds of more minor incidents.[2] None of these incidents involved direct conflicts between troops of the two superpowers, although there have been conflicts between troops of one superpower and those of allies or surrogates of the other. The degree of hostility expressed between the United States and the Soviet Union has varied, however; there have been periods of détente breaking the cold war and some important negotiated agreements (e.g., the nuclear test ban treaty).

In addition to conventional conflicts, there has been a nuclear arms race with each country developing massive stockpiles of nuclear weapons, capable of destroying the world several times over. Nuclear weapons have not been used since World War II, and there have been several attempts to reduce their numbers (or at least reduce their rate of growth), but the stockpiles of these weapons represent a crucial factor that defense policymakers must always take into account.

Allies

The United States also has friends in the world, although its allies do not always agree with the United States on defense issues. The most important alliance for the United States is the North Atlantic Treaty Organization (NATO), which links nations in Europe and North America for their mutual defense. NATO is responsible for the defense of Western Europe and the North Atlantic, and the United States commits by far the largest share of men and material to the alliance.[3] The Soviet Union also has allies, and its equivalent to NATO is the Warsaw Pact. The United States also has important defense agreements with Japan, South Korea, Israel, Australia, and New Zealand.

By the early 1980s, all was not well with the Western and other alliances. A number of European countries made commitments to deploy the new *Pershing II* and Cruise missiles with nuclear warheads on their territory, which provoked strong demonstrations from peace movements in those countries. Political pressures, for example, forced the Dutch government to postpone (perhaps indefinitely) the deployment of the missiles. In 1984 the New Zealand government refused to allow American nuclear submarines with nuclear weapons on board to use New Zealand ports, and there were major protests against nuclear weapons in Japan. On the American side, there were feelings that its treaty partners were unwilling to bear their fair share of the burden in providing for their defense, and there was fear that peace movements would force further problems with missile deployment.

Technology

The technology of modern warfare has advanced far beyond what was available even during the Korean conflict thirty years ago. Nuclear armaments are a major part of the technological change, but systems for delivering weapons have increased even more rapidly. In the 1950s it took hours for a plane to fly from the Soviet Union to the United States; a missile can now make that journey in fifteen minutes, and a missile launched from a submarine can arrive in five minutes. There is even discussion of war in space, with "killer satellites" and orbiting weapons.[4] The technology of conventional warfare also has advanced and now includes laser-guided weapons, infrared night-vision scopes, computers, and the potential for laser weapons.

The advance of weapons technology has several implications for defense policy. One is that defense is now a constant activity; there is no longer any time to raise an army and then go to war. A standing army historically is something of an anathema to many Americans, but in the 1980s the U.S. military numbers approximately 2 million uniformed personnel plus over 1 million civilian employees in the Department of Defense. Another feature of the increased technological component of modern warfare is cost. This is in part a function of having to maintain a large standing military establishment, but it goes beyond that. One air force bomber costs several *billion* dollars; one army tank costs several millions. So any discussion of improving the size and quality of American military forces must be conducted within the context of very high costs.

Public Opinion

Finally, American defense policy is made in a relatively open political arena and is definitely influenced by public opinion. As is true for many public issues, public opinion about defense is ambiguous. There are few committed advocates of unilateral disarmament in the United States, and all politicians advocate a strong defense for the United States. Nevertheless, there are a number of questions about program costs, about whether many of the high-technology weapons purchased actually contribute that much to the security of the United States, and about the manner in which the military power of the United States should be used (e.g., in Central America).

Nuclear weapons constitute an even greater public opinion problem. A significant portion of the population, although favoring a strong defense for the United States, opposes the nuclear arms race between the United States and the Soviet Union and would like to see a negotiated freeze on nuclear weapons or a reduction in the numbers of such weapons stockpiled by both sides. There is virtual unanimity on the one point that the United States should not be the first to use nuclear weapons in a conflict. The Strategic Arms Limitation Treaty (SALT-II), signed but not ratified, placed a limit on the number of strategic weapons that the two superpowers could deploy. Even if that treaty was ratified, the ability to add multiple warheads to missiles (MIRVs) and to add weapons such as Cruise missiles outside the framework of the treaty means that the arms race would continue largely unabated. There were no arms negotiations of any significance during the first Reagan administration, and the stockpile continues to grow. With nuclear weapons, the defense of the United States to a large extent depends on weapons that a large segment of the American public opposes and that would be disastrous to use.

The Strategic Balance

Table 13.2 lists the balance of strategic weapons between the United States and the Soviet Union in 1985. Both powers depend on a nuclear "triad" of inter-

TABLE 13.2
STRATEGIC NUCLEAR FORCES, UNITED STATES AND USSR,
1985

	United States	USSR
Intercontinental ballistic missiles	1049	1398
Submarine-launched ballistic missiles	544	950
Bombers	328	250
Total	1921	2598

SOURCE: U.S. Department of Defense, *Soviet Military Power, 1985* (Washington, D.C.: Government Printing Office, 1985).

continental missiles, submarine-launched missiles, and armed bombers. The table figures do not include "theater" nuclear weapons, such as American *Pershing II* and Soviet *SS-20* missiles. The Soviet Union has somewhat more delivery vehicles, and its missiles are capable of carrying larger payloads than are most American missiles. However, when the number of warheads is counted, the two countries are not very far apart, and each has the ability to destroy the other even in the event of a surprise attack. There are some questions about the reliability and utility of some of the U.S. delivery vehicles. For example, forty-nine of the missiles listed are Titans, which have been in silos for twenty years and which, because of their liquid fuel, require a good deal of time to get into the air. There are also very real questions as to whether the U.S. B-52 bombers can penetrate improved Soviet air defenses. Thus, there have been pressures to upgrade the missile component of the triad with MX missiles (see below) and to fit the B-52 fleet with air-launched Cruise missiles or replace them with the B-1 bomber.

TABLE 13.3

CONVENTIONAL WEAPONS, NATO AND WARSAW PACT NATIONS,

1985[a]

	NATO	Warsaw Pact
Troops	4,880,000	4,760,000
Tanks	19,500	61,000
Armored combat vehicles	39,000	80,000
Artillery	14,000	29,000
Antitank missiles	23,000	36,000

SOURCE: See table 13.2.

a. Includes all forces, not only those deployed in Western Europe. All numbers are approximate.

The balance in nonstrategic forces is more lopsided. Table 13.3 gives the balance of conventional forces between NATO and Warsaw Pact countries. The Warsaw Pact has clear superiority in all categories, especially in the number of tanks. It is hoped that the superior technical capabilities of some of the NATO weapons, as well as superiority in the number of attack aircraft, will level this balance if there ever is a war in Europe. Nevertheless, the relative weakness of the NATO forces makes the use of theater nuclear weapons more likely in the event of such a conflict. This, in turn, makes European members of NATO more vulnerable to demonstrations by antinuclear and peace activists.

Table 13.4 shows the balance of naval forces between the potential adversaries. The NATO countries have something of an edge in surface ships and are close to the Warsaw Pact countries in the number of general-purpose sub-

TABLE 13.4
NAVAL FORCES, NATO AND WARSAW PACT NATIONS,
1985[a]

	NATO	Warsaw Pact
Principal surface combatants	490	295
General-purpose submarines	230	300
Mine warfare craft	310	460
Patrol craft	390	700

SOURCE: See table 13.2.
a. All numbers are approximate.

marines. The numerical superiority in surface ships may in fact underestimate the strength of the U.S. Navy, given the capabilities contained in one of the attack-carrier battle groups. In addition, superior detection equipment and satellite tracking makes the small Soviet lead in submarines less impressive. Thus, despite pressures for greater naval construction, and the far-flung missions that the U.S. Navy must serve, on balance the edge seems to go to the naval forces of the NATO allies.

If nothing else, this toting up of personnel and weapons systems demonstrates the huge destructive potential that can be unleashed in a few moments by either side. Such great power carries with it great responsibility and the need for effective strategic doctrines to prevent the use of nuclear weapons—or, hopefully, any weapons. These strategic doctrines have been the subject of a great deal of debate by the civilian and military officials over the past four decades.

The Development of Nuclear Strategies

Once the world received the "gift" of the atomic bomb, nations had to develop strategies for including a weapon of such great destructive potential in their defense strategies. As long as the United States was the only atomic power (from 1945 to August 1949), this was relatively simple. The United States very early declared that the atomic bomb was a weapon of last resort. When, in 1949, the Soviet Union broke the American atomic monopoly, the development of a nuclear strategy became more important and more difficult, and concepts of deterrence began to be heard in defense policy. The initial U.S. response, expressed in a policy paper from the National Security Council (NSC-68) in 1950, was that the United States would be vulnerable to a surprise attack by the Soviet Union, and since the Soviet Union was conceived as an aggressor nation, the only possible solution for the United States was to try to maintain its superiority in weapons and build up its air and civilian defenses. Also, ef-

279

forts were made to strengthen conventional forces, in part as a response to the Korean war.

In 1954, John Foster Dulles, secretary of state for President Dwight Eisenhower, announced the doctrine of "massive retaliation," arguing that any confrontation with the Communist powers would be met with massive retaliation with nuclear weapons. This policy was intended to deter aggression, but it also had economic roots. It allowed the conventional forces of the United States and its allies to be kept at a minimum level; any attacks would be met with nuclear weapons. As the doctrine evolved during the course of the Eisenhower administration, it became "flexible retaliation" as much as massive retaliation, for the development of tactical nuclear weapons allowed more measured responses to confrontations. In addition, during the latter part of the 1950s the doctrine of limited war began to emerge as an alternative to the cavalier utilization of nuclear weapons in any confrontation.[5]

While the bellicose strategies of Dulles and his allies prevailed during the 1950s, several schools of civilian strategists were being developed.[6] Their common strand was an interest in stability and deterrence rather than in the rapid utilization of nuclear weapons in a controversy. Some of these civilian strategists come to the fore in the Kennedy administration, with Robert McNamara heading the Department of Defense along with his "whiz kids." A most important feature of the strategies emerging from this group was an emphasis on counterforce attacks in the case of war, rather than the destruction of civilian targets. With this approach, it was seen as possible to contain even a nuclear exchange to a military exchange and to prevent massive destruction and loss of life. However, because of the difficulties of insulating civilian targets from the military targets—would an attack on Norfolk, Virginia, be an attack on a military or a civilian target?—and the necessity of buying very large quantities of weapons in order to survive a first strike, the "counterforce strategy" was reversed in favor of the doctrine of "assured destruction." This doctrine was almost exactly the opposite of the counterforce strategy. It depended on the U.S. ability to be able to inflict "unacceptable levels of damage" on any aggressor, even after a surprise first strike.

The assured destruction concept quickly evolved into the doctrine of "mutually assured destruction," or MAD. The idea of MAD was that a stable "balance of terror" could be established if both sides knew that the other was capable of destroying it, whether or not a surprise attack was launched. In such a situation it would be totally irrational to begin a nuclear exchange because the potential "victor" would be destroyed along with the vanquished. Despite the unfortunate acronym, MAD contained more sanity than some approaches to nuclear weapons, and it may have made nuclear war less likely.

During the early 1970s the consensus on MAD as the most acceptable nuclear strategy began to erode. This change was in part a moral response to the strategy, labeling it something out of the Dark Ages, involving the mass destruction of hostages.[7] It was also attacked on strategic grounds, because any threat that involved the destruction of the threatener was not a very credible threat. MAD therefore locked the United States into a strategy for only one kind of attack—a large-scale first strike by the Soviet Union—instead of allowing greater flexibility in the potential utilization of its armed forces and even nuclear weapons. MAD was also vulnerable to technological change. With the development of MIRVs (Multiple Independently Targetable Reentry Vehicles) and the improved accuracy of these reentry vehicles, each side began to have the capacity to destroy all of its adversary's weapons, except submarine missiles at sea, on a first strike. These changes in the nature of the nuclear environment were one of the principal reasons for the two sides to begin the SALT negotiations (see below).

Arising from SALT and the "essential equivalence" in weapons it produced was the search for new strategies to meet the changed environment. One of the first moves was the "Schlesinger doctrine," named after James Schlesinger, who, as secretary of defense in 1974, proposed that American strategy would not be an all-out attack on cities in case of attack but more moderated and possibly counterforce attacks. The idea was to build in a great deal of flexibility for a President and to prevent a rapid escalation. Unfortunately, it was pointed out that the Soviet Union has a historical proclivity for large-scale first assaults, and an equal proclivity for large-scale responses to an attack. It appeared that only one side was playing the "nuclear game." The search for a more flexible response has continued in the 1980s. President Carter planned for the possibility of a protracted but limited nuclear war.[8] The Reagan administration has proposed doctrines that turn back in the direction of MAD and has increased the U.S. nuclear stockpile. It also has deployed Cruise missiles in Western Europe, countered by the deployment of new Soviet rockets in Eastern Europe, so, by the mid-1980s, both sides have even greater levels of destructive capacity available to them.

The Reagan administration also made one of the most destabilizing recommendations in the arms race that has occurred since the 1950s. This was the Strategic Defense Initiative, sometimes called "Star Wars." President Reagan proposed the development of antimissile weapons that would orbit in space and prevent weapons launched by the Soviet Union from reaching the United States. Although he also proposed that the United States might *give* this technology, once developed, to the Soviet Union in order to maintain stability, the proposal was potentially destabilizing. If the United States were successful in developing the new technology (many scientists found that doubtful), it would mean that the missiles of the Soviet Union would become obsolete overnight. This might give the Soviets an incentive to use those weapons *before* a "Star Wars" system could be put in place and they were, for all practical purposes, disarmed. Even if that Armageddon vision did not take place, there would be strong incentives to build more weapons to try to "flood" a defensive system, and thereby to escalate the arms race.

Arms Control

Given the destructive potential and the economic costs of nuclear weapons, both the United States and the Soviet Union have strong incentives to negotiate arms limitation or reduction. There have been ongoing differences between the two sides, with issues such as the verifiability of the number of weapons and other technical questions often taking the place of more substantive issues about the number, size, and destructive potential of the weapons on each side.

The first significant arms-control agreement between the United States and the Soviet Union was SALT I, with SALT standing for Strategic Arms Limitation Talks.[9] The SALT talks were completed in 1972 and produced two major results. The first was a treaty limiting the deployment of antiballistic missiles (ABMs). The treaty limited each side to two ABM sites: one in defense of its national capital and the other in defense of an ICBM base. While the Soviet Union has completed these two bases, the only U.S. ABM facility was deactivated a few years after construction. In the rather perverse logic of deterrence, the elimination of ABM systems assured that a strategy of mutually assured destruction could be valid; each side could be sure of inflicting "unacceptable damage" on the civilian population and defense installations of the other.

The executive agreement covered offensive weapons. It limited the two sides to the number of missiles they already had deployed or under construction. They also were limited to the number of missile-launching submarines that were operational or under construction. Both limitations assured the superiority of the Soviet Union in numbers of missiles.

It would seem that the Soviet Union gained significantly from the SALT talks, but the benefits were actually distributed more evenly. For one thing, the agreement slowed the relatively rapid expansion of Soviet missile forces. In addition, manned bombers were not covered by the agreement, and at that time the United States had a marked superiority (since somewhat eroded) in bombers. In addition, medium-range nuclear weapons in Europe and the British and French nuclear forces were not counted as a part of the limitations, so a significant number of missiles that could reach the Soviet Union were not included. Further, the placing of MIRVs was not limited by SALT I. Thus, as in most successful negotiations, both sides could feel that they got something from the agreement.

Both sides continued weapons developments after the signing of SALT I, with the Soviet Union completing a force of very large missiles (*SS-18s*) that could carry ten MIRVs. They also developed a new bomber (the *Backfire*) that was capable of reaching targets in the United States. The United States made largely technical improvement in its forces with relatively little in the way of new strategic weapons systems. These developments set the stage for a second round of strategic arms talks—SALT II.

The results of SALT II, which emerged in 1979, were more complex than SALT I, in part because of the increasing complexity of the weapons.[10] There were a number of important provisions:

1. A limit of 2250 on strategic nuclear delivery systems (i.e., missiles and bombers).
2. A limit on the number of MIRV missiles and the number of bombers carrying Cruise missiles.
3. A ban on new heavy missiles, thereby ensuring Soviet monopoly with the *SS-18*.
4. ICBMs were limited to ten MIRVs, submarine-launched missiles to fourteen MIRVs, and bombers to twenty Cruise missiles, although the size of the warheads was not limited.
5. Testing and deployment of new ICBMs was to be limited to a single light ICBM on each side (e.g., the MX in the United States).
6. A ban on rapid reload of ICBM launchers. Many Soviet launch sites are "cold" launchers and can be reused; almost all American sites are "hot" and are destroyed by the launch.
7. There was an agreement not to interfere with methods of verification, such as photographic satellites.
8. In exchange for an agreement by the United States not to test or deploy new Cruise missiles before 1982, the Soviet Union agreed to limit production of *Backfire* bombers to thirty per year.

Despite the hope held out for SALT II, the treaty never was put into effect. Ratification was delayed in the U.S. Senate, and in 1980, when the Soviet Union invaded Afghanistan, the treaty was formally withdrawn from the Senate by President Carter. This put an end to détente between the two superpowers and ushered in a colder phase of the cold war. However, it was not only the invasion that produced skepticism about SALT II. The treaty seemed to give too many advantages to the Soviet Union, and to prevent the United States from developing new weapons, especially the Cruise missile, on which it had a technological lead. Thus the treaty would have had a difficult time receiving the necessary consent by the Senate.

In the 1980s, the Reagan administration "upped the ante" in arms negotiations; instead of having "limitation" talks, they proposed talks about the reduction of the number of nuclear weapons deployed by both sides. These came to be called START negotiations, for Strategic Arms Reduction Talks. These talks were premised on the superiority of the Soviet Union in strategic weapons, so any limitation would only confirm that superiority. Thus the United States wanted to reduce the number of weapons on both sides to a more equal level. These negotiations were stalled, or nonexistent, during most of President Reagan's first term. The cold war grew colder, the Soviet leadership was in flux, and the Soviets appeared to have little incentive to engage in talks. The only demonstrable result of negotiations was an improvement in the "hotline" linking the President of the United States and the Soviet Premier in case of an emergency. Negotiations also were complicated by political pressures in the United States, and among its allies, for a nuclear freeze — an end to production of nuclear weapons at the current levels. As noted, this would preserve the Soviet numerical superiority, although supporters of the freeze argue that given the destructive potential of either side, there is ample strength for the logic of deterrence to work.

Problems in Defense Policy

In addition to the very broad strategic problems discussed above, maintaining the defenses of the United States present several specific policy problems, none of which can be solved readily. These problems involve the interaction of specific defense issues (e.g., the acquisition of weapons and manpower) with either fundamental features of the economic system or fundamental American values.

Military Procurement

The first major defense problem is the problem of acquiring new weapons systems.[11] In a modern, high-technology military force, new weapons are not bought "off-the-shelf" but represent years or even decades of research and development. This in turn presents several problems for the military managers who seek to acquire the weapons. Their first problem is deciding what form of competition to demand among potential suppliers of the weapons. One option is to have possible competitors develop full-scale, operating systems and then test those weapons against each other. The other option is to settle on a vendor for the weapons system very early in the development process and then work with the contractor to develop the weapon. Although the former option corresponds to the usual ideas about bidding for contracts and getting the most "bang for the buck" from the Department of Defense's money, it may ultimately produce more expensive and less effective weapons. If a firm must develop fully operational weapons in order to compete for a program, it may choose simply not to compete; hence many potentially useful ideas (especially from smaller firms) will be lost. Second, if this kind of competition is carried out, then any firm competing for government contracts may have to amortize failures across winning contracts in order to make a profit, and consequently the costs of weapons systems will increase.

On the other hand, awarding contracts for major weapons systems on the basis of only prototypes and engineering projections may produce numerous disappointments and cost overruns. Despite screening by skilled military and civilian personnel in the Department of Defense, good ideas on the drawing board may not work when they are brought to full-scale production and deployment. There are a number of examples in recent weapons systems; the F-14, the Bradley Fighting Vehicle, and several missile systems, for example, have not performed as expected. Even if the manufacturer is capable of making the system work as promised, there may be large cost overruns, as with the C-5A where the delivered price was several times the projected price. Given that most contracts for weapons are "cost plus" and virtually guarantee the manufacturer a profit, manufacturers have a strong incentive to bid low on projects and allow costs to escalate later. The Department of Defense has instituted controls to try to prevent the most flagrant violations of this contracting system, but it is difficult to control genuine cases of cost underestimation when a project is well into production. If a workable product can be attained, it will almost certainly be better to go ahead and allow cost overruns than begin again at the beginning.

Another problem arising from the procurement process is that a manufacturer awarded a contract for a particular weapons system becomes the "sole source" for that system and for the parts that go along with it. This allow firms to charge exorbitant prices for spare parts and tools; simple wrenches costing a dollar or less have been billed to the Department of Defense for several *thousand* dollars. Again, curbs have been instituted to stop some of the greatest abuses, but the underlying problem remains.

The division among the armed services may also produce problems in procuring weapons, or at least may make weapons cost more than they should. Again, there are two options. One would be to attempt to force the services to use the same weapons, if at all possible; the other would be to allow the services to acquire systems more suited to their individual needs. For example, both the air force and the navy fly airplanes that perform similar missions; why can they not use the same planes? In addition to the long-standing rivalries between the services, there may be a danger that weapons resulting from an integrated procurement process would be neither fish nor fowl. For example, the weight necessary for a plane to make carrier landings for the navy may make it less suitable as an air-superiority interceptor for the air force. However, procurement of a number of different weapons may produce higher costs, for the research and development costs of each can be amortized across fewer units of production.

Finally, the budgetary process of the United States presents problems for weapons procurement. Unlike the large majority of countries, the United States has an annual defense budget, and there is a possibility (and real examples) that an ongoing weapons system may not be funded. This, of course, presents problems for both contractors and the military. To date, proposals for a multi-year procurement process have been unsuccessful, for Congress wishes to maintain its control over the public purse.[12]

Thus the process of equipping a modern army is a difficult one, and it is made more difficult by the budgeting process in the United States. It is made even more difficult by the close ties between the Department of Defense and their defense contractors—the military-industrial complex—that may make an independent evaluation of some projects difficult to obtain. These problems are hard to solve because Congress wants to preserve its budgetary powers and the Defense establishment needs the cooperation and abilities of contractors; however, given the importance of hardware and technology for the modern military, attention must be given to these questions.

Updating the Strategic Deterrent

Much of the strategic deterrent force of the United States is aging; in some cases, it may be obsolete. The B-52 bomber entered service in the 1950s and, despite updates and modifications, is a very old weapon. The Minuteman missile is by no means obsolete but is vulnerable to a Soviet first strike. These problems with existing weapons have led to the development of two new weapons systems—the B-1 bomber and the MX missile—both of which have been at the center of controversy.

The B-1 bomber is designed as a supersonic penetrating intercontinental bomber that can fly to the target and return, depending on speed and electronic countermeasures for its survival. After several prototypes were built and tested, the Carter administration canceled the project in 1977, arguing that bombers may not be as efficient as Cruise missiles, and that the development of the "stealth" technology, which would make an airplane less visible to radar, would make the B-1 obsolete quickly. This decision caused a great deal of negative reaction in the military—especially in the air force—and was reversed by the Reagan administration, which called for a force of 100 B-1 bombers.

The MX missile presents an even more difficult problem. The MX was designed to reduce the vulnerability of the current Minuteman missiles, as well as to upgrade the accuracy and number of warheads in the U.S. nuclear arsenal. While the existing *Minuteman III* missiles have three MIRVed warheads, the MX could carry ten. The most important controversy about the MX was the original "racetrack" deployment strategy of the Carter administration. The idea was to put each of the (then) 200 MX missiles on a transporter, which would move around an oval "racetrack" containing 26 hardened launch sites; it was assumed that the Soviets (or any other power) would not know where the missiles were at any time and could not destroy them without using at least 5200 warheads (200 missiles times 26 sites). The Reagan administration rejected this proposal, in part because of strong opposition from the western states (sites probably would have been in Utah and Nevada) where thousands of acres would have been needed for the racetracks, and in part because the administration thought there could be means—with spy satellites, for example—by which the Soviets would indeed know where the missiles were. The Reagan administration therefore decided to proceed with the production of 100 MX missiles and appointed a bipartisan Commission on Strategic Alternatives (the Scowcroft Commission) to make suggestions for basing the MX. This commission recommended placing the missiles in reinforced Minuteman silos. The commission also recommended the development of a new, small, and highly mobile missile that could be fired from a mobile launcher and therefore moved almost anywhere, much as Cruise missiles can be. This suggestion soon came to be known as the "Midgetman" missile. The Midgetman would have only a single, rather small warhead, but given its *relatively* low cost and its *relative* invulnerability, it could present a serious deterrent, especially given the destructive capacity of even a small warhead.

The All-Volunteer Military

During the Vietnam war, the use of conscription to provide manpower for the armed forces became increasingly unpopular in the United States. Therefore, in 1975, the draft was phased out and replaced by an all-volunteer force. While this was politically desirable, the policy decision has presented several problems for the armed forces in the 1980s.[13]

The most obvious problem is that the military must now compete directly with civilian employers for the same pool of young people, instead of being able to train young people in the military for a short time and perhaps induce some of them to stay in the service. Given the risks associated with serving in the military, it is not surprising that there have been difficulties in filling enlistment quotas. There are special difficulties in attracting educated and skilled personnel to the armed forces, for these are the people whose services are in demand in the civilian labor market. Thus, for much of its history, the all-volunteer force has been plagued by stories of low-quality recruits. This diminished during the recession of the early 1980s, which made *any* job seem attractive, but may well resurface after the economy has recovered somewhat. The military has lessened its demand for young men somewhat by using women in jobs formerly filled by males (although still not in combat positions) and by using civilians in jobs once filled by uniformed personnel. There is still a problem, however, in attracting highly skilled personnel to a military increasingly dominated by technical weapons systems. There seems to be an increasing disparity between the skills required to function effectively in a modern armed force and the personnel generally available to the military.

Associated with the general problem of attracting personnel is the problem of paying them. An obvious means of attracting and retaining people in any job is to pay them adequately; this is especially true in the military, given the dangers and hardships associated with being in the armed forces. Unfortunately, however, military pay is generally not competitive with private-sector pay, even when the value of allowances and benefits is included in the comparison. Military pay is much better than it was before the introduction of an all-volunteer military, but it is not yet capable of attracting as many of the best personnel in the labor market as the armed forces requires. Nevertheless, military pay has become more expensive in the aggregate and now accounts for a larger percentage of the defense budget than it did before the all-volunteer force.

Associated with the general problem of pay for military personnel is the especially difficult problem of retaining those people that the armed forces have trained. For example, someone who trains as a pilot in the air force is frequently able to command twice his military pay working for a private airline. Even skilled enlisted personnel, such as machinists and radar operators, have found that the private sector offers them a much greater economic reward than continuing in the military would offer. The retirement option available to military personnel (full retirement benefits after thirty years) may make staying in the service more desirable, but the loss of crucial skilled personnel continues, and there are some pressures to make military retirement less generous. For example, one of the principal recommendations of President Reagan's private survey of government costs was to make military retirement much more like retirement programs in the private sector.

Finally, there are philosophical and constitutional questions about the development of an all-volunteer military. Given historical patterns and perhaps continuing discrimination in the labor market, an all-volunteer force may be composed increasingly of members of minority groups. This may be seen as imposing an excessive cost of national defense on these groups. More generally, the traditional ideal of the U.S. military has been that of the "citizen-soldier"; traditionally we have rejected the ideas of a professional standing army. The policy of an all-volunteer force makes it more likely that we will have a professional military force and that we will not have large numbers of young Americans serving for a time in the armed forces. This, in turn, may make the military more of a group apart from the rest of society and may make them less amenable to civilian control. Thus, paradoxically, although we may need a professional military to be able to handle the highly sophisticated weapons in the contemporary arsenal, we may lose some control over those weapons and their massive potential for destruction. There is little evidence to support a claim that a "warrior caste" has developed in the United States, but the current personnel system of the armed forces may make that development more possible than it would be with conscription.

Conventional Forces and Strategies

With all the concern about nuclear weapons and nuclear strategy, it is easy to forget that the most likely use of force by the United States would be with conventional forces. These forces were, in fact, used twice in the first Reagan administration — once in Lebanon and once in Grenada. In addition, the navy has been used to "show the flag" in the Caribbean, the Mediterranean, and the Persian Gulf. While these activities were taking place, American troops remained on duty in Western Europe, South Korea, Okinawa, the Philippines, Guantanamo Bay in Cuba, and several other places around the globe. The ability of the United States to respond to threats to its interests around the world with conventional forces is an important element in defense planning.

One of the important elements in the ability of the United States to project its presence around the world is the Rapid Deployment Force. This is a force of troops ready to be deployed by air on very short notice. Materials have been positioned in places around the world so that troops can be supplied during the time that might be required to have seaborne supplies delivered to them. The Carter and then the Reagan administration have positioned supplies for up to six divisions (a program called POMCUS) in Western Europe; in the event of a confrontation with countries in the Warsaw Pact, troops could be flown to Europe without the need to air-lift heavy equipment and munitions. Both these programs are designed to make the U.S. armed forces more flexible and mobile, and thereby to enable them to deal with much larger Soviet and Warsaw Pact ground forces.

Another means of counteracting the numerical superiority of the Warsaw Pact is to improve the quality of the weapons available to NATO troops. As we discussed in the section on procurement, this presents difficulties because it is difficult to determine in advance if any new weapons system will perform as intended. In addition, there is some evidence that the modern weapons may not in fact be an improvement over older, low-technology weapons. The fundamental problem is that newer and more complex weapons have more components that can go wrong; thus, even if the firepower and accuracy of weapons are enhanced, reliability may be diminished. Therefore, not only are there budgetary problems with procurement but there are real problems with selecting reliable and survivable weapons for the armed forces.

Even with the potential problems of modern weapons, many have proven to be extremely effective. For example, early exercises with the M-1 tank in West Germany indicate that it is an extremely reliable, fast, and effective weapon. The problem then becomes acquiring enough of these weapons fast enough to meet the needs of the armed forces. But what are those needs? What should the armed forces be preparing for? The current doctrine is that the armed forces should be preparing for one-and-a-half wars; that is, the armed forces should be preparing for one major and one minor conflict to occur at any one time. Even that level of conflict might strain the available resources, especially if the conflicts were not in Europe and Korea.

Planning to meet contingencies with conventional forces is important not only for the ability to project the forces of the United States needed to implement national policy. It is also important because a strong conventional force would make the use of nuclear weapons, meaning primarily theater nuclear weapons, less likely. Plans exist for the use of such weapons in the event of apparent defeat by conventional forces; once the use of those weapons begins, it will be difficult to contain their escalation. This is especially true given that the difficulty in distinguishing between a theater nuclear weapon and a strategic weapon; some "theater" weapons in Western Europe can reach the Soviet Union. Thus the availability of nuclear weapons makes conventional forces that much more important.

Summary

Making defense policy is exceedingly difficult. It involves planning for an uncertain future that contains adversaries whose strengths and strategies are not readily predictable. It also involves allies whose commitments to a common purpose and a common set of policies is uncertain. Defense policy also involves making prospective decisions about weapons that may take years or even decades to develop and that may not perform as well (or perhaps even better) as intended. Finally, defense involves huge costs that may be politically unpopular even when the public strongly supports a strong military posture for the United States. Defense policymaking is a series of gigantic gambles about the future, gambles that most of those involved hope never actually have to be taken.

Defense policy has been the subject of intense and sustained political debate during the Reagan administration. Although Ronald Reagan came into office promising to modernize and strengthen America's armed forces, and won reelection stressing the same themes, his ambitious program of military procurement and expansion has come into conflict with the increasing federal deficit. Some programs have been delayed, others have been scaled down, and a few have been eliminated. The tradeoff between a strong military and fiscal soundness will likely continue during the second Reagan administration.

Notes

1. The levels of employment in defense and the expense of the defense establishment have been highly variable. See B. Guy Peters, "Public Employment in the United States," in Richard Rose et al., *Public Employment in Western Democracies* (Cambridge: Cambridge University Press, 1985).

2. Unlike after previous wars, the size of the U.S. military did not return to prewar levels after World War II. There is now a large, seemingly permanent military force.

3. Julian Critchley, *The North Atlantic Alliance and the Soviet Union in the 1980s* (London: Macmillan, 1982).

4. For an analysis of the now famous "Star Wars" technology, see Congressional Budget Office, *Analysis of the Costs of the Administration's Strategic Defense Initiative, 1985-89* (Washington, D.C.: Congressional Budget Office, May 1984).

5. Lawrence Freedman, *The Evolution of Nuclear Strategy* (New York: St. Martin's, 1983), 98ff.

6. William M. Kaufman, *The McNamara Strategy* (New York: Harper & Row, 1964); and Desmond Ball, *The Strategic Missile Program of the Kennedy Administration* (Berkeley: University of California Press, 1980).

7. Albert Wohlstetter, "Optimal Ways to Confuse Ourselves," *Foreign Policy,* 1975, 170-98.

8. Desmond Ball, *Developments in U.S. Nuclear Policy under the Carter Administration* (Berkeley: Seminar on Arms Control and Foreign Policy, 1980).

9. John Newhouse, *Cold Dawn: The Story of SALT* (New York: Holt, Rinehart and Winston, 1973).

10. Strobe Talbott, *Endgame: The Inside Story of SALT-II* (New York: Harper & Row, 1979).

11. Gordon Adams, *The Politics of Defense Contracting: The Iron Triangle* (New Brunswick, N.J.: Transaction, 1981).

12. Herschel Kanter, "The Defense Budget Process," in *The Federal Budget: Economics and Politics,* ed. Michael J. Boskin and Aaron Wildavsky (San Francisco: Institute for Contemporary Studies, 1982), 281-97; and Michael D. Hobkirk, *The Politics of Defense Budgeting* (Washington, D.C.: National Defense University, 1983).

13. Martin Binkin, *America's Volunteer Military* (Washington, D.C.: Brookings Institution, 1984).

PART FOUR

Policy Analysis

Introduction

Now, after discussing the processes through which policies are adopted and some characteristics of certain policy areas, we must look at the means of evaluating policies. Methods of evaluation are of two disparate types. Although they are almost diametrically opposed, both means are central to understanding why some policies should be preferred over others.

The first approach to policy analysis is economic and quantitative. Although there are a number of such methods, cost-benefit analysis is the one most commonly used. This form of analysis attempts to reduce all the costs and benefits of a proposed project to a common economic measuring rod. By so doing, it gives the decision maker a relatively clear choice among the alternatives competing for the use of scarce resources. Using this approach, a project that produces the greatest net benefit for the society would be chosen over other options for funding.

The second approach to policy analysis is ethical. Whereas cost-benefit analysis applies strictly utilitarian standards to issues of policy choice, ethical analysis spreads the net of human values much more broadly and seeks to apply other forms of valuation to the outcomes of the policy process. In addition to the economic good created by policy choices, other values, such as life, liberty, and equality, can be pursued through the policymaking process. Thus, ethical analysis may give very different, albeit much "softer," answers if applied to the same policy.

14. Cost-Benefit Analysis

Much of this book has been concerned with the process through which policies are adopted and with the characteristics of policies adopted in the United States. This chapter extends those interests by discussing one principal method of policy analysis used when making policy choices: cost-benefit analysis. Because governments operate with limited resources and limited ability to predict the future, they must employ some techniques to help them decide how to employ those scarce resources. Cost-benefit analysis is the most commonly employed technique — other than the informal techniques arising from intuition and experience. The fundamental principle of cost-benefit analysis is that the project should produce a benefit for society greater than the cost of the project.[1] Second, when several projects promise to yield positive net benefits and all cannot be undertaken because of limited resources, then the project that creates the greatest net benefit to the society should be undertaken. This technique is perhaps most applicable to capital projects, but it can also be applied to other kinds of public programs.

There is obviously a decided utilitarian bias underlying cost-benefit analysis.[2] The costs and benefits of a project are all collapsed onto the single measuring rod of money, and those that create the greatest net benefit are deemed superior. This implies that the dominant value in society is economic wealth and, further, that more is always better. This is presumed to be true even if rather perverse distributional consequences arise from the program. I discuss the philosophical and practical issues that arise with cost-benefit analysis later in the chapter. These implications may be sufficiently troubling, especially in a democratic political system, to argue for alternative means of evaluating policies. But cost-benefit analysis does have the advantage of reducing all the costs and benefits of public programs to that single dimension, whereas other forms of analysis may produce apparent confusion by lacking such a dimension.

Principles of Cost-Benefit Analysis

In the world of cost-benefit analysis more is always better. Although it does have serious intellectual foundations, which we explore in a moment, the method is in many ways no more than a systematic framework within which to collect data concerning the merits and demerits of a public program. And it is not a new idea: The Army Corps of Engineers used the technique as early as 1900 to evaluate the merits of proposed improvements to rivers and harbors. The basic idea is to enumerate the positive features of a program and attach a monetary value to them, and at the same time to enumerate the negative features and attach a monetary value to them. The net balance of costs and benefits will then determine if a program is economically feasible, although many other questions may still remain.

One principal idea underlying cost-benefit analysis comes from the tradition in welfare economics that has sought to develop an acceptable social welfare function, or a socially desirable means of making decisions.[3] One of the first criteria of this sort was the Pareto principle, which argued that a policy move was optimal if no move away from it could be made to benefit someone without hurting someone else.[4] Stated another way, a Pareto optimal move is one that benefits someone without hurting anyone. Clearly, in the real world of political decision making, moves of this kind are rare indeed, and politics is frequently about who gets what at the expense of whom. A substitute criterion was advanced by Kaldor and Hicks. They argued that a policy change was socially justified if the winners gained a sufficient amount to compensate the losers and still had something left for themselves.[5] This does not imply that those winners necessarily will compensate the losers, or that they could even identify them, but the idea is that the society as a whole is better off because of the overall increase in benefits. This obviously, then, is a justification of the reliance of cost-benefit analysis on any benefits and on the production of the greatest net benefit possible.

A second fundamental idea underlying cost-benefit analysis is that of the consumer's surplus.[6] Stated simply, this is the amount of money a consumer would be willing to pay for a given product, minus the amount he or she must actually pay. Consumers tend to value the first unit of a product or service they receive more highly than the second, and the second more than the third; the first quart of milk where there has been none is more valuable than the second. But these units are not priced marginally; they are sold at an average price. This means that the utility of increased production will give consumers a surplus value from the production. Thus, any investment that reduces the cost of the product or service produces a benefit in savings that increases the consumer surplus. The investment by government in a new superhighway that reduces the cost to consumers of driving the same number of miles—in time, in gasoline, and in potential loss of life and property—creates a consumer surplus. And as the time, gasoline, and lives saved by the new highway may be used for other increased production, the actual savings represent a minimum definition of the improvement to society resulting from the construction of the new highway.

Also important in understanding cost-benefit analysis is the idea of opportunity costs: Any resource used in one project cannot be used in another. For example, the concrete and labor used to build the superhighway cannot be used to build a new dam. Consequently, all projects must be evaluated against other possible projects to determine the most appropriate way to use resources. Again, the basic idea of getting the most "bang for the buck" is important in understanding cost-benefit analysis.

Finally, in evaluating costs and benefits, we must be concerned with the role of time. The costs and benefits of most projects do not occur at a single time, but accrue over a number of years. If our superhighway is built, it will be serviceable for fifty years and will be financed over twenty years through government bonds. Policymakers must be certain that the long-term costs and benefits as well as the short-term consequences are positive. This, of course, requires some estimation of the shape of the future. We may estimate that our new superhighway will be useful for fifty years, but oil shortages may so reduce driving during that period that the real benefits will be much less than anticipated. Or, conversely, the value of gasoline may increase so much that the savings produced are more valuable than assumed at present. These kinds of assumptions must be built into the model of valuation for it to aid a decision maker.

In part because of the uncertainty of future costs and benefits, and in part because of the general principle that people prefer a dollar today to a dollar next year, the costs and benefits of projects must be converted to present values before useful cost and benefit calculations can be made. That is, the benefits that accrue to the society in the future have their value discounted and are consequently worth less than benefits produced in the first year of the project. Likewise, costs that occur in future years are lower than costs that occur in the first few years. Thus, cost-benefit analysis would appear to favor projects that have a quick payoff rather than greater long-term benefits; but perhaps higher maintenance and operation costs. While there may be a good logical justification for these biases in the method, they do certainly influence the kinds of program that will be selected and that will have definite social implications, not least of all for future generations.

Doing Cost-Benefit Analysis

To better understand the application of cost-benefit analysis we now work through the steps required to justify the construction of a new dam on the Nowhere River. This project is being proposed by the Army Corps of Engineers, and we have to determine whether or not the project should be undertaken. We first have to decide if the project is feasible and acceptable and then if it is preferable to other projects that could be funded with the same resources.

Determining Costs and Benefits

One of the most important things to consider when performing a cost-benefit analysis, especially of a public project, is that all costs and benefits should be enumerated. Thus, unlike projects that might be undertaken in the private sector, public projects require an explicit statement of the social or external costs and benefits. In the public sector, projects whose strictly economic potential may outweigh their costs may not be adopted because of the possibility of pollution or the loss of external benefits such as natural beauty. In fact, one of the principal logical justifications for the public sector is that it should take into account these external factors and attempt to correct them in ways not possible in the private sector.[7]

Thus, for our dam project, we can think of two lists of attributes (see table 14.1). On one side are the costs of the project, the main one being the economic cost of constructing the dam, which should reflect the market valuation of the opportunity costs of using the same resources for other purposes. Also, the dam will impose an economic cost by flooding the houses and farmland of present inhabitants of the area. But there are also social, or human, costs involved here, as these farms have been in the same families for generations, and the farmers have resisted the project from the beginning. Finally, there are further social costs in that the proposed dam will impound a river that currently has some recreational value for canoeists and is essentially an unspoiled natural area.

TABLE 14.1
COSTS AND BENEFITS OF DAM PROJECT

Costs	Benefits
Construction costs	Hydroelectric power
Flooded land	Flood control
Relocation of families	Irrigation
Loss of recreation	New recreational opportunities

On the other side of the ledger are the benefits of the program. First, the dam will provide hydroelectric power for the region. In so doing it will provide a source of power that does not consume scarce fossil fuels and does not create the pollution that would result from producing the same amount of electricity with fossil fuels. Also, the dam would help control the raging Nowhere River, which every spring overflows its banks and floods a number of towns and cities downstream from the proposed dam. Also, the impounded water behind the dam will provide irrigation water for the remaining farmers, enabling them to grow more crops. Finally, although canoeists will lose some recreational benefits as a result of the building of the dam, those who enjoy boating and water-skiing will benefit from the large lake behind the dam. Thus, although this dam does impose a number of costs on the society, it also provides a number of benefits in return, and we must now begin to attach some figures to these costs and benefits in order to be able to make a decision as to the feasibility and desirability of the project.

Assigning Value

Assigning a real monetary value to all the costs and benefits of this mythical project would be difficult. For some costs and benefits the market directly provides a value. For example, we know or can estimate the costs of building the dam and the value of the hydroelectric power it will produce. Although such costs are generally measurable through the market, the market may not fully measure the costs and benefits. For example, if our dam is to be built in a remote area with little more than subsistence agriculture, bringing in a large number of highly skilled and highly paid workers may distort prices and increase the costs of building the dam. Likewise, not only is the hydroelectric power salable but it may produce substantial secondary benefits (or perhaps costs) by stimulating industrialization in this rural and remote area. The experience of the Tennessee Valley Authority and its impact on the Tennessee Valley as a result of the development of cheap electric power illustrates this point rather nicely. We cannot fully predict these secondary benefits, nor can we rely on them to make the project feasible, but they do frequently occur.

Some other costs and benefits of the project, although not directly measurable through the market, can be estimated in other ways. For example, we have to estimate the dam's recreational value to the people who will use the lake to water ski and its cost to those who will no longer be able to use the river for canoeing. We can do this by estimating the people's willingness to pay for their recreation.[8] Just how much time and money are they willing to invest to enjoy their recreation? This will provide some measure of the economic value of the lake, or the free-flowing stream, to the population.

This means of valuation returns to the idea of the consumer's suplus. The first unit of a particular commodity is valued more highly than any subsequent units, so that as production is increased each unit is marginally less valuable to the consumer. In our dam example, if there have already been a number of impoundments in the area, as there have been in the Tennessee Valley, then a new lake would have less value to consumers, and they would be less willing to pay than if this were the first lake in an area with a large number of free-flowing streams. Likewise, one more hydroelectric power station in an area that already has cheap electrical power is less valuable than it would be in an economically backward area, and consequently citizens would be less willing to pay for that new power plant.

Finally, on some aspects of the project, the market provides little or no guidance about valuation. For the farmers who are displaced by the project, we can place an economic cost on their land, their houses, and their moving costs. However, we cannot readily assign an economic value to those houses that are the ancestral homes of certain families and that are therefore more valuable than ordinary houses. Likewise, there is some value in not disturbing a natural setting, simply because it is natural, and this is a difficult thing to which to assign an economic value. As a result, at times absolute prohibitions are built into legislation to prevent certain actions, so planners cannot depend entirely on net benefit ratios. The Environmental Protection Agency's guideline for preserving the habitats of endangered species, which resulted in the now notorious case of the snail darter in the Little Tennessee River, is an obvious example of the application of regulations to prevent some actions regardless of the relative costs and benefits.

It is fortunate that the dam we are building does not require any direct decisions about loss of life or injury to human beings. For projects that do— for example, building the superhighway as a means of saving lives—we come to perhaps the most difficult problem of valuation: estimating the value of a human life.[9] Although it is convenient to say that life is priceless, in practice decisions are made that deny some people their lives when that loss of life is preventable. If this is the case, then some subjective, if not objective, evaluation is being made of the worth of lives. One standard method of making such a judgment involves discounted future earnings. In this method the life of the individual is worth whatever the individual could have earned in the course of his or her working life, discounted to present value. Therefore, a highly paid corporate executive's life is worth more than that of a housewife or a college professor. This mechanism for evaluating lives clearly conforms to the basic market valuation, although it can be clearly disputed on humane grounds. Another means of assessing the value of lives in performing a cost-benefit analysis uses the size of the awards to plaintiffs in legal cases of negligence or malpractice that resulted in loss of life. This constitutes another version of the market, albeit one in which considerations of human suffering and "loss of companionship" have a greater (some would say too great) impact on values.

Another means of assessing the value of a human life is somewhat similar to the "willingness to pay" criterion. Presumably individuals would be willing to pay almost anything to preserve their own lives and the lives of their loved ones. However, individuals engage in risky behavior and risky occupations all the time, and when they do so, they make a subjective statement about the value of their life.[10] Because we know how much more likely it is for a coal miner to be killed at work than it is for a construction worker—either in the mines or as a result of black lung—we can estimate from any differences in wages how much the individual would appear to value his life. This method does, of course, imply a certain level of knowledge that individuals may not have, and it assumes that the collective bargaining process, through which wages of coal miners are determined, accurately reflects both individual preferences and the market values of lives. It does, however, offer another feasible means of estimating the value of life, one that uses the assessment of individuals themselves rather than that of the market or the courts.

Discounting

We now return to the problem of time. The costs and benefits of a project do not all magically appear the year the project is completed, but typically are spread over a number of years. Table 14.2 shows the stream of benefits coming from the dam on the Nowhere River over a twenty-year period. This is the projected feasible lifetime of the project, as the Nowhere River carries a great deal of silt and the lake behind the dam is expected to fill with silt after that period. How do we assess these benefits and come up with a single number that we can compare with costs to determine the economic feasibility of the project?

TABLE 14.2

HYPOTHETICAL COSTS AND BENEFITS OF DAM PROJECT FOR TWENTY YEARS
($ millions)

| | \multicolumn{20}{c}{Year} |
	1	2	3	4	5	6	7	8	9	10	11	12	13	14	15	16	17	18	19	20
Costs	5	8	7	2	1	1	1	1	1	1	1	1	1	1	1	1	1	1	1	1
Benefits	0	0	0	3	4	5	5	5	5	5	5	5	5	5	5	4	4	4	3	2

To calculate such a figure, we must compute the present value of the future benefits. We have already decided on the time span of the project; the only task that remains is to determine the discount rate that should be applied to a public investment. And, as with the valuation of costs and benefits, disagreements may arise about what that rate should be.[11] One method is to use the opportunity costs of the use of these funds. Presumably any money used in a project in the public sector will be extracted from the private sector by some means such as taxation or borrowing, and consequently the rate of return these resources could earn if they were invested in private-sector projects is the appropriate rate of discount for public-sector projects. This is not always a practical solution, however, as rates of return differ for different kinds of investments, and investors apparently choose to put some money into each kind of investment. Is building a dam more like building a steel mill or more like investing in a savings account? And which of the many possible rates of return should be selected?

Several other issues arise with respect to the selection of a discount rate. First, in discussing projects for which most benefits are to accrue in the future, there is an element of uncertainty. In our example we have assumed that the probable life span of the dam will be twenty years, but in reality the lake may fill up with silt in fifteen years. Consequently, it may be more prudent to select a discount rate higher than that in the market because we cannot be sure of the real occurrence or real value of the benefits. And because these benefits are expected to be further away in time, they are less certain; therefore, even higher rates of discount should be applied. Also, with inflation and the uncertainties about the increase of oil supplies, we may need to be more conservative about discount rates.

Second, some argue that there should be a "social rate of discount" lower than that set by the market.[12] Such an arbitrarily set discount rate would be justified on the basis of the need for greater public investment and the need to provide a capital infrastructure for future generations. Further, as the size of the public sector is to some degree determined by the rate of discount, that rate should be set not by the market but by more conscious political choices concerning the level of public activity. But the economic argument is that in the long term the society will be better off if resources are allocated on the basis of their opportunity costs. If a public project is deemed unfeasible because of the selection of a market-determined discount rate, then the resources that would have been used in that project will produce greater social benefit in a project that is feasible under that rate of discount, regardless of whether the project is public or private.

Finally, a question arises about intergenerational equity. What do we owe our posterity or, put the other way around, what has posterity ever done for us? If the discount rate is set lower than that determined by the market, then we will tend to undertake projects that have an extended time value and will benefit future generations. But we will also deprive our generation of opportunities for consumption by using those resources as investment capital. This is as much a philosophical as a practical issue, but it is important for our understanding of alternative consequences arising from alternative choices of a rate of discount for public projects.

Using several discount rates, let us now work through the example of levels of benefit from the dam. At this writing, the prime interest rate in the United States is approximately 10 percent. If we use this market-determined interest rate, the $100 in benefits produced after one year is worth

$$V_P = 100/1.10 = \$90.91$$

And $100 in benefits produced after two years would be worth

$$V_P = 100/(1.10)^2 = \$82.64$$

And $100 in benefits produced in the twentieth year of the project would be worth only $14.87 in present value. Thus, if we use this rate of discount in evaluating a project, the net benefit of that project at present value is positive. This project has a rather high cost during its early years, with the benefits occurring gradually over the twenty years. With a higher discount rate such a project is not feasible. If we use a discount rate of 18 percent, which would have seemed very reasonable in the late 1970s, then the net benefit of the dam at present value would be negative and the project is economically infeasible.

Discounting is a means of reducing all costs and benefits of a project to their present value, based on the assumption that benefits created in the future are worth less than those created immediately. Philosophically or ideologically one might want a low discount rate to encourage public investment, but object to the entire process of discounting. Should we simply not look to see if the stream of benefits created is greater than the total costs, no matter how they occur? This would, of course, be equivalent to a discount rate of zero. This point might be valid philosophically, but—until the argument is accepted by economists, financiers, and government decision makers—public investment decisions will be made on the basis of present value and on the basis of interest rates that approximate the real value of the rate of return in the private sector.

Choosing among Projects

We have determined that our dam on the Nowhere River is feasible, given that a benevolent deity has provided us a discount rate of 10 percent for this project. But it is not yet time to break ground for the dam. We must first compare our project with the alternative projects for funding. Thus, the opportunity-cost question arises not only with respect to the single project being considered and the option of allowing the money to remain in private hands but also with regard to choices made among possible projects in the public sector.

We have said that the fundamental rule applied is to select the project that will produce the greatest total benefit to society. If we apply the Kaldor-Hicks criterion, we see that this project is justified simply because it will create more benefits to spread around in the society and presumably compensate those who lost something because the project was built. Thus, in the simplest case, if we were to choose to undertake only a single project this year—perhaps because of limited manpower for supervision—we would choose Project D from table 14.3 simply because it creates the largest level of net benefit. By investing less money in Projects A and B we could have produced slightly more net benefit for society, but we are administratively constrained from making that decision.

TABLE 14.3
COSTS AND BENEFITS OF ALTERNATIVE PROJECTS
(*$ millions*)

Projects	Costs	Benefits	Net Benefit
A	70	130	60
B	90	140	50
C	200	270	70
D	150	250	100

More commonly, however, a particular resource—usually money—is limited and, with that limitation in mind, we have to choose one or more projects that will result in maximum benefits. Let us say that the ten projects listed in table 14.4 are all economically feasible and that we have been given a budget of $50,000 for capital projects. Which projects should we select for funding?

TABLE 14.4
CHOOSING A PACKAGE OF PROJECTS BY NET BENEFIT RATIO
(*$ millions*)

Project	Costs	Cumulative Costs	Benefits	Net Benefits	Net Benefit Ratio
A	2	2	12	10	5.0
B	4	6	20	16	4.0
C	10	16	40	30	3.0
D	10	26	35	25	2.5
E	8	34	28	20	2.5
F	16	50	51	35	2.2
G	2	52	6	4	2.0
H	15	67	42	27	1.8
I	10	77	26	16	1.6
J	18	95	45	27	1.2

In such a situation, we should rank the projects according to the ratio of net benefits to initial costs (the costs that will be reflected in our capital budget), and then we should begin with the best projects, in terms of the ratio of benefits to initial costs, until the budget is exhausted. In this way, we will get the greatest benefit for the expenditure of our limited funds. And projects that we might have selected if we were choosing only a single project would not be selected under these conditions of resource constraint.

This problem of selecting among projects demonstrates the first of several problems that arise from the application of the basic rule of cost-benefit analysis. Given the budgetary process and the allocation of funds among agencies, we may produce a case of "multiorganizational suboptimization." This is a fancy way of saying that if our agency has been given $50 million, we will spend it, even if our agency has a project that will produce a greater benefit to society but that exceeds our budget. Thus, if I had the money, I would continue to fund the projects listed in table 14.4 even though several of them have relatively low cost-benefit ratios and even though there were better projects elsewhere in the government. Of course, I will have been asked what benefits my proposed projects would produce when the capital budget was being considered, but because of political considerations my budget is excessive for the benefits that could be produced from alternative uses of the money. This is not, of course, a flaw in the method; it is a flaw in the application of the method in complex government settings.

A not unrelated problem is that cost-benefit analysis places relatively little importance on efficiency or cost effectiveness. It looks primarily at total benefits rather than at the ratio of costs produced. It could be argued that this tends to favor the ax over the scalpel as a cutting tool. In other words, the method tends to favor large projects over small projects. This may be an inefficient use of resources and may also lock government into costly projects, whereas smaller projects might provide greater flexibility and greater future opportunities for innovation. Capital projects are inherently lumpy, so that only projects of a certain size are feasible, but the concentration on total net benefits in cost-benefit analysis may exaggerate the problems of size and inflexibility.

We have now worked our way from the initial step of deciding what costs and benefits our project provides to deciding if it is the best project to undertake, given our limited resources. At each stage we had to use a number of assumptions and approximations to reach a decision. The cost-benefit analysis does provide a "hard" answer as to whether or not we should undertake a project, but that answer should not go unquestioned. We now discuss some criticisms of cost-benefit analysis and some possible ways of building greater political and economic sophistication into the use of the method.

Criticism and Modification

We have discussed some critical problems regarding cost-benefit analysis. Such things as the difficulty of assigning monetary values to nonmonetary outcomes, the choice of time ranges and discount rates, and the reliance on total net benefit as the criterion all introduce uncertainties about the usefulness of the outcome. We now discuss more basic problems that arise concerning the method itself and its relationship to the political process. Perhaps the most important is that some naive politicians and analysts might let the method make decisions for them, instead of using the information coming from the analysis as one element in their decision-making process. If the method is used naively and uncritically, its application can result in decisions that many people would deem socially undesirable. For example, all costs and benefits are counted as equal in the model, and, even if they could be calculated accurately, some individuals would argue that the cost of death might be more important than other costs. Thus, we might wish to reduce deaths to the lowest possible level and then perhaps apply a cost-benefit analysis to other aspects of the project. We might use this "lexicographic preference" as a means of initially sorting projects, when a single dominant value such as life or the preservation of endangered species is involved.

Perhaps the most socially questionable aspect of the cost-benefit analysis is that it gives little attention to the distributive questions involved in policies.[13] All benefits and costs are counted equally in the method, regardless of who receives or bears them. A project that increased the wealth of a wealthy man by several million dollars and was financed by regressive taxation of $100,000 would be preferred in cost-benefit calculations to a project that produced a benefit of $900,000 for unemployed workers and was financed by progressive taxation of $200,000. This is an extreme example, but it does point to the distributional blindness of the method. Of course, advocates of the method justify it by saying that the society as a whole will be better off with the greatest increase in benefits, and presumably winners can later compensate losers. In reality, however, winners rarely if ever do so, and usually losers cannot be directly identified anyway. Redistributional goals may be included directly in the analysis by attaching some weight to positive changes in the salaries of low-income persons, or redistributional objectives may be imposed on the analysis after the fact. However, because government exists in part to attempt to redress some of the inequities produced in the marketplace, some attention must be given to redistributional goals when evaluating public projects.

Furthermore, the utilitarian and "econocratic" foundations of cost-benefit analysis may not be entirely suitable for a functioning political democracy.[14] In cost-benefit analysis, money is the measure of all things, and decisions made according to the method can be expected to be based on the economic rather than the political values involved. (I discuss in chapter 15 some possible ethical alternatives that may be more suitable in a democracy.)

Finally, cost-benefit analysis has been referred to as "nonsense on stilts."[15] This means that there are so many assumptions involved in the calculations, and so many imponderables about the effects of future projects, that cost-benefit analysis is the functional equivalent of witchcraft in the public sector. Although these criticisms have been phrased in exaggerated language, to some degree they are well taken. It is difficult if not impossible to know the value of eliminating an externality, just as it is difficult to know just how much life, health, and snail darters are worth. Cost-benefit analysis can be used to avoid difficult political decisions and to abdicate responsibility to experts who can supply the "correct" answer. Of course, this fundamental abdication of political responsibility is indeed an "insidious poison in the body politick." Only when the results of analysis are integrated with other forms of analysis, such as ethical analysis, and are combined with sound political judgment can the "correct decisions" ever be made.

Notes

1. Edith Stokey and Richard Zeckhauser, *A Primer for Policy Analysis* (New York: Norton, 1978), 137.

2. Duncan MacRae, "Present and Future in the Valuation of Life" (paper presented to the 1980 convention of the American Political Science Association, Washington, D.C., August 1980).

3. See, for example, Kenneth Arrow, *Social Choice and Individual Values,* 2d ed. (New York: Wiley, 1963).

4. Richard Zeckhauser and Elmer Schaefer, "Public Policy and Normative Economic Theory," in *The Study of Policy Formation,* ed. Raymond A. Bauer and Kenneth J. Gergen (New York: Free Press, 1968), 45-53.

5. Ibid., 58-60.

6. E.J. Mishan, *Cost-Benefit Analysis,* expanded ed. (New York: Praeger, 1976), 24-54.

7. E.J. Mishan, "The Postwar Literature on Externalities: An Interpretative Essay," *Journal of Economic Literature,* March 1978, 1-28.

8. Stokey and Zeckhauser, *A Primer for Policy Analysis,* 149-52.

9. Steven E. Rhoads, ed., *Valuing Life: Public Policy Dilemmas* (Boulder, Colo.: Westview, 1980).

10. Jack Hirshleifer and David L. Shapiro, "The Treatment of Risk and Uncertainty," in *Public Expenditure and Policy Analysis,* ed. Robert H. Haveman and Julius Margolis, 3d ed. (Boston: Houghton Mifflin, 1983), 145-66.

11. For a good general discussion of the problems of discounting, see Robert E. Goodin, "Discounting Discounting," *Journal of Public Policy,* February 1982, 53-71.

12. W.J. Baumol, "On the Social Rate of Discount," *American Economic Review,* September 1968, 788-802.

13. Edward M. Gramlich, *Cost-Benefit Analysis of Government Programs* (Englewood Cliffs, N.J.: Prentice-Hall, 1981).

14. Peter Self, *Econocrats and the Policy Process: The Politics and Philosophy of Cost-Benefit Analysis* (London: Macmillan, 1975).

15. Peter Self, "Nonsense on Stilts: Cost-Benefit Analysis and the Roskill Commission," *Political Quarterly,* July 1970, 30-63.

15. Ethical Analysis of Public Policy

All the mathematical and economic capabilities in the world and all the substantive knowledge of policy areas are of little consequence if we have no moral or ethical foundation on which to base our evaluation of policies. Most of the important questions concerning policy analysis have as much to do with the "should" questions as with the "can" questions. That is, most important policy decisions involve an assessment of what should be done by government as much as they involve the feasibility question of what government can do. The range of technical possibilities is frequently broader for policymakers than the range of ethically justifiable possibilities. But, unfortunately, many values that should affect policy decisions in the public sector conflict with one another. Analysts frequently face choices among competing values rather than clear-cut decisions about options that are either all right or all wrong. In making almost all allocative decisions, policymakers must choose among worthy ends; they do not have the luxury of picking the only acceptable policy. This chapter presents several of the important ethical premises that influence policy decisions and some of the difficulties of implementing those values in real public-sector decisions.

Fundamental Value Premises

Any number of premises have been used to justify policy decisions. These range from vague concepts such as "Americanism," "Aryan purity," or the principles of Marxism-Leninism to well-articulated philosophical or religious principles. The main difficulty in ethical analysis of policy decisions is finding principles that can be consistently applied to a number of situations and that produce acceptable decisions in those situations.[1] Words like "justice," "equity," and "good" are thrown about in debates over public policies in a rather cavalier fashion. The analyst must attempt to systematize his or her values and learn to apply them consistently to all types of issues. The analyst must be a moral actor as well as a technician, or else remain what Meltsner refers to as a "baby analyst" throughout his or her career.[2] As we pointed out in discussing the application of cost-benefit analysis (see chapter 14), values are embedded throughout the policy process. In order to understand what one wants, one must explicate and examine those values. In this chapter I discuss four important value premises for making policy decisions: preservation of life, preservation of individual autonomy, truthfulness, and fairness. These values would probably be widely accepted by the public as important standards for assessing policies, and they have a rather wide range of applicability. As I point out, however, they cannot be applied unambiguously, and conflicts are embedded in each issue as well as across the several issues.

The Preservation of Life

The preservation of human life is one of the most fundamental values that we could expect to see manifested in the policy process. The sanctity of life is, after all, a fundamental value of Judeo-Christian ethics and is embodied in all professional codes of ethics.[3] Despite the importance of human life as an ethical criterion, a number of conflicts arise over its application.

One obvious conflict exists between identifiable lives and statistical lives. Here we are faced with the tendency of individuals to allocate resources differently if known lives are at stake from how they would evaluate them if some unspecified persons would be saved some time in the future. If we know that certain individuals will die in the near future, we tend to give them the resources they need, even though the same resources could save many more—unidentifiable—lives if we allocated them differently. In medical care this is manifested in the conflict between acute and preventive medicine. Preventive medicine is almost certainly the most cost-effective means of saving lives that could be lost as a result of cancer, circulatory diseases, or accidents, but it is difficult to identify the direct beneficiaries. However, the victims of the disease are clearly identifiable, have identifiable families, and consequently are more difficult to refuse care than the unknown statistical beneficiaries of preventive medicine. This pattern was referred to earlier as the "mountain-climber syndrome," in which we may spend thousands of dollars to save a stranded mountain climber, even though we could save many more lives by spending the same amount of money on highway accident prevention.[4] It is virtually impossible to say no to mountain climbers and their families, although if the appropriate ethical criterion is to save as many lives as possible, that is what we should do.

But even if all the lives at stake in a decision are identifiable, in some instances allocative decisions must be made. Table 15.1, although it concentrates on a relatively small number of individuals who are potential users of a kidney machine, points out the broader problem of being forced to choose among lives. Each individual in table 15.1 is worthy of receiving the lifesaving treatment simply because he or she is a human being. But because kidney machines are scarce

TABLE 15.1

WHO SHALL LIVE AND WHO SHALL DIE?

Patient	Sex and Age	Occupation	Home Life	Medical Stability	Civic Activities and Other Considerations
A	M 55	Cardiac surgeon on the verge of a major new technique	Married, two adult children	Bad long-term prognosis, maybe 2 years	Philanthropist with very high net worth; rumors of unfaithfulness
B	F 38	Owner of successful designer shop	Widow, three children, ages 4, 8, and 13	Good	From out of state; excellent violinist in community orchestra
C	M 46	Medical technician	Married, six children, ages 8 to 14	Good	Union boss
D	M 29	Assembly-line worker	Single	Good	Retarded—mental age, 10 years; ward of the state
E	F 36	Well-known historian, college professor; Ph.D.	Divorced, custodian of one son, age 5, ex-husband alive	Fair prognosis, but odd case which would allow perfection of new surgical technique	Excessive eater, drinker, and smoker; very popular professor; other medical conditions
F	M 60	Ex-state senator; now retired	Widower	Good	Criminal record (extortion)
G	M 45	Vice-president of local bank	Happily married, three sons, ages 15 to 25	Good	Deacon of local church, member of Rotary Club

SOURCE: *Washington Post*, 22 March 1981.

and because the demand for them exceeds the supply, decisions must be made that will allow some people to live and force others to die. What criteria can be applied in making such a choice? One might be a utilitarian criterion: The individuals who will contribute the most to the community will be allowed to live. Another criterion might be longevity: The youngest persons should be allowed to receive the treatment, thus saving the greatest number of person-years of life. Another criterion might be autonomy: Individuals who have the greatest probability of returning to active and useful lives after treatment should receive the treatment. Certain other criteria could also justify one choice over another. But additional allocative questions arise from this example: How many kidney machines should be purchased to treat any number of patients who might need this care, regardless of the cost and the underutilization of the machines most of the time? Or should only enough be purchased to meet average demands?

Even though the preservation of life may be an important value for public policymaking, in many situations the definition of life itself is in question. The use of therapeutic abortion as a means of birth control presents one problem of this sort: determining when human life begins.[5] Issues concerning artificial means of prolonging life even when a person would be considered dead by many clinical criteria illustrate the problem of defining life at the other end of the life cycle.[6] Thus, while all policymakers and all citizens may agree on the importance of preserving human life, serious disagreements arise over just what constitutes a human life.

Finally, in some situations the government sanctions and encourages the taking of human lives. The most obvious example is war; others are capital punishment and, in some instances, the management of police response to threats. The question here then is what criteria we can use to justify the taking of some lives while we prohibit the taking of others?[7] Obvious criteria that we might apply are self-preservation and the protection of society against elements that could undermine it or take other lives. But to some degree there is a definite inconsistency in the arguments here, and we must justify placing higher values on some lives than on others. Again, the fundamental point here is that although there may be broad agreement in society on the importance of preserving human lives as a goal of all public policies, this criterion is not obviously and unambiguously enforceable in all situations. We must have a detailed analysis of all situations and some understanding of the particular application of the criterion in each of those varied situations.

The Preservation of Individual Autonomy

Another criterion that should be applied to policy choices, especially in democratic political systems, is the preservation or enhancement of the autonomy of individual citizens. That is, policy choices should be made that enhance the ability of individuals to determine their own fates and the fate of their society. One of the most basic principles underlying democratic political thought is that the individual should be allowed to make his or her own choices in an informed and intelligent manner.

This principle also underlies a considerable body of conservative political thought which assumes that the interests of the individual are more important than those of the society as a whole. Thus, child labor, sweatshops, and extremely long working hours with low wages were all justified at one time because they preserved the right of the individual to choose his or her own working conditions.[8] With such an extreme definition of individual autonomy the public sector would be excluded from almost all forms of social and economic activity. But even with this extreme version of autonomy the state did intervene to protect individuals against fraud and breach of contract, and it did to some degree protect children and other less competent individuals more than it did adults, who presumably were able to make their own decisions.

Several interesting questions arise in the public sector in regard to individual autonomy. One involves an extension of the above comments. What groups in society should the state attempt to protect, either against themselves or against those who would defraud them or otherwise infringe on their rights? Children have traditionally been protected—even against their own parents—because they have been assumed to be incapable of exercising full, autonomous choice. The state has been empowered to operate *in loco parentis* to try to preserve the rights of children. Likewise, the state has protected mentally incompetent adults who cannot make rational, autonomous choices. Less justifiably by most criteria, the state has operated to limit the choices of welfare recipients, unwed mothers, and individuals who, although they may have full mental capabilities, are stigmatized in some fashion. Again, what criteria should be used to decide which groups the state should treat as its children?

The state may also intervene to protect the life of an individual who has made an autonomous decision to end his or her life. Legislation that makes suicide a crime and attempts to prevent individuals from purposely ending their lives indicates the apparent belief that the value of preserving life supersedes the value of preserving individual autonomy. In this hierarchy of values, the decision to end one's own life is taken by definition to indicate that the individual needs the protection of the state. The same principle is apparently applied to individuals who have made it clear that they do not wish to be kept "alive" by artificial means when all hope of their recovery to a fully conscious and autonomous life is lost. In such an instance there are several conflicting values:

What actually constitutes a human life? The problems of preserving life and preserving autonomy become even more confused here because an individual who once made an autonomous choice about how he or she would like to be treated may at some point be no longer able to decide anything autonomously and may, in fact, never be able to do so again.

In less extreme instances, the state may also remove the autonomy of an individual for the sake of protecting him or her. Consumer protection is an obvious example; government may disregard *caveat emptor* and simply prohibit the sale of potentially harmful products in order to protect the citizen. On the one hand, the conservative, or any other person interested in preserving individual choice, would argue that such protections are harmful inasmuch as the paternalistic actions of government prevent citizens from being truly free actors. On the other hand, the complexity of the marketplace, the number of products offered for sale, and the absence of full information may prevent individuals from making meaningful judgments. As a consequence, government is justified in intervening, especially as many of the products banned would affect those incapable of making their own informed choices—for example, children.

Professional licensing and laws that control the licensing of drugs have been criticized on the same grounds. It is argued that individuals should have the right to select the form of treatment they would like, even if the medical establishment deems it quackery. So, for example, the prohibition of laetrile in most states is said to deny individuals the right to exercise choice in the treatment of cancer. Of course, the counterargument is that this restriction is justified because it increases the probability that the individual will receive treatment that is more likley to contribute to the cure of the disease.

Lying

Most systems of ethics and morality prohibit lying.[9] People generally regard lying as wrong simply "because it is wrong." It can also be deemed wrong because it allows one individual to deprive another of his or her autonomy. When one person lies to another, the liar deprives the other person of the ability to make rational and informed decisions. In some instances, telling "little white lies" may prevent awkward social situations. But perhaps special criteria should be applied to justify lies told in government.

Lying to the public by public officials has been justified primarily as being in the public's own good. Those who use this paternalistic justification assume that public officials have more information and are unwilling to divulge it either for security reasons or because they believe that the information will only "confuse" citizens. They may therefore lie to the public to get average citizens to behave in ways that they—the public officials—prefer, believing that the citizens would behave in the same way if they had adequate information. Even if citizens would not behave as public officials want them to, officials think that they should behave in that manner, and the lie is therefore justified as a means of protecting the public from itself.

Such lying obviously limits the autonomy of the average citizen when making policy choices or evaluating the performance of those in office. Even white lies are questionable; the importance of autonomy in democratic political systems may demand much closer attention to honesty, even though the short-term consequences of telling the truth may not benefit the incumbents in office.

Other white lies told by officials to the public involve withholding information that might cause panic or other responses that are potentially very dangerous. For example, a public official may learn that a nuclear power plant has had a minor and apparently controllable accident that is not believed to endanger anyone. The official may withhold this information from the public in the belief that doing so will prevent a panic; a mass flight from the scene could cause more harm than the accident. But, as with other ethical situations, the decision to lie about one thing and not about others makes it difficult to behave consistently. Perhaps the only standard that can be applied with any consistency in this case is the utilitarian criterion: The harm prevented by the lie must outweigh the ill effects caused by the lie. Determining this is relatively easy when we are balancing deaths and property damage from a minor nuclear accident against a widespread and violent panic. Continued lying, however, will eventually cause a public loss of trust in government and its officials, and the cost of such skepticism is difficult to calculate.

A special category of lying is the withholding of information by public officials to protect their own careers. This is a problem for the "whistle blowers" as well as for the liars, and it happens in the private as well as the public sector,[10] placing many individuals in difficult situations. For example, the man who blew the whistle on government cost overruns on the Lockheed C5A lost his job, as have many other conscientious officials in less dramatic circumstances. The problem caused when someone blows the whistle on a lie is especially difficult to analyze when the individual at fault does not lie directly but simply does nothing. The whistle blower must go to some lengths in order to make the information about the lie known to the public. And as a consequence policymakers may want to devise ways to encourage whistle blowers and to protect them against reprisals. In the absence of mechanisms for encouraging officials to divulge information, legislation such as the Freedom of Information Act can at least make it more difficult for government to suppress information.

Thus, in addition to the general moral prohibition, lying carries a particular onus in the public sector because it can destroy an individual's ability to make appropriate and informed choices. Although a lie may be told for good reasons, it must be questioned unless it has extremely positive benefits and is not told just for the convenience of the individual. The long-term consequences for government of even "justifiable" lying may be negative. Citizens who learn that government lies to them for good reasons may soon wonder if it will not lie to them for less noble reasons.

If strictures against lying are to some degree dependent on a desire to preserve the political community and a sense of trust within it, then somewhat different rules may apply in international politics. Although there is a concept of the international community of nations, the bonds among them are weaker than the bonds that exist within a single nation. Further, a political leader's paramount responsibilities are to his or her own citizens. Therefore, lying in international politics may be more acceptable; political leaders have the problem of "dirty hands," which seems to be part of the job of being a political leader in an imperfect world.[11]

Fairness

Finally, fairness is a value to which citizens expect government to give maximum importance. One standard justification for the existence of government is that it protects and enforces the rights of individuals. Further, it is argued that governments can redress any inequities in the distribution of goods and services that result from the operations of the marketplace.[12] Government, then, is charged with making sure that citizens are treated fairly in the society.

But just what is "fair treatment of citizens"? In different schools of social and political thought the word "fair" has had different meanings. To a conservative, for example, fairness means allowing individuals maximum opportunities to exercise their abilities and allowing them to keep what they earn in the marketplace with those abilities. Some conservatives consider it fair that people who cannot provide for themselves should suffer, along with their families. The doctrine "from each according to his abilities to each according to his needs" implies a very different standard of fairness.[13] In other words, all members of the society, provided they are willing to contribute their abilities, are entitled to have their material needs satisfied. According to this standard of fairness, those with lower earning capacities need not suffer, although the doctrine does not imply a standard of absolute equality.

The standard of fairness applied in most contemporary welfare states is something of a mixture of the two standards, although it lacks the intellectual underpinnings of either extreme. The mixed-economy welfare state that operates in noncommunist, industrialized societies usually allows productive citizens to keep most of their earnings and at the same time asks them to help build a floor of benefits under the less fortunate so that they can maintain at least a minimal standard of living. Unlike the situation in the Marxist state, this redistribution of goods and services to the less fortunate from the more successful is conducted in the context of free and open politics.

Can these operating principles of the contemporary welfare state — principles that arise largely from political accidents and pragmatic evolution — be systematized and developed on a more intellectual plane? One promising approach can be found in philosopher John Rawls's concept of justice in a society. In his essay "Justice as Fairness,"[14] Rawls develops two principles of justice for a society. The first is that "each person participating in a practice, or affected by it, has an equal right to the most extensive liberty compatible with like liberty of all." This is a restatement of the basic right of individuals to be involved in governmental decisions that affect them, a principle not incompatible with the cry "No taxation without representation!" This first principle of justice would place the burden of proof on anyone who would seek to limit participation in political life; it can therefore be seen as a safeguard for procedural democracy in contemporary societies. Thus, Rawls places a strong emphasis on the decision-making procedures employed when evaluating the fairness of those decisions and the fairness of the institutions of society.

The second principle advanced by Rawls is more substantive and also more problematic. Referred to as the "difference principle," it states that "social and economic inequalities are to be arranged so that they are both *(a)* to the greatest benefit of the least advantaged and *(b)* attached to offices and positions open to all under conditions of fair equality of opportunity."[15] This principle places the burden of proof on those who attempt to justify a system of inequalities. Inequalities can be seen as just only if all other possible arrangements would produce lowered expectations for the least-well-off group in society. To help a society that is striving for equality, citizens are asked to think of their own place in society as shrouded behind a "veil of ignorance," so that it cannot be known to them in advance.[16] Would they be willing to gamble on being in the lowest segment of the society when they decide on a set of inequalities for the society? If they are not, then they have good reason to understand the need of the society to equalize the distribution of goods and services. Of course, it is impossible to apply the logic of the veil of ignorance in existing societies, but it is useful in understanding rational acceptance of redistributive government policies.

Several interesting questions arise with respect to Rawls's difference principle. One is the place of natural endowments and individual differences in producing inequalities. Should those who have special natural abilities be allowed to benefit from them? One is reminded of a Kurt Vonnegut story in *Player Piano*, in which individuals' particular talents are balanced by the "great handicapper." Individuals who can run particularly fast, for instance, are required to wear heavy weights to slow them down and those who have creative gifts are required to wear earphones through which come loud and discordant noises to distract them from thinking. Does Rawls regard such a homogeneous and ultimately dull society as desirable? One would think not, but he does point out that natural endowments are desirable primarily because they can be used to assist those in the lowest segment of society. Thus, *noblesse oblige* is expected of those who have natural talents.

Does the same hold true for those whose endowments are economic rather than physical or intellectual? It would appear that in Rawls's view equality is a natural principle that can be justified by the veil of ignorance as well as by the cooperative instincts that Rawls believes are inherent in humans. Again, in his view, these endowments should exist only to the extent that they can be used for the betterment of the lowest segments in society.[17] Quite naturally, critics point to the natural rights of individuals to retain their holdings and to the potential incentives for work and investment that are built into a system of inequalities. Inequalities are argued to be useful to society in that they supply a spur to ambition and an incentive to produce more, which in turn will benefit the entire society.[18] These incentives should influence artistic as well as economic production. Thus, to critics of Rawls's philosophy, the tendency toward equality may be inappropriate on ethical grounds because it would deny individuals something they have received through either genetics or through education, and it may be wrong on utilitarian grounds because it reduces the total production of the society along several dimensions.

Finally, the Rawlsian framework is discussed primarily within the context of a single society, or a single institution in which cooperative principles would at least be considered, if not always followed. Can these principles be applied to a broader context; in particular, should they be applied to a global community? In other words, should the riches accumulated in the industrialized countries be used to benefit the citizens of the most impoverished countries of the world? Such a policy would, of course, be politically difficult at best. However, the ethical underpinnings of foreign aid may be important, especially as the world moves into a era of increased scarcity.

While opinions may differ as to the applicability of Rawls's ideas to the real world, and the desirability of such application if it becomes possible, his work does raise some interesting ethical questions for those attempting to design public policies. Many industrialized countries have been making redistributive policy decisions for years. These decisions have been justified on pragmatic or political grounds. The work of Rawls provides intellectual underpinnings for these policies, even though no government has gone as far in redistributing income and wealth as Rawls's difference principle would demand.

Ethics and Public Policy: Alternatives to Utilitarianism

The ethical system most often applied to public policy analysis is utilitarianism. As noted in chapter 14, this principle underlies such approaches as cost-benefit analysis. In this chapter we have discussed several ethical questions that arise in making and implementing public policies, as well as some possible answers to these questions. Ultimately, no one can provide definitive answers to these questions. Likewise, public officials may face ethical questions that have no readily acceptable answers. Values and ethical principles are frequently in conflict, and the policymaker must frequently violate one firmly held ethical position in order to protect another.

Despite these practical difficulties, it is important for citizens and policymakers to think about policy in ethical terms. Perhaps too much policymaking has been conducted without attention to anything but the political and economic consequences. Of course, those consequences are important as criteria on which to base an evaluation of a program, but they may not be the only criteria. Both the policymaker and the citizen must be concerned also with the criteria of justice and trust in society. It may be that ultimately justice and trust make the best policies—and even the best politics.

Notes

1. Victor Grassian, *Moral Reasoning* (Englewood Cliffs, N.J.: Prentice-Hall, 1981).

2. Arnold Meltsner, *Policy Analysts in the Bureaucracy* (Berkeley: University of California Press, 1976), 3-25.

3. Abraham Kaplan, "Social Ethics and the Sanctity of Life," in *Life or Death: Ethics and Options,* ed. D.H. Labby (London: Macmillan, 1968), 58-71.

4. See Guido Calabresi and Philip Bobbitt, *Tragic Choices* (New York: Norton, 1978), 21.

5. See J. Feinberg, ed., *The Problem of Abortion* (Belmont, Calif.: Wadsworth, 1973).

6. See John A. Behnke and Sissela Bok, *The Dilemmas of Euthanasia* (Garden City, N.Y.: Anchor, 1975).

7. See Jonathan Clover, *Causing Deaths and Saving Lives* (Harmondsworth, England: Penguin, 1977).

8. This ideology was expressed in a number of Supreme Court decisions in the late nineteenth and early twentieth centuries. See, for example, *Lochner v. New York* (1905).

9. See Sissela Bok, *Lying: Moral Choice in Public and Private Life* (New York: Vintage, 1979).

10. See Edward Weisband and Thomas M. Franck, *Resignation in Protest* (New York: Penguin, 1975).

11. Michael Walzer, "Political Action: The Problem of Dirty Hands," *Philosophy and Public Affairs,* Winter 1973, 160-80.

12. Geoffrey K. Fry, *The Growth of Government* (London: Frank Cass, 1979).

13. Karl Marx, *Criticism of the Gotha Program* (New York: International Universities Press, 1938), 29:14.

14. John Rawls, "Justice as Fairness," *Philosophical Review,* 1958, 164-94, esp. 166.

15. John Rawls, *A Theory of Justice* (Cambridge, Mass.: Harvard University Press, 1971), 11-17.

16. Ibid., 19.

17. For a critique see Robert Nozick, *Anarchy, State and Utopia* (New York: Basic Books, 1974), 149-63.

18. Kenneth P. Jameson, "Supply-Side Economics: Growth versus Income Distribution," *Challenge,* November/December 1980, 26-31.

Glossary

ADMINISTRATIVE PROCEDURES ACT. Passed in 1946, specifying the details of procedures to be followed by federal administrative agencies. Especially important in defining the process through which these agencies can issue regulations.

ADVISORY COMMISSION ON INTERGOVERNMENTAL RELATIONS. An independent commission composed of congressmen, senators, and representatives of state and local governments advising the federal government in matters of changes in the federal structure of the United States.

AGENDA. The set of issues to be considered when making a public decision. Unless an issue is put on the agenda, it cannot be acted on by government. Agendas may be systemic, or the total range of issues under consideration by the public sector, or institutional for a particular institution such as Congress or the President.

AID TO FAMILIES WITH DEPENDENT CHILDREN (AFDC). The major welfare program in the United States. It provides benefits to families that lack an income earner. In general, this means that the family is headed by a woman without any male in the household.

ANTITRUST POLICY. Beginning with the Sherman Anti-Trust Act (1890), a major component of business policy in the United States. The basic idea is to ensure competition in business and prevent the formation of monopolies.

AUTHORITY. The ability of political systems to have their decisions accepted without opposition. This may be contrasted to power, or the ability to have decisions accepted in spite of opposition.

AUTOMATIC FISCAL STABILIZERS. The effects of tax receipts and social expenditures automatically regulating the economy. In an inflationary period tax receipts increase and social expenditures tend to fall, while in a recession the opposite would be true. This would put money into circulation during a recession and take it out of circulation during inflation.

BACK-DOOR SPENDING. The practice of agencies gaining the authority to spend money through letting of contracts or borrowing of money without specific congressional authorization.

BALANCE OF PAYMENTS. The balance of imports and exports. Countries seek to have a positive balance of payments, or at least break even, in international trade.

BROWN V. BOARD OF EDUCATION (1954). A Supreme Court case deciding that the "separate but equal" school systems segregating blacks and whites were inherently unconstitutional. This was the beginning of the fight to desegregate southern school districts.

BUREAUCRACY. Formally, an arrangement of offices in government characterized by hierarchy, rules of procedure, and permanence in office; connotatively, a system characterized by red tape, lethargy, and incompetence.

CATEGORICAL GRANTS. Intergovernmental grants, generally from the federal government to state or local governments, providing funds for specific purposes or programs. These can be contrasted with block grants, which give funds for broad purposes (e.g., education), or general grants such as revenue sharing, which have no restrictions.

CERTIFICATE OF NEED. A requirement that all new or expanded health-care facilities demonstrate that they are necessary and do not duplicate existing facilities.

CLEAN AIR ACT (1963). The basic legal framework for controlling air pollution. As amended in 1970, it requires setting ambient (surrounding) air-quality standards, and mandated significant reductions in the emissions of both stationary and mobile (automobile) pollution sources.

CLEARANCE POINTS. In the study of implementation, the points through which a decision must be processed before it is put into effect. The greater the number of clearance points, the less the probability that the program will be implemented as intended.

COLEMAN REPORT. By sociologist James S. Coleman on the effects of school desegregation. Findings were that the achievement of blacks improved in desegregated schools while that of whites was not affected significantly except in predominately black schools.

COMMON CAUSE. One of several "public-interest groups" attempting to lobby for the public at large rather than for special interests.

COMPETENCY TESTING. Requirements that students be able to pass a test in English and mathematics before being awarded a high school diploma; used as a means of trying to improve the quality of education.

CONGRESSIONAL BUDGET AND IMPOUNDMENT CONTROL ACT (1974). Established the Congressional Budget Office and restricted the President's ability to impound funds. It represented an attempt by Congress to take a more equal part in the budgetary process.

CORPORATISM. A pattern of interaction between organized interests and government in which the interests serve as legitimate sources of influence and advice, and as mechanisms for the implementation of policies. In such a system, citizens are represented less as residents of a geographical area than as members of segments of the economy or society, e.g., labor, management, senior citizens, students, women.

COST-BENEFIT ANALYSIS. A form of economic analysis used in making policy decisions enumerating, in monetary terms, the costs and benefits of proposed policies. The fundamental decision rule is to select the policy that produces the largest net benefit.

COUNCIL OF ECONOMIC ADVISERS. A group of economists in the Executive Office of the President advising the President on economic policy and budgetary policy.

CURRENT SERVICES BUDGET. A submission to Congress by the Office of Management and Budget projecting total federal expenditures if the current level of services is maintained.

DECISION ANALYSIS. A set of techniques used to aid decision makers faced with difficult decisions. In its simplest form it relates the probability of the occurrence of certain events and their expected value or cost in an attempt to discover which decision would produce the highest expected value.

DECISION PACKAGES. In zero-base budgeting, the discrete programs or additions to programs that are used to decide the level of funding appropriate for an agency. This will allow the development of expenditure priorities and more precise attribution of costs to program developments.

DEFERRALS. A decision by the President to delay spending some funds appropriated by Congress. He is permitted to do this unless one house of Congress passes a resolution in opposition.

DELANEY AMENDMENT. An amendment to the 1958 Food and Drug Act that prohibits using any food additive known to cause cancer in humans or animals.

DIAGNOSTIC RELATED GROUPINGS. A form of paying hospitals for Medicare patients based on their diagnosis rather than the costs actually incurred; an attempt to reduce the costs of Medicare and health care more generally.

DISCOUNTING. In cost-benefit analysis, the process of reducing future costs and benefits to a present value. Benefits produced in the future are worth less at present than are those available now, just as money available to an individual two years from now is less valuable than money available at present.

ECONOMIC GROWTH. Increase in the total goods and services available in the economy. It is important to maintain this growth, especially in a country that has an increasing population. Also, economic growth provides a "fiscal dividend" of increased tax revenue for government.

EDUCATION CONSOLIDATION AND IMPROVEMENT ACT (ECIA) OF 1981. Major federal support for elementary and secondary education, providing for support for school districts with disadvantaged students, education of the handicapped, adult education, and aid for federally impacted school districts.

EFFICIENCY (IN GOVERMENT). The pursuit of maximum output for money spent in public programs.

EFFLUENT CHARGES. The charge governments make to polluters, instead of prohibiting the discharge of pollutants. While some argue that this charge would improve economic efficiency, others argue that it only creates a market in death and disease.

ELEMENTARY AND SECONDARY EDUCATION ACT OF 1965. The first major federal subsidy program for elementary and secondary education. Although intended primarily to aid poor urban school districts, the formulas devised to distribute the funds have spread them to virtually all school districts.

ELITISM. A perspective on the policymaking process that argues that a powerful elite controls policies in the United States. This approach is contrasted with the more open perspective of PLURALISM.

EMPLOYMENT ACT OF 1946. Act declaring the responsibility of the government of the United States to maintain full employment. In 1946 this was defined as no more than 4 percent unemployed, but that definition has been increased to 5 percent.

ENTITLEMENT PROGRAM. Any program, such as Social Security, Medicare, or unemployment insurance, to which citizens believe they have a right on the basis of payments or citizenship.

ENVIRONMENTAL IMPACT STATEMENT. A statement of the environmental effects of a proposed project; used as a means of preventing environmental degradation as the result of federally funded projects.

ETHICS. Moral and humanistic values that should guide the selection of policies. These values are frequently put into contrast with economic methods of decision making, such as cost-benefit analysis.

EVALUATION RESEARCH. Assessment of the effectiveness and efficiency of public programs. This requires knowledge of the goals of the program, the measurement of the effects of the program, and a set of values to assess the outcomes.

EXECUTIVE OFFICE OF THE PRESIDENT. The personal advisory staff of the President, including the Council of Economic Advisers, the Office of Management and Budget, and the White House Office.

EXTERNALITIES. The social costs (or benefits) of production that are not reflected in the price of the product. For example, pollution imposes costs (reduced health, reduced durability from paints, etc.) and disamenities.

Government intervention is justified as a means of reducing these external effects.

FEDERALISM. A division of the powers of government between the central government and the state governments in a manner that preserves significant autonomy for the subnational governments.

FEDERAL RESERVE BOARD. The controlling body for the Federal Reserve banking system. This board determines the major aspects of monetary policy in the United States.

FISCAL NEUTRALITY. A "good tax" should not discriminate among different kinds of income and expenditure so that resources are used according to their best economic usage rather than for tax advantages.

FISCAL POLICY. Use of the public budget as a means of controlling the economy. When the economy is inflationary, government should take money out of the economy by running a surplus; if there is a recession, government should run a deficit to put more money into circulation.

FLAT-RATE TAX. A plan to simplify the federal tax laws by removing most deductions and exemptions and taxing all income at a few (lower) rates.

FOOD STAMPS. A program of the U.S. Department of Agriculture to provide the needy with stamps redeemable for food. This program began with a small appropriation in 1966 but swelled to several billion dollars by the 1980s.

FULL-EMPLOYMENT BUDGET. An approach to budgeting that calculates revenues and expenditures as if the economy were at full employment. Any deficit in excess of that which is the result of the failure of the economy to operate at full employment is seen as a political deficit coming from the unwillingness of politicians to impose sufficient taxes to cover their expenditures.

GARBAGE-CAN MODEL OF DECISION MAKING. In this analytic model of the way in which organizations function, solutions seek out problems rather than the other way around. In the public sector this means that the availability of a known technology such as social insurance will be used to "solve" problems for which it is actually inappropriate.

GENERAL ACCOUNTING OFFICE (GAO). A legislative office responsible for auditing all federal expenditures and then reporting any discrepancies to Congress. Since the mid-1970s the GAO has also been involved in making recommendations for effective use of money, as well as its legal use.

HEALTH MAINTENANCE ORGANIZATION (HMO). A program of prepaid medical care that attempts to alleviate some of the problems caused by fee-for-service medicine. In particular, by removing the fee incentive for physicians to administer treatments for surgery, the program should help slow the growth in medical-care costs.

HEALTH PLANNING ACT OF 1974. A major attempt of the federal government to slow the growth of medical costs by controlling the expansion of medical facilities. The law establishes a program of "certificate of need" legislation administered through state governments and local health system agencies.

IDEOLOGIES. Patterns of belief concerning the nature of government, society, and policy. Examples are Marxism, fascism, and liberalism. Bureaucratic agencies also develop their own ideologies for their particular policy areas.

IMPLEMENTATION. The conversion of legislation, money, and manpower into real operating programs. Numerous barriers, both within the administrative structures of government and in the environment, limit the ability of government to implement programs effectively.

INCENTIVES. Rather than mandate that citizens do certain things, or directly provide a service, government provides incentives for them to do those things. For example, the tax system provides numerous incentives, but there is no certainty that citizens will accept the incentives.

INCREMENTALISM. Descriptively used to depict the pattern of growth of public budgets as stable percentages of the previous year's expenditures. Prescriptively it is argued that decisions should be made in small steps rather than through major changes in existing policies. It is argued that policymakers can never have full information and full knowledge of the consequences of their actions and therefore decisions should be small and reversible changes from the status quo.

INDEPENDENT REGULATORY AGENCIES. A number of regulatory agencies independent of direct executive authority. Beginning with the Interstate Commerce Commission in 1887, these agencies were established to remove important economic regulations from politics but have resulted in the "capture" of the agencies by the very interests they were intended to regulate.

INDEXATION. Adjustment of taxes or benefits for changes in the level of prices. Social Security benefits are indexed so that they increase every six months as prices increase; since the Reagan tax program passed, taxes are indexed.

INFANT MORTALITY. The number of deaths in the first year of life per 1000 live births. This is a standard indicator of the quality of health care in a country.

INFLATION. An increase in the price level; a reflection of an increase in the money in the economy relative to the supply of goods and services.

INITIATIVE. A form of policymaking by the voters in which, by petition of some percentage of the registered voters (in the range of 5 to 10 percent), an issue can be placed on the ballot. This allows citizens to bypass their elected officials entirely.

INTEREST GROUPS. Otherwise known as PRESSURE GROUPS. These are the representatives of organized interests in society. These groups lobby actively for their particular interests and, depending on the perspective taken, may be crucial to understanding the characteristics of public policies.

INTERSTATE COMMERCE COMMISSION. Established in 1887 to regulate the rates and practices of railroads, this was the first of the independent regulatory agencies. Arguably, this agency has become an advocate of the railroads it was intended to regulate, as well as of interstate trucking interests, which it also regulates.

IRON TRIANGLES. The relationship between interest groups, administrative agencies, and congressional committees, which isolates each individual policy area from others and inhibits effective control of the policies adopted. Each of the members of the triangle needs the political power of the others, and there is little incentive for them to adopt policies more in the public interest.

KALDOR-HICKS CRITERION. The "fundamental rule" of cost-benefit analysis that policies should be adopted to maximize the total economic production of the society. It is assumed that if this is done, winners can compensate losers in the process of production, and there will still be a surplus for the society at large.

KEYNESIAN ECONOMICS. An approach to governmental management of the economy stressing the importance of the size of the public deficit or surplus as a means of regulating effective demand and thereby regulating the economy. From the end of World War II to the mid-1970s it was assumed that Keynesianism was an effective means of controlling the economy, but the "stagflation" of the late 1970s and early 1980s ended most faith in this approach.

LEGITIMACY. Acceptance of the government of a country as an appropriate and legal government. A government accepted as legitimate can rule without significant opposition from its citizens. In policymaking, the use of accepted procedures attaches the legitimacy of government to individual policy decisions.

LOGROLLING. Developing winning coalitions in a legislative body by trading votes on issues. A legislator who is indifferent about issue A may well be willing to trade his vote on that issue for the vote of another congressman on issue B, about which he has intense opinions.

MEDICAID. A program of health care for the poor, passed in 1965 by Congress but administered through the states. Eligibility and benefits for Medicaid differ significantly across states; the Reagan administration has attempted to tighten eligibility for the program.

MEDICARE. A program of medical insurance for the elderly, adopted at the same time as Medicaid. Hospitalization insurance is available for all recipients and additional coverage can be purchased for a fee.

MODEL CITIES PROGRAM. A component of the war on poverty attempting to assist cities in improving the quality of life for their populations. One of the major components of the program was to coordinate numerous services being delivered to residents of economically deprived neighborhoods.

MONETARY POLICY. An approach to economic policy stressing the importance of the money supply in controlling inflation and recession. The money supply is regulated by control of the interest rate, reserve requirements in banks, and the sale and purchase of government securities.

MUTUALLY ASSURED DESTRUCTION (MAD). A doctrine concerning nuclear war and arguing that the best way of preventing a nuclear exchange is to ensure that both sides have the capacity of destroying each other in spite of a sneak attack.

NATIONAL DEFENSE EDUCATION ACT. Passed in response to the launching of *Sputnik I* by the Soviet Union, provided money for scientific and area-studies education at both the secondary and postsecondary levels.

NATIONAL ENVIRONMENTAL POLICY ACT. Passed in 1970, establishes guidelines for environmental controls for projects involving the federal government; contains the requirements for environmental impact statements.

NATIONAL HEALTH INSURANCE. Proposed programs for national, i.e., public, health insurance. Since the Truman administration, proposals range from catastrophic coverage for serious illnesses to general coverage, but none has been acceptable to those fearing "socialized medicine."

NUCLEAR TRIAD. The ability of both the United States and the Soviet Union to deliver strategic nuclear weapons in three ways: airplanes, intercontinental ballistic missiles, and submarine-launched missiles.

OCCUPATIONAL SAFETY AND HEALTH ADMINISTRATION (OSHA). An agency in the Department of Labor responsible for improving the health and safety of the workplace. OSHA has been the subject of a great deal of criticism for its numerous, and sometimes onerous, regulations.

OFFICE OF MANAGEMENT AND BUDGET. An office in the Executive Office of the President with responsibility for preparing the President's budget and improving the standards of management in the federal government.

OVERHANG. Money that has been obligated, but not spent, in previous years by an agency. Otherwise referred to as money "in the pipeline," the money in the overhang may be greater than the amount of money in the annual budget. This makes the conduct of fiscal policy more difficult as appropriations can control only a portion of total spending authority.

PLANNING-PROGRAMMING-BUDGETING SYSTEM (PPBS). Otherwise known as

PROGRAM BUDGETING. This approach stresses the need to understand what government does, not in terms of organizations but in terms of the intended activities of government. To budget requires the identification of goals, the attachment of resources to those goals, and the investigation of alternative means of reaching the goals. Although this approach would potentially enhance the rationality of budgeting, it has not proven acceptable to most decision makers on political grounds.

PLURALISM. An approach to policymaking stressing the number of interests involved in making decisions, the absence of any single controlling elite, and the openness of American politics to competing interests. This approach may be contrasted with ELITISM.

POLICY ANALYSTS. Individuals assisting political or administrative decision makers in making policy decisions. Although sometimes regarded as technical or apolitical, the more mature policy analysts will be active participants in the policy process.

POLICY FORMULATION. The task of devising a response to a problem identified as needing a response of government. Difficult because of the inadequate knowledge of the facts in many policy areas, and inadequate knowledge of the process of causation.

POLICY OUTCOMES. Effects of the activities of government on citizens. For example, in health care, a policy outcome would be the level of infant mortality or the level of life expectancy.

POLICY SUCCESSION. Substitution of a new program, or the modification of an existing program, in response to demands for policy change. As government activities have become more widespread, there has been a greater need for policy succession.

PORK BARREL. Distribution of the benefits of public programs, especially programs involving capital projects, as widely as possible. This can be important for building a coalition in favor of a program.

PROFESSIONALS (IN THE POLICY PROCESS). Professionally trained personnel in government. These individuals represent a problem as they tend to be more motivated by their professional careers and ethics, and present difficulties as they push for new ideas and change.

PROFESSIONAL STANDARDS REVIEW ORGANIZATION (PSRO). Established in 1972, organizations composed primarily of physicians and charged with the responsibility of quality and cost of care provided in Medicare and Medicaid.

PROSPECTIVE REIMBURSEMENT. A means of approaching the problem of medical-care costs. This program would require insurance companies to pay a set amount in advance for a particular condition, with any additional costs subject to substantial justification and documentation.

PUBLIC CORPORATIONS. Public corporations, organized like private corporations with stock, boards of directors, etc., existing in government. They typically are organized to provide services of a sort that could potentially be marketed in the private sector.

PUBLIC GOODS. Goods and services that are not readily produced in the private sector. Examples are national defense and police protection.

PUBLIC INTEREST. The overriding interest of the entire population, or a majority of the people, as contrasted to the special interests manifest in interest groups. Although such an interest may exist, it is difficult to identify and difficult to organize politically because no individual has any incentive to organize a group.

QUASI-GOVERNMENTAL ORGANIZATION. An organization having some of the characteristics of a government organization and some of a private organization. For example, Amtrak in the United States has both public and private directors.

RATIONALITY. One of the never-ending quests in government. For some, rationality can only be achieved by a comprehensive review of all policy options and the examination of all their consequences, and the selection of the option that maximizes utility. For others, rationality can be achieved through the incremental decision process of small changes, with constant examination of the effects of those changes.

RECISSION. The refusal of a President to spend a portion of the funds that have been appropriated to him. The President must inform Congress of his desire to withhold the funds and cannot do so without approval of both houses of Congress.

REFERENDUM. An instrument of direct democracy in which a legislative body places an issue on the ballot for the voters to decide on.

REGULATION. Use of the legal power of government to prohibit or mandate an activity. Regulation has been the manner in which the United States has approached managing many of the problems in its economy, as contrasted to the use of public corporations in most European countries.

REORGANIZATION. A changing of the organizational structure of government with the aim of improving efficiency of operation or the quality of the policy decisions made. The Carter administration proposed an extensive reorganization of government, some of which was implemented (e.g., civil service reform and the Department of Education).

RESOURCE CONSERVATION AND RECOVERY ACT (1976). An act giving the Environmental Protection Agency the authority to establish a system for disposing of hazardous wastes.

RISK-BENEFIT ANALYSIS. A means of comparing the risks of the occurrence of certain undesirable outcomes to the benefits that would be derived from a program or project. For example, are the risks associated with nuclear power justified by the benefits derived from this energy source?

SAN ANTONIO SCHOOL DISTRICT V. RODRIGUEZ. A 1973 ruling of the Supreme Court that financing education through the local property tax did not constitute a denial of the equal protection clause of the Constitution and that states did not have to equalize educational finances across districts.

SEPARATION OF POWERS. The constitutional doctrine that the legislative, executive, and judicial powers of the federal government are separate and that each should serve as a check on the other. While designed to prevent tyrannical government, this doctrine has tended to make policymaking slow and cumbersome.

SERRANO V. PRIEST. A 1971 ruling of the California Supreme Court that the use of the local property tax as a means of financing education denied equal protection to children of poor parents. School districts with lower tax bases would either have to tax themselves more heavily or provide lower-quality education if the property tax is the principal means of finance.

SOCIAL SECURITY. A program of social insurance providing benefits for the elderly, survivors of insured workers, and the disabled, as well as providing health insurance for the elderly through Medicare. This system is financed entirely through a payroll tax on workers, and in the 1980s is faced with financial insolvency.

SOCIAL WELFARE FUNCTION. A decision rule, or set of decision rules, that would allow the compilation of individual preferences and the production of a decision that would be the most acceptable to the population. A number of difficulties, such as the difficulty of measuring intensity of preferences, make the construction of a function of this kind virtually impossible.

STAGFLATION. Economic conditions prevailing in the late 1970s and early 1980s, periods of both high unemployment and high rates of inflation. The standard remedies of Keynesian economic management did not prove effective in coping with this situation.

STANDARD OPERATING PROCEDURES. Standard procedures for processing information from an organization's environment and then making responses. While these procedures are useful in providing uniformity of action and more rapid response than if there had to be a new decision in each case, the organization may depend excessively on such procedures and lose the ability to adapt to change and to truly unique situations.

SUASION. Attempting to gain action from the public by persuading people that something is the appropriate thing to do; especially effective for issues of national security.

SUNSET LAWS. Laws requiring the review of all agencies at regular intervals, such as every twenty years. The intent is that agencies that had become outmoded or ineffective could be terminated, thereby reducing the costs of government and the volume of regulation.

SUPERFUND. A program passed by the Carter administration for dealing with hazardous wastes. It taxes the chemical and petroleum industries in order to have funds to clean up toxic waste sites.

SUPPLEMENTAL SECURITY INCOME. A program of the Nixon administration that put the previous categorical aid programs for the elderly, blind, and disabled into a single program and added some general assistance benefits. This was seen as the beginning of a national minimum income.

SUPPLY-SIDE ECONOMICS. The economic program of the Reagan administration predicated on the assumption that if taxes are reduced, citizens will save the money returned to them and this saving will in turn generate investment and increased economic growth. As investment is crucial to the argument, it is therefore justifiable in this plan to aid differentially the more affluent in the tax reductions.

SYNFUELS. Include the generation of methane and methanol from biomass (decaying vegetation), as well as coal gassification. With the declining reserves of natural fossil fuels, there has been a movement toward developing synthetic substitutes (synfuels).

TARGET POPULATIONS. The particular segment(s) of the total population who are intended beneficiaries of a program. Frequently, because of political pressures, the nature of the target population becomes confused and benefits are spread across the entire population.

TAX EXPENDITURE. Not collecting taxes on certain kinds of expenditures or certain categories of revenue, thereby having the same effects on the economy as if an expenditure had been made for the same purpose. For example, by not collecting taxes on the money spent for interest on home mortgages, the effect is the same as if government had spent the same amount for housing programs for the middle class. Tax expenditures are a special kind of incentive.

TECHNOLOGY-FORCING REQUIREMENT. Provisions of the Clean Air Amendments required reductions in the emission of carbon monoxide and hydrocarbons, although there was no known technology to produce those reductions. These requirements were adopted to attempt to force the manufacturers to develop the technology.

THINK TANKS. Organizations established to develop policy ideas. Two of the most important are the Brookings Institution, usually associated with the Democratic party, and the American Enterprise Institute, usually associated with the Republican party. Recently, more conservative think tanks, such as the Heritage Foundation, have been influential.

TRANSFER PAYMENTS. Public expenditures that involve the transfer of money from government to an individual or organization for the final consumption decision. These are contrasted to exhaustive expenditures that involve government decisions about what to buy and how many people to employ.

THE "TROIKA." The Council of Economic Advisers, the Office of Management and Budget, and the Department of the Treasury. Leaders of these three organizations advise the President on budgetary policy, especially in setting the annual target for total expenditures.

TUITION TAX CREDITS. A proposal of the Reagan administration to allow a tax credit for parents sending their children to private schools. This is intended, as are educational vouchers, to create more competition and greater quality in education.

UNCONTROLLABLE EXPENDITURES. Expenditures that government has little capability of controlling, except by major program revisions. For example, expenditures for Social Security are determined by the number of people eligible and the value of their benefits. Unless government is willing to pass legislation restricting eligibility or changing the value of the benefits, nothing can be done about controlling expenditures.

VALUE-ADDED TAX. A tax, levied on the value added at each stage of production and then reflected in the price of the product. This form of taxation, largely invisible to the public, has been considered to supplement the payroll tax for Social Security.

VALUES—PATERNALISM. Government operating in the role of a parent to prevent its citizens from doing things they might later regret. For example, government might require citizens to wear seat belts, thereby reducing individual freedom and responsibility but saving many lives.

VALUES—UTILITARIANISM. A system of values that assesses the activities of government, using the standard of the greatest good for the greatest number (Bentham) or, more simply, the greatest increase in production; obviously closely associated with the use of cost-benefit analysis in policy analysis.

VOLUME BUDGETING. Making out a budget in terms of the volume of service to be provided rather than in terms of the current costs of those services. This involves setting a stable price system for government services and then budgeting in terms of those constant dollars.

VOUCHER PLANS. Plans that would give parents vouchers good for the education of their children. These could be used in public or in private schools. The concept is to create something of a market in education to increase the diversity of the options and to improve quality.

WAGE-PRICE POLICY. A form of economic policy in which allowable rates of wage and price increases are established. This is usually used as a means of temporarily controlling inflation.

WAR ON POVERTY. A series of programs in education, urban and regional development, and social welfare. The majority of these programs were administered by the Office of Economic Opportunity.

WELFARE STATE. The structuring of government in a way to provide at least minimal levels of health, economic security, housing, and education for all its citizens. The effects of most welfare states have not been to radically redistribute income but to build minimal levels below which citizens do not have to live.

WHISTLE BLOWERS. Members of the public bureaucracy, or other organizations, who expose errors and wrongdoing within their own organizations, even at the expense of their own careers.

ZERO-BASE BUDGETING. Fundamentally, a budgeting system that requires spending agencies to justify their entire budget each year. Given the difficulty of actually dealing with such a huge volume of information, in practice the system sets survival levels of funding below which it is not possible to run the program at all, and then adds decision packages reflecting increases in services and increases in costs. Decision makers can then choose levels of costs and benefits according to their own values.

ZERO-SUM SOCIETY. A society in which per capita economic growth is slow or nonexistent. In such a society any increases in benefits to one group implies reduced benefits for others. The politics of policymaking in such a setting would be much more contentious than in a society with economic growth.

Index